Changing Politics of Canadian Social Policy

Second Edition

A consistent bestseller since its publication in 2000, *Changing Politics of Canadian Social Policy* is a one-of-a-kind resource in the fields of political science and social work. Examining current conditions affecting the development of social policies in Canada, this book offers in-depth critical analysis of how these policies first arose and the implications they pose for future policy development.

This new edition of *Changing Politics of Canadian Social Policy* features updated chapters while retaining the first edition's analytical focus on economic globalization, societal pluralization, and social protection. The authors offer fresh considerations of gender relations and families, community agencies and the voluntary sector, as well as the social policy activities of all levels of government in the Canadian federation. *Changing Politics of Canadian Social Policy* will continue to provide the much-needed groundwork for students and policy makers, as well as propose real solutions for the future.

JAMES J. RICE is an emeritus professor in the School of Social Work at McMaster University.

MICHAEL J. PRINCE is Lansdowne Professor of Social Policy in the Faculty of Human and Social Development at the University of Victoria.

Changing Politics of Canadian Social Policy

Second Edition

JAMES J. RICE AND MICHAEL J. PRINCE

UNIVERSITY OF TORONTO PRESS
Toronto Buffalo London

© University of Toronto Press 2013
Toronto Buffalo London
www.utppublishing.com
Printed in Canada

ISBN 978-1-4426-1217-4

Printed on acid-free, 100% post-consumer recycled paper with
vegetable-based inks.

Library and Archives Canada Cataloguing in Publication

Rice, James J.
Changing politics of Canadian social policy / James J. Rice and Michael J.
Prince. – 2nd ed.

Includes bibliographical references and index.
ISBN 978-1-4426-1217-4

1. Canada – Social policy.   2. Social security – Canada.   3. Welfare state –
Canada.   I. Prince, Michael John, 1952–   II. Title.

HV108.R518 2013   361.6'10971   C2012-907962-6

University of Toronto Press acknowledges the financial assistance to its
publishing program of the Canada Council for the Arts and the Ontario
Arts Council.

  Canada Council Conseil des Arts
for the Arts du Canada

University of Toronto Press acknowledges the financial support of the
Government of Canada through the Canada Book Fund for its publishing
activities.

Contents

Preface to the Second Edition

We are gratified that the University of Toronto Press has asked us to do a second edition of *Changing Politics of Canadian Social Policy*. Short-listed for the Harold Adams Innis Prize for best social science book in 2000, the book has been widely adopted across universities and community colleges in Canada and well received internationally. In the first edition we argued that changes in the economy that threaten people's security lead to renewed community demands for social protection and redistribution; and that changes in society are creating demands for the recognition of diverse identities. Events in recent years – a global financial crisis, economic recessions in most industrial nations and tentative recoveries in many, the challenges of economic globalization, debates over cultural fragmentation and the reasonable accommodation of different faiths, and calls for social protection and social investments – are as urgent as ever. For our theoretical approach, we drew on the work of Karl Polanyi, including his notion of the double movement, to understand international and national economic issues and their interactions with states and community responses.

The problems of unemployment and the Employment Insurance program illustrate the double movement by highlighting the tension between the needs of workers for social protection on one side and the effects of markets and economic liberalism on the other. Both historically and in current times, workers have fought to protect themselves from the insecurities of labour markets by calling for employment insurance to protect individuals, families, and even communities against the loss of earnings. Invariably, there are pressures from business interests and employers to limit the costs of these programs by containing the scope and generosity of benefits; this has led to tighter eligibility requirements and limited benefits. In responding to these demands, the government must create social policies and unemployment programs that balance the needs of both sides. An examination of the evolving employment insurance program provides insights into which side of the argument is being heard. Over the past ten years the government has restricted the eligibility rules for these programs and reduced benefits, leaving many working people and families at risk.

Since our first edition, there has been increasing interest in Polanyi's ideas with regard to historical applications, conceptual details, and recent empirical developments (Stiglitz 2001; Arrighi and Silver 2003; Block 2007; Saul 2009; Piore 2009; Dale 2010; Peck 2010). For students of social policy, Polanyi's idea of a double movement draws attention, first, to economic and other societal structures and to the importance of material relations, and second, to the agency of humans, the importance of social values and relationships, and the possibility of community actions. If the focus is only on general structures, the risk is fatalistic pessimism; if only on personal agency, the risk is idealistic naïveté. Both human agency and systemic structure must be included in an account of social policy developments and political trends. For the twenty-first century, Polanyi remains a relevant thinker.

Another notable feature in the first edition was our close attention to the ideas and influence of Leonard Marsh, especially his *Report on Social Security for Canada*, with regard to the development of Canadian social policy from the 1940s into the 1970s and beyond. It is encouraging to see renewed interest in Marsh's work among social policy scholars (Echenberg 2004; Jenson 2004; Maioni 2004; Palier 2004; Banting 2006; James 2006). His concepts of universal social and employment risks and the contingencies of life remain perceptive, as do his policy ideas regarding seniors, health care, and people with disabilities; the central need for family income security; and national investments in housing and other social infrastructure. These themes and others are reflected in the growing literature on the welfare state and social policy in Canada (Olsen 2002; Lightman 2003; Westhues 2006; Finkel 2006; Peach and Warriner 2007; Raphael 2007; Graham, Swift, and Delaney 2008; McKenzie and Wharf 2010).

To this ongoing tension between economic liberalism and social protection, the book adds an examination the politics of cultural recognition, broadly defined in *Changing Politics of Canadian Social Policy* as including various social movements, marginalized identities, and disadvantaged groups. One example is the prejudice towards, and economic exclusion of, racialized groups in Canada (Galabuzi 2006; James, Este, Bernard, Benjamin, Lloyd, and Turner 2010). This politics of recognition also entails redress of historical and contemporary injustices for some groups, such as the Japanese Canadians interned during the Second World War (Miki 2005), as well as positive recognition for other groups, such as gays and lesbians (Rayside 2008; Badgett 2009). The literature on indigenous peoples – First Nations, Inuit, and Métis – is growing, particularly with regard to their struggles for self-determination (Alfred 2005; Belanger 2008). So too is writing on diversity, immigration, religious tolerance, and multiculturalism (Abu-Laban and Gabriel 2002; Banting, Courchene and Seidle 2007) – or, as it is termed in Quebec, interculturalism (Oakes and Warren 2007; Bouchard and Taylor 2008; Leroux 2010). There are also works that criticize multiculturalism policies; some of these are well argued, while others are weak and unpersuasive – what Ryan (2010) gives the name "multicultiphobia." Notwithstanding recent critical analysis, much of the recent literature on differences and pluralism in Canada is generally positive in outlook (Bloemraad 2006; Adams 2007; Dhamoon 2009).

Since 2000, when the first edition appeared, Canada has passed from a period of economic growth, government budget surpluses, a Liberal majority government, and renewed investments in health and social programs, to a period of global financial crisis and economic recession in 2008–9, during which the national unemployment rate rose for the first time in fourteen years, federal deficits were projected until 2015, the Conservatives came to power in Ottawa (with minority governments from 2006 to 2011, followed by the first Conservative majority in a generation), critical social policies were reversed, and relative disinterest overall was displayed by the federal government with regard to income security, equality and human rights, community and social services, and public health. Yet over this same period, several provincial and territorial governments introduced comprehensive poverty reduction strategies – a significant political development in Canadian social policy, and one that we examine in some detail in this new edition. Continuities aplenty characterize much of Canadian politics, governance, and social policy. Inequalities are deeper; dependence on food banks is greater; homelessness is rising; racism, discrimination, and stigma persist towards various groups, such as people living in poverty and individuals with mental health conditions; unemployment rates are staggeringly high for people with physical and cognitive disabilities. Many Canadians participated in and/or supported the "Occupy Movement," which began in New York City around the Wall Street financial district and spread from there around the globe. These activists were protesting deepening economic inequalities, extreme concentrations of wealth, and government actions and inactions. Most governments across Canada lack a workable vision regarding the voluntary sector and community capacity building. *Changing Politics of Canadian Social Policy* addresses these shifting contexts and continuing problems and examines the claims formulated and advanced by different sectors of society in the ongoing politics of social policy.

In this second edition we retain our analytical focus on economic globalization, societal pluralization, and social protection. We offer an updated consideration of gender relations and families, community agencies and the voluntary sector, and the social policy activities of all levels of government in the Canadian federation. We examine the political discourse and policy-relevant processes of fiscalization and marketization, and retrenchment and reinvestment.

We have revised all of the chapters, some of them quite extensively, as well as the bibliography. We have kept the chapters on historical development largely as they were. Feedback from colleagues and reviewers indicated that these were important features of the book. New to this second edition are the following features:

- An original chapter on the global financial crisis and economic recession of 2008–9 and the implications of both for the politics and policies of the Canadian state.
- Material on the social economy, as well as expanded discussion of civil society and voluntary sector developments under the federal governments of Paul Martin and Stephen Harper.
- Examination of the Universal Child Care Benefit introduced in 2006 and of recent debates on universality and selectivity in social policy.
- Expanded and updated material on gender relations, and new material on social reproduction, social provisioning, and women's work.
- Additional discussion on the Charter of Rights and Freedoms and its impact on social programs.
- New material on the renewed attack on poverty in Canada, with clear reference to recent poverty reduction strategies in several provinces and territories.

- A revised final chapter on social policy reform that addresses matters of social justice, economic participation, income security, intercultural relations, and shared citizenship.

As authors, our collaboration now spans more than thirty years. Once again, we appreciate the opportunity to work together on the ever fascinating, always compelling and still changing politics of Canadian social policy. We wish to thank the two reviewers who provided useful feedback on the outline of the new edition and a special word of appreciation to Matthew Kudelka for his careful copy editing of the book. We dedicate this book to our families.

James J. Rice, Campbellford, Ontario
Michael J. Prince, Oak Bay, British Columbia
January 2013

Preface to the First Edition

Changing Politics of Canadian Social Policy examines the current conditions affecting the development of social policies in Canada and offers a sweeping historical examination and contemporary account of the welfare state and social security. As Canadians enter the twenty-first century, they are grappling with the legacy of the fiscal crisis of the state alongside the tensions between the globalization of the economy and the pluralization of the community. After nearly a generation of neo-conservative politics and retrenchment of governments, this book argues for a new balance between the market, the state, and civic society. We maintain that Canada's welfare state and social programs remain relevant and essential precisely because of economic globalism and the growing diversity of community life; and that the role of social policy will increasingly become concerned with the protection of communities and groups against market turmoil, and the recognition of various social and cultural identities within Canadian society.

The scope of the book is an analysis of Canadian social policy, with various examples from other countries. While it focuses primarily on income security and social services, it examines a range of social programs provided by the federal and provincial governments and the non-profit sector. The structure of the book leads the reader to understand how the political context is restructuring the fundamental ideas of the welfare state to meet the needs of the global economy.

Our methods include an assessment of the changing economic and political conditions affecting the development of social policies; an analysis of the changing ideologies influencing the way governments think about social policy issues; and a review of the literature to determine how advocates, service users, and experts believe social policies will evolve in the future.

We have written this book with three audiences in mind: first, students and teachers in the fields of child and family studies, disability studies, education, health administration, nursing, political science, public administration, social work, sociology, and women's studies; second, activists, clients, and workers in community groups and social movements; and third, policy analysts, decision makers, administrators, and practitioners within governments and other public sector organizations – those who wish to understand the evolution of social policy and the welfare state in Canada, including where we are now and where we may well be heading. We have tried to write the book in a way that speaks to each of these groups in a style that is accessible, stimulating, and, at times, personal.

Every book expresses the values of its writer or writers, so first let us be clear as to our beliefs, assumptions, and backgrounds. We believe that to understand Canadian society, social policy, and the welfare state requires a careful consideration of the processes of globalization and pluralization, and the political structures which partially mediate these macro-processes. We believe it is essential to view society from a historical perspective, taking lessons from the past and applying them to the future. We also believe in the importance of finding new ways of building community capacity in order to maintain strong social cohesion, foster environmentally and socially responsible firms and corporations at national and international levels, and democratize the state with a renewed social role. We believe every society must find a balance amidst the forces that drive economic production, foster democratic governance, and maintain a civil society.

A key underlying assumption in our writing is that context influences policies and practices. For us, context includes the economic, social and political realms, with special consideration given to the diverse nature of people. Another assumption is that contemporary agencies, programs, and helping professions are influenced by past choices, conflicts, and achievements. History is important. Finally, we assume that social movements, ideas, and programs can and do affect the way people choose to live.

We come to the study and practice of social policy from different disciplinary perspectives and work experience – social work and political science. Together we have been working and writing on aspects of social policy since the early 1980s. The collaboration, we believe, has resulted in a richer and broader approach to social policy theorizing and analysis.

For encouragement, guidance, and feedback thanks are due to Marie Campbell, Bruce Doern, Demi Patsios, Marge Reitsma-Street, Katherine Teghtsoonian, and special thanks to Brian Wharf for his careful review. This book would not have been written and completed without the love, patience, and sacrifice of our families: Robin, Chandra, and Sara; and Karen, Jessica, and Kathleen.

Changing Politics of Canadian Social Policy

Second Edition

Introduction

Three dominant forces are changing the way Canadians think about social welfare: the neoliberal globalization of the economy; changing human risks and needs for social protection; and the desire by diverse groups for community recognition. These three forces are altering the social policy agendas of governments, community groups, interest groups, and social activists. They are creating new debates about the impact of social interventions on economic markets, the relationship between social benefits and labour market involvement, and the implications for social rights for disadvantaged and oppressed groups. The purpose of this book is to explore how and when these three conditions arose and to analyse the implications they pose for the development of new social policies.

This introduction indicates how the present study approaches and contributes to the literature on welfare states and social policies. We then present our analytical framework for understanding the politics of Canadian social policy, historically, in current times, and in likely developments. Concepts central to the framework include Karl Polanyi's ideas on the commodification of human labour, on the detachment of market forces from social fabrics, and the subsequent "double movement" of social change (Polanyi 1944). We also introduce preliminary remarks on the nature of social policy making vis-à-vis three overarching policy orientations that are highly significant to the debates and practices of contemporary social policy and to Canadian politics more generally. These orientations are economic liberalism, social protection, and cultural recognition. Each is ideological, historically situated, and politically shaped by specific actors, groups, and institutions. This means that each is a partial, contested, and shifting ensemble of ideas, interests, and instruments of policy and practice.

The changing politics of social policy are the result of tensions between global economic forces that are constraining governments' ability to provide social protection on the one hand, and diverse groups that are claiming recognition and benefits from social programs on the other. Governments are under pressure from multiple directions: corporations are demanding open markets and freedom from the constraints of social policies and, in recent times of crisis, financial aid and tax benefits; many citizens are demanding protection from the ravages of quickly changing economic conditions, while others, at the best of times, struggle for belonging. Pressures from various sides are reshaping the old ways of thinking about the welfare state and creating conditions for the development of new social policy conceptualizations and interventions (McKeen 2006). Canada is a liberal welfare state regime in which social policy includes mainly the following: means- or needs-tested social assistance and other income-tested programs; limited coverage in supports for housing, training, and disability insurance; general or universal coverage on health insurance and on elementary and secondary education; a few universal income entitlements; a major reliance on employment-based programs (such as the Canada Pension Plan, Employment Insurance, and workers' compensation); minimal investment in active labour market programs to promote employment opportunities; modest levels of income support or earnings replacement programs; a heavy reliance on personal responsibility, private sector, and voluntary sector provision of services and benefits; and an implicit set of family policies that make gender-based assumptions about male and female roles.

Most of the contemporary literature on national and comparative social policy, and on the crisis of the welfare state, has focused on globalization. The malaise of the welfare state is explained in relation to economic problems of inflation, low growth, business imperatives, and work disincentives. Major issues examined in this literature include deindustrialization, the changing distribution of work, and the impact of economic globalization on labour markets and on the sovereignty of nation-states. A trade-off is commonly held to exist between economic growth and international competitiveness on the one hand, and social protection and redistribution on the other.

Typically, the literature on globalization examines the question of what the role of the state should be. Some argue that social programs must be altered – that is, made to be more "active" and supportive of market forces. This new line of social policy debate focuses on the notion of the "responsible" citizen whose main goal should be to fit successfully into the labour force and be a contributing member of the economy. The analysis argues that the state ought to be downsized and many interventions deregulated or privatized. To be sure, for the past fifteen to twenty years, governments have been adapting and adjusting programs to what have been called "the new world economy" and "new fiscal realities."

A second body of literature focuses on domestic politics and social trends. The welfare state is viewed as either (a) a set of programs and rights offering a social safety net, or (b) a cultural form concerned with the construction of identities and status through the dominant discourse and public policies. This stream of writing treats the welfare state as a political project concerned with nation building and province building and, more recently, Aboriginal self-government. Here, social programs and services interact with demographics, identity politics, and intergovernmental relations, and examined issues include population aging, gender relations, new social movements, and the changing racial and ethnic composition of Canadian society. In this line of analysis, many of the challenges facing the modern welfare state derive from the mismatch between existing social programs and the needs and aspirations of a multiplicity of groups. Typical reform ideas call for making institutions, professions, laws, and programs more representative, culturally sensitive, and respectful of differences – in other words, the state needs to be further democratized. For these reformers the politics of social policy relate to the state's struggle to incorporate diverse people into the broader structures of society. This second body of literature thus assumes that the state retains a significant capacity, if not sovereignty, to exercise authority and to determine how people interact.

In *Changing Politics of Canadian Social Policy*, we connect these different bodies of writing on the state, economy, and society. In examining economic globalization and social pluralization together, we find that the trade-off is not only between economic expansion and social programs, but also between the quality of life that Canadians will have in the new century, the rights and responsibilities people will bear, the nature of their social relations, and their access to resources. The changing politics is about the struggle over who should benefit from the changing economic conditions and how these benefits should flow to groups within the country. It is about what rights and resources corporate interests claim, and the powers they exercise in relation to the state. It is about social status for different groups, and access to health care, education, and housing. It is about how groups in civil society are mobilized, and which ones succeed in obtaining a voice and recognition – or fail to do so. It is about investment, trade agreements, and markets as well as ethnicity, gender, age, and disability. It is about creating new mechanisms for income redistribution that meet the emerging needs of Canadians while improving productivity and economic efficiency. Social policies are the instruments, and the welfare state is the institutional complex through which new politics must develop if Canada is to become a more socially and economically inclusive society.

A Framework for Understanding the Magnitude of Current Changes

To understand what is happening to interrelationships among the economy, the state, and the community, we find it useful to look at the principles identified by Karl Polanyi (1944/2001) regarding the transformation from pre-industrial society to a post-industrial social system. His analysis of this transformation provides a powerful parallel for us to use as a way of thinking about how today's society is changing under the pressure of economic globalization and community pluralization. Two crucial ideas emerge from his analysis. The first describes the ways in which community members can be separated from their own economic activities as governments create new economic structures, which lead in turn to social degradation and the inability of community members to care for themselves. The second describes how community members respond to these changes by demanding from their governments greater social protection against the debilitating effects of market liberalization.

In his analysis of pre-industrial society, Polanyi demonstrates how economic activities are deeply embedded in social relationships. That is to say, while people labour to earn their living (economic activities), they are involved in their communities and act in ways that ensure community well-being, protect social harmony, and foster social cohesion (social relationships). Community members also maintain social ties through mutual reciprocity and the redistribution of resources. Reciprocal acts bind community members together as they give and receive help in meeting the demands of daily living; in difficult times, for example, community members redistribute food and resources to those in need, and those who contribute the most often receive the highest regard from the community. In this way the community maintains social cohesion.

Polanyi then describes how economic activities were disembedded from the community as pre-industrial societies were transformed into industrial societies. Governments, which were basically the instruments of the new capitalist elites, created markets to allow the owners of capital to produce and sell products. To create markets, governments placed constraints on community rights, limited community access to common property, removed traditional barriers to trade and finance, and allowed the owners of capital to treat land, labour, and capital as if they were commodities. Since land, labour, and capital are not natural commodities, the governments had to enforce this fiction through the mechanisms of contracts and laws.

The most damaging part of the fiction as just described is that it undermines the cooperative aspects of civil society. To maintain the civil society's separation from the economy, business interests and governments sympathetic to them undervalue both the cooperation of community members and the importance of reciprocity and redistribution. At the same time, governments enshrine the notion of private property and reinforce the idea that people should care for themselves and become competitive individuals who willingly forsake their communities to find work in the new industrializing societies. Polanyi provides a powerful description of the results when human beings and their communities are treated solely as commodities:

> In disposing of a man's labour power the system would, incidentally, dispose of the physical, psychological, and moral entity "man" attached to that tag. Robbed of the protective covering of cultural institutions, human beings would perish from the effects of social exposure; they would die as the victims of acute social dislocation through vice, perversion, crime, and starvation. Nature would be reduced to its elements, neighbourhoods and landscapes defiled, rivers polluted, military safety jeopardized, the power to produce food and raw materials destroyed. Finally, the market administration of purchasing power would periodically liquidate business enterprise, for shortages and surfeits of money would prove as disastrous to business as floods and droughts in primitive society. Undoubtedly, labour, land, and money markets are essential to a market economy. But no society could stand the effects of such a system of crude fictions even for the shortest stretch of time unless its human and natural substance as well as

its business organization was protected against the ravages of the satanic mill. (1944:73)

How does all of this relate to contemporary social policy in Canada? We believe that in the changing politics of social policy, the global economy is being separated from the state in the same way that the economy was disembedded from social relationships in Polanyi's analysis of industrialization. The nation-state has less control over economic forces than it did twenty years ago, and the globalization of the economy has lessened the ability of states to control economic development within their own borders. Governments are creating vehicles for enhancing the power of international corporations – vehicles such as the World Trade Organization – through legislation such as the North American Free Trade Agreement; and they are continuing to seek ways to protect the rights of investors over the rights of citizens. As they have gone about creating the global economy, corporations and governments have been prepared to increase the risks that community members must bear in meeting the demands of daily living, while reducing their collective capacity to deal with these risks. Governments have allowed corporations to take enormous risks in the name of making higher profits; yet the ensuing losses from such economic gambles fall mainly on taxpayers. At the same time, governments have cut back on social benefits, dismantled parts of the welfare system, and removed support for people who are unable to find employment.

Polanyi's analysis tells us that community members respond to conditions such as these, acting to protect themselves and their neighbours from the most damaging effects of economic change. He posits that community members band together to demand the enactment of policies to protect them from the destructive forces of change. He paints a detailed picture of how people developed social movements to defend themselves and their environment from the forces of the unregulated market. They called for factory laws, they organized unions, and they created self-help organizations, and all of these activities contributed to the foundations of the modern welfare state.

A brief look at this process in Canada helps us understand better Polanyi's argument. When Canada was developing its economy in the 1800s and early 1900s, people faced complex challenges that were inherent in living in an urbanized environment: to maintain social cohesion under stressful conditions; to find and keep steady employment; to protect children in an increasingly dangerous world; and to balance the demands of family, kin, and community. The problems created by the forces of economic development included unemployment, sickness, disability, industrial accidents, poverty in old age, and the poverty that was so often the result of large families. For families, it was not just a matter of making small adjustments in how they lived or how they got along with their neighbours. The problems were deep and systemic.

To protect themselves, people turned to their local communities. But charities and municipal governments could deal only with local and immediate issues, such as providing emergency shelter or food; so families and local communities increasingly turned to higher levels of government for protection from the destructive forces of self-regulating markets. The provincial and federal governments, sometimes on their own and sometimes in collaboration, sought ways to deal with the risks created by industrialization. Over time, structures for administering and providing services changed from those of a local and non-professional nature to those that were relatively centralized and professional. New social policy instruments were found to deal with the breadth and complexity of social problems. First social assistance, then social insurance, and finally universal programs were developed to protect citizens. These programs re-created the two fundamental structures found in pre-industrial society: reciprocity and redistribution. They took resources from members of the community who were making money from industrialization and urbanization and distributed them to other members to ensure social cohesion and a sense of community.

Throughout the twentieth century, the social policies applied in the construction of the welfare state created and maintained a new relationship between market forces and the needs of communities. Governments in the industrialized economies organized a variety of programs to deliver health care, housing, education, income support, and social services. At the same time, they intervened in the market to maintain high levels of employment, economic growth, and social stability. The result was a civil society in which a large portion of the population was protected from the turmoil created by economic development. Through political action, community members forced governments to intervene in the markets to ensure a fairer distribution of the fruits of everyone's labour. Governments increasingly taxed individuals, families, and corporations and then redistributed the resources to people who were unable to manage successfully in a competitive market environment. Polanyi describes these activities as a double movement:

the action of two organizing principles in society, each of them is setting itself specific institutional aims, having the support of definite social forces
and using its own distinctive methods. The one is the principle of economic liberalism, aiming at the establishment of a self-regulating market,
relying on the support of the trading classes, and using largely *laissez-faire*
and free trade as its method; the other is the principle of social protection aiming at the conservation of man and nature as well as productive
organizations, relying on the varying support of those most immediately
affected by the deleterious action of the market primarily, but not exclusively, the working and landed classes and using protective legislation,
restrictive associations, and other instruments of intervention as its methods. (1944: 132)

It is inaccurate to suggest, as some writers have done, that this double
movement is a pendulum that swings back and forth between business
markets and civil society groups. There is no automatic cause and effect at work here. Nor is the double movement some spontaneous phenomenon that immediately emerges from the actions of markets and
the reactions of communities. Rather, the relationship is contextual –
contested to be sure, and thus contingent – which means that the results are not predetermined or always predictable. The concrete nature
of the double movement varies over time and across policy issues and
jurisdictions. This movement is shaped by the capacity and sustained
activism of environmentalists, anti-racist groups, youth projects, raging
grannies, fair trade groups, disability advocates, indigenous peoples,
artists, community land trusts, homeless people and affordable housing activists, immigrant workers, unionists, and others (Shragge 2003;
Choudry, Hanley, Jordan, Shragge and Stiegman 2009; Whitmore, Wilson and Calhoun 2011). While successes occur from time to time, struggles are constant companions of community activism.

Governments in our day continue to use social policies to create the
social protection described by Polanyi in this double movement. For example, social policies construct relationships between workers and the
labour market. They create regulations that govern the age at which a
person can normally start working and the age at which people can expect to retire. Social policies establish minimum wages, provide workers with rights to organize and bargain collectively, provide pay equity
between the genders for work of equal value, and provide unemployment insurance protection when people are laid off from their jobs. Social policies require employers to create safer working environments,

pay better wages, provide job security, and offer employment benefits such as holidays and pension plans. Social policies regulate workers' relationships with their employers by creating labour boards to settle employment disputes and human rights legislation to provide protection from discrimination or sexual harassment. Of course, social policies go beyond the relationships people have with work itself. They provide social security programs based on citizens' rights to old age security, child benefits, health care, social services, and social assistance. Such policies aim at maintaining or improving the status of individuals, families and community groups. Much more than a corrective for market failures and adverse economic consequences, social policies distribute and redistribute resources, invest in the human and social development of the community, and enact a range of rules and laws, including for the recognition of particular groups in the political community. The social field "remains the focus of intense and unsettling desires – for security, improvement, success, solidarity and better ways of life (of very different kinds)" (Clarke 2007, 984). In later chapters we examine versions of this field in terms of social security, social investment, social capital, social economy, and social reproduction.

Over the past twenty years, economic globalization has put welfare programs under the same strain as the social system experienced when capitalism was being developed and markets were being created. We argue that as threats from the global economy have increased, people have closed ranks and looked for new forms of protection. New social movements represent groups of people who are attempting to articulate their own stories concerning their identity and their history, which in many cases has included oppression and subjugation. Members of these groups are expressing ideas that challenge many of the stereotypes contained in existing social policies. Black Canadians, gays and lesbians, people of colour, people with disabilities, people living in poverty, and community activists, for example, are seeking to maintain or reintroduce the old processes of reciprocity and redistribution.

People seeking to re-establish the importance of reciprocity and income redistribution are creating a new language for social policy. They want to demonstrate that social problems "are part of much wider discourses such that political struggles for welfare occur in many different sites: in the social and cultural relations of sexuality, gender, race and ethnicity and age, for example" (Penna and O'Brien 1996, 54). These struggles go beyond class relations, worker–employer relations, and family relations, while being part of all of these. A new struggle for recognition is developing that respects the differences among people while accepting universal commonalties. These new ideas are altering fundamental ideas about what is politically left or right by cutting across political boundaries to create new politics based on social identity rather than political orientation.

In addition to economic liberalism (globalization) and social protection (the welfare state) a third movement can be observed, that of cultural recognition. Like the others, this movement provides an organizing principle in society. It has definite aims and the support of specific classes and groups, it uses distinctive methods, and it has preferences for particular forms of social provision, policy, and the welfare state. The cultural recognition movement aims to redress oppressive relations and establish structures for self-determination. It relies on the support and mobilization of marginalized and disadvantaged groups (Drache and Cameron 1985). Economic liberalism, social protection, and cultural recognition amount to three distinct orientations to social policy analysis; each has its own aims, supports, methods, and institutional structures. Table 1 provides an overview of these policy orientations.

The history of cultural recognition is a long narrative of recurring efforts and battles. In Canada, it can be said that the most recent period emerged in the 1970s. This movement employs affirmative action, employment equity, human rights petitions, and – for Aboriginal or indigenous peoples – land claims and treaty negotiations. Other methods include converting private troubles into public issues by raising awareness, challenging stereotypes, and altering the language that people use to label peoples and behaviours. The institutional sites of struggles for cultural recognition are wide ranging; they include First Nations, community groups, new social movements, and families and kinship networks.

Generally speaking, the vision of social policy and the welfare state advanced by groups seeking cultural recognition is one of an active and more facilitative state for citizens, one that is enabling rather than overly administrative and controlling. These groups believe that policy development should be more inclusive and respectful of differences while advancing equitable treatment.

That these three policy orientations exist today, playing out across several policy fields and program areas, challenges sweeping claims that the social investment state is the new paradigm in public policy or that neoliberalism is having an overwhelming impact on the welfare

Table 1. Three Policy Orientations

Organizing principle	Economic liberalism	Social protection	Cultural recognition
Aims	Establishing "self-regulating" markets	Conserving people and the social and natural environments	Redressing wrongs, gaining acceptance of identities, achieving self-determination
Support	Trading classes, business think tanks, and transnational corporations	Working classes, the young, aged, sick, poverty groups, social justice movements, and the unemployed	Various social movements and marginalized groups: people with disabilities, ethnic and racial minorities, GLBTQ
Methods	Laissez-faire, free trade, contract law, commodification	Redistribution and reciprocity through public intervention, protective laws, mutual aid, trade unions, and self-help associations	Land claims and treaty negotiations, challenging stereotypes, changing every-day discourse, advocacy, and community action
Institutional sites	Domestic and global economies, World Trade Organization, NAFTA, APEC, etc.	Governments, organized labour, social economy, and voluntary sector	Indigenous nations, families, communities of shared interest or identity, civil society organizations
Periods of ascendancy or emergence	1800s–1930s 1980s–2000s	1940s–1970s	1970s–present
Vision of social policy and the welfare state	Residual social programs and a minimalist welfare state; night watchman or law-and-order state	National system of social security; the social investment state	Diverse range of facilitative empowering programs and a more democratic set of states; the inclusive state

Source: Adapted in part from Polanyi (1944), and substantially elaborated by the authors.

state and contemporary public administration. The original view of "the social investment state" – a view that continues to prevail – locates it in relation to two ideological approaches, as a "third way" of governing situated between liberalism/neoliberalism and social democratic politics – what may be called a "hybrid welfare regime." In our terms, the social investment state model corresponds to economic liberalism and social protection. Its goals are economic opportunity and inclusion; policy initiatives regarding labour markets, child benefits, education, and tax supports for working families; and partnerships in service delivery with business firms and/or voluntary sector associations. What the social investment state model largely misses is our third policy orientation – the politics of cultural recognition and the role of identity-based groups and social movements. Moreover, social investment policies have changed in recent years to some degree in response to economic downturns and financial crises, and to some degree in response to the agendas of several provincial governments. And of course, debates ensue *within* each policy orientation as well, across all three orientations. Social policy approaches and working practices can and do contain a variety of blends of purposes, ideas, methods, and institutional sites.

The Challenges

Since the social policy world is always being made and unmade, it is never entirely clear or agreed upon as to what this policy world looks like now or what it *will* look like. We can make some preliminary observations. First, many of the old social risks and problems remain. Indeed, economic and social inequalities, income poverty among young and older people, unemployment and precarious employment, and multiple forms of sexism and racism may all be worse than before, though the contexts of these problems and the responses to them are changing. For example, in 1980 there were no food banks in Canada, yet by 2010 nearly 870,000 Canadians were using food banks every month – the highest level of food bank use on record. This does not include seniors in Canada, who receive food through meal programs delivered at their homes or provided at community centres. About one-third of food banks across the country ran out of food in 2010, closing early and turning people away (Food Banks Canada 2010). Virtually unheard of just a few decades ago, food banks are today an entrenched part of Canada's charitable meal provision system, along with soup kitchens, school breakfast and lunch programs, shelters, and drop-in centres. Second, the old evils of homelessness and begging have re-emerged and poverty is on the rise. These issues are connected. The rising need for food banks is in part the result of people facing greater difficulty finding both work and affordable housing, or obtaining employment insurance or receiving social assistance. This reflects the impact of Canada's economic downturn in 2008–9. Third, many "new groups" are seeking help or protection from the government as well as reasonable accommodation for legitimate differences. Issues in this regard include Islamophobia with respect to Muslim identity and homophobia and transphobia with respect to sexual identities (Hamdon 2010; Haskell and Burtch 2010). Harassment, abuse, date rape, and neglect of the elderly,·issues that for decades were personal and private, are moving into the public sphere. For example, discrimination and violence faced by people due to their gender identity or gender expression (transsexual and transgender individuals) is emerging on the agendas of educational institutions, human rights commissions, and legislatures in Canada, albeit slowly. In the field of health care, more people are demanding that they be allowed to die with dignity and to determine for themselves when to stop medical intervention. Still others need help in their struggle to live with the ravages of cancer, HIV/AIDS, and other life-threatening illnesses. Advances in biomedical, neonatal, and reproductive technologies are presenting new choices and new ethical concerns regarding the formation of families. Fourth, in a world of instant communications, there are new concerns about individual privacy and identity theft; another concern is that the Internet will continue to serve as a vehicle for disseminating pornography and hate literature. As a result of these concerns, new ideas are entering the welfare debate; new relationships between the public, private, and community realms are being forged; new programs are being developed to deliver welfare services; and new volunteer organizations are being created to help the state manage its social welfare responsibilities.

The challenge for Canadians is to analyse these ideas, interests, policy instruments, and institutions in order to determine how they will influence the development of social policy. It is clear that the welfare system needs to be redesigned to allow for new relationships among civil society, the market, and the state. New policy designs must be able to absorb wide differences in family structures, work patterns, learning and training experiences, sexual identities, and ethnic and religious beliefs. Those new designs must contribute to the country's social capital by creating social harmony, safety, and trust while encouraging people to think about the relationship between individual responsibility and social responsibility. The changing politics of social policy must open the process so that the public feels included, and the advice of those affected by the system must be sought. The more people are part of the deliberations, the more ownership of social policy outcomes they will have.

As with all politics, people differ in their views about how the system should be changed. Some want to dismantle existing welfare programs and allow markets to solve social problems. Others want to redesign and rebuild the system in the hope that it will work better. Still others want to leave the system more or less as it is. Debates about how to change health and welfare systems are raging. The greater the differences among people's views, the hotter the debate. In this book we examine how these debates are shaping social policy. We examine the ideas of conservative thinkers who believe that the existing system has failed to solve social problems. We compare these with the ideas of people who believe that we must find new ways of providing state-sponsored welfare. To this we add the views of those who are seeking a middle way by holding on to the best parts of the existing system while finding new designs that are more inclusive and that achieve more integrative goals.

Overview

We have organized *Changing Politics of Canadian Social Policy* in a way that traces the building of the Canadian welfare state and that examines how social programs connect to the demands and pressures of the global economy, to personal and communal needs for social protection, and to organized claims for recognition by different populations. The book rests on a fundamental argument: *changes in the economy that threaten people's security lead to renewed community demands for social protection and redistribution, and cultural and political changes in society are creating demands for the recognition of diverse identities*. In short, what characterizes the broad political texture of Canadian social policy is the persistence of economic neoliberalism in policies and practices, the resilience of many educational, health, and social service programs, and the prominence of claims by assorted and overlapping groups for inclusion, respect, and self-determination. These three policy orientations link in various ways through the economic, political, and cultural spheres, generating the tensions and urgent trends of our times.

An illustration of the presence and interplay of these three orientations is the recent immigration policy of Stephen Harper's Conservative government. Our example is a passage from a study by Jehad Alieweiwi and Rachel Laforest on citizenship and immigration under the Conservatives, in which we note in brackets the three policy orientations: "Welfare state restructuring and offloading [informed by ideas from economic liberalism] has meant cuts into many important programs and services [social protection] that have been felt at the local level [seeds of the double movement]. Unequal access to resources and social infrastructure has in effect created a greater segregation of minorities [politics of cultural misrecognition and racialization of poverty] in impoverished and decaying communities. It has reinforced their sense of exclusion and undermined their sense of fairness" (Alieweiwi and Laforest 2009, 140). Throughout, this book examines the implications of this set of arguments for the development of Canadian social policy.

Chapter 1 examines in detail the two main forces that we feel are effecting the changes to the welfare system: the globalization of the economy and the pluralization of the community. We argue that the changing politics surrounding the welfare state are the result of tensions between global economic forces and the demands being made by community interest groups for greater protection from the risks created by globalization. Pressures from both sides have undermined the support for the existing welfare system as we enter a new era of social policy development.

Chapters 2 through 5 deal with the historical background of the welfare state in Canada and the politics surrounding it. Chapter 2 examines the roots of social policies in Canada and explores the implications these have for the politics of social policy. Beginning with the pre-colonial era and extending to the years of the Great Depression, we focus on the movement from local private practices of providing charity to the establishment of federal–provincial programs of social assistance. We describe the four major changes that took place in relation to the following: those who took responsibility for providing welfare services; the levels of government involved in social programs; the structures for administering and providing services; and policy instruments and processes. As we will see in later chapters, these four factors came to play an important part in the development of Canada's welfare state.

Chapter 3 explores the development of the modern welfare state between 1940 and the early 1970s. We examine how the debate changed
as a new set of ideas came to dominate the social policy agenda. The
Great Depression had left no doubt among Canadians that it was social
conditions, not individual behaviours, that determined the fate of most
families. During the 1930s, unemployment had risen dramatically, leaving hundreds of thousands of people looking for work. With community groups demanding government intervention, governments turned
to the theories of John Maynard Keynes for guidance in their efforts to
provide social policies that would not hinder economic development.
It was Keynes's contention that by encouraging consumer demand
through public expenditures, the government could encourage employment, sustain economic growth, and maintain economic stability.
During and after the Second World War, the Canadian government had
a number of reports prepared that described how it could use Keynes's
ideas to protect its citizens against most of the evils witnessed during
the Depression. The most important of these was the Report on Social
Security for Canada (Marsh 1943), which urged the government to intervene in the economy by creating programs to help people deal with
the problems created by modern industrial society. The chapter examines the effect this and other reports had on the development of a number of essential social programs.

In chapter 4 we examine what we call the crisis politics of the welfare state. By the 1970s, critics had begun to complain that the economic
system could no longer sustain the welfare system's costs. There was
growing rejection of the Keynesian idea that the welfare system could
be used to create economic stability, and new monetarist ideas and practices came into vogue. The right argued that the welfare system's costs
were destroying the economy's ability to grow; therefore, it followed,
social programs would have to be dismantled and the market would
have to be allowed to develop in an unfettered way. Writers from both
the left and the right developed critical reviews of the welfare state.
Feminists and other community members soon concurred with this
critical analysis of the welfare state. While many people benefited from
the support of the welfare system, it was not without faults. The bar-
rage of critiques succeeded in destroying the confidence of many people in the welfare system. Chapter 4 then explores these criticisms and
adds the critical voices of people working within the welfare system as
well as those of clients who received benefits through the programs.

Chapter 5 describes three broad policy strategies that governments might resort to in responding to changing conditions: dismantling programs and policy paradigms; remixing the social economy of welfare; or maintaining existing systems of benefits and rights. The Canadian government has used aspects of all three approaches. It has dismantled its universal income security programs, eliminated the Canada Assistance Program, privatized parts of the social service system, and cut back many employment insurance and social assistance benefits. At the same time, the federal and provincial governments have maintained policy commitments to universal health care and education, workers' compensation, and income support for the elderly. The chapter argues that the cumulative impact of these changes has been a lowering and fraying of Canada's social safety net.

In chapter 6 we argue that globalism must be examined in broad terms. Globalization has had not only economic impacts but also cultural and community ones. We examine the views of those who champion globalization and compare it with the views of those who raise doubts about its benefits. Generally, Canadian governments have championed economic globalization. They have signed free trade agreements and opened the Canadian economy to the world, in the process changing how Canadians see themselves. We also analyse the effect that globalization is having on new conceptions of the welfare state – conceptions that depict welfare programs as handmaidens to the economy in that they make social investments directed towards training and mobility, wage subsidies, and the development of human capital. Seen in this way, such programs do not interfere with globalization but rather prepare people to live in a more globalized world.

Chapter 7 examines the financial and economic crisis that unfolded between 2007 and 2009 and its effects on the development of social policy in Canada. The chapter explores the causes and nature of the crisis, the responses to it that have developed around the world, and the implications for the national economy. The analysis suggests that this latest crisis has not led to a disintegration of economic globalism, or to the end of neoliberalism, or to the resurgence of a social role for the state. However, the era of unbridled neoliberalism is apparently over, the championing of economic globalism has diminished, and claims that the private sector can solve most problems have been undermined. This presents opportunities for renewed debates on the market economy, the state, and social policy.

Chapters 8 through 11 speculate about the way the politics of social policy will unfold over the next ten years. They deal, in turn, with diversity and equality in the economy, gender and the family, the community, and a proposed policy agenda.

Chapter 8 examines the changing politics of social policy in light of the new social movements. Community groups are struggling to have their needs met in the context of economic globalization; but they have found themselves caught in the tensions created between the benefits provided by social policies and the control these policies have over the lives of community members. One critical perspective sees the state as an extension of patriarchal power whose interests solely benefit men. Another, less critical perspective assumes that there are competing power sources, predominantly reflecting patriarchal power but leaving room for the development of wider community involvement in social policy issues. We argue that the new social policy politics has entailed a shift away from universalism, standardization, and uniformity and towards particularism, fragmentation, and diversity, in such a way that subjectivity and difference are emphasized rather than universal and homogeneous experiences.

In chapter 9 (and in part of 10), we examine the changing politics of social policy for women. The needs of women, children, and families have always been secondary in the welfare state. Feminist writers point out that policies have supported the dominant role of men in both the workplace and the family. Much of the welfare state was originally constructed to meet the needs of people directly engaged in the paid labour force; these policies were based on the assumption that families are the basic building blocks of the community. The retrenchment of the welfare state has had different implications for women and men, and the shift back to a more residual welfare system has heightened the tensions regarding entitlements and reinforced many of the inequities and disadvantages facing women. The chapter also explores the changing roles of women in relationship to the welfare state.

Chapter 10 examines the implications of the changing politics of social policy for community development. It examines the nature of communities and the web of interconnected relationships in which people share resources and care for one another. It compares this with the neoliberal view, which maintains that individuals are independent agents looking out for their own best interests. We argue that people's connections in the community (be it communitarian or neoliberal) shape their ability to help one another. If communities are bound too tightly, members look only towards the community and are not prepared to care for strangers. If communities are made up of independent individuals with little or no connection with one another, no one will share with others for fear of being taken advantage of. When a balance exists, community resources can be used to address social problems. The chapter also looks at how a community's capacity can be used to address social welfare issues. Here, our analysis leads to the conclusion that communities can deal with local problems, particularly those that require one-on-one interactions, but find it much more difficult to deal with systemic problems of poverty or unemployment. The chapter also examines the ways in which governments have been shifting some responsibility for solving problems back onto communities. This realignment of responsibilities – particularly as it relates to personal caring – has the greatest implications for women, and caution is required in terms of how communities are expected to provide care.

The final chapter brings together the book's main arguments. We contend that the changing politics of social policy are the result of tensions arising from the interplay between economic globalization and the pluralization of society. The impact of this interplay can be seen in the restructuring of the welfare system, the changing ideas about the welfare state, the use of new policy instruments, and the changing institutions that have been created to deliver welfare services. The basic assumptions of this policy regime are that citizens are the fundamental building blocks of the economy and that social policy, instead of protecting people from market failures, should be preparing them for fuller engagement in the market. Neither purely neoliberal nor purely social democratic – a social investment state. We examine the implications of these changes for the fate of the Canadian welfare state and ask what will happen as we move into the next millennium. We argue that a new relationship between market and community must be found and that a new welfare agenda must be forged.

Throughout the book our focus is on the realm between theories and practices, a realm that is filled with the events, people, and politics that make up the social policy-making process. We are concerned with the questions about how the community takes care of its members, and why. The story we tell does not explore, except in passing, the actual programs and services offered by the state, private organizations, and the not-for-profit sector. We do not spend much time exploring the regulating and implementing of particular policies; rather, we concern ourselves primarily with the values that shape social policies and the ways these values are translated into interests, instruments, and institutions that determine the course of social policy.

Our analysis is based on the assumption that social change is not part of an evolutionary process leading to greater stability and integration; rather, it generates both positive and negative outcomes. Some changes move the system towards instability and disintegration; other changes do the opposite. To hypothesize about the direction of the changes, policy analysts must be aware of the history of the issues and the context in which the changes are taking place. We seek to demonstrate that the development of social arrangements such as industrialism, capitalism, and the development of the welfare state are interrelated and that one area cannot be understood without an appreciation of the others.

1 Changing Politics: Social Policy in a Globalizing and Pluralizing Context

This chapter describes and assesses two trends: economic globalization and societal pluralization, worldwide developments that we examine here in the contemporary Canadian context. Economic globalization is, of course, the latest expression of market liberalism and the latest stage in the development of capitalist economics, whereas societal pluralization refers to the increasing divisions among people based on gender, ethnicity, sexual orientation, family form, and age or relationship to the labour market. We devote more space to explaining pluralization because that concept, as we use it, adds an analytical dimension to the social policy field. Both of these trends embody much of what is changing the politics of social policy and shaping the future directions of markets as well as relations among markets, communities, and states in the early decades of the twenty-first century.

Economic Globalization

We have all experienced the rush of globalization. Information travels around the world at the click of a button. Twitter, Facebook, YouTube, blogs, and podcasting have become common in recent years. Capital can move from one country to another in seconds. We have become part of an international culture and international economy. This rapid flow means that issues spread instantly from country to country – ideas, new products, and medical discoveries travel at the speed of the Internet. Problem-solving social interventions used by one nation are soon on the political agendas of others. Positive and negative events travel at the same split-second pace. Remote famines and wars are part of the regular six o'clock news; and meanwhile, the CBC, the BBC, and CNN provide worldwide coverage of every conceivable topic, twenty-four hours a day. People are connected in an ever-tightening communications web and are able to communicate more often and far more quickly than ever before.

This new communication and production technology is having a profound effect on the politics of social policy. But before we jump into a discussion of globalization's effects, it is important for us to consider how it affects the world economy. Thus, we must first examine the three major impacts that the new global technology is having on the economy: it increases the ability of corporations to transfer resources and technology from one country to another; it increases the concentration of economic power in the hands of multinational corporations; and it opens domestic markets through the removal of trade barriers.

Increase in Corporations' Ability to Transfer Resources

New telecommunications and computing processes have created new organizational connections (Doern, Pal, and Tomlin 1996, 3). Corporations have developed a global perspective wherein international markets are as important as national or domestic ones. This new orientation has led corporations to tailor their investment and production decisions to take advantage of changing market conditions. Companies segment markets and organize production to benefit from low labour costs and the availability of natural resources. A large pool of non-unionized labour is viewed as a ready asset in the same way that the discovery of oil or nickel once inspired corporations to locate production facilities in remote areas.

Globalization has made every corporate decision an interconnected one. A decision to take advantage of low wages in Mexico can hasten the closure of an assembly plant in Nova Scotia, which in turn can alter corporate investment decisions about locating a plant in Nagpur, India. The economic freedom offered by globalization means that more businesses can seek conditions that favour their productive capacities. To maximize profits, companies pursue situations that offer the least regulation, the cheapest labour, and the smallest social welfare burden. In their relentless quest for favourable economic and social conditions, corporations will bypass countries that have laws and regulations limiting business profitability.

Concentration of Power

We hear almost weekly about large companies merging to form mega-corporations. Mergers can be accomplished with so much ease largely because of the speed with which resources and capital can be transferred. The concentration of corporate power is staggering. Corporations are so powerful that they have more influence on the global economy than most national governments.

In today's world, 40,000 corporations are operating on the international level. Of these, 200 control one-quarter of the world's economic activity. Sarah Anderson and John Cavanagh (1996) point out that "instead of creating an integrated global village, these firms are weaving webs of production, consumption, and finance that bring economic benefits to at most, a third of the world's people." Anderson and Cavanagh claim that these corporations' activities are hurting the bottom 20 per cent of people in rich countries and the bottom 80 per cent of people in poor countries. To support their claim, they provide a brief overview of the extent of corporate concentration. Of the 100 largest economies in the world, 51 are corporations. The top 200 corporations' combined sales are larger than the combined economies of all countries minus the largest nine. These same corporations have almost twice the economic power of the poorest four-fifths of humanity. The top 200 corporations have been net job destroyers in recent years, and in 1995 they had combined revenues of $7.1 trillion. Because these corporations have become so powerful, they can make demands for special consideration as they seek out new locations in which to invest.

Opening of Domestic Markets through Removal of Trade Barriers

Economic globalization has increased the influence of corporations on the public agenda. Corporations prod and push governments to pass laws that increase privatization, deregulate industries, and expand free markets; they also lobby for tax reforms that shift burdens from the corporation to the individual. In response to capital's increasing mobility, governments are removing trade barriers, eliminating national standards, and opening domestic markets to free trade. Governments that refuse to take such steps are risking rejection by corporations that are seeking new investment opportunities. The global economy appears to reward those states that are open and flexible. A frightening example of the new power of corporations is the Multilateral Agreement on

Investment (MAI), which was debated in the mid-1990s (Cohen 1997b). Twenty-nine member countries of the Organization for Economic Co-operation and Development (OECD) tried to introduce these new policies. Some of the rights contained in the agreement would have allowed corporations to challenge government decisions regarding the state's internal activities. For example, corporations from other countries would be able to challenge a government's provision of public or not-for-profit social services. Corporations could also encourage the dismantling of public services and social programs as well as the marketization of services provided by public or not-for-profit organizations. If a government was unwilling to introduce legislation favourable to corporate interests, a company could sue the government or, if all else failed, simply hunt for a different investment market. However, the power of globalization does not flow only in one direction. When a draft of this proposal became public in 1997, the Internet was used for the first time to organize a protest against an international agreement. Cohn (2005) describes how a coalition of NGOs argued that the MAI would lead to a "rush to the bottom" as countries lowered their employment standards in an effort to attract investment. The head of a Canadian NGO, Tony Clarke, provided important leadership during this social policy fight, and Maude Barlow, another Canadian champion of social rights, supported the campaign. The efforts of social policy protesters from around the world led to the withdrawal of the proposal and the introduction of the "voluntary" Policy Framework for Investment (2006), which offered a set of OECD "good practices" for attracting investment.

Globalization has shaped both sides of policy developments. It has placed enormous pressure on governments to adjust to the flexibility, power, and demands of corporations. As governments attempt to court corporations they are encouraged to privatize, deregulate, decentralize, and downsize public services as well as weaken laws and rights. In doing so, governments give up some of their power to solve or even address social problems. Yet at the same time, opponents to these new initiatives can communicate internationally, mobilize opposition through the Internet, and seek to introduce the theme of "civil society" into social policy debates. These citizens' campaigns demand that international negotiations take into account the needs of citizens, including social needs.

To understand more fully how globalization is affecting the social policy agenda, we examine how globalization is influencing the politics of social policy. In a nutshell, globalization undermines job security, changes the relationship between citizen and state, and limits

Figure 1: The Effects of Globalization on Social Policy

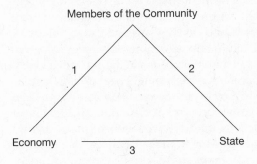

Members of the Community

Economy   State

1 Job insecurity and inequality
2 Transformation from citizens to customers
3 Limits on government

governments' influence over the economy. Figure 1 depicts these changing relationships.

Globalization Undermines Job Security and Polarizes Labour Markets

Globalization undermines workers' employment security. For example, engineering technology allows machines to replace people; new communications technology enables corporations to shift production from countries with expensive labour and restrictive laws to countries with cheap labour and few regulations; and the opening of domestic markets reduces the need for domestic products, which threatens the jobs of workers involved in their production. Workplace automation, the exportation of jobs, and the importation of products all mean fewer jobs. The result has been a steady increase in unemployment, which has not been below 7 per cent in Canada for the past twenty years. And those who become unemployed are without a job for longer periods. More people in the past ten years have had part-time or temporary jobs without benefits. Furthermore, Canadian wage rates have fallen in real value over the same period. The result has been a growing division between those who have "good" jobs, with security and benefits, and those who have "poor" jobs, without security or benefits – a gap, in other words, between privileged and precarious forms of employment (Vosko 2006).

New production processes and distribution systems have strengthened the forces of globalization, resulting in fewer workers. Jeremy Rifkin, in *The End of Work* (1995, 198), points out that "in every advanced economy, new technologies and management practices are displacing workers, creating a reserve army of contingent labourers, widening the gap between the haves and have-nots, and creating new and dangerous levels of stress." Those who have been unable to compete have suffered economically and socially; those who have succeeded in the expanded global markets have improved their economic well-being. The resulting increase in inequality places the state in a contradictory position: it seeks to keep its economy competitive by harmonizing regulations, tax structures, and welfare policies; it must, however, contend as well with the social stresses that develop when citizens are excluded from the labour market by these changes. Keith Banting (1996, 32) comments that this "emphasis on adaptation and flexibility conflicts with the emphasis on security and protection that was embodied in the historic conception of the welfare state."

Globalization Changes the Relationship between Citizen and State

John Ralston Saul (1995) contends that the growth of corporate power is disfiguring the ideal of the public good. Any corporation, be it a bank, a developer, a business, or a producer, is interested primarily in its own bottom line. Like the corporatist movements in the 1920s, corporations seek to "shift power directly to economic and social interest groups; push entrepreneurial initiative in areas normally reserved for public bodies; and obliterate the boundaries between public and private interests – that is, challenge the idea of the public interest" (91). The shift in power from the state to the corporation has transformed the relationship between the government and the public by turning citizens into customers. This shift is evident in the "marketization" of social discourse and social programs, a process we examine in chapter 6. Universities, hospitals, and social service workers, for example, are encouraged to think of students, patients, and clients as consumers. But citizens have rights and duties conferred by the state and benefits that accrue from these rights, whereas customers have only choices that are defined by their purchasing power. This change from citizen to customer has the potential to undermine the social fabric of the community. It encourages public institutions to abandon their social obligations.

Globalization Limits Government Influence over the Economy

Globalization is reducing governments' ability to solve social problems by limiting their power over the economy. To keep corporations from moving production out of Canada, federal and provincial governments have been dismantling parts of their welfare programs, reducing corporate taxes, overlooking or underenforcing environmental regulations, and helping ensure a compliant workforce by allowing the perception to grow that there is general insecurity in the workplace. Globalization, it has been suggested, has constrained the capacity of governments to act in socially compensatory ways, by reducing their willingness to deficit finance, given the ability of currency speculators to punish government borrowing; by weakening states' ability to levy taxes (as a consequence of tax competition, tax havens, and the transfer mechanisms of multinational corporations); and by impeding the work of organizations such as the WTO. A final point is that states become impoverished when transnational organizations introduce capital, technology, and management without any accountability to the host countries.[1]

Societal Pluralization

Economic globalization generally looks "out" from the nation-state; societal pluralization looks "in." Pluralization, a trend found in many countries, relates primarily to affairs and circumstances *within* the nation-state and society. Pluralization describes the growing divisions within Canada based on the social characteristics of groups of people. It is a multidimensional process that reflects the increasing diversity of people's cultural, economic, social, and political orientations. People with different orientations have different ways of knowing, seeing, and understanding the world and explaining how it functions, and they want those differences reflected in the state's social policy development. A result is that the policy process becomes more fraught with tensions and controversies as people struggle to have their needs recognized. Pluralization encourages the development of new identities, which leads to personal empowerment and group recognition for people who have felt excluded from society's mainstream. But pluralization also creates fear and leads to attacks on groups that are seen as different.

Canadian governments have supported economic globalization. They have also supported pluralization through their policies on Aboriginal governance, divorce and family law, immigration, official languages, multiculturalism, employment equity, and the public funding of non-governmental groups. Pluralization is entrenched in the Charter of Rights and Freedoms. Thus pluralization relates to and is affected by the forces of economic globalism and by calls for social protection and for the recognition of diverse identities and life circumstances. Other factors contributing to pluralization are social trends such as Canada's aging population and cultural trends such as the decline of deference and the growth in the acceptance of differences (Adams 1997; Reid 1997).

Pluralization is intrinsically a multidisciplinary concept, and various aspects of pluralization are addressed by various practitioners, organizations, and academic disciplines. As an overarching concept, pluralization encompasses what has at different times been called the politics of difference, identity politics, labour market polarization, and elements of postmodernism. Thus, economists have tended to examine the growing incidence of irregular patterns in employment and careers; gerontologists have traced the decline of age sixty-five as the normal age of retirement from the labour force; demographers and statisticians, among others, have highlighted the shifts in family forms, sizes, and roles in recent times; anthropologists and sociologists have made a distinctive contribution to Canadians' image of their country by studying the ethnic and racial composition of society; critical theorists, feminists, pollsters, and social workers have contributed to the deconstruction of prevailing ways of thinking about and explaining modern society and the political economy; political scientists and legal scholars have assessed the implications of the Charter of Rights and Freedoms and changes in intergovernmental relations as they apply to the distribution of public power and the status of various groups.

In this chapter we examine the following elements of pluralization in present-day Canadian society: the increasing variation in education, work, and retirement patterns; the expanding forms of family structures and relationships; the changing ethnic, linguistic, and racial composition of the population; the declining consensus on the postwar welfare state and the deconstruction of common ideas and theories; the proliferation and networking of interest groups; the decentralization of governmental authority and program delivery; and the constitutional recognition of several groups and identities.

Pluralization Reflects Variation in Patterns of Education, Work, and Retirement

One important aspect of pluralization is that people are approaching education, work, and retirement in new ways. Over the past generation, educational careers have become more varied, secure careers less common, and employment histories more diverse. Judith Maxwell (2003) describes what she calls the Great Social Transformation in Canada. She maintains that men and women, and parents and non-parents, are facing a serious time crunch as they balance work, study, and family responsibilities; and that families and individuals are being asked to carry more risk on their own shoulders and must finance more of their own (and their children's) learning, finance a greater share of their own benefits and pensions, cover the costs of frequent job change, and face the risk of being trapped in a low-paid job. Even young people who invest in education have no guarantee they will find a career job. This transformation has increased the responsibility on family members for providing or financing health and social services. It has also reduced access to the shared public services that people need to manage their daily patterns of family and work life efficiently, as well as increased the risk of social marginalization. For many people, at least some of these transitions across the lifespan do not call for personal choices. As we discuss in chapters 6 and 9, jobs are increasingly taking non-standard forms such as contract, part-time, temporary, shared, and self-employed. Part-time workers now form a larger share of the employed labour force, and there are more non-standard work hours. These trends have resulted in a polarization of work and earnings between high- and low-skilled jobs in the Canadian labour force. A 2006 report on minimum wages points out that on average, minimum-wage workers now receive 20 per cent less in real dollars than they did thirty years ago (CUPE Economic Brief 2006).[2] Closely linked to all of this is what Grant Schellenberg calls the destandardization of retirement: "People are leaving the labour force through different pathways and for different reasons than in the past" (1996, 151). The ages at which people are retiring from the labour force, as well as the causes and the ways, have become more diverse. Retired people in Canada are not necessarily "old people" or senior citizens.

Pluralization Fosters Viewing Families Differently

A second aspect of pluralism is the diversification of family forms in Canada. The nuclear family – that is, the heterosexual couple with children – was once Canada's predominant family structure, accounting for 42 per cent of all families in 2001, compared to 40 per cent in 2006. Yet even within this category there has been a growing number of "blended families" consisting of couples with the mother's, the father's, or both partners' children from previous marriages or common law unions. Other family types include single parent, joint custody, three parent, adoptive, teenage parent, later-life parent, grandparent, childless couple, queer parent, and extended families (Fox 2009; Goldberg and Brushwood Rose 2009; Vanier Institute of the Family 2010). In 2006, for the first time, the Canadian government collected census information on same-sex married couples; it reported that there were 45,350 same-sex couples, most of which were common law (Statistics Canada 2010).

During the expansionist era of the Canadian welfare state, from the 1940s into the 1970s, the main reason for being a lone parent was widowhood (Evans 1991). Today the primary reasons are that people have never (or are not yet) married, or they are divorced or separated. The proportion of lone-parent families, of which women head over 80 per cent, has increased substantially since the 1970s; in 2006 they represented 15.9 per cent of all families (Statistics Canada 2006). Common law families jumped in number from 6 per cent in 1981 to 16 per cent of all families in 2006 (most are in Quebec) – the largest increase over this period in the number of children in a particular family form. Common law unions are becoming more popular among older as well as younger people. Statistics Canada in 2006 began to track the numbers of same-sex couples, both with and without children; it found that these family forms are increasing in number and that they have been gaining recognition since the law was changed in 2005 and since the introduction of programs in some Canadian jurisdictions. The growing diversity in family forms has implications for household incomes, social care and informal support, child rearing, family law, employment standards legislation, and human rights.

Pluralization Recognizes Increasing Racial, Ethnic, and Linguistic Diversities

A third dimension of pluralization is society's growing racial, ethnic, and linguistic diversity. Ethnic differentiation is not new in Canada. Many years ago in *The Vertical Mosaic*, John Porter observed: "If not its one distinctive value, that of the mosaic is Canada's most cherished. Legitimization for the mosaic is sought in the notion of collective or group rights" (1965, 558). What may be relatively new is the *pace* of change in the Canadian mosaic's design and composition. What remains an important insight in Porter's work is the connections he made between race and ethnicity on the one hand, and class and power on the other;

he carefully documented the vertical or hierarchical relations among Canada's many cultural groups. Another legacy from his work is his insightful reminder that Canadian society is not simply pluralistic – it is also stratified into groups with unequal power and status. More recent analyses have added the dimensions of age, disability, gender, and sexual orientation, plus others, in exploring the nature of inequality and authority in societies. We consider these issues in various ways in chapters 4, 6, 8, and 9.

Regarding ethnic diversity, Andrew Armitage (1996, 23) observes that "Canada has become, through immigration, a polyethnic multicultural state in which Aboriginal peoples and peoples of French, British, other European, Asian, and African origins live together using common social institutions." The 2006 census found that immigrants represented over 20 per cent of Canada's population; that was the largest share in more than five decades. In addition, for the first time in the twentieth century, most immigrants to Canada were coming from Asia and the Middle East. Immigrants from Central and South America, the Caribbean, and Africa were also increasing in proportion. The proportion of immigrants living in Canada who were born in Europe declined from 67 to 47 per cent between 1981 and 1996. The 2006 Census identified more than 200 ethnic origins in Canada. This recent immigration-based diversification of the population was concentrated in three provinces and in urban centres. Almost 90 per cent of immigrants were living in Ontario, Quebec, and British Columbia. About one-fifth of the populations of Toronto and Vancouver were immigrants who had come to Canada since the early 1980s.

Canada's linguistic character is changing. Over the past decade, according to the 2006 census, the share of the population whose mother tongue is English or French has been declining: close to 20 per cent of the population now is allophone – that is, people whose mother tongue is neither of the official languages. Also, most of the recent immigrants to Canada – about 80 per cent – report a language other than English or French as their mother tongue, compared to 54 per cent in the 1960s. In the 1990s, Chinese surpassed Italian as the most common non-official language among Canadians. Among the top ten language groups in Canada other than English and French, four languages – Chinese, Punjabi, Arabic, and Tagalog (Filipino) – were not on the list twenty-five years ago; these have replaced Greek, Dutch, Hungarian, and Yiddish on that list. Indeed, the 2006 census found that 18.7 per cent of the population described their ethnic origin as Canadian; 17.1 per cent as from the British Isles; 9.5 per cent as French; 26.3 per cent as some combination of the above groups; 2.7 per cent as Aboriginal; and 25.7 per cent as other ethnicities. People in Canada with Aboriginal ancestry belonged to 608 First Nations, comprising 52 cultural groups and languages. Between 2001 and 2006, 1.1 million immigrants came to Canada. The majority were from Asia (58 per cent) (including the Middle East), but there were still a large number from Europe (16 per cent), Central and South America and the Caribbean (11 per cent), and Africa (11 per cent).

In 1996 the Canadian census, for the first time, provided information on the numbers and characteristics of visible minorities, defined by the federal Employment Equity Act as "persons, other than Aboriginal peoples, who are non-Caucasian in race or non-white in colour." That census reported that 11.3 per cent of the Canadian population – nearly 3.2 million – were people of colour, an increase from an estimated 6.3 per cent in 1986. The percentage rose again in 2006 to 16.2 per cent. Statistics Canada has forecast that as a share of the Canadian population, visible minorities could double to about 23 per cent by 2016 – a significant change in a relatively short period. In our view, Armitage is correct in concluding that what he calls the paradigm of British/French/Other European discourse, "no longer represents the basis on which social policy can be developed" (1996, 24).

Pluralization and the Adoption of New Ideas Regarding the Human Condition

A fourth strand of pluralization is the deconstructing of dominant ideas and conventional wisdom regarding the human condition, social theories, and politics. Public opinion analyst Angus Reid writes of the "attitudinal mosaic" in the values and beliefs of Canadians (1997; see also Bibby 2006). Pollster Michael Adams in *Sex in the Snow: Canadian Social Values at the End of the Millennium* (1997) argues that traditional forms of social consensus and conformity are breaking down and that people now define themselves by their personal priorities and life choices. Adams argues that this goes beyond talking in terms of being members of a particular generation, such as the baby boomers (1947–1966), the Generation Xers or baby-bust group (1967–1979), and the millennial generation or the baby echo cohort (1980–2008). Adams's survey research suggests that Canadians divide into thirteen social value "tribes" with different demographic characteristics, motivations, values, and philosophies both across and within generations (Adams 2007, 2010).

As it pertains to social policy, deconstruction involves questioning critically – and perhaps ultimately rejecting – taken-for-granted assumptions about such key concepts as citizenship, universalism, the public interest, and work. It also involves the assertion that alternative perspectives and social relationships are valid and legitimate. As Iris Marion Young (1990, 102) has argued, "reason cannot know the whole and cannot be unified." From this perspective, claims to impartiality and to universality of policies and practices are a fiction: "No one can adopt a point of view that is completely impersonal and dispassionate, completely separated from any particular context and commitments" (1990, 103). Rather, everyday life is a "plurality of moral subjects and situations" characterized by group affiliations and differences, by needs and desires, by particular perspectives, and by passionate beliefs.

Postmodern thinkers are challenging official expressions of a "general public good" and of a dichotomy between public and private spheres of life. In their place, they are advancing the idea of the heterogeneous public, emphasizing the particularities of ethnicity, race, gender, culture, age, religion, sexual orientation, ability, social class, and geography as separate spheres. Implicit in the idea of the heterogeneous public, suggests Young (1990, 120), are "two political principles: (a) no persons, actions or aspects of a person's life should be forced into privacy; and (b) no social institutions or practices should be excluded a priori from being a proper subject for public discussion and expression."

New theoretical approaches to analysing society, the economy, and the state have in recent decades been challenging prevailing notions as they relate to scientific social knowledge, government planning, and the management of human affairs. Many of the new ways of thinking and theorizing about the welfare state embrace a conflict model of society – one that emphasizes struggle, coercion, and oppression – rather than a consensus approach that suggests stability and unity. The newer theories view conventional notions of social integration as partial and exclusionary; they also question claims concerning the benefits of industrial growth, pointing to the adverse consequences of industrialism for communities and the natural environment. These challenges have contributed to a weakening of the progressive liberal and social democratic intellectual underpinnings of the postwar welfare state (Mishra 1984, 1990a), as we show in chapter 4. Moreover, in the domain of policy practice and social provision, ideas about retrenchment, fiscal constraint, and making the welfare state more responsive to market conditions gained predominance in the 1980s and 1990s.

The social policy response to retrenchment, fiscal constraint, and making the welfare state more responsive to market conditions is reflected clearly in the policy shifts in social housing. Canada has historically relied almost exclusively on private markets to meet the housing needs of Canadians. Fifty years ago, however, it developed a public housing program to provide rental housing for low-income families. By the mid-1970s it had shifted to a not-for-profit and cooperative housing policy in which community groups received government subsidies to develop and build housing and rented these units to families with low and modest incomes. By the mid-1990s, Canada was beginning to decentralize social housing, which forced local governments to deal piecemeal with housing issues.

Pluralization and the Proliferation of Interest in Policy Fields

The challenges to ways of thinking about economic and social issues are closely connected to a fifth aspect of pluralism: the proliferation of interests within most public policy fields. More groups are forming, and they are claiming a direct interest in public issues and programs; furthermore, they expect to participate in policy reviews and consultations. "In the past two decades," Canadian political scientist William Coleman (1991, 204) has noted, "the number of interest groups representing all facets of social, cultural, and economic life has grown more rapidly than at any previous time in Canadian history. There has also been a significant professionalization of interest groups, as these have become institutionalized participants in public policy making." Types of groups include client-based organizations such as those for pensioners; producer groups such as teachers' federations and nurses' associations; public interest organizations such as anti-poverty groups; think tanks and social planning councils; voluntary social service agencies; and health advocacy groups. Canada's mainstream political parties have been partly eclipsed as vehicles for political participation and policy development. The result of these developments has been a greater range of values and views brought to bear on policy debates and processes, although a dominant policy focus may persist. Daniel Drache and Duncan Cameron (1985) use the term "popular sector groups" for those organizations that express counterdiscourses of politics, economics, and social welfare. This alternative approach focuses on human well-being and the needs of the poor and marginalized; it supports significant new roles for government in the economy; and it stresses the importance of social investments through training, job creation, and active engagement of those seeking employment.

Alongside the more traditional forms of parliamentary, electoral, linguistic, and intergovernmental politics are newer forms and styles. These include politics of ethnicity, gender, sexuality, disability, intergenerational relations, Aboriginal self-determination, and the Charter of Rights and Freedoms. The new social groups represent people from a variety of backgrounds: gays and lesbians, blacks, single parents, people with disabilities, Aboriginal peoples, and women. There are new religious or faith groups, new movements fighting for the rights of disadvantaged people, new ethnic groups struggling for their cultural identities, and new advocacy groups finding ways to strengthen their communities (Fagan and Lee 1997, 143). These new social movements are community based (Fisher and Kling 1994, 8). People do not have to become formal members; instead, they can federate themselves loosely with the group. Blogs, Facebook, Twitter, and e-mail lists are all providing ways for groups to communicate with their members and to inform them of activities. The fight to establish identity and raise social status is now taking place on the streets and the Internet, and in the press and the courts, instead of through the governmental policy process.

Innovative social movements are beginning to influence policy making (Scott 1990, 16). Social movements seek to obtain some of the resources and rights enjoyed by older, work-oriented collectives. Each group seeks input into the policy process, and governments respond by opening up the process, by ignoring the groups, or by making policy changes. Within policy communities, new social movements challenge more established interest-group structures and at times succeed in altering them. At one level, all of this may make it easier for governments to manage the policy process: with so many contenders in the policy arena, they can play groups off against each other, seeking and finding support with some while rejecting the advances of others. At a deeper level, however, pluralization and the pursuit of cultural recognition seek to redefine, and to democratize, the social contract that underpins both policy and the Canadian welfare state.

The differential retrenchment of social programs, which we examine in later chapters, has contributed not only to the segmentation of clientele and other group interests, but also to the broader distribution of authority in the Canadian federation. Divided jurisdiction and regional political identities are long-standing features of Canadian federalism and governance. What is distinctive in the current era, particularly for social policy, are the following developments: the entrenchment of the Charter of Rights in the 1980s; the retreat of the federal government from its postwar (1940s to 1980s) leadership role; the founding of the Green Party; the emergence at the federal level in the 1990s of the Bloc Québécois and the Reform Party, both representing strong regional discontents and resolutely advocating more decentralization; the assertiveness if not aggressiveness of the provinces in the later 1990s regarding the further delegation of funding and powers; the concerns of municipalities as well as hospital and school boards concerning the offloading of responsibilities for programs and services from the senior levels of government; the establishment of Nunavut in 1999 as a new territorial government in the eastern and central Arctic, with the transfer of health care, public housing, and other social programs taking place between 1999 and 2009; and the (re)building of First Nations governments in Aboriginal communities across the country. Clearly, the political process is being pluralized.

We now comment briefly on one of these developments – the introduction of the Charter to Canada's constitutional order – to illustrate the implications for societal pluralization and social policy. In the original British North America Act of 1867, which established Canada as a political union, a few groups were identified, such as Indians, aliens, and denominational education schools. In the Constitution Act of 1982, which entrenched the Charter of Rights and Freedoms, many more groups gained constitutional recognition. In addition to those of Indians, the existing rights of Inuit and Métis peoples were recognized; also, rights and protections were specifically granted to women, official language minorities, visible ethnic and racial minorities, people with mental or physical disabilities, and northerners. Our political system, policy discourse, and processes now rest on a far more pronounced, politicized, and constitutionalized form of pluralism.

Conceptions of citizenship in Canada have deepened and become more complex. The Charter has undoubtedly added to the rise of the individual- and group-oriented rights discourse so evident today. Alan Cairns (1991, 173) claims, with considerable reason, that "the Constitution is now the crucial instrument for defining one's place in Canadian society." Of course, the paid labour market remains the crucial economic institution for defining one's place in society. For groups that do not see themselves in the Charter, such as gays, lesbians, and bisexual or transgendered people, the Constitution remains an exclusionary document, and any subsequent process of reforming the Canadian Constitution has prompted and will continue to prompt groups to advance their claims for recognition (Smith 2008). Yet legal scholar Andrew Petter (2010) questions the promise of constitutional rights and the politics of the Charter. Petter contends that "the *Charter* is not a productive instrument of progressive politics" and that it has achieved relatively little in improving the living conditions of socially disadvantaged Canadians over the past three decades (2010, 10). He argues that "the *Charter*'s most powerful political influences have been to legalize political discourse and to legitimize neo-conservative policies" by relying on judicial arenas, with key decisions of the courts favouring the rights of market-based interests over those of other groups (2010, 13). For Petter, a more rewarding approach to politics for changing social policy is democratic mobilization and citizen engagement.

Conclusions

Economic globalization and community pluralization tend to push and pull societies, economies, and states in uncharted directions. The external forces of globalization draw governments towards an opening up of their domestic economies; they also push for a retrenching of social and other public programs and expose communities to market upheavals. International corporations looking for new investments press governments to reorganize the fiscal, monetary, industrial, and social sectors so that they can maximize profits. At the same time, we believe, the internal forces of pluralization are moving countries towards increased diversity and fragmentation as well as new forms of social identity and inclusion. A multitude of groups are demanding that public programs and services be reorganized or devolved to better meet their members' needs. These changes are having similar effects on what constitutes public space or the "commons." Globalization encourages corporations to seek ways to take economic control of public space by creating new forms of ownership for such things as the air, the sea, and outer space. At the same time, pluralization encourages the transformation of public space into territorial space as particular groups come to control public institutions such as schools, hospitals, and other public organizations.

In support of economic globalization, various classes and interests pressure governments to cancel social programs in order to create an "even playing field" for international competition. With corporations shifting capital from one country to another, most governments find it difficult to maintain social programs that place real or supposed burdens on the corporate sector. Policy harmonization with other countries encourages governments to relinquish national sovereignty to other political structures by transferring powers through international agreements. Thomas Courchene (1987, 18), an enthusiastic champion of economic liberalism, identifies two social policy challenges in this process: "first, to ensure that the incentives within the social policy network will encourage, rather than inhibit, the required adjustment on the economic front; second, to ensure that the social safety net evolves in a manner that reflects the changing needs of citizens as they adapt to the new economic order." We explore this and contending views of globalization in chapter 6; and in chapter 11 we offer an alternative vision of the social policy challenges and choices facing Canadians in the coming decades.

Community pluralization both reflects and reinforces diversities within the Canadian polity and society. It also creates a means for people to express their own needs, and in doing so, they contest and alter the beliefs and practices underpinning the social contract. As a consequence, we are witnessing a transformation of the social sphere and the welfare state. To appreciate the scale and significance of this transformation, in the next two chapters we discuss the history of this system of social security.

2 Early Developments in Canadian Social Welfare

Histories of welfare states are much more than collections of facts and chronologies of programs. They are also compilations of human memories and myths, of political conflict and struggle, of compassion and sharing, and of aspirations and achievements. They are the stories of community members coming together to protect themselves and organizing to encourage their governments to create security against unforeseen misfortune. And they can teach us so much.

The fundamental lesson we can learn from these histories is that today's politics are rooted in yesterday's social policy legislation, and that the principles established during the early period of social welfare development can still be found in today's policies and debates (Blake 2008; Finkel 2006; Graham, Swift, and Delaney 2008; Warrier and Peach 2007).

Our intent in this chapter is to examine the key ideas that informed the building of the social fabric of Canadian society and how these ideas were transformed into social policies.

Colonial Origins of Welfare

Dennis Guest (1985, 9) traces the origins of modern Canadian social policy back in time to the late sixteenth century in England and France. These colonial legacies came to be reflected in Canada's first constitutional document, the British North America Act of 1867, which regarded matters of social welfare as local and private and thus under provincial jurisdiction. Colonial arrangements for social welfare included local and provincial jails, penitentiaries, and asylums; government funding and supervision of private charities; and municipal/provincial systems of public relief for the poor and destitute. Most of the elements of pre-Confederation social policy are captured in the name of the administrative agency, the Board of Inspectors of Prisons, Asylums, and Public Charities, established in Upper Canada (Ontario) in 1859. In Quebec, public responsibilities for social welfare were assigned to the church (Guest 1985, 13).

Community members generally believed that social problems were the immediate consequences of people's behaviour. Members of the community often assumed that poverty was a symptom of personal weakness and that an inability to take care of oneself was a sign of failure. They believed that families could and should be able to solve their own problems with a little help from the community. Four principles of social provision were established during the colonial era that reflected the way people thought about welfare at the time. These principles have continued to influence the politics of social assistance into the present day.

The first principle was that social assistance should be residual to what was available from other sources. Private philanthropy, good neighbours, voluntary organizations, and the churches were all looked to as important and legitimate sources of help for people in need. Indeed, colonial administrations delegated or contracted out the responsibility to care for the poor and destitute to charities and religious orders. Only after all other sources of help had been used up could people legitimately turn to the government for help. Public relief was usually financed and administered by local governments from a rather restricted tax base, and rudimentary bureaucracies provided the services.

The second principle was that social assistance should be targeted to particular groups. Public support for the poor was intended for certain "deserving" groups – the old, orphans, the mentally ill, and the disabled. An able-bodied unemployed person (someone Canadian governments now call an "employable") who applied for public assistance was expected to perform work as a condition for receiving it (Guest 1985, 37). This was called the "workhouse test" or "work test." For the children of poor families there were apprenticeships.

The third principle was that assistance should be conditional on the applicant engaging in certain civic duties or activities, with penalties for those who did not comply. In the colonial era, the laws concerning relief to the poor included sections on parents' responsibility to care for their children and on older children's responsibility to help care for their parents and grandparents.

The fourth principle – that of "less eligibility" – was that assistance should be minimal, not optimal or even average in amount. Thus, anyone collecting social assistance should receive an amount less than that of the lowest-paid worker so as not to encourage dependency on relief or to undermine the work ethic and low wages. This principle is evident to this day in discussions of welfare rates, minimum wages, and the work (dis)incentives supposedly built into welfare and employment insurance. For observers of welfare reform and of debates over "workfare" in Canada in recent years, this all should sound eerily familiar.

The dominant ideology of the colonial era stressed the importance of private initiative and individual responsibility. It was rooted in a strong belief in the work ethic and self-improvement. The broad assumption was that successful families were hard working and frugal, whereas people living in poverty were lazy or unwilling to make sacrifices. Sometimes the poor were thought of as "down on their luck." However, those who were indigent and dependent were viewed in the same way as criminals and the mentally ill – that is, as responsible for their fate and deserving of their "lot in life." The ethos of individualism, the pioneer experience, and (later) industrial capitalism fostered the notion that the first line of defence against poverty was the family. Where that institution failed, charities, voluntary organizations, church groups, missions, child welfare societies, and neighbourhood settlement houses were expected to respond by developing and maintaining social programs for those in need. The word "relief" appropriately described social welfare in this early stage because it implied the state's limited acceptance of a "public" responsibility to care for those who were unable to care for themselves. The belief in self-reliance encouraged the notion that governments should involve themselves as little as possible in the private affairs of citizens.

Growing Country, Growing Community Needs: 1867 to the Early 1900s

Social ideas evolved slowly. Elisabeth Wallace (1950, 383) suggests that the origins of the Canadian welfare state can be traced to the first thirty years or so after Confederation, from 1867 to 1900, "when the proper function of government was a matter of general concern and wide debate." During this period, economic and social conditions as well as public opinion on what constituted a proper society "underwent a marked transformation." Given the changing social conditions, governments in Canada – especially municipalities but also the provinces – were being required to intervene more and more in the social sphere. After Confederation, as people left their farms for work opportunities in the growing towns and cities, they found that their lifestyles changed. There was less allegiance to and reliance on the family. The separation from the family and the farm created new situations that required people to find new ways of meeting their needs. Gone or declining were the rural communities with their unambiguous social structures. Gone, too, was the sense of community that had seemed to protect individuals or families as a matter of course. Going or gone was the reliance on a self-sufficient environment.

New ways of life were emerging. Towns were growing, as were urban slums. Urbanization was creating new eating and drinking habits. Spending and consuming patterns were changing, as were health and sanitary practices, and new norms for personal interaction were evolving. Problems of infant mortality, child neglect, and juvenile delinquency were becoming more evident as well as more serious. In the 1890s and early 1900s, men and women viewed these social problems in different ways. Thelma McCormack (1991, 31) points out that "men saw the industrial system, the factories, women saw the slums and households; men saw exploited workers, women saw women exhausted by child-bearing; men saw unemployment, women saw sick and underfed children; men saw industrial accidents, women saw the impact of alcoholism on the family." Men pushed for policies relating to factory conditions, workers' compensation, and pensions. It was not uncommon for women to push for policy measures concerning public health, family planning, mothers' pensions, and, later, family allowances.

With urbanization, Canadian society became fragmented and differentiated. A wage labour class emerged that was heavily reliant on others for income. Unemployment was always a threat. As all these changes took place, new stresses and strains were placed on people to find ways to cope. Individuals were forced to turn more and more to their communities for help. As J.S. Woodsworth (1972, 178) observed in 1911: "In a small community it is easy to give relief to the occasional needy family. There exists a personal relationship which largely precludes imposition, and which goes far in encouraging thrift. But in the city the situation is quite changed. The well-to-do are separated from their less fortunate neighbours by distance and by social cleavages of many kinds. The very numbers make personal knowledge and sympathy almost an impossibility."

Table 2.1. Provincial Social Expenditure (Gross), 1871–1977

Year	Social Welfare %		Health %	Education %	Protection %
1871	–	9.5	–	22.5	12.8
1881	–	12.7	–	16.6	8.1
1891	–	13.4	–	16.8	10.8
1901	–	14.7	–	15.1	8.9
1911	–	11.1	–	14.2	7.7
1921	3.9		8.6	20.0	9.2
1931	5.8		8.1	18.0	6.2
1941	10.8		9.6	13.7	B
1951	14.1		17.1	16.1	5.1
1961	11.0		24.8	22.9	3.8
1971	11.3		26.7	26.8	3.4
1977	14.6		24.3	23.6	3.5

Source: Allan Moscovitch and Jim Albert, eds. The Benevolent State: The Growth of Welfare in Canada (Toronto: Garamond, 1987), 22.

In the later decades of the nineteenth century, public attitudes were shifting as well, and the ideas of "laissez-faire and individualism were being challenged by notions of social justice, by a concern for the well-being of the group and of the wider interests of the community as a whole" (Guest 1985, 24). As people became separated from their families and communities by the process of industrialization, they found it more difficult to meet their needs. There was growing cultural disorganization, secularization, and individualism.

The new social stresses encouraged the provinces to involve themselves in social welfare. Table 2.1 shows that from the beginning of Confederation, the four provinces were spending more than 40 per cent of their budgets on social welfare, health, education, and protection. These figures fluctuated as new provinces joined Confederation and the country lived through two world wars, but they never fell below one-third of all provincial expenditures. This contradicts the common perception, as disseminated in some history texts and in today's media, that the provinces did little to address social issues while the country was being formed and that "rugged individuals" took care of themselves.

As industrialization transformed Canadian society, old structures and processes were found to be inadequate. Through social and political action, citizens encouraged the provinces to take on more responsibility for certain groups: the aged, the sick, children, and people with mental disabilities. The provinces provided an ever-expanding range of institutions: tuberculosis hospitals, homes for the aged and infirm, child welfare services, and other specialized programs. In 1874, Ontario passed the Charity Aid Act, which established a uniform structure for government grants to voluntary social welfare organizations – from now on, such grants would be determined in accordance with the services actually performed and the amount of funds received from other sources. Another key principle in the legislation was that voluntary agencies receiving provincial grants would be subject to provincial supervision or monitoring. The Charity Aid Act amounted to a recognition on politicians' part that voluntary agencies would play a continuing role as instruments of provincial social policy.

"Although it was not until the twentieth century that the phrase social security was invented, and emphasis placed upon the need for *prevention* as more important than cure in attacking social problems, the germ of the idea may be found well before 1900" (Wallace 1950, 387). By 1893, 32.4 per cent of the Ontario budget was being devoted to social welfare spending. Splane (1965) suggests that this increase in expenditures through the 1880s and 1890s indicated the emergence of a philosophy of prevention. The prevention of illness, disability, and dependency was the essence of the province's new public health program and factory inspection measures. Beginning with Ontario in 1884, followed by Quebec in 1885, Manitoba in 1900, and the other provinces later, the provinces enacted Factory Acts to regulate the conditions of industrial work. A child welfare program "represented the willingness of the province to launch a new non-institutional type of programme aimed at preventing crime and dependency through timely assistance to the neglected and dependent child" (Splane 1965). This philosophy of prevention and increasing provincial action on social welfare was partly the result of efforts by pioneer social researchers and reformers and partly the result of advocacy by Canadian trade unions, the urban reform movement, and the Social Gospel movement.

Throughout this period (1800 to 1900), the radical idea of "public" education was being promoted by church groups, concerned citizens, and a group of "school promoters." In many ways the development of public education reflected general changes in the way people thought about the government's responsibilities. Families had long been viewed as responsible for educating their children, either by sending them out to work with older, more experienced family members or – if they had the means – by sending them to private grammar schools (1807). It was not until 1816 that Ontario introduced its first Elementary Schools Act, which set up eight school districts in the province. The other provinces slowly took Ontario's lead as "school promoters" encouraged provincial action. This early education was as concerned with solving social problems such as crime, poverty, and idleness, and with integrating immigrants into the British social system, as it was with teaching children to read, write, and do arithmetic. Reformers such as Egerton Ryerson (in Ontario), Jean-Baptiste Meilleur (in Quebec), and John Jessop (in British Columbia) worked to develop a system of public education in Canada.

By the beginning of the 1900s, provincial and municipal governments and school boards were providing free, widely available public education with compulsory attendance. Also, free public libraries were being established in many towns and cities across Canada, as were playgrounds, parks, community centres, and art galleries (Wallace 1950; Cassidy 1947; Manzer 1985).

The Shift to Provincial and Federal Responsibility for Income Security Policy: 1914 to the 1930s

Growing industrialization and urbanization created many new problems for families in Canada. There was increased risk of industrial accidents, sickness from living in an urban setting, and unemployment as a result of volatility in the economy. There was also increased likelihood of mental illness due to social stress as well as a rising threat to families from crime. Because market mechanisms were unable to provide employment for all Canadians, governments needed to provide welfare programs. Municipalities were unable to create the necessary programs in any systematic and effective way, and this forced people to turn to higher levels of government. The provincial and federal governments both responded to the demand. Next, then, we examine the role of the provincial and federal governments in social programs, especially with regard to income security reforms.

Provincial Responsibility

The provinces agreed to take over more responsibilities. This meant having to expand the programs they offered and the services they provided. New programs and organizational structures introduced in one province were soon copied or adapted in several others, and still later by the rest, though often with a lag of ten to twenty years. This pattern of social policy innovation, diffusion, time lag, and convergence was to be repeated numerous times throughout the twentieth century. Between 1914 and 1939, there were four major developments that reflected this pattern of welfare provision with respect to income support – changes that together represented a modernization of income security policy in Canada. Each of these developments has been examined at some length in the literature, so we need only briefly note them here.

First, workers' compensation was introduced, initially in Ontario (1914), followed soon after by Nova Scotia (1915), British Columbia (1916), Alberta and New Brunswick (1918), and Manitoba (1920). About a decade later, Saskatchewan (1929) and Quebec (1931) enacted comparable legislation, and much later Prince Edward Island (1949) and Newfoundland (1950) did the same. Workers' compensation was based on the principle of insurance and rooted in the rights of workers under the common law. The insurance principle fitted well with the ethos of industrial capitalism. It was an accepted market mechanism, even though it altered the employment contract by creating new obligations between worker and employer. It brought the state further into the worker/employer relationship by making government party to the contract.

Second, most provinces introduced mothers' pensions or allowances, beginning in western Canada with Manitoba (1916), Saskatchewan (1917), Alberta (1919), and British Columbia (1920). Ontario followed soon after (1920); there was then a lag until Nova Scotia (1930), Quebec (1937), New Brunswick (1943), and Prince Edward Island (1949) introduced similar programs. Program design varied across the provinces in terms of the range of single-mother situations covered, residence requirements (if any), and other eligibility criteria. All of the mothers' allowance programs, however, provided means-tested public assistance to certain indigent mothers with children. For the most part, private charities and voluntary agencies were still strong believers in individualism and self-reliance; suspecting that government aid weakened people's will to work and bred dependency, they were unsympathetic if not hostile to the idea of income support for needy mothers (Guest 1985, 52–61).

Third, provincial minimum-wage laws were another advance in income security policy. The early wave of legislation began with British Columbia and Manitoba (1918), then Quebec and Saskatchewan (1919), Ontario (1920), and Alberta (1922). Nova Scotia enacted a law in 1920 but did not implement it until 1930. Other provinces introduced minimum wage laws even later.

Fourth was the provision for old age pensions (examined in detail later in this chapter). The Old Age Pensions Act was passed in 1927. The four western provinces and Ontario accepted the plan within a year or two; then it took nearly ten years for the Maritime provinces and Quebec to enter into the agreement (Bryden 1974).

These four reforms represented a modernization of the concept of social assistance. Social assistance had evolved from the traditional private practices of poor relief by private charities, churches, and municipalities into a public responsibility addressed in legislation and administered by trained civil servants. The four program reforms provincialized income support. They were provincially financed in whole or in part, with some costs shared with employers (the case with workers' compensation and minimum-wage rates) or with municipalities and the federal government (the case with old age pensions).

The Federal Government's Expanding Social Policy Role

The British North America Act of 1867 assigned the provinces major responsibility for much of what today we call social policy. Thus the stories typically told about the rise of state social welfare in Canada over the first sixty years of Confederation emphasize the role of the provinces and local governments. The limitation of this approach is that it overlooks the federal government's key social roles, which leads to a narrow view of what constitutes social welfare and whom social policies and programs have affected.

Under the Constitution, the Canadian Parliament's original legislative powers relating to social welfare encompassed the military, and hence veterans; marine hospitals; the census and statistics; regulatory powers over trade and commerce as well as weights and measures; immigration, naturalization, and aliens; Indians and lands reserved for

Indians; marriage and divorce; and the criminal law and penitentiaries. These functional responsibilities were underpinned by fiscal powers that gave Ottawa the authority to raise money by any mode of taxation and by borrowing on public credit.

Deficit financing was pursued by successive federal governments from the 1870s to the 1890s in the face of three economic recessions and the imperatives of nation building (Gillespie 1991; Wallace 1950). Between 1917 to 1923 the personal income tax, the corporate income tax, and the manufacturers' sales tax (the predecessor to the goods and services tax [GST] introduced in the late 1980s) were inaugurated. Over the following decades, these taxes would become the major sources of revenue for the federal government.

The composition of a political cabinet tells us something about the policy functions and priorities of a government, as well as about the times in which they govern. In 1867 the federal public service contained thirteen ministerial departments, two of which were concerned with social policy: Justice and Agriculture, the latter having responsibilities for health and for immigrants. The Department of the Interior, created in 1873, was responsible for Canada's Native populations. Indian Acts were passed in 1876, 1880, and 1884. In 1880 the ministerial position of Superintendent General of Indian Affairs was established. The federal Department of Labour was formed in 1900. A small number of new federal social ministries were created at or near the end of the First World War – specifically, the Departments of Immigration and Colonialization in 1917, the Department of Soldiers Civil Re-establishment in 1918, and the Ministry of Health in 1919. The latter two were relatively new fields of activity for the federal government (Hodgetts 1973), though the Department of Health did bring together health services from a number of other federal departments, along with the Dominion Council of Health, which was formed at the same time. The council was an early example of administrative federalism with an element of citizen participation; it consisted of the federal Deputy Minister of Health as chair, the deputy minister or executive director of each provincial Department of Health or Board of Health, and up to five other people appointed by the federal cabinet. In 1928 the Department of Health and the Soldiers Civil Re-establishment Department were merged to form the Department of Pensions and National Health to provide veterans with pensions, medical treatment, and sheltered employment. So over the course of twenty years the federal government moved from two to six ministerial departments dedicated to social policy.

But the federal government was not limited to the policy side. Like the provinces, it also became involved in income security. The federal government's earliest meaningful entry into income security came with the introduction of financial benefits for veterans.[1] Andrew Armitage (1996, 197) explains: "Federal involvement was a product of high regard for veterans but also of social unrest, including the Winnipeg General Strike. Returning veterans were not assured work and found a marked contrast between the society's rhetoric and their destitute circumstances." Between 1916 to 1939, the federal government was quite active in veterans' policy development, passing two Orders in Council and five key pieces of legislation, as well as another dozen acts that amended legislation. In 1916 the federal cabinet instituted a Board of Pension Commissioners to award and administer pensions to veterans of the First World War. Pension regulations were established that replaced the pay and allowance regulations of the Department of Defence. Under the previous rules, a disability or death had to be directly due to service to qualify for payments; the new regulations introduced the insurance principle.

In 1918, just after the war ended, the cabinet amended the regulations to introduce the principle of "prospective dependency" for parents of deceased members of the armed forces. Earlier that year, legislation establishing the Department of Soldiers Civil Re-establishment had been passed, and that department was given responsibility for helping reestablish First World War veterans in civilian life and for offering care to their dependants. The 1919 Soldier Settlement Act defined as a "settler" any person who, at any time during the 1914–18 war, had been engaged in active service with a military force from Canada, Britain, or any British dominion or colony; and the widow of any person who would have been eligible if he had lived. A Soldier Settlement Board was created and authorized to issue free land of up to 160 acres to any settler; to make provision for instruction in agriculture and economics for settlers; and, among other benefits, to make cash advances of up to $1,000 for permanent improvements to land.

The Pension Act of 1919 was the other key piece of legislation for veterans in the aftermath of the war. Under this measure, the federal government committed itself to providing pensions for disabled members of the armed forces and their dependants, on a scale based on the degree of disability and the military rank of the veteran. Pensions were also provided for dependants on the death of a veteran, the amount geared to military rank. Here, for the first time, the principle of income support as partial compensation for disability or death was introduced into federal policy. Equally noteworthy, disability pensions awarded under the Pension Act were the first universal income benefit in Canadian social policy, for neither the entitlement to a pension nor the amount of that pension was determined by the veteran's financial circumstances. (We discuss the topic of universality and selectivity in social programs fully in chapter 7.) During the 1920s and 1930s the Pension Act was amended several times in the direction of expanding eligibility of benefits, increasing benefit amounts, and establishing and reorganizing the structures that would allow hearings and decisions on appeals when such pensions were refused.

Despite all the social security measures for veterans, the programs did not "deal adequately with the problem of the prematurely old (burnt out) veteran, and, in 1930, under considerable pressure from veterans organizations, Parliament passed the War Veterans Allowance Act" (Bryden 1974, 79). This program provided means-tested allowances for veterans aged sixty or over and for veterans who were permanently unemployable because of a physical or mental disability; it also extended allowances to their wives and dependants. The basic benefit was the same as under the Old Age Pensions Act of 1927 but was available at a younger age. Under the old age pension law, benefits were payable to certain individuals seventy years of age or over; while the war veterans' allowance was available to certain veterans at age sixty.[2]

With the Old Age Pensions Act of 1927, the federal government formally entered the social security arena in a major way for the second time. The legislation authorized federal reimbursement of 50 per cent to any participating province for pensions to British subjects (Canada did not pass a citizenship law until 1947) aged seventy or over who had resided in Canada for at least twenty years and in the province for at least five years. Native Canadians were excluded from the program. The maximum pension, which was means tested, was initially $240 a year, an amount unchanged until the 1940s.

The responsibilities of the federal and provincial governments for old age pensions, acknowledged in the legislation and fulfilled through conditional grants, meant there was no politically easy way to alter existing programs in the short term; both levels of government had to agree on the problems and the solutions. Guest (1985, 79) claims that as far as early pensions were concerned, this was an unintended benefit. It would have been difficult for either party to alter the agreement, and this made for "a degree of stability from the beginning which enhanced the programmes' worth, particularly during the depression of the 1930s when many government programmes had to be severely curtailed."

The 1930s: The Depression Decade

The Great Depression profoundly affected many Canadians and deeply influenced how governments and the public thought about social policies. The economics, ideas, and politics that had influenced the development of the Old Age Pension and other federal, provincial, and municipal programs were dramatically altered by the depression, which spanned the entire decade of the 1930s with worldwide consequences. By 1933, in the depths of the depression, the Canadian economy had shrunk by one-third from its level in 1929. Over the same period, the official unemployment rate rose from about 3 per cent to 25 and then 30 per cent of the work force (Goffman 1968; Marsh 1975). Industrial production fell by half; exports fell by two-thirds, and construction dropped to one-tenth of its previous level. With hundreds of thousands out of work, family dislocation, social unrest, and political dissatisfaction were heightened. Canadians increasingly came to believe that unemployment and poverty were not the result of individual characteristics or failures, but rather of larger social and economic forces, both domestic and international.

The social and economic chaos generated by the depression forced individuals, families, and communities to look for new ways to protect themselves from economic instability and other risks. The search for security undermined earlier ideas about self-sufficient individualism. A wider range of ideologies became popular in various segments of society: socialism, communism, and fascism, to name a few. There was, too, rapid growth in alternative political organizations: the Social Credit Party, the Co-operative Commonwealth Federation (CCF; precursor to the New Democratic Party), the Union Nationale, farmers' unions and cooperatives. Each of these organizations sought to protect individuals from the uncertainties of unbridled capitalism. There was a growing belief that government had to provide some form of assistance for those who could not protect themselves against unemployment and other risks. These beliefs and the resulting demands shaped a new "social contract" under which people were prepared to live and work.

The costs for relief programs had to be met by the provincial governments, whose sources of tax revenue were declining in the 1930s. Local municipalities – the traditional level of government for responding to such needs – could not deal with the magnitude of the problem, so the provision of relief shifted in large part to the provinces. This centralizing tendency was not to be reversed. The change in social policy structures and resources can be seen in the shifting shares of social welfare expenditures by municipalities and provinces. In 1913, local expenditures on health and welfare were twice the provincial ones. Just twenty-five years later, the situation was more than reversed. By the end of the 1930s the provinces were spending more than twice as much on social welfare as the municipalities were.[3] With harsh economic conditions persisting throughout the decade, the costs of unemployment relief hopelessly exceeded the financial resources of municipal and provincial governments. The federal government was required to provide substantial assistance to the provinces. Through a series of special grants, federal help was delivered, even while the provinces' constitutional responsibilities for welfare matters were respected. Harry Cassidy (1947, 52) called these relief arrangements the first nationwide service of economic security for the Canadian population: "The result was a great emergency system of unemployment relief administered mainly by the municipalities according to traditional poor-law methods but financed largely by the Dominion Government and the provinces through grants-in-aid. This system lasted 10 years, from 1931 to 1941; involved total expenditures of about one billion dollars, and at its peak (in April 1933) supported nearly 1,600,000 persons, about 15 per cent of the total population."

The Department of National Defence established relief camps for the unemployed and indigent, but these were deeply unpopular. Their intent had been to offer some relief and work as well as to maintain public order. The camps were located in remote areas, where unemployed men lived in bunkhouses and were paid a dollar a week to do menial labour. As Leonard Marsh (1975, xiv) reported many years later about these camps, "growing resentment culminated in the March to Ottawa, and the confrontation with the police in Regina, in 1935. Following a change of [federal] government in that year, they were discontinued."

Besides providing grants-in-aid to the provinces for unemployment relief, the federal government undertook other social policy initiatives during this decade, some of them successful, others dramatically not. For example, we have already mentioned legislative measures with respect to veterans and old age pensioners made in the 1930s that extended benefits. Another related measure was an amendment in 1937 to the Old Age Pensions Act that provided for pensions to blind persons aged forty and over, with a maximum monthly payment equal to that of the old age pension. A third policy initiative, this one a response to the prolonged drought in western Canada, was the Prairie Farm Assistance Act, passed in 1939. The Canadian Wheat Board also was formed in this period.

In addition, the federal government entered the field of housing policy.[4] The Dominion Housing Act of 1935 authorized federal assistance in the construction of houses for persons with moderate incomes, by making loans available through private lending institutions. The National Housing Act of 1938 replaced the earlier legislation and extended the scope of assistance; the purpose here was to improve housing conditions and stimulate the construction and building materials industries. The new legislation, administered by the Minister of Finance, also enabled the federal government to make direct loans to local housing authorities to assist in the construction of low-income rental housing. This legislation began the trend of using housing policy as a tool of economic stimulation and development (Prince 1995).

The social policy initiatives described above were all successful. We now turn to the ones that failed. The most ambitious policy effort at federal intervention in social and economic affairs, and the most dramatic failure, was the Employment and Social Insurance Act, passed in 1935, at the end of R.B. Bennett's Conservative government. This legislation was revolutionary in the Canadian context, given the broad scope of planned new public programs and the potential extent of intervention by Ottawa into what were provincial, local, and private-sector domains. The legislation provided for action on unemployment insurance and on health care. An employment and social insurance commission was to be formed to administer a national employment service and a program of unemployment insurance for certain classes of workers. Insurance contributions were to be made by both employees and employers. For persons excluded from insurance coverage, assistance would be provided during periods of unemployment. As well, training would be offered, in cooperation with educational institutions, to rehabilitate unemployed persons. Regarding health care, the legislation charged the commission with collecting information and submitting to cabinet implementation proposals for providing – in cooperation with the provinces, municipalities, corporations, and other groups –benefits for medical, dental, and surgical care, including medicines, drugs, appliances, or hospitalization; as well as compensation for loss of earnings arising out of ill health, accident, or disease. Bennett also promised improvements to old age pensions, a federal minimum wage, and a shorter work week. Mackenzie King returned to power in the 1935 federal election, and in the face of sharp provincial attacks on Bennett's "New Deal" legislation, referred the law to the courts for a ruling on its constitutionality.[5] In 1937 the Judicial Committee of the Privy Council in Britain (at that time the final court of appeal for Canada) declared the Employment and Social Insurance Act *ultra vires*, or beyond the powers of the federal government as granted under the Constitution.

This constitutional ruling brought the country to an impasse. Most authority for social policy resided with the provinces and the municipalities, yet the staggering events of the 1930s had made it clear that these governments were unable financially to provide programs and services that would prevent starvation, offer relief and hope, and proffer a modicum of economic security. At the same time, even though the federal government may have had sufficient resources and even the inclination to involve itself more deeply in the social security of Canadians, key provinces were unwilling to relinquish jurisdiction to Ottawa, and the King government was loath to intervene in these areas without provincial support. In true Canadian political fashion, "this complex constitutional issue was referred in 1937 to the Royal Commission on Dominion–Provincial Relations (the Rowell–Sirois Commission), which did not submit its report until the beginning of the war. By then the needs for relief had greatly diminished, and the Dominion–provincial controversy regarding the social services was, temporarily, at least, subordinated to other issues" (Cassidy 1947, 53). Thus the most ambitious social policy initiatives of the time were never implemented.

Conclusions

As we have seen throughout this chapter, social welfare as a communal and governmental activity predates the rise of the welfare state in the 1940s as well as the academic discipline of social policy. The origins and extent of public intervention in social welfare are found perhaps unexpectedly early in Canadian history.

Over the period surveyed, from the colonial era to the end of the 1930s, social policy emerged and evolved along many dimensions, four of which we observe here. First, the sponsorship of social care and control began shifting from the private and charitable sectors to the state sector, with public bodies taking on responsibility for child welfare, public health, education, and the income needs of injured workers, single mothers, soldiers, and seniors. Second, within the Canadian state, the level of government(s) involved in social programs changed from a heavy reliance on municipalities to a reliance on the provinces and on federal initiatives and federal–provincial arrangements. Local bodies kept an important role outside of income support, however, in matters such as education, public libraries, policing, parks, and recreation. Third, the structures for providing and administering services changed from being local and non-professional in nature to being more centralized, provincial/federal, and professional (Cassidy 1947; Rice 1979). Fourth, the policy instruments applied by governments for designing and implementing social programs changed over this period. Several innovations took place: there came to be an early emphasis not simply on remedial measures but also on preventive services; the first social insurance program, Workers' Compensation, was created; the first universal income benefit, disability pensions for war veterans, was established; and federal–provincial cost-sharing agreements were negotiated with respect to health care, old age pensions, and unemployment relief.

Social welfare policy in Canada has developed in response to and in interaction with several factors. At one level are broad socio-economic trends and political events: the rise of industrial capitalism, urbanization, and immigration, as well as the profound effects of the First World War, the depressions of the late 1800s, and the Great Depression of the 1930s. We have discussed how these forces affected individuals' lives, family and community structures, and the economy and the labour market. At a second level is the role of ideas and beliefs, which of course intermingle with material circumstances. By the 1890s, "social and economic conditions had so altered that public opinion was demanding government action on matters held in 1867 to be primarily personal and of no concern to the state" (Wallace 1950,384). Liberal individualism, Christian charity, private altruism, trade unionism, and socialist thought all influenced, in different degrees and ways, the development of social welfare policy. Also significant was the prevailing philosophy of public finance and government budgeting. This was a view of the state as modestly active, influenced by a concern for balanced budgets. The state was like the household and should live within its means (Maslove, Prince, and Doern 1986; Gillespie 1991). International experiences were also important – a factor we give attention to in the next chapter. Finally, at a third level are political forces and governmental factors. These include the impact of the Constitution, judicial

rulings, and the evolution of intergovernmental relations; the role of social movements, businesses, and interest groups; the limited tax base of
municipalities, and the later development of local government in Newfoundland and the Western provinces; and processes of social policy
experimentation and dispersion across Canadian jurisdictions. In practice, woven together, these three levels of factors constitute the political context in which the social welfare and diswelfares of people are
experienced. This context simultaneously displays changes and continuities, and embodies forces that both support and resist the development of social programs as well as the rights and duties of citizenship.

3 Envisaging and Establishing a System of Social Security for Canadians

Having reviewed the ideas informing the early developments in social welfare, we now examine the first period of modern social policy and the formation of a welfare state in Canada between approximately 1940 and the early 1970s. We begin by looking at what community activists and politicians came to think about social issues and their ideas concerning how to solve some of the social problems facing Canadians. Thinkers such as Leonard Marsh, Harry Cassidy, Charlotte Whitton, C.A. Curtis, and J.J. Heagerty wrote important reports or chaired important committees, while federal civil servants such as Joseph Willard, George Davidson, and Robert Bryce helped design the systems. Many of these ideas were put into practice between 1940 and the early 1970s. Our goal is to identify the thinking behind social security proposals and to discuss the forces that affected the major social policy developments over this period.

Envisaging a Social Security System

The process of envisaging a social security system for Canadians began in the 1930s and intensified during the 1940s. Social researchers and government bodies gathered information and drew lessons from the harsh experiences of the Great Depression; they also looked at the social risks, needs, and hopes of Canadians during the Second World War (1939–45). In planning for the postwar reconstruction of Canada's economy and society, they contemplated better ways of addressing a variety of social problems. As Leonard Marsh (1975) remarked at the end of this period, whatever the war represented in terms of death and destruction, it was a time of political agitation and of a fundamental rethinking of economic management and social policy making. The events of the 1940s were epoch making for social security in many countries. As Ed Broadbent (2010) has pointed out, the 1948 Universal Declaration of Human Rights was based on a fundamentally radical social policy idea: every woman and man has an inherent and equal right to a life of dignity. The term "welfare state" – itself coined during the war – generally referred to government responsibility for providing a range of services, benefits, and rights for citizens (who in turn had their duties). A welfare state or system of social security entailed governments financing, organizing, and delivering varying levels and forms of health care, housing, education, income support, and social services. Government was also to play an active role in steering the economy towards the goals of high and stable levels of income and employment. In Canada, governments – especially the federal government – were seen as providing leadership in developing a comprehensive and nationwide social security system.

A community of reformers, intellectuals, and public administrators – the "government generation" (Owram 1986) – played an energetic part in redefining the Canadian state's social role. New ideas concerning the relationship between state and citizen and the purpose of social programs were conceived and considered. It can be said that the initial wave of thinking about a social security system for Canada took place between about 1937, when the Rowell–Sirois Commission began its work, and 1945, when federal proposals for postwar reconstruction were presented at a federal–provincial conference. A second wave of taking stock and contemplating the future of social policy took place during the late 1960s and early 1970s, at the end of this period of establishment and expansion.

How important were ideas in directing the formation of social policy in Canada? One view is that they were influential but that the process of development was deeply affected by circumstances of the day. Alan Cairns and Cynthia Williams (1985, 16) have argued that "the Canadian welfare state is a classic example of incrementalism. Its development was ad hoc and subject to the complexities of the division of powers. No articulate philosophy guided its halting early development and subsequent consolidation." A different view holds that besides economic and social forces, visions of the welfare state "powerfully shaped" the evolution of Canadian social policy. Keith Banting (1987, 147) has argued that "social policy making inevitably proceeds within a broad conceptual framework that defines the critical problems facing society, the goals that should guide government action, and the range of relevant policy alternatives. These underlying assumptions about the domain of social policy need not always be comprehensive, internally consistent, or explicitly elaborated. Nonetheless, they are critical; decision making is inevitably guided by a general conception of the social role of the state."

Looking back from today's vantage point, it is true that the Canadian network of social programs took thirty years or more to build. That network was built program by program in response to various needs. It was conditioned by the politics of federalism, including at times provincial pressures for federal action. It was an incremental process. Yet if there was no articulate philosophy, there was a set of ideas, expounded in an intelligible fashion to the public and to politicians, about a new economic and social role for the state. These ideas reflected the growing belief that governments could solve some of the problems facing Canadians. Richard Splane (1987, 246) has written of what he refers to as "the initial agenda for the development of a comprehensive social security system for Canada," a hypothetical agenda "conceived and nurtured by the findings of royal commissions and comparable studies conducted from the 1930s into the 1960s." Here, we will examine the thinkers and the documents that set this agenda.

The Ideas of Keynes and Beveridge: Intellectual Foundations of the Welfare State

Two seminal works came out of Britain in the late 1930s and early 1940s: John Maynard Keynes's *The General Theory of Employment, Interest, and Money* (1936), and Sir William Beveridge's report, *Social Insurance and Allied Services* (1942). Both had a dramatic influence on the development of social policy in Canada and elsewhere. Prior to the publication of Keynes's book, economic theorists claimed that full employment was assumed to be part of the natural order of things. Periodic unemployment and recessions were considered aberrations that would be solved through natural market processes. Any person wanting to work would be able to find employment if they looked for it and were willing to accept the wage rate of the day. The theories at the time claimed that high unemployment would only result when wages were kept at unnaturally high levels. The mass unemployment of the 1930s, however, was difficult to explain using accepted economic theory. A million or more individuals were certainly willing to work for any wage in Canada, but there were no jobs for them. Even in the face of these problems, the message from economists was to wait for the downswing to flatten out, as this would eventually turn into an upswing on its own accord.

Keynes argued against this perspective, calling for government spending to stimulate the economy. He contended that the level of unemployment is determined by the level of output, which in turn is determined by the level of effective demand. Effective demand is affected by expenditure, which is affected by the supply of income. Keynes divided income into consumption and investment and demonstrated that individual decisions made about consumption and investment would not necessarily create full employment. The policy implication was that if the community wanted full employment, then its governments would have to take steps to modify the levels of consumption and investment.

The importance of Keynes's critique and prescription for social policy was clear. Up to this point, social policy had been seen as a means of providing relief to those who were unable to provide for themselves. It was now evident that environmental conditions played a large part in one's ability to find and keep work. It also became evident that social policy could play a much larger role than just that of welfare – it could be used as an important tool for economic management. Keynesian economics postulated a direct link between social policy and economic development. Each area might have its own goals, but achievement in the one area could have positive outcomes in the other. By encouraging consumer demand through public expenditures, the government could promote full employment, a goal of economic policy. The government could sustain economic growth by fuelling the economy; if prices became inflationary, it could withdraw expenditures and thereby cut back on economic stimulation. Politically, this happy marriage of the welfare function and the economic management function reduced the hostility towards the introduction of large-scale social programs (Rice 1979).

The emergence and at least partial acceptance of Keynesian thinking by governments in Canada and other industrial countries in the 1940s changed the language of social policy. The debate was described no longer in terms of a struggle between capitalism and socialism, or between the exploitation of workers and the sanctity of unregulated private enterprise, but rather in terms of the economic necessity of stabilization, regulation, and stimulation. Social welfare programs became countercyclical benefits rather than anti-capitalist intrusions in the economy. From Keynes's perspective, mass unemployment was not simply a result of "private troubles" that families were expected to endure on their own; rather, it was the result of economic conditions and was a public issue to be addressed through public policies. Strengthened by fresh memories of the Great Depression, the realities of wartime mobilization – which had required strong central government intervention – and the desire to avoid another economic downturn after the war, Keynesian concepts provided a practical blueprint for government involvement in economic and social management.

The Beveridge Report attracted great attention on both sides of the Atlantic. Beveridge is widely regarded as the principal architect of much of British social legislation in the 1940s, including the 1944 Education Act, the 1945 Family Allowance Act, the 1946 National Insurance and National Health Service Acts, and the 1948 National Assistance Act. He believed that the need for public assistance and means-tested relief would dwindle to a minor role after a system of social security had been introduced. Though the British government did not adopt all of Beveridge's notions, Canadian thinkers introduced many of his ideas into the debates about social security and used his model as the foundation of the welfare state.

In 1940, Beveridge chaired an interdepartmental committee of civil servants established by the British government to undertake a comprehensive survey of existing national schemes of social insurance and affiliated services, including workers' compensation, and to consider adding health benefits to others not covered by social programs. Unlike Canada, Britain by the early 1940s had a fairly extensive system of social security programs in place. A good part of the Beveridge report therefore entailed extensions of existing policies and the integration of various administrative arrangements. A main proposal, for instance, was the unification of social insurance and public assistance programs with respect to contributions and administration. Beveridge described a plan for social security that would attack what he called the five giants facing modern society – want, disease, ignorance, squalor, and idleness – all of them great obstacles on the path of social progress. The principal reforms that Beveridge recommended included a universal national health service; a universal children's allowance; a comprehensive social insurance plan to address interruptions or loss of earning power due to unemployment, disability, old age, or sickness; and maternity and funeral grants.

Canadian Thinking on Social Security

The flow of ideas from overseas had a profound effect on Canada. Canadians came to believe that governments should become more involved in economic management and the provision of social programs. Just how the governments were to involve themselves was a matter of public debate, which was fuelled by six key documents published between 1940 and 1945. These documents were a turning point in the broader politics of social policy, for they proposed a range of mechanisms for transforming ideas and lessons into concrete programs that would eventually become the foundation of Canada's social security system. The ideas proposed by each report follow.

THE ROWELL–SIROIS COMMISSION

When Prime Minister William Lyon Mackenzie King announced the formation of the Royal Commission on Dominion–Provincial Relations in 1937, Canadian federalism was in fiscal crisis. The provincial governments of Manitoba and Saskatchewan, battered by the depression and severe droughts, were financially unable to provide essential public services and meet their budgetary commitments. That same year, King proposed to the provinces the idea of a national unemployment insurance (UI) scheme, but three premiers rejected the transfer of constitutional power over UI to the federal Parliament. The commission's major task was to re-examine the economic and financial basis of Confederation and the distribution of legislative powers in light of the economic and social developments of the past seventy years. The commission was asked to examine the constitutional allocation of revenue sources and governmental burdens placed on the federal and provincial governments; to determine whether the allocation of taxation, public expenditure, and public debt was as equitable and efficient as could be devised; and to investigate federal subsidies and grants to the provincial governments to meet their needs. The supplementary reports to the commission, known as the "Red Books," reviewed all existing social programs: social services, old age pensions, widows' pensions, mothers' allowances, health care, social insurance, and education.

The commission argued that despite serious financial problems facing the provinces, Canada, as a population with diverse origins, traditions, and goals, should remain a federal state. Its report noted that most legislative powers dealing with "pressing social questions" rested with the provinces and should so continue. But it also recognized that the provinces were unable to finance their social welfare responsibilities without financial assistance from the federal government, so it recommended that a system of unconditional adjustment grants be provided to the poorer provinces so that they might provide adequate public services without excessive taxation. The commission also recommended that the federal government take over responsibility for personal and corporate income taxes and that it assume responsibility for the unemployed, the elderly, and provincial debts arising from the Great Depression. However, the provinces rejected these recommendations.

What did come out of the Rowell–Sirois Report was the argument for a national standard for social programs as well as for a national system that would equalize the provinces' fiscal capacities. The report warned that if provincial governments were unduly limited in spending on education or social services, disparities would develop that could have critical implications for national unity and the general welfare. This idea has reverberated through the politics and practices of Canadian federalism ever since, symbolized by the principle of equalization payments, which was enshrined in the Constitution in 1982. Contemporary debate about the social union and national standards in social policy can also be traced back to this landmark study of public finance and Canadian federalism. In 1940, following the Rowell–Sirois Report, Prime Minister King did secure agreement with all the provinces on a constitutional amendment to the British North America Act enabling the federal government to enact legislation on a national UI scheme. UI contributions began the following year; UI benefit payments to eligible unemployed Canadians commenced in 1942.

THE MARSH REPORT

The *Report on Social Security for Canada*, authored by Leonard Marsh and presented to the House of Commons Special Committee on Social Security in 1943, has been called "the most important single document in the history of the development of the welfare state in Canada ... a pivotal document in the development of war and postwar social security programs, the equivalent in Canada of the Beveridge Report in Great Britain" (Bliss 1975, ix). Like Beveridge's report, the Marsh Report contemplated a comprehensive package of social programs for Canadians. Unlike Beveridge's, however, Marsh's report was a preliminary appraisal, not a final blueprint with all the details included on matters such as rates of benefits or levels of contributions.

The three central ideas of Marsh's report were social insurance, children's allowances, and national investment. The Marsh Report argued for greater use of social insurance methods in place of public assistance methods; it also set out the rationale for, and the elements of, an extensive system of social security. The principle of social insurance held many advantages over the public assistance method of relief and means testing: it held recipients partly responsible for meeting the program's costs through mandatory contributions and/or general taxation; it encouraged a feeling of self-dependence; it identified who was eligible to receive benefits; it ensured a broad financial base through the pooling of risks and funds; and as a policy mechanism, it did not have the "flavour of charity." As Marsh (1943, 14) expressed it, "the genius of social insurance is that it enlists the direct support of the classes most likely to benefit, and enlists equally the participation and controlling influence of the state, at the same time as it avoids the evil of pauperization, and the undemocratic influence of excessive state philanthropy."

Marsh distinguished in his scheme between "universal risks," applicable to all persons, or to all persons of a working age; and "employment risks," which are applicable to and insurable for wage earners only. Under the employment group of risks, Marsh recommended a national investment program that, while not a part of the ordinary social security structure, would be included to complete the postwar employment strategy. In contrast to Beveridge, who favoured flat-rate benefits, Marsh proposed that employment-related benefits be largely related to prevailing wage scales. But income maintenance benefits for meeting universal risks would principally be at a standard rate, rather than dependent on past income or wages or the actual amount of the premium or contribution paid. Here again, as discussed in chapter 2 with respect to veterans' disability pensions, was the principle of universality in income support.

The Marsh Report envisaged a federally financed and administered children's allowance for all children, whether or not there were one or two parents and regardless of whether the parents worked or were unemployed.[1] These two categories of benefits would together lay the base for a national minimum, provided as a right; this still, however, left considerable leeway for individual insurance provision and for additional social services. Marsh estimated that the full application of his scheme would cost something approaching $1 billion. That was about four times the total of direct expenditures by all three levels of government in Canada on public welfare in the late 1930s, and represented about 20 per cent of the federal budget for 1942–3.

As part of a "grand economic strategy," Marsh recommended a government-sponsored program of peacetime investment and social and economic development, perhaps lasting for three years or more. Such a national investment program would make work available; by offering wages rather than subsistence support, it would also provide social security for Canadians. Marsh was almost certain that a great range of enterprises could only be undertaken through public initiatives – for example, the redevelopment of blighted urban areas to remove "wastes, eyesores, and social costs." Reflecting the influence of Keynesian economics, Marsh (1975, 83) reminded those who worried about the cost of reforms that "the creation of a social security system brings about directly a stronger demand for what might be called collective consumer goods or social utilities – housing, hospitals, schools, libraries, urban and rural recreation facilities, and so forth."

The federal government's initial reaction to the Marsh Report was not encouraging. According to one social policy historian, the government ignored the report, which was never tabled in Parliament (Guest 1985, 124). Fairly or not, critics argued that the report's scheme was too interventionist, too expensive, and, within Canadian federalism, too centralizing. Nonetheless, a universal family allowance program was introduced in 1945. The Marsh Report's impact over the next few decades was far more significant. Angela Djao (1983, 25) has observed that "not all of Marsh's recommendations were followed or implemented in the ways he suggested. But the general contours of Canada's social welfare programs since the Second World War were sketched out in his grand plan, and, in the main, the same rationale was used."

THE HEAGERTY REPORT

The same day the Marsh Report was released, the *Health Insurance Report* (1943; Heagerty Report) was also published. This report set out plans for a joint federal–provincial health and medical insurance scheme that would be administered by the provinces with financial assistance from the federal government. The report "envisaged the whole population being covered for a full range of benefits in kind, including medical, dental, pharmaceutical, hospital and nursing services" (Guest 1985, 138). Its recommendations, like those in the Marsh report, were based on the social insurance principle, with annual premiums sufficiently low that the program would be universal. After considerable alterations, its proposals were included in the recommendations made by Ottawa to the Dominion–Provincial Conference on Reconstruction in 1945.

THE CURTIS REPORT

The Marsh and Heagerty Reports were followed the next year by the Curtis Report on Housing and Community Planning, which recommended massive federal intervention in the housing market and in town planning. This comprehensive report contended that an adequate and modern housing policy demanded bold action by the public, private, and cooperative sectors. It called for special attention to be paid to low-rental housing, farm housing, and home and farm improvements.

The Curtis Report was a milestone in the enunciation of the federal government's social responsibility in the housing field. Curtis's view of housing policy was a thorough mix of market-assisted and social-based housing (Prince 1989). His vision was breathtaking in its scope; the impact of his ideas, though, was disappointing, perhaps inevitably so. Marsh (1975, xxxi) himself noted thirty years later that "few of the recommendations were followed with any dispatch, in spite of its documentation of the urgency of the situation."

A new National Housing Act, passed in 1944, was designed to promote the construction of new houses, the modernization of existing ones, and the expansion of employment in the postwar period. The Central Mortgage and Housing Corporation (CMHC) began operations in 1946, and a rental housing program for veterans was launched in 1947. However, many of Curtis's recommendations were largely ignored. There was no strong federal leadership in town planning and little action on slum clearance. Priority was not given to low-rental housing until the mid-1960s, to cooperative housing until the mid-1970s.

These first four reports – Rowell–Sirois, Marsh, Heagerty, and Curtis – were all written by advisory committees. Running through these reports were a number of themes reflecting the shifting context and politics of social policy: the economy was not self-regulating and if left unattended would collapse, leading to social upheaval; individual self-reliance had been dramatically altered by urbanization and industrialization, and in dire economic circumstances people could no longer count on family members, charity, or the market to meet their needs; the federal and provincial governments separately and cooperatively would have to become dominant actors in providing protection against income disruption; and social policy instruments and administrative organizations had developed to the point where they could be used to provide comprehensive social security. These themes found voice in claims that the state should accept three fundamental responsibilities: the stabilization of the economy so that the overall risk to wage income would diminish; the creation of high levels of employment; and the development of a social safety net. Broadbent (2010, 3) claims that "what emerged from this thinking was a Canada characterized by a wide range of new social and economic entitlements: government pensions, universal health care, trade union rights, comprehensive unemployment insurance, the expectation that every boy and girl with ability could go to university – and all were paid for by adequate levels of progressive taxation. Benefits that were once available mainly as means-tested charitable benefits had become citizens' rights guaranteed by the state."

The wartime cabinet of Prime Minister King was aware of the growing popularity of these themes and ideas, as demonstrated by public support for the CCF, which had become the official opposition in Ontario in 1944. King's Liberals knew that in the long run, steps would have to be taken to capture the political support these new ideas were attracting. At the same time, a number of influential people in the civil service – intellectual allies of the authors of these reports – were prepared to translate those reports into programs that were ideologically acceptable to the governing party. Thus the Canadian government, as distinct from the advisory committees, released two federal documents in 1945: the White Paper on Employment and Income and the Green Book Proposals to the Dominion–Provincial Conference on Reconstruction.

THE WHITE PAPER

Ideas in the White Paper were previewed in earlier Speeches from the Throne, which spoke of the government's intent to prevent unemployment after the war and, more positively, to secure adequate incomes and full employment for Canadians. Robert Campbell (1987, 3) accurately depicts the White paper as "a precise Keynesian statement of the government's plan to respond to the new socioeconomic public expectations in a particular way." The government's particular Keynesian policy response was economically optimistic, politically restrained, and generally explained in the technocratic language of economics. David Wolfe (1985, 129) contends that over the next three decades, the White Paper would provide the basis for a substantial degree of ideological consensus regarding the conduct of public finance. The White Paper declared that the government had adopted as a major aim of employment policy the creation and maintenance of "a high and stable level of employment and income." The White Paper conveyed the King government's optimism regarding the capacity of private sector investment and enterprise to create sufficient jobs; it also stated that the government did not think it desirable or practicable to expect that further expansion of government would provide the additional employment required.

Thus the White Paper did not call for a significant extension of public ownership. It proposed only a modest program of public works, and it signalled the government's intent to reduce taxation as rapidly as possible. Furthermore, the transition from a wartime to a peacetime economy would involve substituting private-sector expenditures for most public-sector ones. Other ideas in the Marsh Report, however, were visible in the federal government's Green Book submissions to the Dominion–Provincial Conference on Reconstruction, held just a few months after the White Paper's release.

THE GREEN BOOK

The federal submission to the reconstruction conference outlined Ottawa's goals as a high and stable level of employment and income, support of national minimum standards of social services, and a greater degree of public responsibility for economic and social security. The main federal proposals concerned public investment, major reforms to intergovernmental financial arrangements, and several social security initiatives. The social security proposals sought to provide small, regular payments as a protection against the risks and hazards of unemployment, sickness, and old age. The federal proposals were designed to fill three main gaps in the Canadian social security system: health insurance, national old age pensions, and unemployment assistance. More specifically, those proposals offered grants for a national health insurance plan, hospital construction, and a range of public health services; they offered to assume 100 per cent of the cost of a universal old age pension for those aged seventy and over and to contribute 50 per cent of the costs of provincially administered means-tested old age pensions for those between sixty-five and sixty-nine. In addition, the federal government offered to assume responsibility for the able-bodied unemployed not covered under unemployment insurance, through an unemployment assistance program. Grant-in-aid programs would be provided for community planning, housing projects, and slum clearance, and training services would be extended, along with unemployment insurance coverage and benefits. We can see here some – but by no means all or even most – of the recommendations of the Curtis, Marsh, and Heagerty Reports. In relation to the Rowell–Sirois Report, the Green Book "rejected the equalization principles and the concept of effective provincial autonomy" (Black 1975, 53), but it did embrace the notion of national standards for certain public services. Rowell–Sirois had conveyed a view of cooperative federalism; the Green Book communicated a centralist concept that would place greater powers at the federal level.

Compared to the comprehensive social security plans envisaged by policy specialists and social workers in Canada and in other countries, the King government's social security proposals were fairly limited in scope and were based far less on the principle of social insurance. Dennis Guest (1985, 137–8) suggests that this distinctive and meagre policy agenda was partly the result of the government's real priorities: reducing spending and taxes, and balancing the budget. Guest also suggests that the proposals were not framed primarily on their intrinsic merits or on welfare considerations. Rather, they were inducements for the provinces to agree to open their personal and corporate income tax fields and succession duties to Ottawa in return for some form of unconditional grants. In part, too, they were viewed as economic tools for maintaining consumer demand. Finally, by choosing public assistance and universal income policy instruments, the federal government was hoping to sidestep the challenging process of securing agreements to amend the Constitution. In one sense, the 1945 conference on reconstruction ended in failure because of the federal and provincial governments' inability to come to agreement on tax rental arrangements. Consequently, the federal government's modest plans for reforming the social security system were put aside. They were not, however, off the national policy agenda for long. For although the ideas and recommendations of these six documents were not all acted upon immediately, they did fuel the debate about how governments should involve themselves in the management of the economy and in the provision of social programs for years to come. We next discuss some of the programs that were developed over the years in response to the ideas generated by the reports.

Establishing a Comprehensive Social Security System: Implementing an Ordered Series of Measures: 1945 to the Early 1970s

Close to the end of the Marsh Report (1975, 260) the question was raised "whether comprehensive social security should be inaugurated completely or as an ordered series of measures over a period." The report itself offered possible priorities concerning which categories of social need should be given earlier consideration than other categories. The chronicle of the Canadian welfare state shows clearly that a comprehensive social security system was not set up in the space of one government's mandate. Instead, it took more than ten mandates – from the end of the war to the early 1970s – for virtually all of the social security proposals made by the federal government to the provinces at the reconstruction conference to be introduced. Thus the history of social policy in this period is less about sweeping reform than about ordered change; it is less about disjointed incrementalism and more about directed incrementalism; it reflects a sequence of actions by governments implemented one by one over time, but guided and connected by a general conception of, and policy agenda for, the state's social role. Given the broad sweep of program areas in the field of social security, we can discuss only some areas. The following review focuses on the six categories of social need identified by the Marsh Report: unemployment; sickness and medical care; disability; old age and retirement; premature death; and family needs.[2] And as it had the largest impact, we will focus on the Marsh Report as the body of ideas that were acted on.

Unemployment Insurance

As noted earlier, unemployment insurance (UI; much later EI) began as a federal policy initiative a few years before the Marsh report was commissioned. The UI program was amended six times in the nine years between 1946 and 1954, in response to pressures for coverage to be extended to groups of workers hitherto excluded. Coverage was extended by adding particular sectors under the program, such as loggers and nurses, and by raising the annual earnings ceiling to include more middle-income employees. Contribution rates and benefit rates were also increased. In 1945 the federal government introduced a vocational school assistance program, and in 1948 the Vocational Training Act was passed, which led to agreements with the provinces over the next decade (Campbell 1987). Perhaps the most significant change to UI in this period was the introduction in 1950 of extended or supplementary benefits, worth about 80 per cent of regular benefits, to reflect the greater difficulty of finding work during the winter months. Supplementary benefits were originally set for the months of January through March; by 1957 they spanned the period from December to mid-May. A new Unemployment Insurance Act in 1955 replaced the original 1940 legislation. The new act contained a mix of cuts in some areas and enrichments in others. For instance, the maximum duration of benefits was reduced from fifty-one weeks to thirty-six weeks, while the supplementary benefits were replaced with seasonal benefits of the same value as regular benefits. Coverage was again extended to include municipal police forces and certain types of work in agriculture, horticulture, and forestry. Whereas the 1940 act covered 42 per cent of the labour force, the 1955 legislation applied to 75 per cent of workers (Pal 1988). In 1957, coverage was further extended to include employment in fishing.

Between 1946 and 1956 the national unemployment rate in Canada averaged 3.2 per cent; it then rose to 4.6 per cent in 1957 and to 7 per cent in 1958, and stayed around that level for the next three years. In 1959 the UI program was amended to increase the maximum duration of benefits from thirty-six weeks to fifty-two, reversing the change made in 1955. The earnings ceiling and the contribution rates were also raised. From the early to mid-1960s, the Canadian unemployment rate continued to decline, and only a few modest changes were made to UI in that decade.

A major reform to UI took place in 1971. The new act expanded coverage of the workforce, increased benefits and introduced new ones, eased eligibility qualifications, and consolidated regional elements in the program design. The earnings ceiling was eliminated, and coverage was extended to nearly all people in an employee–employer relationship – that it, over 96 per cent of the labour force. The benefit rate for UI was increased to two-thirds of average insured earnings, and the maximum weekly benefit was automatically indexed to changes in the wage rates. New sickness, maternity, and retirement benefits were added to the program for persons with twenty or more weeks of insured earnings. Another innovation was that benefit duration for regular benefits was now to be determined by the number of weeks of insurable employment, as well as by regional and national unemployment levels. Moreover, the 1971 policy provided that employer and employee contributions would cover the costs of the new benefits and the regular benefits when the national unemployment rate was lower than 4 per cent. Also, the federal government would pay the cost of regular benefits when the national unemployment rate was over 4 per cent.

Even with the extensions in coverage made to UI since the early 1940s, many of the unemployed were not insured and thus were ineligible for benefits. In the Green Book proposals, besides promising to extend the UI system, Ottawa offered to assume responsibility for able-bodied unemployed workers not covered by UI and to create a national scheme of unemployment assistance. To permit such a scheme, in 1956 the Unemployment Assistance Act was approved. Rather than being delivered under federal auspices as the Marsh Report (1943) favoured, the plan relied on the existing provincial and local welfare bureaucracies. The federal government was authorized to reimburse a province 50 per cent of the amount spent by provincial and municipal authorities on financial assistance to unemployed persons in need. Activities and programs not cost-shareable included mothers' allowances, payments to inmates in public and charitable institutions, health care costs, and payments to clients of other federal and federal–provincial income benefits. Within three years, all ten provinces had signed agreements with the federal government.

In 1965 the federal government offered the provinces tax abatements in return for the provinces taking full responsibility for the administration and financing of unemployment assistance and related welfare programs. In 1966 much of the Unemployment Assistance Act was replaced by the Canada Assistance Plan (CAP), a significant needs-tested social welfare measure. The parts remaining of the Unemployment Assistance Act included programs that were means tested rather than needs tested, and thus not covered under CAP. The Unemployment Assistance Act was also amended that year to allow for the cost sharing of provincial mothers' allowance programs.

Hospital and Medical Care

Ottawa's reconstruction proposals included a federal–provincial system of medical care for the whole population as well as federal grants to assist the provinces in mental health and public health. In 1948 a national health grants program was established to assist the provinces in building their health services and infrastructure. Grants were made available for the following: health surveys; research and professional training; hospital construction; crippled children; mental health; general public health; and the control of cancer, tuberculosis, and venereal disease. In 1953 the program was extended to allow grants for child and maternal health, laboratory and radiological services, and medical rehabilitation. The impetus for the health grants program apparently was a threat by a prominent Canadian neurosurgeon that if federal support on health care was not forthcoming he would be forced to close his institute and move to the United States (Guest 1985, 141).

This modest health initiative was followed by the Hospital Insurance and Diagnostic Services Act of 1957, a far more ambitious health policy measure. The legislation authorized federal payments from general revenues to provincially administered programs of hospital insurance as well as laboratory and other diagnostic services. Exceptions included mental hospitals, nursing homes, and tuberculosis sanatoria, all of which were already publicly funded in most provinces. Heedful that health care was primarily a provincial jurisdiction under the Constitution, the legislation stipulated that federal contributions would not commence until at least six provinces, representing at least half the Canadian population, had entered into agreements with Ottawa (a "six and fifty" consensus threshold).

After nearly twenty-two years in power, the Liberals were defeated in 1957 by the Progressive Conservatives led by John Diefenbaker of Saskatchewan, a province that had long pioneered many innovations in health care and social services. On the health insurance issue, Diefenbaker acted quickly, amending the legislation in 1958 and withdrawing the provision that no federal contributions would be forthcoming until a new cost-sharing program had been developed (Johnson 1987, 40). By 1961, agreements were in place between the federal government and the provincial governments. The intent was that hospital care, as a universal social program, would now be available to all residents of a province, and on the same terms and conditions.

In 1962, Saskatchewan again led the way in Canadian social policy when, unswayed by a doctors' strike, it introduced the country's first universal medical insurance plan (Badgley and Wolfe 1967). Notwithstanding the conflict, the plan proved to be immediately popular and of great interest in other provinces as well as at the federal level of party politics. Ottawa established the Health Resources Fund and made $500 million available to it between 1966 and 1980. The intent of this new fund (as with the earlier fund) was to share costs with the provinces, on a 50–50 basis, for the construction, acquisition, and renovation of health facilities and equipment. In 1966 the Medical Care Act was passed, though it did not take effect until two years later due to budgetary concerns of the federal finance minister. In introducing the legislation, the responsible minister described its purpose as "to insure access to medical care to all of our people regardless of means, of pre-existing conditions, of age or other circumstances which may have barred such access in the past." To receive federal contributions, provincial and territorial medical care plans would have to meet five key criteria: the coverage must reach and be maintained at 95 per cent or more of each province's population; the plans must include all the benefits deemed to be medically necessary services provided by physicians; the plans must be portable from one jurisdiction to another within the country; the plans must be not-for-profit and administered by a provincial or territorial public authority accountable to the legislature; and services must be available on reasonably equal terms and conditions to all insurable residents by ensuring that any health insurance premiums paid by residents did not financially impede or preclude access to medically necessary services. By 1972, all provinces and territories had entered into agreements with the federal government, which, through the Medical Care Act, had positioned itself as an ongoing and prominent actor in health care policy. Canadians now had a universal medical care system with access to insured services regardless of ability to pay.

Social Programs for People with Disabilities

Aside from workers' compensation and veterans' programs, until the 1940s few provincial or federal policies recognized disability as a category of social need. People with various kinds of disabilities were seen as "worthy poor," yet often they were given public or private charity instead of being granted regular citizenship rights (Bach and Rioux 1996). The Marsh Report, however, regarded non-industrial disability as a universal risk facing Canadians – a risk, moreover, that called for special provisions as part of the social security system. The income support needs of blind persons had been addressed under the Old Age Pensions legislation since the late 1930s, and increases were made to pensions for the blind four times during the 1940s. In addition, the age of eligibility for such pensions was lowered from forty to twenty-one.

Marsh's vision of a comprehensive, national social insurance program for disability was not taken up. Instead, a number of means-tested programs for people with specific disabilities were instituted. Michael Bach and Marcia Rioux (1996, 318) describe the pattern and consequences of this policy approach as follows: "Investment in institutional facilities, special education, segregated vocational training, and employment and community services exclusively for persons with disabilities grew substantially in the postwar period. In this way the postwar framework for securing the welfare and well-being of Canadians ironically institutionalized exclusion for people with disabilities."

For persons with visual impairment, for instance, the Blind Persons Act of 1951 offered allowances to blind persons aged twenty-one to sixty-nine, cost-shared with the provinces on a 75 per cent federal, 25 per cent provincial basis. The residency requirement of twenty years under the previous Old Age Pensions Act was changed to ten years, and an earlier provision that excluded Indians was dropped. The maximum allowance of $480 a year was the same as for a blind person under the repealed old age pensions law, although the total allowable income for a recipient, including the allowance, was initially raised an average of $10 a month, rising again in 1955 and twice more in 1957. The eligibility age for the blind allowance was lowered from age twenty-one to eighteen in 1955, and the allowance itself was twice raised in 1957, by the Liberals before the federal election and by the victorious Conservatives after the election. The allowance was next raised around the 1962 and 1963 federal elections.[3] The Blind Persons Act was amended in 1966 to allow provinces to switch the financing and administration of the program under the new CAP legislation. That reform, coupled with the transfer of federal tax points to the provinces, under fiscal arrangements for financing this and other welfare programs, essentially removed the blind persons allowance from the federal agenda.[4]

The 1950s also saw initiatives relating to income support for persons with total and permanent disabilities and to the vocational rehabilitation of disabled persons. In 1951 the federal government formed the National Advisory Committee on the Rehabilitation of Disabled Persons. The committee had thirty-seven members, comprising representatives from the federal and provincial governments, health and welfare voluntary agencies, the medical profession, employers, organized labour, and universities. Representatives from disability groups themselves were not specified as interests deserving designated membership on the committee.[5] In 1953, medical rehabilitation was added to the list of services funded under the National Health Grants Program. Also that year, the federal cabinet authorized the Minister of Labour to enter into agreements with the provinces to develop activities for the rehabilitation of disabled persons.

Under the Disabled Persons Act of 1954, the federal government offered to share, on a 50–50 basis with the provinces, the cost of allowances to permanently and totally disabled persons aged eighteen to sixty-nine. A person was deemed totally and permanently disabled if he or she were suffering from a major impairment that was likely to continue without substantial improvement and that severely limited the ability to handle self-care and daily activities. There was a ten-year residence requirement, and the allowance was not payable to recipients of other federal and provincial income benefits. By the end of 1956, agreements had been reached between the federal government and all the provinces. This program, too, was means-tested rather than based on the social insurance principle. The subsequent story of the disabled persons program is the same as for blind persons in terms of periodic increases around federal elections in the late 1950s and early 1960s; the influence of new intergovernmental fiscal arrangements and the CAP in the mid-1960s; and the eventual cancellation of the legislation in the 1980s.

Under the Vocational Rehabilitation of Disabled Persons Act, passed in 1961, the federal government offered to split 50–50 with the provinces and territories the costs for a range of vocational rehabilitation services designed to help people with physical or mental disabilities become capable of pursuing a gainful occupation. The federal government's financial obligation was open-ended – that is, a function of how much provinces wished to spend on these services. Except for Quebec (which eventually did participate, in the late 1980s), all the provinces entered into two- or three-year agreements with Ottawa and regularly renewed over the years (Prince 1992).

Old Age Pensions and Retirement Insurance Provisions

"The universality of old age" in the human condition, observed the Marsh Report (1943, 153), "is evidenced by the fact that only in the case of old age pensions is there a full acknowledgment of social responsibility by all nine provincial governments [Newfoundland did not join Canada until 1949] and the federal government as well." Marsh then added that none of the provincial pension programs was adequate to address the income or service needs of aged persons. The report discussed possible improvements to old age assistance and recommended the introduction of a compulsory contributory retirement insurance scheme. The trend internationally was away from means-tested old age assistance towards social insurance–based retirement plans – a trend that Marsh viewed as both desirable and irreversible. "Individuals prefer to get their retirement income as a right, on a basis consistent with their idea of human dignity. Means-test procedures, however lightly applied, violate to some extent this conception of the right to retirement income" (1943, 171). The Green Book proposals included, as we noted earlier, a new old age pension and a revamped old age assistance scheme. Action on both these ideas happened fairly rapidly.

In 1947 the federal government amended the Old Age Pensions Act, making three changes along the lines proposed by Marsh: the provincial residence requirement of five years and the British citizenship requirement were eliminated; the maximum pension was increased from $25 to $30 a month; and the total allowable income was also increased. In 1949 the maximum pension was raised to $40 monthly. These amounted to minor repairs to the legislation, given that the age limit of seventy, the means testing of benefits, and the practice of holding adult children responsible for aged parents were all retained.

More fundamental changes to old age pension policy came with the Old Age Security and Old Age Assistance Acts in 1951 and with the revocation of the Old Age Pensions Act. These measures were preceded by a constitutional amendment approved earlier that year giving the Canadian Parliament authority to make laws in relation to old age pensions. The Old Age Security (OAS) Act introduced Canada's third universal income benefit, the one that would eventually be the largest in terms of clientele and program expenditures. A monthly flat-rate pension of $40 was offered to persons aged seventy and over regardless of their financial or family circumstances. The exclusion of Indians under the previous policy was removed. A feature that remained, though, was the residence requirement of twenty years; furthermore, pensioners had their OAS benefit suspended if they left the country even for a few months. The financing for the program, the "2–2–2 formula," was unique: revenues were to be derived from an OAS tax comprising 2 per cent on personal income, 2 per cent on corporate income, and 2 per cent from general budgetary revenue, all to be deposited in a special OAS Fund. The intended political function of the tax and the related fund was to make the public aware of the apparent costs and taxes associated with the new universal benefit, thereby curbing public demands for increases. The tax mix was raised to 3–3–3 in 1959, then to 4–3–3 in 1964, and altered again in later years (Bryden 1974). The OAS tax was formally abolished in 1972, while the fund continued until 1975. Since in practice the OAS program had always been financed from federal general revenues, Bryden (1974, 205) maintains that talk of an OAS tax and fund "was a purely metaphorical way of describing it." However, as we will show in the next chapter, many seniors and pensioners' groups reacted sharply to proposed cuts to the OAS during the 1980s, arguing that they were entitled to the benefits because they had specifically paid for them between the early 1950s and the early 1970s.

Along with the universal OAS for those aged seventy and over, the 1951 Old Age Assistance legislation introduced a revamped means-tested selective program for persons aged sixty-five to sixty-nine. The federal government would cost-share the program on a 50–50 basis with the provinces. Recipients of the blind persons' allowances and war veterans' allowances were excluded, and there was a residence requirement of twenty years. The maximum level of assistance of $40 a month was the same as under the repealed Old Age Pensions Act. Some of the more undesirable features of the earlier law were not continued, such as excluding Indians, making recoveries from the estates of deceased pensioners, and suspending benefits when a pensioner was in a public mental institution.

In 1965, with the introduction of the Canada Pension Plan (CPP), a contributory retirement insurance plan for people age sixty-five and older, the universal OAS program was amended. Beginning in 1966, the eligible age for the OAS pension was lowered, one year at a time, to age sixty-five.[5] The previous residence requirement was again extended to include forty years in Canada after age eighteen. After 1968, annual increases in the OAS benefit were indexed to the consumer price index (a measure of cost of living), subject to a 2 per cent limit.

The introduction of the Guaranteed Income Supplement (GIS) in 1967 marked an innovation in public pension policy. Some commentators believed that it foreshadowed a guaranteed annual income program. The GIS was an income-tested benefit for OAS pensioners on low incomes, determined on a family basis. It was conceived as an alternative to yet another increase in the universal OAS pension (Johnson 1987, 44). The GIS maximum benefit was set at 40 per cent of the OAS pension. The GIS was originally thought of as a transitional program that would fade away as the CPP matured and as more Canadians secured their retirement savings through that program as well as through occupational plans, investments, and private savings. As it turned out, these were heroic assumptions, especially regarding the expansion of private pension plans. The GIS would play a large role in the retirement income system to the end of the 1990s (Prince 1997).

The debate over competing design ideas and the actual implementation of the Canada and Quebec Pension Plans (C/QPP) has been well chronicled elsewhere (Bryden 1974; Johnson 1987). In 1964 a constitutional amendment (the third in twenty-four years) was passed that enabled Parliament to make laws relating to supplementary benefits – including survivors' and disability benefits irrespective of age – in addition to the old age pensions authorized by the 1951 amendment. The CPP came into effect in 1966 with the collection of contributions. Benefits were phased in over the next four years: retirement pensions became payable in 1967, survivors' benefits in 1968, and disability benefits in 1970. Though nearly a quarter of a century had elapsed, many of the Marsh Report's ideas were evident in the design of the CPP, which embodied (as Marsh had urged) the principles of a compulsory, contributory, social insurance retirement program covering most of the working population. The CPP covers employees and self-employed persons between the ages of eighteen and seventy with pensionable earnings in all provinces and territories except Quebec, which has its own parallel plan. At the outset (and continuing to 1986, in fact), contributions by employees and employers were 1.8 per cent of pensionable earnings; for the self-employed, they were 3.6 per cent. The retirement age for eligibility began at age sixty-eight in 1967 and was reduced, one year at a time, to age sixty-five in 1970. The basic retirement pension is graduated, dependent on earnings, and set at 25 per cent of average adjusted earnings. In this way, the CPP offers a basic minimum public pension that allows room for occupational plans.

Marsh (1943, 174) had endorsed this approach: "there is something to be said of regarding a retirement pension as a small nucleus to which private and industrial provisions may be added." In discussing family needs, Marsh had examined the issues of widowhood, survivors' insurance, and funeral benefits. The CPP addressed these issues in part by providing pensions for widows and disabled widowers under sixty-five; flat-rate benefits for children of deceased contributors and children of disabled contributors; and a lump sum death benefit paid to the estate of a deceased contributor. All monthly benefits were initially indexed to changes in the CPI, subject to a 2 per cent ceiling to maintain something of the purchasing power of the benefits. In 1974 the retirement and other benefits became indexed to the full annual CPI increase.

These cycles of reforms pointed to a *pension politique* – that is, party politics had a strong influence on policy making. For instance, during the minority and majority federal governments of Lester Pearson's Liberals and John Diefenbaker's Conservatives, the universal and selective old age maximum benefits were increased four times by the same amounts, rising from $40 a month in 1957 to $75 a month by 1963. In addition, the limits on total allowable income were raised, while the residence requirement for both programs was lowered to ten years. During the minority government of Pierre Trudeau between 1972 and 1975, with the NDP holding the balance of power, the basic OAS pension was increased from $80 to $100 monthly and the GIS rose from $55 to $67 monthly. The benefit payments of both programs were to increase quarterly by the annual rise in the CPI. In 1975 another selective, family-based, income-tested program for seniors was introduced, the Spouse's Allowance. The maximum monthly Spouse's Allowance was set at an amount equal to the monthly OAS pension plus the maximum monthly GIS. At the outset, this program was designed for persons aged sixty to sixty-four inclusive – and thus ineligible for the CPP or the OAS or GIS – who were married to and living with a pensioner, that is, someone age sixty-five or older.

Family Income Maintenance

The reports of Beveridge, Marsh, and others emphasized the risk of personal and societal insecurity that can arise when earnings and income are interrupted or are insufficient for the needs of families with children. A key recommendation in this regard was for a family allowance, of which Canada introduced a version in 1945 (Blake 2008). Several notable changes were made to the Family Allowances program over the next thirty years: Indian and Inuit children were no longer excluded from benefits (1947); the residence requirement for a child not born in Canada was lowered from three years to one year (1949); reductions in allowances for the fifth and succeeding children were abolished (1949); the program was extended to the children of Newfoundland upon that province's entry into Confederation (1949); benefits were increased for children aged five and under and for those aged ten to twelve, by one dollar a month (1957); and a standard monthly allowance of $12 was set in 1973 and then enriched in 1974 to $20 a month. The 1974 reform also allowed provinces to vary federal allowances according to the ages of children and/or the number of children in the family – an option taken up by Alberta and Quebec. The 1973 Family Allowances Act was the first overhaul of the legislation since the original law. Age eligibility was extended to children under eighteen, and special allowances were provided for children under eighteen who were living in foster homes or public institutions. Both types of allowances were to be fully indexed to the CPI, and family allowances became taxable as income.

Other family income programs during this period included family assistance, youth allowances, and mothers' allowances, all patchwork programs. The Family Assistance Program, launched in 1956, paid to families not eligible for family allowances (Canadians resettling in Canada and recent immigrants) a monthly benefit of $5 for each child under age sixteen. Following on a similar initiative by the Quebec government a few years earlier, a federal Youth Allowances Program was begun in 1964; it offered monthly benefits of $10 to parents of youths aged sixteen and seventeen (and so not covered by the Family Allowances Program) who had been attending school or university but who could not continue because of serious illness. Guest (1985, 150) describes this program as "recognition of the increasing years of dependency of the young as the requirements of Canada's technological society called for greater educational preparation." The Youth Allowances Program was a short-lived universal program for a narrow age group; both it and the Family Assistance Program were repealed and subsumed by the comprehensive 1974 reforms of the Family Allowances Program. Mothers Allowances, as discussed in the previous chapter, were among the earliest income programs in Canada, and wholly financed and administered by provinces. This pattern continued in the postwar period. It was not until 1966 that the Mothers Allowances Program was included for federal cost-sharing purposes under the Unemployment Assistance Program.

A Vision of Comprehensive Reform Realized

By the early 1970s the consensus was that the Canadian welfare state was finally complete. All the categories of social need and risk enumerated by the Marsh Report and others had been provided for in some way by federal, provincial, and intergovernmental social programs. According to Johnson (1987, 50), with the introduction of medicare in 1968, "the grand design of 1945" was in place, "not always tidily, not always peacefully, but it was there. There had been some embellishments; there had been some shifts in the balance between elements of the system; there had even been some harbingers of new directions for the future (notably the Guaranteed Income Supplement)." Splane (1987, 246) writes of "the initial agenda for the development of a comprehensive social security system for Canada being completed by the early 1970s." For Splane, the completion date was the passage of the

1971 Unemployment Insurance Act, which extended coverage to nearly the entire labour force, and the introduction of sickness, retirement, and maternity benefits.

Whether called a grand design, a long-term national social policy agenda, or a Keynesian welfare consensus, there was in effect from the 1940s to the 1970s a broadly shared set of beliefs concerning the building of a progressive system of social security. Forged by the experiences and aspirations of Canadians, these beliefs were reflected in the administrative culture of federal and provincial social welfare departments and related portfolios. Outside government, beliefs were reinforced as well as challenged by researchers and academics, client groups, professional associations, and other interests. For Splane, who was one of these reformist bureaucrats – as indeed was Johnson – the overarching objectives were to introduce new programs, to make improvements in coverage and benefits, and to develop a comprehensive, nationwide system of social security. The credo of these reformist bureaucrats included strong support for the concept of public responsibility for social welfare, an agreed-upon recognition of unmet social needs and contingencies facing Canadians, engagement in policy analysis and advice, "and an interest in finding workable solutions to common problems" (Splane 1987, 235). Continuity in implementing the agenda was facilitated at the federal level by the fact that from 1944 to 1972, the Department of National Health and Welfare had only two deputy ministers on the welfare side, both of whom were specialists in social administration with links to the provinces, the voluntary sector, and international welfare agencies.[6] The expectation was that social policy measures would significantly reduce insecurity and poverty. Research has shown that social programs have created a level of protection against unemployment, injury, sickness, old age, and disability and, along with other public policies and the tax system, have mitigated market-generated income inequalities, although poverty persists.

We have reviewed in quick succession many of the key programs put in place during this period of social policy ascendancy. Here we want to emphasize that each program had its own unique political history. Different needs, interest groups, political factors, and social events influenced each program's formation. In general, the ability to establish a comprehensive social security system was shaped by multiple forces. These included the skill and determination of individual ministers and their deputies; support (or lack thereof) from the Prime Minister and other members of cabinet, especially the Finance

Minister; interdepartmental relations; whether a majority or a minority government was in power; the level of public knowledge and the nature of public concerns; the lobbying efforts of interest groups; the state of the domestic and world economies, and the fiscal health of governments; the state of federal–provincial relations and issues of national unity; and any other issues on the public policy agenda that were preoccupying leaders (Splane 1987). Behind these forces, deeper ones were at work, such as the impact of the Great Depression and Second World War and the ongoing industrialization and urbanization of Canada (Johnson 1987). As examples, consider that the populist Diefenbaker government helped entrench equalization payments for the less well-off provinces in an effort to overcome the centralist biases of the previous Liberal government; that the Liberal Party adopted left-of-centre policies during the Pearson minority government, in which the NDP was able to exercise some influence; and that the architects of social programs were able to argue that new programs were not only just but also affordable during the economic expansion of the 1960s.

Conclusions

Envisaging and establishing a national system of social security from the 1940s to the 1970s transformed Canadian social welfare. No longer were benefits allocated based on relief and means testing; social welfare had moved towards a system based on universal entitlement, public service, and social insurance (Blake 2008; Finkel 2006). Needs testing, income testing, and the automatic indexation of benefits also emerged near the end of this era as new social policy instruments. Old Age Security, Family Allowances, and medicare were examples of universal programs providing benefits to the eligible population as a social right. Unemployment Insurance, Workers' Compensation, and the Canada and Quebec Pension Plans were examples of programs designed in such a way that provision was limited to those who paid a social insurance premium. Relief and means-testing devices were maintained for social assistance programs such as Mothers' Allowances, Unemployment Assistance, and the Old Age Assistance Program. The Canada Assistance Plan was based on a needs test, and the Guaranteed Income Supplement for seniors introduced the device of income testing to federal income security. By the early 1970s, several federal programs had been indexed to the CPI.

Social reforms take time and are made in various parts of the state. This review reveals that while the policy ideas of a report may be rejected or ignored in the short term, many are adopted in one form or another in later years. Social policy is forged in many ways, including through legislation in Parliament, cabinet orders and departmental regulations, key court decisions, constitutional amendments, and intergovernmental arrangements. This analysis also reveals that the evolution of Canada's social security system entailed a mixture of minor reforms and marginal measures on the one hand, and fundamental structural changes on the other. It should not be surprising that much of Canada's postwar social policy was crafted incrementally. Given the constraints of limited resources and parliamentary time, and competing issues and interests, each governmental mandate allows only a few social policy initiatives, if any. What is noteworthy, we believe, is that the overall process was *not* disjointed; rather, it was directed by a set of reformist values concerning the state's role in society.

Another important trend during this period was the centralization – perhaps more aptly, *federalization* – of the income security system. Most of the important cash benefit programs designed after 1940 were delivered by the federal government. In other social policy areas, such as hospital insurance and human rights, the pattern was one of provincial innovation and diffusion, as in the pre–welfare state era. The two levels of government were involved in collaborative decision making for social programs; they also accepted financial responsibilities. This was the era of cooperative federalism, explained in part by public acceptance that social policies played a role in the development of a stable and growing economy. There was not always easy agreement on specific arrangements, and in many instances the provinces protested that the federal government was encroaching on their constitutional territory; that said, the social policy process developed a system with a greater degree of shared responsibility than could be found in any other policy field (Rice 1985).

The analysis in this chapter has shown that the growth of an extensive system of social security recast the character of politics and governing in Canada in several ways. With the entrance of Keynesian economics – even a modest version of it (Campbell 1987) – into public budgeting and policy making, the historic strain between social welfare and "free enterprise" was diminished. Keynes demonstrated that it was possible through social policies to achieve both welfare functions and economic management functions. A new set of rationales and terms for debating and justifying social policy arose, and the reduction of existing tensions cleared the way for a wide variety of social policies. On the constitutional front, amendments were made granting powers to the federal government on matters of income security – exclusive powers in the case of Unemployment Insurance, and concurrent powers (with the provinces paramount) in the case of old age pensions and contributory pensions. Despite these amendments, most legislative powers on social questions remained with the provinces, as the Rowell–Sirois Commission had urged. In public finance, a complex array of fiscal arrangements developed between the federal and provincial governments on tax sharing, equalization payments, and shared-cost programs. In terms of the distribution of expenditures on health and social security by level of government, the federal share jumped dramatically during the war, from about 49 per cent in 1940 to nearly 72 per cent in 1945, and stayed near that level into the 1960s, declining gradually to about 65 per cent in the early 1970s.

The share of social spending by the provinces grew steadily over the postwar period, from 21 per cent in 1945 to 34 per cent in the 1970s, while the share by municipalities declined over the whole period, from a substantial 17 per cent in 1940 to 7 per cent in 1945, down to less than 2 per cent by the mid-1970s (Guest 1985, 242). Finally, while acknowledging that the state did not have a monopoly with respect to social policy formation and provision, the vision and discourse tended to concentrate on the state. A state-centred conception of social care and social intervention became apparent in the Canadian literature in political science, sociology, social work, and public administration, among other disciplines. As the next chapter shows, the crisis politics of social policy in the later 1970s and 1980s directly and profoundly challenged both the effectiveness and the desirability of this focus on the welfare state.

4 The Crisis of the Welfare State: Canadian Perspectives and Critiques

No sooner had the Canadian postwar social policy agenda been seemingly completed than critics began lamenting its effects on public and private budgets, the economy and community, the status of women, and clients and service providers. As a federal Royal Commission observed in the mid-1980s: "With the major elements of the welfare state in place, a loss of momentum and a growing uncertainty about the next steps were perhaps inevitable. But this hesitancy was reinforced by economic difficulties of the last decade and the criticisms from both right and left" (Canada 1985, 578). Viewed historically and comparatively, these economic difficulties were neither minor nor exclusive to Canada; they were unprecedented in the postwar period and struck industrialized economies around the world. Between 1973 and 1975, "the combined GNP of the Organization for Economic Co-operation and Development (OECD) countries fell by 5 per cent, industrial output plummeted, and world trade declined by 14 per cent. Unemployment climbed to a staggering 15 million in all OECD countries combined. At the same time, inflation accelerated" (Gough 1979, 132).

Beginning during this period, complaints arose that the economic system could no longer function with ever-increasing levels of taxation to support the welfare state apparatus constructed over the previous several decades. The business community contended that governments were adding to inflation by borrowing money to finance social policy and that greater numbers of people were becoming dependent on the welfare system. The list of denunciations grew, with commentators deploring that welfare programs were soaking up monies that would be better spent on economic investment. Such criticisms were reinforced by the view that the social policy agenda, in any case, was failing to address problems effectively and with due speed. The mounting pressure of these attacks came to be referred to as the crisis of the welfare state, a period in Canada that roughly spanned the mid-1970s to the late 1980s.

The welfare crisis was defined and influenced from both outside and inside the system. Here, we survey five main perspectives on Canadian social policy during this period – left, right, feminist, community, and insider – and examine a number of the critiques they raised. Left-leaning academics and politicians expressed disappointment that inequality and poverty persisted amidst obvious prosperity. Right-leaning academics and politicians were concerned about the contradictions between social programs and economic structures. Feminists critiqued the role that social policies were playing in marginalizing women, keeping them "in their place," and concealing the burdens they were having to bear as governments abandoned policy initiatives (see chapter 9). Community members voiced their opposition to the welfare system's disregard for clients trapped in bureaucratic organizations. People within the system – service providers, caregivers, and clients – criticized the ways in which welfare programs were institutionalizing recipients, as well as how discretionary administrative powers were being exercised in determining who should receive benefits and how the system was forcing people to live in poverty.

This analysis does not provide an overview of the crisis period, or even a detailed review of the central tenets of each argument. These have been thoroughly analysed in the literature.[1] Rather, here we make the case that the welfare crisis as articulated in Canada during this period amounted to a series of contending ideas, issues, and developments that significantly challenged and strained the consensus on which the social security system had been built.

Critique from the Left

The political left – a mixture of community activists, welfare-oriented liberals, social democrats, labour leaders, Marxist thinkers, and other critics – developed penetrating analyses of the welfare state. In the Canadian context, it was the left initially, starting in the early 1970s, that argued that many social programs were no longer meeting people's needs, if they ever had. Thus the left called for a review of the social security system. This was part of the background of the 1973–6 social security review by the Trudeau Liberal government, as well as of the social security review by the Chrétien Liberal government in 1994–5. The right's interest in restructuring social programs, beyond the simple mantra of rolling back benefits and regulating clients, followed later (Lightman 1995, 356).

Three themes serve to illustrate the left's critique of the welfare state: the way governments used welfare systems to control and blame the poor; the effect of economic contradictions on the welfare state; and the impact of new forms of capitalism on states' capacity to solve social problems.

The first theme – that governments use welfare systems to control and blame the poor – focuses on the harmful ways in which governments employ social policies to address social issues. Frances Fox Piven and Richard A. Cloward (1971, 40), early critics of welfare, studied how the system was maintaining social and economic inequalities while forcing people to take low-paying jobs. Their research showed how governments use welfare programs to regulate the poor during periods of social upheaval. They argued that governments introduce social policies or increase benefits in order to quash civil disorder during periods of mass unemployment. These same programs are then restricted during times of economic growth. Equally important to Piven and Cloward was that governments abandon programs and services designed to support the poor during periods of economic growth in favour of programs supporting workers and the middle class. Far from providing liberal benefits, the welfare system is "periodically expanding and contracting relief rolls as the system performs its two main functions: maintaining civil order and enforcing work" (Piven and Cloward 1971, xv). Through the 1970s and 1980s, this cyclical nature of social welfare could be observed in Canada.[2] The ideals of full employment, the war on poverty, and support for Trudeau's Just Society were declining; social spending was increasingly viewed as a burden; and despite several social policy reviews at the federal and provincial levels, concrete reforms were insubstantial compared to the expectations and achievements of earlier decades. With respect to income and wealth redistribution, the Canadian welfare state was not the Robin Hood many thought it was meant to be or perceived it to be in practice (Gillespie 1978; Osberg 1981), due in part to regressive features and gaps in the tax system.

Other critics on the left claimed that governments were constructing welfare programs in ways that blamed the victim. William Ryan examined the process of victim blaming, disguised often as kindness and concern. Unlike the conservative ideologies that dismiss welfare recipients as "inferior, genetically defective, or morally unfit," blaming the victim allows the humanitarian to have it both ways: "He can all at the same time concentrate his charitable interests on the defects of the victim, condemn the vague social and environmental stresses that produced the defect (some time ago), and ignore the continuing effect of victimizing social forces (right now)" (Ryan 1971, 7). Ryan's criticism stressed that welfare programs blame the victim by failing to take into account social stratification, political struggle, inequalities of power and income distribution, and ethnic and racial group conflict.

In examining the ideology of the welfare state in Canada, Angela Wei Djao (1979, 301–2) conducted an empirical study of public perceptions and beliefs. She found that "the ideology comprised some factual statements about the welfare system for the poor, some misconceptions about those dependent on the welfare system for the poor, and general concealment of the welfare system for the non-poor." She concluded that "the ideology of the welfare state is based on individualism in the liberal tradition. Its key components are desirability of state intervention in promoting social welfare and suspicion towards the poor. State intervention should, however, be interpreted with caution. The official goal of state intervention is to reduce income inequality in society; in practice, state intervention amounts to a few programs providing subsistence income to the poor. The ideology masks the real workings of the welfare state, so that the structure of inequalities in society is left intact" (1979, 314).

Throughout this period of crisis politics, many on the left drew attention both polemically and analytically to the welfare system of tax breaks, subsidies, and grants for corporations (Lewis 1972; Clement 1975; Calvert 1984; Tudiver 1987), as well as to the hidden welfare system of tax expenditures, cash transfers, and services for the well-to-do in Canada (National Council of Welfare 1976, 1978).

A second theme from the left concerned the contradictory nature of the welfare system. Internationally, James O'Connor (1973), Ian Gough (1979), Ramesh Mishra (1984), and Claus Offe (1984) all raised theoretical questions about the state's capacity to support ongoing welfare. Their book titles indicate, respectively, the direction of this critique: *The Fiscal Crisis of the State, The Political Economy of the Welfare State, The Welfare State in Crisis,* and *Contradictions of the Welfare State.* In Canada, edited works by Leo Panitch (1977), Allan Moscovitch and Glenn Drover (1981), and Allan Moscovitch and Jim Albert (1987) provided similar critical assessments of the welfare state's viability within a political economy approach.[3]

These writings suggested that the crisis of the welfare state was actually a crisis of the capitalist state in maintaining a comprehensive welfare function. For the moderate left in Canada – social democrats and welfare liberals – the relationship between social programs and market economics was not contradictory at root; rather, it involved a tension that could, through a judicious mix of policy instruments, be managed. The more radical left's position, vividly articulated by O'Connor, described the crisis as a basic contradiction between the rising expenses of social welfare and the declining ability of states to meet these costs. According to O'Connor, every capitalist state has two central functions: ensuring the private accumulation of wealth, and legitimizing the capitalist social structure in a way that maintains social order. To achieve these functions, governments develop policies that support social investments and social consumption on the one hand, and social expenses of production on the other. Social investments such as cheap electricity, highways, education, and job training for the working class are meant to increase labour productivity. Social consumption expenditures on projects and services such as social insurance are meant to reduce the costs of labour. Such programs include child care, tax credits for children, and income support programs for families. Finally, governments try to ensure social stability by providing support for people who must leave or are left out of the labour market in the form of unemployment benefits, pensions, and compensation for injured workers.

O'Connor argues that the more programs a government creates, and the more services it provides, the more people will want access to them. This growth of the welfare system requires additional resources to finance new programs. At some point the government comes to the limit of its ability to find new resources; it can no longer manage both the growth of welfare and the growth of the economy, and the deep contradiction between the two is what defines the crisis that confronts welfare states.

Canadian academics and activists quickly took up O'Connor's framework. They used his categories and arguments to evaluate taxation policies, the status of public employees, regional economic underdevelopment, and social spending (Deaton 1973; Armstrong 1977; Kuusisto and Williams 1981; Moscovitch and Drover 1987). Data on the functions and levels of expenditures and on tax revenue sources confirmed O'Connor's thesis that Canadians were facing a fiscal crisis. In an analysis of public expenditures, Allan Moscovitch and Glen Drover (1987, 37) found that there was "a trade-off between transfers to persons and aid to business and industry. In the postwar period, when transfers to persons increased, spending on capital declined. Conversely, when spending on capital increased, transfers to persons declined." On the tax side, they found that "during a downturn, it has become easier for government to reduce taxes on capital than to increase public expenditures, producing the net effect of continuously shifting the tax burden from corporations to persons."

The contradictions exposed by O'Connor created a new language to describe the welfare system: *a fiscal crisis* – that is, there was a large structural gap between what governments were spending on programs and what they were raising from taxes. This criticism allowed elites to blame welfare for the large deficits of the 1980s' slow or no-growth period. The fiscal crisis analysis undermined the notion that protective welfare systems create political conditions to encourage the rapid movement of resources that finance economic growth. In our view, the analysis failed to see that large-scale social and economic transformations have taken place without social upheaval and that urbanization, industrialization, commercialization, and dramatic labour force changes have revolutionized society. These transformations were only possible because of the security offered by the social welfare state.

A third theme dealt with the impact of new forms of capitalism on the state's ability to solve social problems. Offe and other critics suggested that the conditions of capitalism altered as the economy shifted from organized capitalism to disorganized capitalism (Offe 1985, 6; Lash and Urry 1987). Organized capitalism reflected a period of mass production of standardized goods, often called Fordism.[4] Large, vertically integrated companies employed many semi-skilled workers to make products for largely undifferentiated markets. This coincided with the development of large unions engaged in collective bargaining for workers. These structural conditions supported the development of the welfare state. The welfare state grew from the 1920s into the 1970s because there were organized political parties, labour unions, and, to a limited extent, interest groups. These structures provided ways for the working class to fight for rights and social security in the context of a capitalist society (Offe 1985, 7).

*Dis*organized capitalism, on the other hand, reflected growing divisions between highly skilled and unskilled workers, as well as declining roles for national and subnational states. New forms of capitalism began to take shape with the introduction of new production processes, which spread quickly from the United States to Japan and other parts of the world. These changes included the weakening (and even the destruction) of the union movement, the introduction of robotics, the development of small-batch production, the expansion of horizontal integration between producers, and the introduction of multipurpose production strategies. Corporate activities became more targeted, with increases in local production designed for niche markets. Just-in-time processes eliminated the need for vast stockpiling of products; specialization in production allowed parts to come from all over the world to low-cost assembly plants. These new processes led to a fragmenting of the production process as well as to a declining demand for semi-skilled labour.

The restructuring of the economy led to a decline in the role of labour unions and in labour protection practices. Similarly, governmental regulation of markets began to weaken as producers searched for the least expensive places to produce their goods. As a result of these changes, governments found it much more difficult to address internal issues. As the economy changed, a "coalition of neo-liberal politicians, internationally competitive industries, finance ministries, central banks and private financial institutions emerged within and across states and sought to reduce the size and scope of government" (Bernard 1994, 225).

In exploring the changes that were taking place, some critics on the Canadian left challenged their colleagues to reassess long-standing Keynesian prescriptions and to adjust their policy agendas to new economic circumstances. In *Rethinking the Economy* (1984), James Laxer, a prominent member of the New Democratic Party, pointed out that the world was moving "towards a new international division of labour and a basic technological transformation." He argued that social democrats in Canada needed to shift their attitudes concerning the economy. They needed to change their preferred policy tools while maintaining their goals of full employment and fair social programs. Laxer called for an abandonment of traditional Keynesianism, a stronger focus on production (especially in manufacturing), renewed economic nationalism, and the democratization of the workplace. His analysis was controversial and, at the time, quite divisive within the NDP.

The control of the poor, the contradictions within the welfare state, and the changing nature of the economy together cast a light on the tensions between social and economic investment. These tensions will be explored further in chapter 6. The point here is that the changing politics of social policy reflect this division between the social and economic spheres.

Critique from the Right

The enormous expansion of the welfare state in all industrial democracies has encouraged many conservatives and neoconservatives to critique governments' development of sweeping social programs. While they accept the need for some forms of government intervention, these commentators are troubled by the impact of ever-expanding social programs. In particular, they point their fingers at the welfare system. In the 1970s some new groups on the right appeared in Canada. The Canadian Federation of Independent Business and the Business Council on National Issues joined traditional business groups such as the Canadian Chamber of Commerce and the Canadian Manufacturers Association. These new business associations were public policy oriented; they spoke out on matters of social programs, among other issues; and they actively lobbied governments (Doern and Phidd 1983, 85). Right-wing policy institutes and think tanks were also established during this period. The most notable of these were the moderately conservative C.D. Howe Institute and the more radical Fraser Institute. The latter envisioned (and still does) a society based on free markets, private property rights, individual responsibility, and limited government. All of these groups believe in market solutions for social problems. In the 1970s and 1980s, they sought "to redirect public attention to the role markets can play in providing for the economic and social well being of Canadians."[5]

Three themes capture the neoconservative critique: the evolution of Canadian social policy and the changed economic context; the notion that the welfare system infringes on individual liberty and creates dependency in the recipient population; and the notion that social policies provided by the state commonly use resources inefficiently.

The first theme – the evolution of Canadian social policy and the changed economic context – is based on a particular interpretation of how the Canadian welfare state was founded and is being maintained. Thomas Courchene (1980, 1987, 1994) has argued that the welfare state supplanted traditional sources of protection and support, such as the family and local communities, and politicized economic affairs. Moreover, the welfare state as it was built in Canada conferred a comprehensive range of generous social benefits and rights. According to this view of our history, social policy moved strongly away from selective programs towards universal programs. Most significantly, this network of social programs assumed a life of its own because of the steady flow of tax revenues from the sustained economic growth of the 1950s and 1960s. Social policy making became detached from market discipline and the imperative of wealth creation. Michael Walker, the director of the Fraser Institute, called the Canadian welfare state a fiction in that "the state does not create welfare or wealth or economic production of any kind" (1985, 21). An "explosion" in the expansion of social programs was virtually costless in political terms, Courchene claims, because of the growing economy and fiscal surpluses. In addition, "the nature of demands on government in the name of social policy altered rather dramatically" from economic security and human needs to economic compensation and human wants (Courchene 1987, 8–9).[6]

Conservative critics emphasized that the good old days of easy growth were gone and that social programs therefore had to adapt to a much harsher economic context. To quote Courchene (1987, 11) again: "The 1980s are very different from the 1960s. Productivity has been flat for the better part of the past decade, and unemployment has been unacceptably high. Fiscal deficits are nothing short of staggering. In addition, the world economy is anything but tranquil. Economies everywhere are restructuring, and the new world trading environment is becoming more, not less competitive." As a consequence of these new economic, fiscal, and global realities, "social policy has to facilitate and assist the occupational, industrial, and often geographic relocation that the new economics requires of the current generation of Canadians. We no longer have the luxury of designing social policy independently of the underlying economic environment."

A second line of criticism by the right was that the welfare state infringed on personal freedom and created dependency. Some critics on the right dismissed the welfare state on principle, maintaining that governments had little or no place in regulating the economy and that social programs were deterring people from making choices about their own lives. The Fraser Institute created the idea of "Tax Freedom Day," reporting for each province how many days and months of an average worker's total annual income was needed to pay all the taxes to all the various levels of government. In effect, the message was that for the first five or six months of each year, Canadians' incomes were going entirely to the tax collectors. Taxes were portrayed as a necessary evil at best, as the public confiscation of private wealth at excessively high levels. Walker described the welfare state as "a coercive system of paying for things" (1985, 35). Since taxation is mandatory and automatic, individuals do not get to decide if they will "participate as sponsors of the welfare state." Transfers of wealth through social programs are neither voluntary nor personal in contact. Walker expressed doubt that people would willingly support the overall welfare state apparatus if they had the choice, and pointed to tax evasion and the growth of the underground economy as evidence of such resistance to tax burdens.

Critics from the right asserted that welfare assistance was encouraging people to rely on social programs rather than take care of themselves. Impoverishment was the result of pathological behaviours, part of a "culture of poverty," where the poor take on values and norms that are different from those of mainstream society. Anthropologists and sociologists writing in the 1960s had used the concept of the culture of poverty to describe the *effects* of poverty on the beliefs and lifestyles of families and communities. Neoconservatives over the next few decades used the term as a causal *explanation* of poverty. In its original meaning, the culture of poverty referred to the reaction and adaptation of people to high rates of unemployment and underemployment, low wages, lack of property, inadequate social benefits, and marginalization from mainstream social institutions and government agencies. A culture of poverty became the way of life for many of the poor caught in these structural features of the market economy and society. Those on the right twisted the concept, arguing that a subculture of poverty with dysfunctional work values and family structures had been created and was being perpetuated by the welfare programs themselves.

Neoconservatives claimed that welfare as a way of life was being transmitted from parent(s) to children as a result of repeated or long-term reliance on social assistance or unemployment insurance.[7] In the United States, more so than in Canada, neoconservative writers blamed welfare for poor parenting and the breakdown of the traditional family, for a weakening of the work ethic, and for defeatist attitudes among the poor. Charles Murray (1984) argued that the rules governing the availability of welfare were making it profitable for the poor to behave, in the short term, in ways that were destructive in the long term. He claimed that the welfare system ignored three premises: that people respond to incentives and disincentives (i.e., that sticks and carrots do work); that people are not inherently hard working or moral (i.e., in the absence of countervailing influences, they will avoid work and be amoral); and that people must be held accountable for their actions (1984, 146). By rejecting these premises, the welfare system had created dependency.

In the late 1960s and early 1970s, a federal task force on urban issues, and Senate committee reports on poverty and on aging, demonstrated to the right (and indeed to some other Canadians) the problems of the welfare system. These documents maintained that social housing produced ghettos, that income maintenance programs failed the poor and reduced people's willingness to work, and that public pensions were encouraging citizens to spend and not save for their old age. Neoconservatives in particular perceived the poor as rejecting the work ethic and as accepting instead a life based on handouts and transfer payments. Where social policies were needed to address social problems, right-leaning critics advocated selective benefits so as not to encourage people into welfare. Those arguing for limited government involvement believed in having the poor arm themselves for the future through educational and/or training programs. The poor needed to be forced into work through reductions in social welfare benefits; the more stringent the requirements for receiving benefits, the more rapidly people would return to taking care of themselves. In particular, the right favoured workfare programs, as well as a more general emphasis on duties and obligations, to counter the welfare state's emphasis on rights and entitlements.

A third theme was the assertion that welfare programs were an inefficient use of resources and that they should not be allowed to interfere with the economy. Rightist critics rejected the notion that the state should try to create full employment, arguing that when it did so, it disrupted the natural workings of the market, thereby creating greater unemployment. For the capitalist system to work, workers must be obliged to sell their labour at the prevailing market price. In this way, the capitalists could use labour to produce wealth. Neoconservative critics maintained that governments were spending vast sums of taxpayers' money without achieving many results; their evidence for this was that welfare programs had not changed the living conditions of the poor, nor had large-scale programs affected the distribution of income in capitalist countries. The right contended that the costs of social programs had placed an unfair burden on taxpayers, creating disincentives for investment; that such programs encouraged people not to work; and that these programs were structured in ways that allowed government to intrude on people's lives, thereby threatening their liberty. Conservatives rejected many aspects of the welfare state: universal programs such as education and health care, as well as social insurance programs such as public pensions and employment insurance. These kinds of social programs reduced the choices of individuals while simultaneously requiring massive tax burdens that undermined the economy's vitality.

In essence, this was a public burden model of welfare, with the right depicting social policy expenditures as a drain on the economy's productive capacity.

For Walker (1985, 24), inefficiency was a central flaw of the Canadian welfare state in that "of the income taken from them [the public] allegedly to support people whose means are less than their own, only one dollar in five is used to that end." He contended that some Canadians at the poverty line were contributing to the support of more fortunate citizens, and that the universality of income programs financed by general taxation had resulted in the poor transferring some of their income through the tax system to the rich. Many health and social services, he argued, were inefficient "because the government sector often operates under conditions of monopoly" in such a way that "there is no efficiency-inducing competition for the production of the service" (1985, 35).

The following is a summary of the social policy prescriptions offered by the Canadian right during this period: Major reform of the welfare state is necessary for economic, fiscal, and social and cultural reasons. Social well-being can be brought about through deregulated markets in which individuals compete for jobs, income, and social status. Collective interests are undermined by the idea that competition is healthy and desirable. All collective actions – unionization, consumer and community group activities, environmental regulations – undercut individual well-being. Social programming needs to move away from entitlements and towards assistance. A safety net is necessary, but it should be far more residual than the social security system established during the expansionist era of the 1940s to the 1970s. Income security programs must be much more targeted, with little or no universality. A selective, means-tested negative income tax (or tax credit) is one way to restructure the multitude of income programs.

The right called for greater "welfare pluralism" in the sense of retrenching the role of the federal government and the public sector in social policy; at the same time, the roles of the provinces, the market, the voluntary sector, and families should all be increased (Courchene 1980, 1987; Walker 1985). In particular, the market sector could be expanded in a number of ways: by introducing and increasing user charges for social services; by terminating certain public policies such as rent controls; by allowing private-sector firms to enter the education field; by contracting out health care services; and by transferring public-sector activities such as social housing to the private sector. In addition, social policy needed to be coordinated with – or even subordinated to – economic, industrial, and trade policy. In short, the right was calling for a dramatic retrenchment of Canadian social policy in terms of programs, the overall system, and the very paradigm of the postwar welfare state. Courchene (1987, 16) realized that all of this was controversial, predicting that "there will be organized resistance to these initiatives, at least initially, since they represent a turning back from the philosophy that dominated the expansionist era in Canadian social policy."

Feminist Critiques

The emergence of second-wave feminism in the 1960s and early 1970s coincided with the final years of the expansionist era of welfare states in Canada and other countries. A crucial event and process in the Canadian context was the creation in 1967 of the Royal Commission on the Status of Women (RCSW), which reported in 1970. As Heather MacIvor (1996, 80) notes, "the commission travelled across Canada, listening to women in shopping malls and church basements as well as hotel ballrooms and legislatures. Women who read or heard about these meetings in the media were astonished to hear their own personal experiences in the words of others. The RCSW was a gigantic national consciousness-raising exercise. It helped build a bridge between the older, more traditional feminists of the YWCA (Young Women's Christian Association) and VOW (Victoria Order of Women), and the younger, more radical feminists emerging from the campuses and the new social movements."

The RCSW had several effects on the women's movement and the politics of social policy (Brodie 1995, 42–4). It provided an agenda of issues and strategies for popular mobilization and policy advocacy by women, an agenda that holds to this day. It threw attention onto the state as the principal site for addressing many of the concerns and claims of women for equality and equity. The RCSW provided a rationale for the formation of bureaux for women within federal, provincial, and even some municipal public service bureaucracies. These included the Canadian Advisory Council on the Status of Women within the federal government. The RCSW also prompted the formation and consolidation of women's organizations outside of government.

Between 1972 and 1976, in what may be called the transition years between the expansionist and crisis phases of the welfare state, eight national women's organizations were established: the National Action

Committee on the Status of Women (NAC); the Canadian Abortion Rights Action League; the Native Women's Association of Canada; the Canadian Teachers' Federation; the Canadian Association of Women Executives; the National Association of Women and the Law; the Canadian Research Institute on the Advancement of Women; and the Women's Bureau of the Canadian Labour Congress.

The NAC was created initially to track and assess the implementation of the RCSW's recommendations, particularly by the federal government. It evolved into a multi-issue, multi-perspective umbrella association for the Canadian women's movement, with 570 affiliated groups by the late 1980s (MacIvor 1996, 328). In the 1980s, several other national women's organizations were formed, most of these representing the interests of various groups of minority women: the Congress of Black Women; the Canadian Congress of Learning Opportunities for Women; the Inuit Women's Association of Canada; the Disabled Women's Network; and the National Organization of Immigrant and Visible Minority Women (Burt 1994, 213). There was, then, a growing organization and pluralization of feminist views in Canada.

In addition to all this were events such as the International Women's Year in 1975 and the constitutional reform process of the early 1980s. During the latter, after considerable lobbying by women, a sexual equality clause was entrenched in the new Charter of Rights and Freedoms. All of these events mobilized and expanded the women's movement. Thus over the course of the crisis period, even while the welfare state was coming under increasing attack, the women's movement grew in both complexity and influence. Marjorie Cohen (1992, 217) recalls that "in the 1980s government and employers had accepted women's intervention in issues like equal pay, maternity leave, and the movement of women out of traditional occupations. They also accepted our right to speak on daycare, reproductive choice, pornography – anything that could be seen as a women's issue." Efforts, however, to speak out on issues beyond traditionally understood notions of social policy and women's issues, such as trade policy and fiscal and monetary policy, were challenged by governments and business interest groups as outside the expertise and mandate of women's groups.

Feminist critiques of the welfare state are but one part of a broader feminist analysis of all contemporary social institutions: the community, the education system, the family, the legal system, the mass media, the political system, the religious orders, and the wage system. Feminists argue that all social policies reflect stereotypes about family, the role of women, the raising of children, and relationships between men and women (Abramovitz 1988). Three themes from the feminist critique demonstrate this concern about stereotypes: governments' use of the policy process to marginalize women's issues; the way policies keep women "in place"; and the way policy initiatives conceal gender issues by resorting to apparently neutral terms.[8]

Feminists claim that governments develop most social programs in ways that marginalize women's issues by maintaining the dominance of patriarchal structures. In *Women and the Welfare State*, perhaps the first book to approach modern social policy from a feminist perspective, Elizabeth Wilson (1977, 9) stated that "social welfare policies amount to no less than the *state organization of domestic life*. Women encounter State repression within the very bosom of the family." Wilson and other critics argued that welfare systems were marginalizing women socially, politically, and economically (Williams 1989; Firestone 1979). Welfare policies were encouraging women to assume roles based on reproduction and reproductive relations. As such, these policies were heightening the importance of maternal relations based on birth, nurturing, and the rearing of children – relations that were the crux of how welfare treated families. In the political arena, the welfare system was dividing women into subgroups as defined by conditions of eligibility. Policies upheld specific categories: unmarried women, welfare mothers, divorced women, single women, and female lone parents. In the economic sphere, social policies were reinforcing the unequal division of labour in the workplace: women were not being accorded the same rights and benefits as men; instead they were being treated as a reserve of cheap labour (Abramovitz 1988).

When examining the marginalization of women's issues, feminist analysts asked who was benefiting from the dependence of women and the domestic division of labour. They explored the ways in which policies were being used to support the relationship between patriarchal domination and capitalist social relations. Their critiques provided a theoretical explanation of why the state supported social assistance, family benefit programs, and child care for stay-at-home mothers. Dorothy Miller (1990, 21) suggested that "social welfare's treatment of men primarily functions to uphold and serve the economy and its treatment of women, albeit not exclusively, in service to patriarchy." This "patriarchal necessity," as Miller defined it, was the "need among the collectivity of men to separate the sexes and devalue and control women."

The second theme from feminist critiques is that many social policies function in ways that keep women in place. Feminist writers criticized the traditional vision and practices of the welfare state, and also of both the left and the right, for downplaying or ignoring the position and experiences of women. Feminists pointed to how governmental welfare policies were perpetuating the idea that women are caregivers whose primary roles are mother and wife. They believed that policy makers were assuming that married women were dependent on their partners and that this construction of welfare was locking women into a historical dependence on male-dominated social systems. Feminist theory drew attention to the division between the public and private spheres of life and sought to challenge the resulting practices. Men dominated the public domain, women the private domain. The private domain "covers not only the process of bearing children, but also the physical, emotional, ideological, and material process involved in caring for and sustaining others not just children" (Williams 1989, 42). Social policies were one way for men to extend the public domain into the private one, thereby controlling women. Feminists noted that laws developed by men controlled the availability and use of contraceptives; that male-dominated medicine controlled the processes of childbearing and birth; that educational systems structured the process of child rearing; and that employment policies influenced women's relationships with the labour market (Pascall 1986, 25).

A third theme concerns the gendered impact of language and problem formulation in policy making. Women's risks and needs had been inadequately envisaged – and sometimes totally excluded – when the postwar social security system was being developed. The social evil of violence against women needed to be added to the national agenda. Reproductive rights were not then part of mainstream social policy studies or political discourse. A national child care program was beyond the grand design of 1945 examined in chapter 3; that is, it was not part of the Marsh Report or other government studies on the postwar reconstruction of Canada. The Keynesian welfare consensus was essentially a consensus among male-dominated institutions of government, business, and organized labour, with notions of full employment premised on a male breadwinner model of the family. But feminist thinking and advocacy did share with the postwar design a state-centred conception of social care and provision.

Feminists expressed scepticism about policy reforms that sought to shift responsibility for providing support from the government onto families and communities. Such reforms hid the fact that when responsibility was shifted, it was onto women. When policies described "home care" as an alternative to institutional care, feminists pointed out that they really meant low-paid or unpaid care by women. When policies suggested the expansion of "community care," it really meant that the burden was being shifted back onto women. These seemingly gender-neutral descriptions of policy initiatives concealed the fact that the greatest burden within formal community or informal systems of care was being borne by women. Concepts such as the "welfare state" and the "public interest" were seen as mystifying the discriminatory impacts of social laws, transfers, and services on women. Similarly, feminists deplored classifications of social problems that disguised issues that affected women more than men. For instance, the term "elderly" – used in almost all social research – concealed the fact that most elderly people, especially over age eighty, are women. Likewise, the term "child abuse" did not identify men as the major perpetrators. The terms "domestic violence" and "spousal abuse" also blurred the harsh reality of wife battering and male violence. Social policies that discussed "lone parent" problems ignored the reality that these were, and still are, mainly women's families.

Second-wave feminism in Canada began challenging these ideas in the 1960s and 1970s. Feminists contended that new concepts and categories had to be developed that were inclusive, less hierarchical, and more sensitive to power relationships between men and women. Women's groups were no longer willing to be marginalized or kept in place by social policy developments. Feminism demanded equal rights and opportunities, if not results, in the labour force, the law, politics, and the family. In contrast to the right, activities by the women's movement called for a renewed and expanded welfare state.

Critiques from Community Groups

In relation to the welfare state and social policy, "community" refers to formally organized groups based on a common place (locality) and/or a common interest (affinity/identity). Community groups associated with Canadian social welfare traditionally included charitable and philanthropic organizations, churches and other religious groups, cooperatives, service clubs, and social action groups. Starting in the 1960s with poverty groups and social planning councils, and increasingly throughout the crisis years of the welfare state, community-based social service and policy groups expanded greatly. This expansion was prompted by social movement developments in the United States as well as by domestic policy initiatives. These domestic initiatives included the Canadian war on poverty of the mid-1960s (including the 1966 Canada Assistance Plan [CAP]); the 1967–70 RCSW; the 1969 official languages legislation; the misguided attempt at abolishing the Indian Act in 1969–70; the 1971 multiculturalism policy; community employment programs of the mid-1970s; the cooperative housing movement of the 1970s and 1980s; the 1977 Canada Human Rights Act; the 1982 Charter of Rights and Freedoms; and the 1986 Employment Equity Act. These federal government initiatives sought to address claims for social protection and/or cultural recognition.

During this crisis period of the Canadian welfare state, community groups emphasized three major issues: the failure of policy makers to recognize their differences and properly include them in policy development; their alienation from mainstream professional service bureaucracies; and inappropriate and inadequate conceptions of groups, their experiences, and their contributions to society and the economy.

Community groups come together to promote or resist change. They seek to influence the policy process so that new social initiatives will create equality, fairness, or impartiality and address issues of diversity and difference. It is not uncommon for members of these groups to be hostile to professionals, whom they claim regulate the lives of those receiving benefits or services (Wharf 1979, 1990, 1992). These groups almost always find it difficult to directly influence policy making unless they can demonstrate significant political support.

Community groups interested in social policy criticized policy makers for being unwilling to take their issues seriously – issues such as sexism, racism, homophobia, and the struggles of disabled people. They argued that legislators were failing to recognize the economic and cultural conditions in which groups of people were having to live and, as a consequence, failing to include those groups in policy making. As an example, gays and lesbians were routinely excluded from adopting children or receiving spousal benefits from government programs. Many community groups lacked formal representation in social policy processes and had to struggle constantly to have their identities recognized and their views heard. According to Offe (1985), many such groups spun off from existing interest groups and government structures because their communities were excluded in some way from the mainstream concerns of industrial growth and economic development. With less power and influence, new social movements lacked the clout of larger, more established interest groups, and their ambitions to achieve recognition and support were constantly being thwarted by the formal policy-making structures. At times, this prompted more virulent attacks against those structures for their exclusionary, racist, sexist, and homophobic processes.

A second major criticism from community groups was that the welfare state was not meeting the needs of disadvantaged people. Governments were failing to develop policies that took into account a whole array of new needs. Part of this critique centred on the bureaucratic structure of the welfare state, which relied on professionals and on centralized planning and control (Davies and Shragge 1990). For many groups, mainstream social policies were providing general benefits that did not acknowledge adequately the diversity of populations in need of help from the social welfare system. Nor did these policies factor in the contrasting needs of different groups. People with developmental needs, for instance, have other requirements than those of their parents, who may be more concerned with security than with encouraging their children to live independently in the community. We return to this issue in chapter 8.

Andrew Armitage describes Ottawa's failure to institutionalize support for community social services – an important social policy failure that had clear consequences for community groups across the country:

> Towards the end of the 1970s an attempt was made by the federal government to consolidate this pattern [of community-based services] through the establishment of an overall framework for the financing of social services throughout Canada as part of the social security review. If it had succeeded, it would have established an institutional commitment to community social services as a Canadian citizenship right. It failed, however, partly for financial reasons (the first wave of financial restructuring) but also because of provincial opposition to the further extension of federal authority. It is also possible that these government social services were beginning to be affected by the lack of informed community participation and by the alienation that their size and bureaucratization were causing. (1996, 105)

A federal social services act had been agreed upon through intergovernmental discussions by 1976. The following year, federal legislation was tabled, but this was withdrawn. So, too, was a subsequent federal proposal to replace the legislation with a block funding approach to social services. After five years of effort, financing for personal and community social services remained under the Canada Assistance Plan.

A third critical theme was that social policies were typically developed as interventions from above; as a consequence, those with political clout were in a position to influence the policy process, with those in the community having to accept policy dictates as they arrived (Lee and Raban 1988). Gay and lesbian activists, civil liberties and human rights movements, and anti-poverty and anti-racist groups viewed themselves (and often still do) as constantly struggling with dominant groups in society. These criticisms from community groups resulted in a reconstruction of how social problems were framed and talked about. Many deaf people no longer considered deafness a problem but rather a culture with its own language and means of communication. Gays and lesbians reconstructed their way of life as a right rather than a deviance from the norm. People with disabilities started taking control of the organizations that represented them, seeking to shift the community's understanding of disability away from the medical model towards a social one. Disability groups pointed out that an inability to walk, see, or speak was an impairment that only became a disability if there were barriers to access, or no facilities to assist locomotion, or no technical aids to promote communication. That is, the *impairment* might reside with the individual, but the *disability* was a function of how the individual and the community interacted. A disability, it followed, was a shared responsibility that required community action as a human right (Prince 1992, 2009).

In response to growing unemployment, persistent poverty, and the crisis of the welfare state, community groups began to explore new employment and income opportunities. As David Ross (1986, 8–9) put it: "At the centre of this crisis is the quality and quantity of employment opportunities. No longer able to assume that the traditional mixed economy can provide full employment and sustain welfare state activity at expected levels, we must now seek new ways to attain both full employment and provide income security. One promising avenue is local economic initiative." Organizations such as the Vanier Institute of the Family (1979) and the Canadian Council on Social Development (Cameron and Sharpe 1988) explored the relationship between the formal and informal sectors of the economy, the viability of community-oriented economic initiatives, and various concrete measures for job creation. Meanwhile, community groups lobbied governments for stable funding for advocacy efforts, core administrative activities, and service provision.

Critiques from Insiders

"If we look more closely at the crisis of the welfare state," Lois Bryson (1992, 229) has written, "we find that it by no means affects all sections of the population equally. The benefits and the advantages of the better-off have largely been maintained and even enhanced. Most of the belt-tightening has been done by those who are at the bottom of the social hierarchy." With the rediscovery of poverty in Canada and other welfare states in the 1960s, early 1970s, and later in the 1990s, we could add that this is the same as it ever was.

The most morally damning criticisms of the welfare state – though not the most politically influential ones – have come from within the system. People working close to or within the social welfare system have raised many concerns about the impact that programs have had on recipients. Insiders' views describe programs and services from the perspectives of front-line workers and recipients in addition to those of non-recipients (Carniol 2005; McKenzie and Wharf 2010). Such perspectives reflect personal views of how the system actually operates for those who must live with the effects of policies, programs, and rules (Neysmith, Bezanson, and O'Connell 2005). Unlike "expert" perspectives on whether the system is providing adequate compensation or sufficient protection, insiders' views describe how the system is affecting clients and whether they are living better lives as a result, or worse ones.[9]

People who receive welfare benefits know that Canadian social programs have made important differences to their lives. Employment Insurance, Workers' Compensation, medicare, Old Age Security, provincial social assistance, and the Canada/Quebec Pension Plans have improved the lives of people who receive benefits, but they have done so at a cost to those people, a cost that is reflected in the three themes we examine here: the way social programs stigmatize recipients, the difficulty recipients have in dealing with the complexities of welfare programs, and the loss of hope that many people feel once they become part of the system.

Regarding the first theme, social welfare programs have always tended to stigmatize recipients, largely because welfare support is viewed as a sign of personal weakness. Recipients feel they have been branded failures and perceive their reputations as having been damaged by the process of becoming dependent on the state. At a deeper level, becoming a welfare recipient creates feelings of shame. The amount of stigma that individuals feel depends on how social programs go about assessing them for eligibility. Programs such as provincial social assistance are based on needs and are highly selective and thus generate the greatest stigma. Other programs, such as Employment Insurance, are based on contributions, with benefits restricted to those who have paid premiums. People receiving these benefits feel they have a right to support, so these programs are less stigmatizing, although negative connotations remain. Finally, there are programs, such as medicare, that are universal and available to all Canadians. These programs are the least stigmatizing.

The question "Can we afford our social programs?" has a stigmatizing ring to it. Those who were receiving social benefits heard it increasingly· in the charged welfare crisis politics of the 1970s and 1980s. It spoke to them of their value and of the contributions they were making to society. Every "No" answer from the media, from the business community, and from working taxpayers undermined the confidence that recipients had in their own worth and abilities. They thought badly not only of themselves but also of other welfare recipients. Every time they read headlines that included terms such as "welfare fraud" and "welfare cheats," they felt like cheaters and fraud artists, even though they had complied with all regulations. Similarly, every time they heard the phrase "get a job" they were made to feel inferior and dysfunctional even though the unemployment rate was at 8, 9, or 10 per cent or higher. The nature of this stigmatization changed as governments altered classification systems. An example was the reclassification of women with children as "employable" in terms of social assistance benefits. Mothers, who once were thought of as contributing to society by caring for their young children, were now considered employable. Changes like these altered the ways in which such mothers were portrayed: they went from deserving government support to being considered dependent and somehow undeserving of it. For those who were defined as employable but who could not work because there were no jobs and no available child care spaces, there was increased stigma.

A second theme raised by insiders concerned the system's complexity. *Welfare in Canada: The Tangled Safety Net* (1987), a report by the National Council of Welfare, documented "a complex of rules to determine who would be eligible for social assistance, how much they were entitled to receive and how the status of recipients could be monitored on an ongoing basis" (1987, 16). The complexity arose in part because of the piecemeal way in which the system had evolved. As chapters 2 and 3 showed, governments developed new social programs, changed old programs, added or took away benefits, created new categories of recipients, and altered eligibility requirements. Not surprisingly, it became difficult to ascertain who was entitled to benefits and how much they could receive if eligible. Different jurisdictions continue to have different rules, and there is no uniformity in the system. Both recipients and front-line workers struggle to understand the maze of policies, rules, and procedures.

In *Street-Level Bureaucracy* (1980), Michael Lipsky examined the experiences and dilemmas faced by individual citizens and professional workers in schools, police departments, welfare and social work agencies, lower courts, and legal aid clinics. Lipsky was analysing the American welfare state, but his findings resonated with workers, clients, social policy academics, and advocates in Canada as well. He documented how legal aid lawyers, police officers, teachers, and social workers experienced work realities that imposed sharp limits on their aspirations and intentions as service providers and caregivers. The structure of their work typically involved top-down policy directives and hierarchical reporting requirements; large classes or caseloads and seemingly limitless needs; inadequate resources and insufficient time due to budget constraints and cutbacks; uncertainties of work methods; unpredictable clients; and constant pressures from the public. These work realities resulted in frustration and alienation by workers, if not burnout, because of inevitable gaps between personal and work limitations on the one side and service ideals on the other. Lipsky found that workers developed survival mechanisms to cope with the pressures and gaps between the intentions and realities they confronted. Survival mechanisms included establishing routines and stereotypes of clients, simplifying problems and views of clients, and lowering their expectations of themselves and their clients to bridge the gap between work and service ideals.

For those who consumed these public services, there was a loss of individualized service. Citizens as applicants became clients who, in turn, became bureaucratic subjects. In many cases, front-line workers had to interpret the complex rules governing eligibility. It was only natural that these workers differed in their subjective assessments of situations, since the rules governing cases were so complicated. This gave workers broad discretionary powers in deciding who would and who would not get benefits. This might "enable the system to respond to individual situations and diverse local conditions ... [but] it also gives rise to inequities" (National Council of Welfare 1987, 22). Many people requiring support from the welfare system – and this includes more than just social assistance – found applying confusing and difficult. They did not know where to go or what to ask. The system was structured so that if a person did not ask the right questions, he or she could not get the right answers. People in similar circumstances were often treated differently depending on whom they asked and what they asked. Another example from *Welfare in Canada: The Tangled Safety Net* provides an insider's view: "Now that I have a new worker, I walked in to see her two weeks ago. She said as she was handing me my support payments for the month: 'You know, considering that you are unemployable; I don't think it's fair that you should take such a loss. I will go and talk to Mr. M.' She left the office, came back and said, 'You will get an additional $196.' Now I had previously been denied that amount. I walk across the hall and I'm given it from another worker. These are rules I don't understand" (1987, 15).

The welfare system is not really a system. People living in the same conditions can be treated differently depending on where they go within it. Insiders and outsiders agree that there are no unifying principles holding programs together. The government may be providing income protection in one part of the program even while punishing recipients in another part (as a way to encourage them back into the workforce). It is not uncommon for people to find that one section of a program contradicts another. There are hundreds of social programs and laws in Canada, some offered by the federal government, others by provincial or territorial governments, and still others by municipal governments, health boards, and school boards. Every program has its own set of eligibility criteria, and one set does not seem to relate to another. Rather than a system functioning as a whole, to many insiders it is a bewildering hodgepodge of programs.

A third theme from the insiders' critique concerned the lack of hope instilled by existing programs. Many clients and workers inside the system think that welfare is a poverty trap. Two features contribute to making it so: first, the rules and regulations make it difficult to regain independence; and second, people inside the system begin to feel despondent and lose hope of finding a way out. The basic rules for receiving welfare use a budget deficit assessment method that calculates the difference between needs and resources; the latter include assets and income available to meet those needs. This assessment method assumes that those who apply for social assistance will have depleted most or all of their assets before seeking help (depending on the provincial regulations). In a process like this, a person must be reduced to a state of impoverishment before being considered eligible for income assistance. Once all of their resources are gone, it is difficult for welfare recipients to become self-supporting again. The level of benefits provided by social assistance, and the regulations regarding how these benefits may be used, make it impossible to save enough to get off welfare.

In sharp contrast, in other segments of the Canadian welfare state throughout the 1970s and 1980s there was a growing militancy among associations and unions representing nurses, physicians, police officers, public servants, and teachers, as well as other professions and occupations. This trend underscored the power differences that existed among those inside the social policy system, in particular between clients (especially welfare recipients) and providers (especially human services professionals). Within the health care system, for instance, public and political concerns were growing that extra billing by physicians and the increasing use of hospital user fees were threatening reasonable access to medicare. These concerns led to a federal Royal Commission in 1979–80, a parliamentary task force in 1981, and a task force by the Canadian Medical Association on the allocation of health resources. In a move to preserve universal health care, the federal government enacted the Canada Health Act in 1984, with all-party support in Parliament. The act consolidated earlier federal laws on hospital and diagnostic services and medical care passed in the 1950s and 1960s; it also placed financial penalties on any provincial or territorial government that allowed hospital user fees.

Conclusions

The period from the mid-1970s to the late 1980s was the era of the "crisis of the welfare state" in Canada and elsewhere. For some observers, this crisis was the manifestation of inherent contradictions between capital accumulation and social legitimation. For others, it was about regulating the poor and blaming victims. For others still, it involved concepts such as culture of poverty and workfare and the impact of both. The welfare state in Canada became the object of considerable criticism among several segments of society, yet there were signs that not all was lost. As Francis Castles observed in his detailed study of OECD welfare states: "Crisis threats made with increasing stridency since the mid-1970s have remained uniformly unfulfilled" (2004, 168).

Indeed, in the period we have reviewed in this chapter, there was some *expansion* in social provisions and in the number of policy stakeholders. In the area of social rights, there was the enactment of the Canadian Human Rights Act, the founding of the Human Rights Commission, the entrenchment of the Charter of Rights and Freedoms in the Constitution, and the passage of the Employment Equity Act and the Canadian Multiculturalism Act. Yasmeen Abu-Laban (1994) has described the years 1971 to 1981 as ones of consolidation and the years 1981 to 1989 as ones of growth for the development of multiculturalism policy in Canada. Regarding income security for seniors, the Spouse's Allowance Program was introduced in 1975 and expanded in 1985, and the Guaranteed Income Supplement was enriched a number of times.

Within the social policy community, many new organizations and alliances have been created. However, the crisis period also witnessed social policy failures or marginal results. These included the ambitious but largely doomed Social Security Review of 1973–6, the aborted 1977 Social Services Act, and what was called the Great Canadian Pension Debate over the years 1979 to 1984, which yielded less than great reforms.

The final report of the Royal Commission on the Economic Union and Development Prospects of Canada in 1985 rejected the view that the broad postwar consensus on social policy was disintegrating or seriously eroding. The commissioners did concede, however, that political consensus had weakened and that ideological debates were growing stronger (Canada 1985, 577). There was general support from both the left and the right for the basic principles of market economies; for the need to ensure that people lived healthy, secure lives; and for the provision of education and work opportunities. The critics disagreed, however, on how such goals should be achieved. The left remained confident that the state could and should intervene in market activities in ways that ensured social justice and human rights. The right opposed government interference in the workings of the market (except in exceptional cases) in the belief that markets provided the best method of ensuring welfare. Most perspectives, while critical of government's role in social policy, wanted the welfare state to be maintained or enlarged, even if reformed and reconfigured in some fashion. Through their critiques, many groups were actually broadening traditional conceptions of social policy, with their ideas about "corporate welfare bums," the informal economy, the hidden welfare system of tax benefits, and the message from second-wave feminism that the personal is political.

Despite the resiliency of the welfare system, political, business, and media elites increasingly interpreted the crisis as a fiscal crisis of the state. There was a rightward shift in the dominant discourse of politics and policy making, generally towards promoting markets. Faith in the redistributive capacities of the welfare state declined. There was less agreement on the merit or feasibility of expanding government budgets on health and social services. It was argued that the state needed to expand the markets' role, not constrain it. Liberal and Conservative federal governments began acting as if social programs were a hindrance to economic growth and financial responsibility. Federal transfers to the provinces for health and education were restrained. After 1975, unemployment insurance programs underwent a succession of cutbacks. The indexation of the universal Family Allowance and Old Age Security came to an end, and benefits were frozen or capped. Provinces began trimming welfare benefits, and minimum-wage rates either were not raised or were raised only periodically, and then only marginally. In the early 1980s, food banks began appearing in cities across the country. Ultimately the crisis was about (re)defining social policy in terms of how many resources should be allocated through the state sector, by what means, and to address what range and types of human needs and social issues.

Next we examine at length the different ways in which social policy and the welfare system have been redefined and changed, and how the forces of globalization and pluralization have affected the debate. Although the criticisms from the five main perspectives examined in this chapter severely strained the underlying consensus on which the welfare state had been constructed, they were not the only forces at work. In hindsight, the crisis also involved a turning away from the apparently completed postwar social policy agenda, now that it was realized that problems of poverty remained. An awareness of the looming problems of globalization and pluralization only increased concerns regarding what form the social welfare system would have to take in order to survive.

5 Response to the Crisis: Retrenching the Welfare State and Changing Responsibilities for Social Protection

In the 1990s, governments no longer took for granted their role as the dominant providers of social welfare programs. In response to growing criticism, and given the pressure of the forces of globalization and pluralization, all governments were re-examining their role and taking action. Some governments dismantled their welfare systems by eliminating programs and services. Other governments maintained their systems by making incremental adjustments to programs and services. Still other governments remixed social policy, retrenching some parts of the system while leaving other parts relatively untouched (Mishra 1990b; Splane 1987, 246). Here we examine the three broad policy strategies used by governments in Canada.

These three strategies reflect the traditional classifications of welfare programs – residual, integrated, and institutional – so we will be using these terms to discuss the different strategies. A government that dismantles its welfare system is moving back towards a residual model of welfare. It wants a welfare system that only comes into effect as a last resort after the family and private markets have failed to meet social needs. A *residual* welfare system provides only temporary support, and it does so in ways that do not confer social rights and duties. Often these programs are means tested and provide only modest benefits. A government that maintains most aspects of its welfare system but wants to deliver programs in new ways uses an *integrated* model of welfare. It is interested in maintaining a welfare system that uses benefits as a way to support the economy. This policy orientation is based on the notion of social investments and focuses on training and education. Such a government wishes to maintain a clear connection between the economy and the provision of social services, but it is also looking for ways to share its responsibilities with other sectors of society. Finally, a government that seeks to maintain its welfare system as a central function of its society uses an *institutional* model of welfare. Such a government takes an institutional approach by providing welfare as a right based on the notion of universal need. It consciously uses the welfare system as an instrument for social inclusion and cohesion. Changes to social welfare systems can be categorized as primarily fitting into one of these policy responses and the corresponding welfare models (although different types of changes may reflect varying degrees of conformity to the model).

Dismantling the Welfare System: Abandoning Policy Goals, Abolishing Programs, and Altering the Context

Dismantling the welfare system – the most severe response a government can make to the welfare crisis – relies on the assumption that government intervention no longer meets the intended goals or that those goals are no longer relevant or desirable. Governments that want to dismantle their welfare systems must believe that the private sector, families, or local communities can provide social supports more effectively than the state. These governments are turning to the private and not-for-profit sectors to take responsibility for solving social problems. Canada, the United States, Britain, and Australia, among other nations, are introducing changes that are generally pushing their systems in residual directions. These countries are deregulating industry, opening trade, and eliminating or tightening existing welfare programs. There are three strategies that the government can use to dismantle the welfare state: programmatic retrenchment, systematic retrenchment, and paradigmatic retrenchment. We now examine each of these.

Paul Pierson (1994) describes the first two strategies. Programmatic retrenchment refers to cutting the size and expenditures of social programs, building greater restrictions into the design of programs, and generally shifting policies in a residual direction. This strategy involves direct assaults, in the short term, on programs and services by cutting and eliminating them. Systemic retrenchment focuses on institutional and fiscal practices, but with longer-term effects on the politics and nature of the welfare state. Systemic retrenchment alters the broader political environment, including public opinion, interest groups, intergovernmental relations, and government finances, in ways that yield future cutbacks as well as a residualization of the social policy system.

While Pierson sees this political environment as lying outside the welfare state, in Canada the welfare state appears embedded in society and the economy. Because our society is fragmented and politicized, and our welfare state is federalized and dispersed, state and society are intertwined in many ways (Cairns 1986).

We add a third strategy of dismantling and restructuring that we call paradigmatic retrenchment. This strategy involves weakening or dropping support for a set of guiding principles that serve as the basis for policy action, and replacing them with one or other policy frames, political discourses, and cultural assumptions. "More and more scholars recognize that current changes within welfare systems are of a paradigmatic nature, and therefore should include the analysis of ideas, discourse, ideologies and culture in explanations of change and stability" (Orloff and Palier 2009, 406). As we discussed in chapters 3 and 4, Keynesianism was a policy paradigm offering a rationale for state intervention in the economy and in society. In recent years, the Harper Conservative government has emphasized a policy paradigm that includes a more limited role for the federal government in the social union – a paradigm that Harper calls "open federalism" – along with a renewed role for the traditional "night watchman" state, which posits that governments should focus sharply on law and order, the military, and national security.

Whether the retrenchment is programmatic, systemic, or paradigmatic, the goal is to considerably reduce public responsibility for addressing social problems, human needs, and community interests.

Programmatic Retrenchment

As stated earlier, programmatic retrenchment refers to cutting the size and expenditures of social programs, building greater restrictions into the design of programs, and generally shifting policies in a residual direction. In Canada, both federal and provincial governments have taken steps to dismantle or reduce large parts of their welfare systems, and such programmatic retrenchment has had a serious impact on community organizations. Here, we outline the cuts to social programs and how they affect community organizations, using the example of the deinstitutionalization of the mentally ill as an example of programmatic retrenchment.

The cuts to social programs have been both large (cutting entire programs) and small (abandoning certain aspects of programs). The large cuts, of course, have had the most impact. At the federal level, in 1993, Brian Mulroney's Conservative government eliminated the universal Family Allowance, claiming that it was necessary in order to fight the deficit. They replaced it with the income-tested Child Tax Credit and also introduced the Working Income Supplement, in effect abandoning the principle that all families raising children, regardless of income, deserve to be recognized for this fundamental responsibility (Blake 2008).

At the provincial level, in 1993, Ralph Klein's Conservative government in Alberta scrapped the existing social assistance program and introduced the Supports for Independence Program, which stopped more than 54,000 people from receiving social assistance over the next four years (Azmier and Roach 1997). The new program forces people to use all other forms of support before turning to the government for help. It is more difficult for people to get on the system, and benefits cannot exceed the earnings of low-income workers. These and other public expenditure cuts in Alberta have undermined public support for social programs (Taft 1997).

The Mike Harris Conservative government did much the same in Ontario. In 1995, it cut social assistance benefits by 22 per cent and then did away with General Welfare Assistance and the Family Benefits Programs altogether, replacing them with the Ontario Disability Support Program and the Ontario Works policy on workfare. These programs divide welfare recipients into the deserving and undeserving poor. By tightening eligibility requirements, increasing anti-fraud measures, and creating barriers to receiving welfare, the Harris government fundamentally altered the welfare system. For community activists and progressive scholars, the "Common Sense Revolution" of the Harris government meant that Ontario was open for business but closed to people (Ralph, St-Amand, and Regimbald 1997). Ernie Lightman, Andrew Mitchell, and Dean Herd (2010) explored the post-welfare labour market experiences of people who were on social assistance in Canada in 1996. Using data that tracked a panel of recipients over five years, Lightman and his colleagues examined the mixing of work and welfare, the transition from welfare to work, and the hours of work and wages that those in receipt of social assistance encountered in taking on paid work. They found that those leaving welfare for work faced precarious employment opportunities. In particular, those leaving welfare for work earned lower wages, worked fewer hours, and consequently had lower annual earnings than non-recipients. Moreover, while the gap narrowed, it remained significant even after six years. Returns to welfare were widespread. Even after six years, most social assistance recipients were on the fringes of the labour market.

Whether the cuts were large or small, government dismantling has profoundly affected community organizations. It has reduced the capacity of voluntary agencies to provide services. A study carried out in Metropolitan Toronto in 1995 asked 1,862 community-based agencies how government cuts were affecting their plans and programs. The agencies reported that 106 programs were likely to be eliminated in 1996 and that 301 were under review for cancellation (Kitchen 1996, 165). The termination of health and social service programs weakens a community's capacity to respond to social problems.

Besides reducing the service provision capacity of voluntary agencies, funding cuts have had at least four other serious consequences: they have weakened the infrastructure; debilitated communications; forced commercialization; and drowned the political voice of these agencies. First, cutbacks often result in the loss of a paid position for managing volunteers; this squeezes the already limited infrastructure of most agencies and reduces their ability to recruit, train, and oversee volunteer staff. The entire infrastructure that the voluntary agency is based upon is weakened as a result. Second, cuts in grants can increase competition for funding within the voluntary sector, with agencies chasing a limited number of donors, corporations, and foundations; agencies may as a result become less likely to share information and ideas with other groups in their community. Third, community agencies can experience the commercialization of their activities and even their mission, as a consequence of user fees and market pricing for the services and goods they provide; this may place them in direct competition with private-sector organizations. Such commercialization undermines the foundations on which voluntary organizations have been built. Fourth, when they cut grants to voluntary groups, governments typically target non-service functions such as advocacy activities and administrative support for federations and umbrella associations. This weakens the ability of community groups to network and engage in democratic politics; these agencies' political voices are thereby drowned out. Even though interesting pockets of activism and participation continue to exist within community social services (Baines 2010), the future role and vitality of the voluntary sector in Canada is in some doubt, like love in a cold world (Browne 1996). These serious consequences expose the long-standing myth that voluntarism is independent of government support.

The cutting of welfare programs has long historical roots. A case in point was when governments dramatically altered social policies affecting people with mental illnesses. What began with the best of intentions after the publication of James Tyhurst's *More for the Mind* (1963) turned into the deinstitutionalization of large numbers of seriously mentally ill people. The institutionalization of people with cognitive, developmental, and intellectual disabilities had separated them from their families and segregated them in facilities, resulting in absent citizens; their basic needs were perhaps maintained, but their social capacities wasted away. The deinstitutionalization process, which included closing psychiatric institutions, discharging patients, and ending new admissions, was meant to move people out of institutions and into the community (Piat 1992, 202). In the late 1960s and early 1970s, governments in Canada closed close to three-quarters of inpatient beds for people with mental illnesses (Trainor, Pape, and Pomeroy 1997). Patients were shifted to local hospitals and outpatient care, and for many, this meant abandonment. Over time, many could not find a place to live and fell onto the city streets. Myra Piat (1992, 204) points out that poor housing conditions, financial problems, ghettoization, and dependency on drugs have generated social problems such as increasing numbers of homeless persons and the incarceration of psychiatric patients by the criminal justice system. For those who found housing in large boarding houses, these turned out to be not too different from the large institutions, except that they had much less service and no protection from institutional abuse. Deinstitutionalization may mean that people with disabilities are no longer absent from the community; however, without sufficient social supports and public services, they have been marginalized by society (Prince 2009).

The dismantling of programs and services for people who were being deinstitutionalized stimulated the private sector to provide profit-making residential services. Provincial governments allowed the private sector maximum flexibility in establishing and operating lucrative boarding homes in which the mentally ill were now housed. Governments also encouraged the private sector to keep the boarding houses self-regulating and out of the public domain. The deinstitutionalization of people with mental illness also had a profound effect on communities. Community groups were not consulted, informed, or educated in preparation for the arrival of people who had been discharged from institutions (Piat 1992, 205). The community response has been documented by Michael L. Dear and Jennifer R. Wolch (1987), who describe the emergence of the "not in my backyard" (NIMBY) syndrome. This response reflects the deep concerns people have about social problems being pushed back into their communities. Negative attitudes about government downloading have come to infect every social issue, from how to develop accommodations for low-income people to how to provide services for the homeless. It now seems that virtually every issue faces NIMBY resistance as community members express their fear of changes to their local communities.

Systemic Retrenchment

Systemic retrenchment focuses on institutional and fiscal practices. Its measures "alter the broader political economy and consequently alter welfare state politics" (Pierson 1994, 15). Within this type of retrenchment, which happens primarily at the federal level, governments try to dismantle the welfare system by weakening the policy context in which social policies are crafted. Here we outline the different ways that various countries have weakened policy-making processes; we also explore how such activities take place.

The British governments of Margaret Thatcher weakened policy making by weakening the labour unions. Thatcher fought the unions by introducing legislation that limited their ability to represent workers and by supporting plant owners during important strikes (Marsh 1991, 301). Her government also deregulated the labour market by introducing eight employment acts whose intent was to change working conditions and increase the influence of market forces (Pratt 1997, 49).

The U.S. administrations of Ronald Reagan changed the context of social policy making by limiting the amount of money that governments could borrow to support welfare programs. At the same time, the U.S. government lowered taxes on high-income earners, which led to revenue reductions that pressured governments to pay down their deficits (White and Wildavsky 1989).

In Canada the Mulroney and Chrétien governments changed the context of social policy by limiting the amount of financial support the federal government gave the provinces for health care, post-secondary education, social services, and social assistance programs. They also ended a number of cost-shared programs, replacing them with block grants, thereby limiting the growth of welfare programs. Governments that change the context of social policy do not appear to be attacking the welfare system directly; nonetheless, such actions undermine the conditions for making social policy.

On the whole, dismantling the welfare state is publicly controversial and therefore politically difficult. Every program develops constituents over time – that is, people with commitments to existing programs who are prepared to lobby to ensure that their programs survive. Clientele receive direct benefits from the programs, while those who seek to dismantle them enjoy only indirect benefits, such as a small reduction in taxes. Even the most strident anti-welfare commentators recognize that people support existing systems, and governments face strong political resistance when they attempt dramatic changes. David Marsland (1996, 159) suggests hiding the fact that the welfare system is being dismantled. He believes that governments are prevented from making dramatic changes by the political backlash that would result. So, he suggests, the dismantling must be phased in so that people have time to save enough to pay for what they need and adjust to the changes. That, in our view, is a flawed strategy, because how can those who have no money save it?

Governments wanting to hide policy changes often alter their approaches to making policy decisions. When the Conservative government in Ontario began dismantling the welfare system, it chose methods that made it possible to conceal what it was doing. The Social Assistance Reform Act, which came into effect in 1998, gave the provincial cabinet sweeping powers to make radical changes without going through legislative review, public input, or appeal (Torjman 1997a). The same law gave cabinet the power to make regulations concerning every detail of the new welfare system, from determining eligibility criteria to setting benefit levels. The Ontario government can now govern through regulation rather than legislation across a broad welfare front; in this way, it has assumed a vast array of powers while limiting public scrutiny. No longer does the government need to seek input from the community, which can no longer influence directly the retrenchment agenda through its elected representatives. Governments can also restructure the policy domain by shifting the level at which decisions are made. In federated states, it is possible for the central government to either centralize or decentralize authority depending on which tactic will help it achieve its goals. When decision-making responsibilities for cutbacks (along with the blame for them) are shifted to local administrators, future governments find it more difficult to coordinate welfare interventions and/or introduce social policies.

Paradigmatic Retrenchment: Abandoning the Goal of Full Employment

Paradigmatic retrenchment involves reducing support for the under-lying principles guiding policy development. Probably the most im-portant case of welfare state dismantling has been the abandonment of "full employment" as a central goal of public policy. The goal of full employment was closely associated with Keynesian thinking, which from the 1940s to the 1970s was the dominant paradigm in macroeco-nomic policy and a major influence on social security policy (McBride 2005). A government that has decided to maintain full employment will adopt fiscal and economic policies to foster job creation and community development; it will also spend tax money on education and training, on programs and services, and on capital expenditures to keep people employed during economic slumps. To ensure a high level of employ-ment, governments offer opportunities and hope; this in turn reduces demands on the welfare system. Governments that abandon the idea of full employment are in effect allowing market forces to determine the level of unemployment.

We need to understand what the goal of full employment can *mean*, and not simply lament its passing. During the decades when the welfare state was being envisaged and established, full employment in Canada was actually discussed by government leaders in terms of "high and stable levels of employment." In practice, this referred to full-time paid work for men, with the expectation of a career or job mobility in rela-tively secure industrial and resource sectors of the economy. Even in the expansionist era of social welfare, Canada's policy commitment to full employment rested on residual thinking; that is, employment was to be generated primarily by the market economy. The role of government was to create a favourable climate for business, introduce public works projects when the economy slowed or slumped, and have in place pub-lic welfare and unemployment insurance programs as safety nets. A full-employment policy was only partially pursued by Canadian gov-ernments; even so, through the 1950s and into the 1970s a range of pro-grams, laws, and institutions were established that accompanied and supported economic growth, rising incomes, and tax bases, along with a rising standard of living (Campbell 1987; Gonick 1987; McBride 1992).

During the crisis period of the 1970s and 1980s, when the world's economies faced a global oil-price shock, along with rising inflation and no growth, the right effectively challenged the belief that national governments could manage their economies and maintain a policy of

full employment. The goal of full employment dropped off the plat-
forms of both liberal and conservative political parties as well as the
agendas of successive governments in Ottawa. The official discourse of
policy makers and most mainstream economists increasingly referred
to a "natural" rate of unemployment. Definitions of what constituted
full employment in the Canadian economy continually lowered the target from 97 to 95 to 93 per cent (or even lower) of the labour force, as the
average rate of unemployment for each decade continually rose.

In the contemporary economy, the world of work has changed and so
must the concept of full employment. The Commission on Social Justice
has written that "in the 1990s and beyond, it will involve for both men
and women frequent changes of occupation, part-time as well as full-
time work, self-employment as well as employment, time spent caring
for children or elderly relatives as well as or instead of employment,
and periods spent in further education and training. Forty years ago
the typical worker was a man working full-time in industry; today the
typical worker is increasingly likely to be a woman working part-time
in a service job" (1994, 154). We examine these trends and their implications for gender and communities in chapters 9 and 10.

Social Economy of Welfare: Remixing the Provision of Social Care

The mixed or social economy of welfare describes an old practice with a
new name. The old practice, where social welfare programs were delivered by government agencies, not-for-profit organizations, and private
corporations (see chapters 2 and 3), is now referred to as the mixed – or
social – economy of welfare. This approach has been used in varying degrees in all liberal democratic countries. Germany, France, the Nether-
lands, and Italy are currently taking this middle-of-the-road approach to
welfare change. Their approaches have focused on managing the labour
supply through job training, education, and early retirement; at the same
time, they have kept their commitments to major welfare programs.

Governments moving towards a mixed welfare approach generally
believe that welfare systems provide important supports to the economy. They want to alter the provision of the existing system rather
than destroy its principle. They believe there are better ways of delivering programs and services than just public-sector agencies. In taking this approach, governments assume that the social welfare system
will work more effectively if other organizations are involved in developing and delivering programs. Policy makers therefore seek to forge
new linkages and expand on existing partnerships with other sectors of

society. Governments can mix welfare programs and services between the different sectors in a number of ways. All such tactics entail the changing and sharing of responsibility for welfare between governments and other sectors of society.[1] Here we look at two primary ways that a mix is attained: by changing the governing body responsible, and by contracting out with other sectors. But first, a quick look at the different domains within the Canadian mix will help us understand how the mixed economy of welfare works.

The term "mixed economy of welfare" captures the pluralistic nature of the provision of social benefits and the allocation of resources. In Canada's mixed model of welfare there are five primary domains: the public sector, the voluntary not-for-profit sector, the private-for-profit sector, the Aboriginal sector, and the informal sector of families and local communities. Each sector has different attributes. In the public sector, benefits and services are normally funded through the general tax system and provided by public servants working in government agencies. In the voluntary sector, programs are normally funded through community-based fundraising and government contracts with not-for-profit organizations and are provided by employees and volunteers who work in community organizations. Private-for-profit organizations obtain funding through contracts with the government to provide services, or through user fees paid by the people who are receiving services. Employees work in privately owned organizations. It is assumed that private organizations offer more choice to consumers and that they tend to be more efficient and responsive to demand. The sphere of Aboriginal communities, governments, and urban organizations is of growing importance in social policy and in politics more generally, and is funded in large part by the federal government, but also by provincial governments, with associated political issues of public accountability and governance capacity (Abele and Prince 2008; Prince 2011). In the informal sector, benefits and services are funded through the personal contributions of family and friends and are delivered on an interpersonal basis. All of this variety results in social programs with some resilience; but as we will see, the pressure placed on some of these domains as a result of government restructuring has jeopardized these same delivery systems.

Towards a New Social Union: Changing Which Government Is Responsible

A clear example of seeking ways to remix responsibility for welfare is reflected in the intergovernmental discussions and negotiations over

Canada's social union – that is, in efforts to develop a shared political view of social purpose and citizenship.[2] The 1995 federal budget announced a 25 per cent cut in transfers to the provinces and territories for health, education, and social welfare. In response, the Provincial Ministerial Council on Social Policy Reform and Renewal prepared a report on behalf of the provincial premiers and territorial leaders setting out a framework for "rebalancing the federation" and the welfare state. The Provincial Council made recommendations relating to health care, post-secondary education, social services, labour market programs, and arrangements for financing the system. The provinces wanted greater control over social programs as well as increased access to cash transfers and tax points. They also wanted to institute a way of limiting federal involvement in provincial program areas. At the same time, they wanted an agreement that would result in the federal government taking responsibility for all programming for Aboriginal people. All of these recommendations reflected the changing politics of social policy; in general terms, the provinces wanted more authority over welfare.

A Social Union Framework Agreement (SUFA) was signed in 1999 by the federal government, nine provinces, and two territories, but not Quebec. Nor were the voices of national Aboriginal political leaders directly involved (Prince 2002). The agreement aimed to promote equality, universality, and affordability by removing barriers to participation in post-secondary education, training, health and social services, and social assistance. Under SUFA's terms, the federal government would respect the priorities of the provincial and territorial governments as these related to cost-shared or block-funded programs. It would also consult with other governments about funding changes or social transfers one year in advance of any changes; also, it would not introduce changes without getting the consent of a majority of provincial governments. Provincial and territorial governments could invest program funds in ways that reflected the spirit of the new programs and would receive their share of the funding. In the estimation of one political scientist, "the provincial position implied a greater decentralization of social policy in Canada, while the federal response to it sought measures to strengthen the Canadian economic union. Together, this particular combination of decentralization and centralization fits well with the neoliberal approach to federalism" (Harmes 2007, 432).

Subsequent events have made it clear that the SUFA has been more a ripple than a sea change in intergovernmental relations and social policy making in Canada (Prince 2003, 2005). Other factors have proven to be more influential, including, since 2006, the Harper Conservative administrations in Ottawa.

Stephen Harper, "Open Federalism," and Limited Federal Social Policy

It is clear that Stephen Harper's minority Conservative governments (2006–8, 2008–11) approved of the SUFA's principles and rules, especially because these placed formal limits on the federal spending power when it came to new cost-shared programs in areas of provincial jurisdiction. Both before and after coming to power, Harper supported what he called "open federalism." "The Harper government has its own lens through which it views both social programs and the spending power, and its lens is different than that of the Liberal governments that preceded it" (Lazar 2008, 133). Major themes of Harper's open federalism have been to limit the federal spending power in areas of provincial responsibility; to ensure that new shared-cost programs in areas of provincial responsibility have the consent of the majority of provinces; and to recognize the right of provinces and territories to opt out of shared-cost federal programs with compensation if they offer similar programs with comparable goals and systems of accountability.

Shortly after taking office in 2006, the Harper government cancelled a federal–provincial–territorial agreement called the Kelowna Accord, which had been brokered by Paul Martin's Liberal government. That accord would have funded new and expanded measures for Aboriginal peoples and communities in the areas of education, health care, and housing over a ten-year period. In 2007 the Harper government terminated another of Martin's social initiatives – five-year intergovernmental agreements with the provinces that would have supported the development of universally accessible early learning and child care services. These two actions represented major retreats in social policy as well as retrenchments of the federal spending power. Yet around the same time – no doubt conditioned by the exigencies of public opinion at a time of minority government – the Harper government endorsed the Canada Health Transfer (CHT) and Canada Social Transfer (CST) agreements that had been negotiated by the Chrétien and Martin Liberal governments; these will run until 2014. Similarly, the Harper government's policies on equalization payments and financing formulas to have-not provinces and to the territories have been continuations of previous Liberal government policies. Thus, a substantial part of

Harper's new approach to intergovernmental relations is rooted in historic debates and interests within the federation (Bickerton 2010; Lazar 2008). This relative lack of strong federal leadership stands in contrast to the activism of the later Chrétien government (2000–3) and the Martin years (2003–6) in social policy.

Regarding the social policy and intergovernmental record of the Harper government, Harvey Lazar (2008) has concluded that "it has asserted forcefully and explicitly that program areas covered by the Canada Health Transfer and Canada Social Transfer are areas of shared responsibility, and has extended their legislative lives. The Conservative government initially attempted to improve provincial accountability for these programs by substantial intervention. But it has since seemed to lean towards an accountability regime for these two large transfers that focus on clarity of roles and responsibilities. At the same time, the federal government does not appear to have any major new social policy initiatives in mind and it has very significantly reduced its fiscal room for launching any such initiative" (Lazar 2008, 139). Likewise, Adam Harmes has concluded that "limiting the federal spending power, and cutting or transferring federal taxes, amounts to a more decentralized federation" (2007, 422).

Downloading to Municipalities and Other Local Public Organizations

At the same time that the provinces are striving to gain more financial resources from Ottawa, they are looking for ways to share responsibility for social welfare with municipal governments and community organizations. Peter Clutterbuck (1997, 70) contends that the "devolution of responsibility to the municipal level of government and local communities has been a driving force of public policy in the 1990s." This trend of devolution or downloading continued in many provinces during the early 2000s. We can distinguish between devolution and downloading as follows: devolution involves delegating resources along with responsibilities, whereas downloading (at times referred to as offloading) involves passing responsibilities onto other public bodies but not the commensurate resources to undertake adequately those service and policy duties. The process of shifting welfare responsibilities downward moves those responsibilities closer to the community, which in turn raises important questions about how social welfare systems can be financed and sustained. Municipalities (and related local bodies, such as school boards and library boards) are under considerable pressure to avoid or minimize property tax increases; to cut services and lower existing service standards; and to contract out higher-cost service responsibilities to the lowest-bidding commercial operators.

Welfare devolution from federal to provincial to municipal governments has deeply fragmenting effects. When social policy systems are devolved, it becomes harder to maintain standards across the country or across a province. Larger and wealthier jurisdictions are able to afford better and broader services. Where governments cannot provide those services, voluntary and private-sector organizations are invited to participate. This opens the system up to the development of services that some people can afford and that others cannot. Clutterbuck has predicted that devolution will create two-tier systems in health and education and three-tier systems in social services. In health and education, devolution will lead to private hospitals and charter schools for the well-off and poorly funded public hospitals and schools for the rest. In the social services, there will be high-end market services responding to the ability of the well-off to pay for what they need, lower-quality public services for the middle classes supported by regressive taxes, and low-end community services for the impoverished and destitute provided by voluntary agencies supported by charity.

Contracting Out Service Provision

Besides sharing and devolving responsibility for welfare programs, governments are remixing their social policy systems by contracting with not-for-profit and private organizations to provide services. Contracting represents a transfer of property rights and obligations to not-for-profit or private organization (Hirsch 1991). Contracting establishes the activities to be performed, the goals to be reached, and the clients to be served. Governments that resort to contracting to create a mixed economy of welfare are not relinquishing responsibility for welfare; rather, they are creating partners in service delivery. As an example, instead of establishing nursing homes for the elderly, hiring staff, and offering services, a government contracts with a not-for-profit or private organization to provide those services. The government continues to finance the services in full or in part, but it does not directly provide them.

Contracting out provides governments with flexibility in redesigning the welfare system. Governments can enter into contracts with limited periods, sharply identified objectives, specified outcomes, and clearly established costs. Contracting allows a government to develop relationships with many providers offering services in local communities and meeting local needs. By calling for proposals, governments hope to create competition among potential providers. In this way, they should be able to get the best services at the lowest cost. The difficulty is that, while contracting may bring costs down, it does so by allowing contracting agencies to pay lower wages than government departments, with fewer employment benefits and less job security. This has important implications for gender equality, since most workers in contract agencies in the health and social service fields are women.

Also, private providers are not limited by regulations in the same way that public agencies are. As an example, when the government operates a housing program, the public agency must take into account the composition of families when providing accommodations – the state must ensure, for instance, that there are private bedrooms for male and female children over a certain age. The private sector faces none of these regulations. It can rent housing to a family without knowing anything about its members. Similarly, when a local government provides home care it must protect staff from potential risks and clients from potential abuse. When the informal sector provides the same services, it is assumed that the conditions will be safe because they are provided by family members or friends.

Does remixing the provision of social services away from the state towards other sectors constitute retrenchment? This question is too rarely asked, but it *needs* to be asked in the new politics of social policy. Mishra (1990b, 111) offers an approach to exploring the issue of welfare pluralism: "It is one thing to decentralize and privatize service delivery in such a way that entitlement is not weakened. It is quite another to privatize, that is, withdraw public services and public commitment to maintaining standards, without underwriting entitlement or ensuring that equity considerations are met." The reallocation of service delivery clearly has implications for gender relations, the quality of employment, and the actual capacity of sectors to undertake the tasks, as well as for national or provincial standards in social programs. We consider these matters in the chapters that follow.

Maintaining the Existing System

The Nordic welfare states of Sweden, Denmark, Norway, and Finland are working hard to sustain their welfare systems. They have kept public employment high while maintaining the vast majority of their welfare programs.[3] As they maintain the status quo, they deal with threats to the system by making incremental modifications to programs. All of this has kept these countries' systems essentially intact. This strategy is based on the following three premises. First, in order for capitalist economies to develop, there must be a system of underlying supports that allow change to take place without destroying the basic social structure; the welfare system provides these important stabilizing mechanisms. Second, market failures create many social problems that only social interventions can address. Markets tend to create inequality and social unrest, so welfare programs are necessary in order to counterbalance these forces and thereby maintain social integration. Third, if liberal democratic governments want to keep the political support of low- and middle-income families, they must redistribute resources through their welfare systems. Without social interventions to reallocate resources, the standard of living of most citizens would slowly fall, leading to political turmoil.

Some commentators have developed an "irreversibility theory" of social rights (Mishra 1990b, 32). That theory is based on the notion that welfare systems have been created through contributions from workers, who then have a proprietary claim on benefits. The interlinking of contributions and income protections provided through the welfare system creates important structural supports for capitalism. Michael O'Higgins (1985) suggests that governments, even strongly neoconservative ones, have difficulty abolishing existing social insurance systems. The irreversibility theory is not based on the notion that the system will remain the same as long as there are liberal democratic states. Rather, the fundamental structures of welfare – income protection, social insurance, services for meeting basic needs, and measures for preventing and relieving poverty – will remain essential ingredients of democratic societies.

The welfare system may be pushed in one direction by neoconservatives, in such a way that deep resistance develops, leading to a counter-push in the other direction by the political centre-left. The welfare system may exist in contradiction to the markets, yet each makes a contribution to the population's well-being. Many aspects of the welfare state are resilient. Welfare programs stopped many people from falling into destitution during the economic roller coaster of the 1980s and 1990s. People were protected from the worst aspects of economic change, and families were not destroyed, nor were entire communities devastated as they had been during the Great Depression. John Myles and Paul Pierson (1997) point out that while there have been similarities in the policy shifts between Canada and the United States, Canada has offset the rising inequalities in labour market incomes by providing social transfers. The result has been a stable level of poverty in Canada but an increasing level in the United States.

The resilience of the welfare state – or at least of certain kinds of social policies – may also be due to people's suspicions of free markets. Many Canadians are inherently wary of the marketplace and "free enterprise." The principle of *caveat emptor* (buyer beware), and the notion that private enterprise exists only to make a profit at a cost to the paying public, are long-time hindrances to the dismantling of the welfare state. Relatively few people in Canada want their families to be cared for by people who are making a profit at it, especially if those profits result in poorer services than those offered by voluntary or public-sector organizations. Besides, almost everyone who understands the market's workings believes that the economy cannot and will not protect them from the risks created by a changing society. People who look back in history, before the introduction of the welfare state, see what happened to individuals and families during the Dirty Thirties. Social inequalities were vast; families were impoverished if their breadwinners became unemployed or fell sick; a visit to the hospital could lead to economic ruin; and the provision of relief was demeaning and coercive. Few people, if given the choice, want to return to those days.

Changes to Canadian Social Policy

Canada's various social programs and policy areas have experienced various fates. Accounts of the changes that the Mulroney, Chrétien, Martin, and Harper governments have made to Canadian social policy are readily available in the literature – including in our own reviews (Prince and Rice 2007; Rice and Prince 2004) – so we need only summarize those changes here.[4] A substantial amount of Canadian social policy has suffered from retrenchment. With respect to paradigmatic retrenchment, the abandonment of Keynsianism and of the goal of full employment has been particularly significant (see chapter 6). Another important example (see chapter 10) has been the elimination of universality as a central principle of the income security system for families with children, as well as for seniors. Still another has been the termination of the Canada Assistance Plan (CAP), which represents the end of the federal government's forty-year commitment to play a direct and specific role in funding social assistance in association with the provinces. All of these changes illustrate in concrete terms what is meant by the weakening of the social consensus that underpins social policy in Canada.

With respect to systemic retrenchment, public opinion remains supportive of many social programs and services, such as education, medicare, and equalization payments for Canada's have-not regions. The vast majority of Canadians reject calls for the privatization of the Canada Pension Plan or for the formal adoption of a two-tier health care system. In the later 1990s the general public expressed concern that governments were going too far and too fast in reducing deficits, and that additional social spending was needed in critical areas such as child poverty. Public beliefs and claims are shifting, however, given the rise of new social movements and the discourse of diversity. Like previous recent federal governments, the Harper Conservatives have weakened interest groups within the social policy community by cutting their funding, by calling into question their representativeness and expertise, and by ignoring their voices and ideas in policy consultation processes such as parliamentary studies on poverty and homelessness. The discourse of fiscal restraint and deficit reduction has seriously constrained the role and effectiveness of client and advocacy groups.

A distinctive feature of the Canadian version of retrenchment over most of the 1980s and 1990s was the extent of tax increases. Successive Conservative and Liberal federal governments did not "defund the welfare state" (Pierson 1994) by restricting revenue flows to itself for financing programs and debt charges. Canadian governments instead sought to strengthen their fiscal capacities and stabilize their revenue sources.[5] The partial indexation of income tax brackets and of many social benefits has allowed revenues to increase through inflation – a process dubbed "social policy by stealth" (Battle 1990). This process is linked closely to the centralization of power in federal decision-making structures within the Department of Finance (see chapter 6).

Yet the federal government *has* defunded social policy by sharply and unilaterally cutting back transfer payments to the provincial and territorial governments. For most of these governments, transfer payments are vital sources of revenues for financing education, health, income support, and other public services. In 1996 the Canada Health and Social Transfer (CHST) dramatically altered the way welfare budgeting and policy making takes place. The CHST has also fragmented or dispersed access points for welfare groups and poverty advocates across the country (Rice 1995b). The move away from CAP (a conditional cost-sharing arrangement for income assistance and social services) towards the CHST (a smaller and far less conditional block fund) amounts to a fundamental change in the systemic features of the country's social policy. To date, the federal government has resisted provincial demands, expressed through the Premiers' Council and other forums, to change the way such decisions are made – for example, how the principles and standards of medicare as contained in the Canada Health Act are to be interpreted and enforced. The provinces want to develop in cooperation with Ottawa a new approach to the use of the federal spending power in order to avoid future acts of federal unilateralism, which inevitably generate conflict. In the coming decades, much of the intergovernmental politics of social policy will focus on provincial–municipal and municipal–community relations, especially in the metropolitan centres of Montreal, Toronto, and Vancouver, where one-third of all Canadians and the majority of immigrant, refugee, and visible majority populations are located.

Programmatic retrenchment – the erosion of benefits, the contraction of program designs, and the imposition of burdens – is easily visible in a range of benefits, programs, and services at all levels of government. There have been repeated and dramatic cutbacks in Employment Insurance and income assistance. There have also been reductions in spending on post-secondary education, medicare, social housing, old age benefits, family benefits, and retirement and disability benefits under the CPP. Meanwhile, workfare and user fees are being introduced, and the wages of public employees are being frozen. As Frank McGilly (1998, 247) has written, "such coast-to-coast, across-the-board restraint in social programs constitutes a critical juncture for social policy in Canada." Although some of these restraint measures were negotiated and consensual in their introduction, most governments have simply imposed them, at times through stealth.

One measure of this restraint refers to total program spending by the federal government as a share of the gross domestic product (GDP). Between the early 1990s and 2000, federal expenditures on all programs and services declined from about 20 per cent of GDP to less than 12 per cent – the lowest share since the social security system was launched in the 1940s. In the Chrétien and Martin Liberal governments between 2000 and 2006, federal program spending was between 12 and 14 per cent of GDP. Under the Harper Conservatives, in large part due to economic stimulus spending in response to the 2008–9 recession, federal government program spending rose to 15.6 per cent of GDP by 2010, with a medium-term objective of reducing that ratio to 13 per cent by 2014.

The remixing of service and program provision has been pursued through deinstitutionalization, contracting out, devolution, and the transfer of lands, funds, powers, and programs to Aboriginal governments. A remixing of the welfare state can also result from the restraining of public programs (such as old age benefits and pensions) in ways that place the onus for retirement savings on personal and private-sector measures. The consequences of this retrenchment of public programs, and of parallel changes to the market economy, have been emergency shelters, food banks, and soup kitchens.

Several components of the welfare state endure: universal health care, universal education at the elementary and secondary school levels; workers' compensation programs; veterans' benefits; income supplements for seniors; and provincial taxation and shelter assistance programs. The entrenchment in 1982 of the Canadian Charter of Rights and Freedoms was an important development for citizenship and politics in the midst of the crisis era, even if subsequent results have fallen short of progressives' hopes (Petter 2010). Social policies based in the workplace and in the tax system are often overlooked in discussions of the welfare state, but they are important determinants of welfare, and they display continuity. Occupational welfare benefits (see chapter 9) have largely been maintained – indeed, in some cases they have been expanded. Furthermore, a multitude of tax expenditures in the personal and corporate income tax systems, as well as in the GST, have been maintained or even enhanced. Such provisions result in forgone revenue for the public purse and therefore represent spending through the tax regime. Some occupational and fiscal provisions are for social policy purposes, others for economic interests; some are progressive, others are regressive in their impacts on income and wealth distribution, subverting the reduction of inequalities.

Conclusions

In response to the crisis of the welfare state, governments have adopted various strategies. One has been to dismantle social welfare systems through paradigmatic, systemic, or programmatic forms of retrenchment. A second has been to remix the social economy of welfare by seeking partnerships with other sectors. A third has been to more or less maintain existing systems by focusing on incremental adjustments to policies and programs. Elements of all three strategies have been implemented in Canada.

The continuation of health, education, and other social programs has led some commentators to conclude that, despite the efforts of neoconservative governments, the welfare state remains "largely intact" (Mishra 1990b,14; Pierson 1994, 179). Richard Gwyn (1996, 83, 91) has written that "it would be too strong to say that Canadians are entering a post-welfare state era. Medicare and unemployment insurance will be reduced, but they will always be with us ... We've gone through the sound barrier of the near-depression of the early 1990s with our egalitarian ideal, and a fair amount of its substance, still intact."

Regarding federal–provincial relations, in many program areas the Harper government has been backing away from exercising federal powers through new or enhanced initiatives. It is true that federal constitutional powers remain in place and that jurisdictional responsibilities have not been transferred to provinces; also, important federal social programs, such as Employment Insurance, elderly benefits and family benefits, and student grant programs remain more or less in place. But in Canadian social policy overall, the profile and influence of the federal government has diminished relative to that of provincial governments, especially in the larger provinces. The trends in these policy shifts are not new; rather, they reflect a longer dynamic linked to developments traced earlier in this chapter and in the previous one. However, the Harper government's ideology has no doubt furthered this trend. Harper is inclined to view issues of urban life, family needs, health care, and the challenges of poverty primarily as provincial responsibilities rather than as national issues. Moreover, his government has been reluctant if not outright resistant to consider federal leadership on matters such as home care, pharmacare, social housing, and disability income support. We return to this theme of the provincialization of Canadian social policy in chapter 10.

It is also true that some of Canada's social programs are politically durable and have experienced less than radical changes. Many policies and programs, however, have been fundamentally transformed, as have the paradigmatic and systemic features of the welfare state. As a guide for policy makers, the Keynesian welfare consensus has lost much of its influence over government agendas and has sometimes virtually disappeared. The maintenance and expansion of the welfare state is no longer an article of faith among political parties in the way that it was in the 1950s and 1960s. In the current era, all mainstream political parties with perhaps the exception of the NDP are more socially conservative in their outlook, with weak commitments to social planning, redistribution, and job creation. We would also argue that the cumulative impact of fifteen to twenty years of incremental cuts and reductions has been powerful. Social safety nets are now badly frayed and closer to the ground. Welfare caseloads overall hit record high levels in the 1990s; for specific groups, such as people with mental and physical disabilities, welfare caseload numbers continued climbing in the first decade of the new millennium. The labour force is polarizing in terms of the availability, quality, and security of jobs. Faced with these risks and retrenchments, as well as the forces of globalization and pluralization, communities and social movements are striving for new forms of inclusion and protection.

6 Global Capitalism and the Canadian Welfare State: Impacts of Economic Integration, Fiscal Policy, and Market Liberalism on Social Policy

Canadians have long viewed social programs as modifying the play of market forces, offering extra-market allocations, and protecting people inside and outside the labour force. Social welfare values are asserted over economic ones. When the postwar welfare state was being built, social policy was commonly distinguished from economic policy in terms of its goals, which included these: to build identities, to foster community and integration, and to alter how society was structured and how market-generated incomes were distributed. Nicola Yeates (2005) reminds us that "governments and representatives of capital, labour and non-governmental organizations (NGOs) all attempt to advance their interests and endeavour to influence how national territories, institutions and populations are governed by engaging in various types of political action in different spheres (institutional, economic) and at different levels (multilateral, regional, national, subnational)." From a more focused perspective, welfare theorists (Titmuss 1968) referred to these types of activities related to state welfare as a social market distinct in aims and standards from the economic marketplace. Under Keynesian economics, the social and economic markets were linked in a compatible manner, with social spending serving an important role in stabilizing the economy and promoting growth. Even in the debates about the "crisis of the welfare state," no one disputed that the welfare state intervened in economic affairs and had an impact on market forces. The debate was and still is over the scale of such interventions and their consequences for workers, other citizens, businesses, market sectors, and the overall economy.

Ideas have changed during the era of globalization. Today more than ever before, market forces are both defining and delimiting welfare states. It appears that in most areas of public policy, economic values are prevailing over community ones. Using Esping-Andersen's (1990) categorization of welfare states, there has been a shift in support for welfare regimes from the social democratic (or "socialist" as originally termed), to the liberal ("residual"), and more to the conservative ("corporatist") model of welfare. In the changing politics of Canadian society, social policy and the welfare state are being pitted against economic policy and the market, and this has heightened tensions between the two sides. Social policy is being depicted as a "drain" on economic policy rather than as a necessary partner in the capitalist enterprise. Programs that provide protection from the consequences of free markets are viewed negatively. Policies that guarantee union rights, the right to strike, or the right to collective bargaining are deemed to run counter to the essential logic of the capitalist labour market. So too are those policies that provide benefits that give people a choice between selling their labour and any other activity. And, most important, anti-welfare commentators are claiming that social policies are a threat, at least theoretically, to the development of a strong economy.

The tensions between social and economic policy have been deepened and aggravated by economic globalization. The boundaries between domestic and international considerations in policy making are blurring. Canada's welfare state has become a battleground in the struggle over continental and international economic development. Given the dominance of international economies, the role and value of national social programs, and the techniques embodied in them, are being called into question. The very methods and processes embedded in the public policy discourse are being criticized. Globalization is encouraging policy makers to favour the economy over social welfare.

Surprisingly, there is nothing fundamentally new in Canada about economic globalization. From the time the first Europeans arrived here, hoping to find silks and spices and instead finding fish and furs, Canada has depended heavily on exports. Likewise, in the social welfare domain, from colonial times to the present day, international debates and reforms have influenced social policy making in Canada.

What *is* new about globalization over the past twenty-five years or so is the increasing international flow of information and capital. Specifically, globalization in the present day is defined mainly by the geographic expansion of markets, the deepening of global market relationships across a multitude of goods and services sectors and financial activities, and the entrenchment of international institutions and agreements for promoting and regulating global trade. David Brown (1994, 114) attributes this modern phase of globalization to two processes: "a natural process of international economic integration led by market forces, and a policy-driven process composed of trade agreements and other forms of international co-operation that complement the natural process." The so-called natural market forces to which Brown refers are as follows: the growing integration of world financial markets since 1945, which has increased the mobility of financial capital as it searches for the most advantageous places to invest; innovations in telecommunications and other technologies, most notably computers; and the newly industrializing economies of the Pacific Rim, which have spurred the internationalization of production. These "natural" market forces are complemented by the rise of multinational and transnational corporations as well as by increases in foreign investment in many domestic economies. Policies that complement global market forces include international economic agreements and the development of continental, regional, and global trading blocs.

It is important, however, to view globalization's impact as extending beyond international economics. Globalization, we believe, is best understood more broadly than that. It includes not only market forces but also cultural impacts as well as power relations between the private and public sectors. Globalization, that is, is also about the diffusion of particular cultural beliefs and the imposition of certain power relationships. Policy shifts also reflect moves towards more socially responsible globalization: greater concern for social rights; moves towards global labour and health standards; the development of investment and business codes of behaviour; and calls for global economic regulation and taxation. To understand the broad impact of globalization, we briefly examine one facet of the cultural dimension of globalization, one that Andrew E. Cooper and Leslie A. Pal (1996) call the "internationalization of human rights."

The internationalization of human rights entails the spread of universal norms and standards. These norms, which are rooted in Western political thought and history, are contained in global reference documents such as the 1948 Universal Declaration on Human Rights; the International Covenants on Civil and Political Rights and on Economic, Social, and Cultural Rights, effective as of 1976; and, more recently, the 1989 United Nations Convention on the Rights of the Child and the 1995 Social Development Accord. In Canada, the Charter of Rights and Freedoms and the various federal and provincial human rights acts that complement it both legally and symbolically buttress these global codes of moral conduct. International expressions of human rights are providing a set of standards relating to (for example) access, dignity, equality, and self-determination; in terms of these, Canada's social policy groups are able to assess the actions and inactions of the federal and provincial governments.

Another cultural aspect of globalization relates to concerns that as the economy becomes less national and more international, global trade relations and norms will diminish Canadians' willingness to share resources among their country's regions (Simeon 1991). The split between social policy considerations and economic ones is encouraging policy makers to embrace a neoliberal financial perspective that relies more on markets and on the free movement of capital. This has led to the opening up of internal markets – for example, for health care, social services, and the cultural industries.

Given globalization's impact on social policy, this chapter explores three questions. First, *How have the elites and the general public responded to globalization?* Here we outline three positions on globalism – those of champions, competitors, and challengers – and explore where Canadians fit. We also identify the key international economic institutions and trading agreements that provide the context for decision making in contemporary social policy.

Second, *How has economic globalization affected Canada's welfare state and social union?* Here, we consider the sovereignty of the nation-state, the balance of authority and influence within Canadian federalism, and the significance of globalism for governance. Third, and most important, *What are the implications of globalization for the politics of social policy?* This question enables us to probe more deeply than in earlier chapters into the implications of global capitalism for the welfare state. In particular, we examine the ideas and discourse of social policy; the labour market, an institution that is critical to the functioning of the social security system; a range of changes in the substance of social programs, which reveal a process we call the "marketization" of social policy; and the social policy community of clients and interest groups, many of whom are isolated and marginalized by and from the changing politics.

What Are the Responses to Economic Globalization?

Globalization is often discussed as a natural, external, and inevitable trend to which we must adapt or risk economic decline. At times, however, Canadians have hotly debated it, and international trade policies continue to be questioned by many within the social policy community. Economic globalization originates within Canada as well as outside it and is attached to the specific interests of influential corporate actors. It is a highly political process in which the more powerful states, such as the United States and Germany, impose policies on weaker states (Coleman and Porter 1996).

Three Positions on Globalism: Champions, Competitors, and Challengers

John Wiseman (1996) suggests that three types of political responses to globalization have arisen: champions, competitors, and challengers. Other commentators have proposed similar categorizations, which we will note where fitting. Mark Brawley (2008), for instance, discusses the competing perspectives of globalization in terms of economic and social progress, market insecurity, and creative destruction.

The *champions of globalization* include those who, as Wiseman puts it (1996, 116), "are fully and unashamedly committed to enhancing the global power of corporations and reducing the legal and political regulatory power of the nation state." Canadian champions of globalism include the C.D. Howe Institute, the Fraser Institute, and the Business Council on National Issues. Brown (1994) has written of "globalization theorists" – such as Canadian economists Thomas Courchene and Richard Lipsey – who favour policies of economic integration between Canada and the rest of the world, along with social policy reforms to complement this changing economy. There is, of course, an international literature that defends globalization and explains why it works (Bhagwati 2004; Wolf 2004). "Globalists," as Banting (1996, 36) calls those who take this position, "also tend to believe that the effective sovereignty of the nation state is now significantly reduced and that the pressures for harmonization or at least convergence in social programs are narrowing the room for manoeuvre enjoyed by governments. In the long run, social policy that seeks to offset or delay adjustment can only lead to lower economic growth, long-term unemployment, and growing government deficits."

The *competitors* are often "sceptics of globalization" (Brown 1994), but they also accept the need for trade liberalization. According to Wiseman (1996, 116), this perspective "focuses on maximizing the competitiveness of national and regional economies. This commonly involves policies designed to reduce costs through labour shedding [a euphemism for eliminating jobs through layoffs, early retirements, and attrition], wage reductions, [and] deregulating labour markets." Other policies seek to improve "productivity through technological innovation and improvements in infrastructure, training, production processes, marketing, and distribution." In the industrialized countries, trade unions and social democratic political parties – including the NDP in Canada – have adopted variants of this position as they seek to limit the loss of jobs, to maintain employment standards and benefits, and to compensate those who are economically displaced or disadvantaged; at the same time, they call for more "free trade" agreements and for greater export competitiveness.

The *challengers* offer a third type of political response to globalization. This body of opinion contests the basic assumptions of economic globalism and sets out alternative courses of action at the national and international levels (Klein 2007; Saul 2009).[1] As "anti-globalists" (Banting 1996, 37), the challengers are strong opponents of globalization. They include the traditional political left as well as newer progressive groups (environmentalists, feminists, and peace activists) who believe that economic integration policies such as NAFTA are making things worse for the labour markets in Canada and other countries, as well as working against social equality and justice (Brown 1994, 117–18; Cohen 1997b). The reforms proposed by challengers include "the creation of alternative political, financial and legal global institutions which can form a democratic counterweight to the power of transnational capital"; "the enshrinement of trade union and human rights principles in international trade agreements and the creation of multilateral and bilateral social charters"; and the creation of alliances between trade unions, community organizations, and social movements "which reaffirm and give substance to the values of sustainability, social justice, and democracy in an age of global power" (Wiseman 1996, 126–7).

In Canada, the champion perspective seems to dominate, since that is the one favoured by the ruling elites. Canadian business executives, senior government officials, and the leaders of the Liberal and Conservative political parties all subscribe to some variant of the pro-globalist position. Within this prevailing ideology, trade liberalization, increased international competitiveness, and a restructured social policy system are core values. Outside government and the corporate sector, groups in the social policy community tend towards the challenger or anti-globalist outlook (Banting 1996; Cohen 1997b). Undoubtedly, the public's views on globalization are a mix of all three. G. Bruce Doern and

Richard W. Phidd (1992, 19) remark that globalization "has made Canadians more conscious of their interdependence with the rest of the world and with the inevitability of rapid change. Canadians have also developed a greater sense of vulnerability and of being a smaller player in the world stage." Understandably, Canadians tend to value social security, equality, and collective rights more highly than the elites, who prioritize international competitiveness, individualism, and a much smaller welfare state (Reid 1997).

Community groups are encouraging Canada's governments to maintain strong social interventions. They have noted the high risks that globalization has created, and they recognize that if international corporations win in these high-risk activities, the elites will benefit at the expense of the middle and working class. Globalization does not bring with it a commitment to jobs or the workplace. Rather, it is built on the idea that jobs will come and go and that competition and profitability are the order of the day. Given that globalization represents a risk to citizens and that it offers little long-term security, community groups do not want their governments to give away those policy spaces within which local social problems can be solved.

The Context for Contemporary Social Policy

If Canadians are primarily champions, then what are the key international economic institutions and trading agreements that support globalization? International trade agreements and trading blocs are not the stuff that social policy texts have traditionally been made of. Yet, as Ken Collier (1995, 57) points out, events over the past decade or so "now force attention to these topics, because social work educators, researchers and students heading for practice will find our work suffering momentous impacts from them." An array of foreign and international institutions influence domestic social policy making and budgetary decisions. The international state has grown, as has the influence of officials in the international institutions to which Canada belongs. These include the Organization for Economic Co-operation and Development (OECD), the General Agreement on Tariffs and Trade (GATT), the International Monetary Fund (IMF), and the World Bank, all of which were established at the end of the Second World War, as well as the World Trade Organization (WTO), founded in the early 1990s. Canada also belongs to three international economic summit groups: the G-8, established in the mid-1970s and comprising the seven largest capitalist economies in the world, with Russia joining the group in the later 1990s; the Asia-Pacific Economic Co-operation (APEC) group, founded in 1994; and the G-20, established in 1999 as a forum of central bank governors and national finance ministers. Canada hosted the G-8 and G-20 meetings in Huntsville and Toronto in 2010. Canada also belongs to a continental trading bloc with Mexico and the United States: the 1993 North American Free Trade Agreement (NAFTA), signed in 1993, which built on the 1989 Canada–United States Free Trade Agreement.

Community groups and their policy analysts are examining these global instruments and describing the implications that international agreements have for the social policy domain. They recognize that each new agreement further restricts the ability of governments to solve social problems. They are aware that these institutions and agreements share an economic logic of free trade and economic growth through increased exports, as well as a neoliberal discourse on restructuring and reducing the welfare state (Teeple 1995). They contend that the discourse of free trade is undermining the conditions of citizenship. Their view is that free trade negotiations formulate the rules for global competition and promote the reduction or elimination of domestic barriers to trade; they also articulate only voluntary guidelines on the ethical conduct of transnational corporations; and they support economic deregulation, privatization of public enterprises, and other forms of government restraint. Such negotiations affect many areas of national and provincial jurisdiction. This influence can be direct and quasi-regulatory in some instances, or it can entail subtler pressure, brought to bear through the political and professional networks that negotiations foster. This includes, for example, pressure on government finance officials to limit program spending and reduce taxes.

Global capitalism tends, of course, to advocate for less government in general; yet at the same time, it often pushes for *more* government in specific situations – for example, regarding loan guarantees, strategic incentives, and deferred taxation for business interests. If there is a single agreed-upon view among international agencies as to how social policy should respond to globalization, it is that countries should pursue a mixed economy of welfare and shift some responsibilities for the financing and provision of programs away from the public sector towards other sectors.

Foreign institutions of an even more direct kind influence Canadian budgetary and social policy decisions. These include the U.S. Federal Reserve (the American central bank), whose decisions affect interest rates in Canada; and private institutions such as the New York bond rating houses, which assign credit ratings to provincial governments. These ratings can significantly affect the interest rates that governments must pay when they borrow in Canada and abroad. All of these international economic institutions and trade agreements constitute a substantial part of the global context for Canadian social policy.

How Does Globalization Affect Canada's Welfare State and Social Union?

In Canada, globalization has significantly affected the balance between national and international policy as well as relations between the federal and provincial governments. Champions *and* challengers of globalism agree that the sovereignty of nation-states has been reduced as a result of the increased international mobility of capital, the creation and expansion of trading agreements and blocs, and the power of transnational corporations. According to Peter Drucker (1993), we are moving into an era of post-sovereign states; by this he means that states are ceasing to be a nation-states and are evolving into administrative units rather than political entities. Claims that the Canadian state is losing or has already lost real control over domestic policy making are common in the critical social policy literature. Diana Ralph (1994, 80) conveys this belief when she states that "as a result of NAFTA and GATT provisions, the federal and provincial governments no longer have the power to grant even the liberal vision of a social welfare state." Likewise, globalization has significantly affected intergovernmental relations and the social union. As a result of the globalization of culture and international values, east–west relations in Canada have become fragmented and Canadian identity has eroded. Here we examine the impact of globalization on the role of the nation-state and the Canadian social union.

The Role of the Nation-State

Globalization has redefined the role of nation-states in the international arena. Over the past twenty-five years, Canada's federal government has increasingly supported, and participated in the development of, international agreements and agencies to facilitate and regulate the accumulation of capital on a global scale (Teeple 1995, 69). The basic rationale that underlies states (i.e., the promotion of a nationally defined capitalist class) is waning, and states' macroeconomic policies have shifted away from Keynesianism towards a monetarist approach.

Precisely opposite to the Keynesian idea that social and economic policies are interrelated, monetarism separates those policies. According to monetarists, the principal determinant of the level of economic activity is the money supply, and government spending and taxation activities by themselves have little impact on macroeconomic conditions. Monetarists also tend to favour minimal government intervention in the labour force and in other markets. As we have seen, this shift has led to less government involvement in the management of the economy – a more hands-off approach – as well as to a reduced ability for governments to use the economy to solve social problems.

In the 1980s and 1990s, those who advocated a monetarist-minimalist policy argued that the competitive forces of markets must be strengthened in order to restore and enhance economic growth. They contended that to accomplish this, the state must withdraw from many of the areas in which it had come to play an important role in recent decades, because this state intervention was precisely what had weakened the ability of markets to function efficiently. Keynesian-style intervention, they claimed, was ineffective; only a monetarist policy would create the required environment for economic competitiveness.

By the end of the twentieth century, monetarism had become the conventional wisdom for federal governments in Canada (Lightman and Irving 1991). Monetarism was being pursued through a policy agenda that included the following: free trade pacts, deficit reduction, the deregulation of certain markets, the privatization of some public services, limits to collective bargaining rights (and other union powers), a reduction in the number of public employees, the transformation of the tax system, the restructuring of local governance structures (municipalities, hospital authorities, and school boards), and the promotion of charities and other community groups as vehicles for meeting social needs. In short, there was a downsizing of the state, "the abrogation of government responsibilities for the social and economic well-being of society, [and] the redefinition of public duties by the state or the reshaping of the boundaries between civil society and the state so that intervention by the state in the affairs of the civil society are hereafter ... restricted" (Teeple 1995, 101–2). All of this led to a decline of social reform and the promotion of private property rights and markets.

According to Richard Simeon, globalization has constrained the sovereignty of all governments. In all countries, corporate interests are pressuring governments to relax tax and regulatory policies, including through trade agreements. For Simeon, "globalization highlights the growing mismatch between the scope and scale of the issues with which we must cope and the reach of the political institutions through which we must deal with them. The result is that global forces increasingly escape the capacity of states to manage them" (1991, 47–8). In twenty-first-century Canada, the idea of the nation-state is coming under increasing pressure. Globalization underscores the tensions between internal social problems such as poverty and employment and international social problems such as climate change, contagious diseases, and international social development. The nation-state works well at addressing internal problems; it is less effective when it comes to international problems. The financial crisis of 2007–8 has provided a clear example of this – clearly, it takes international dialogue and a co-ordinated effort to address widespread economic and social problems (see chapter 10).

The mismatch between international challenges and national capacities to address them is apparent in many environmental problems such as global warming. Local and national governments are fixed in a territorial space, whereas transnational firms and investment capital are relatively mobile and face few international regulations. Simeon posits that globalization is creating new roles for the state, which must not only protect national trade interests in an increasingly international economic climate, but also cushion the jolt of global stresses on the domestic economy and on society. The state, then, is faced with two contradictory functions: to promote international competitiveness and adjustment, and at the same time to protect workers, communities, and industries against the disruptions arising from global capitalism.

The Social Union of Canada

The basic rationale for the creation of a national government in Canada was the building of an east–west economy. While that original reason may have disappeared with globalization, in contrast to Teeple we see the Canadian state as continuing to serve important sociopolitical and cultural purposes. These include giving political meaning to our lives as governments grant identities, rights, and obligations; defining our sense of community under federalism; and providing an admittedly imperfect process through which to practise democracy (Simeon 1991,

46–7). The globalization of culture and international values is threatening Canada's unity, straining east–west relations. Without connections between the east and the west, north–south globalizing forces will dominate. If Canada wants to maintain its sovereignty, it must take powerful social policy steps to reinforce its east–west connections. The present structures – the CBC, medicare, and equalization payments – are not sufficient.

North American free trade has transformed the political economy of Canadian social policy. Greater continental integration of commerce is producing even more of a north–south trading system; the challenge is how to maintain political support across the country for an east–west system of transfers and equalization payments. With the Canadian economy becoming increasingly regionalized, and with regions remaining economically diverse, political pressure is building in at least some provinces for further decentralization as well as for asymmetry in social programming (Courchene 1994). Labour market policy reform is being shaped by the move away from Keynesian management of the aggregate demand for labour at the national level, as well as by the belief that Canada's economy is now a series of loosely connected regional and urban economies. An example of this regionalization of policy is the change made to the federal minimum-wage legislation in 1996 – the first increase in the federal rate in ten years. The federal minimum wage applies to private-sector industries that are interprovincial or international in scope, such as banks, telecommunications companies, and some federal Crown corporations. There is no longer a standard federal rate per hour across the country; that rate is now adjusted to the general adult minimum-wage rates in each province and territory. In 2010, the minimum wage ranged from a low of $8.00 per hour (after 500 hours' work with the same employer) in British Columbia to $11.00 per hour in Nunavut. Another recent example is the transfer of various federal training and employment-related activities and federal employees to interested provincial and territorial governments and Aboriginal organizations.

Globalization may well affect the assorted levels of government differently. Simeon (1991, 53) suggests that the federal government is especially constrained because it has less jurisdiction "over the kinds of quality-of-life issues that are likely to become the major areas of government innovation in the future. These are largely provincial, so that in Canada – perhaps paradoxically – globalization seems to be fostering decentralization rather than centralization." Quality-of-life issues include education, health care, healthy communities, housing, human rights, multiculturalism, race relations, sports, and recreation. Many of these issues concern the pluralization of Canadian society, and all are issues of social policy. When Simeon made his observation, the federal government was burdened with large annual deficits. By the late 1990s, Ottawa had eliminated the federal deficit and was running a budgetary surplus for the first time since 1970. This turnaround in financial capacity strengthened the federal government's ability to enforce the principles of public health insurance, for instance, and to launch new national projects for social security. By 2008, however, deficits had returned at the federal level. In chapters 9 and 10 we will be examining this shift in the fiscal fortunes of Canadian governments, especially the implications of the 2007–8 recession for future social policy making.

New Challenges for Social Policy

To delve further into globalism's ramifications for social policy, we canvass the ideas and discourse of social welfare. We also examine the Canadian labour market. the substance of social program changes, and the social policy community of clients and advocacy groups. We believe that the forces of globalization are restructuring the ways that Canadians think about social policies. The forces of globalization are making difficult political choices seem to be mere matters of economic determinism. Canadian elites, as champions of globalism, are narrowing the view most people have of social policy by giving priority to economic rather than social issues. This has created a disjuncture between business and government leaders on the one hand and community activists on the other. Globalization is pushing the changing politics of social policy into a fiscal debate about economic implications; lost as a result is any discussion of how to deal adequately with the new insecurity in the labour market. Social policy analysts are being forced to apply the language and tools of private enterprise when deciding which policies should be kept or cut; we will be examining the debilitating effect this is having on advocacy groups. We will be exploring the resulting attitudinal shifts as they relate to the role of welfare (safety net versus springboard) and changes in the workplace. Social policy debates have become fiscalized; they are no longer about dreams and compassion but about dollars and cents.

*From Safety Net to Springboard: The Narrowing Conception of
the Welfare State*

Economic globalization has changed how we think and talk about the
welfare state and social provision. As a result, a new conception of welfare has developed that defies many of the ideas about social security
that have been in place since the 1940s. The goals of a comprehensive
social policy system and high and stable levels of employment have effectively been abandoned by Canadian governments as unattainable
(McBride 1992; Brodie 1995).

Part of the new orthodoxy is that the Canadian network of social programs, while it may have served us well in the past, is outdated now
that globalization is transforming the world's societies and economies.
The postwar welfare state is no longer appropriate to the times we live
in, goes this line of thinking, because of the "new realities" of fiscal constraints, global trade imperatives, and an aging population.

The new conception of the welfare state has thus reframed the role
of social policy as a handmaiden to economic development and labour
market adjustment. Governments that focus their social policies on
training the unemployed and on education are now considered part
of the "social investment" state. From this perspective, policy is directed towards training and mobility, wage subsidies, and investments
in human capital designed to enhance people's capacity to participate
fully in labour markets. Alexandra Dobrowolsky (2003, 1) describes
these as "social policies that are mostly child or youth-centred and ac-
tivation-oriented, from new deals for youth, trust funds for children
and tax credits for working families to child care initiatives and progress made on parental leaves." She notes that in Britain, identity-based
groups such as the anti-racist and women's movements were left out
of most consultations and civic participation processes. Jane Jenson
and Denis Saint-Martin (2003, 81) contend that "many political jurisdictions are shifting the boundaries of the responsibility mix, defining
new forms of security, redesigning the content of social citizenship by
assigning more responsibility for welfare creation to markets, families,
and the voluntary sector. In particular we suggest that the new citizenship regimes taking shape in Canada and in Europe involve an increasing focus on social investment." This involves movement in three policy
areas: reinforcing active labour market policies and (especially) increasing the employment rate; modernizing social protections to make them

sustainable; and stepping up the fight against social exclusion. In actual practice, there is no single social investment state model or coherent social investment state project in Canada. Instead, as we show in later chapters, there are multiple policy agendas, discourses, and programs related to not only social investment but also to social protection, social control, and community and gender relations.

With perhaps a few exceptions, such as cultural industries, the dominant conception now holds that Canadian social policy should not challenge the forces of international trade – indeed, social policy should not even be primarily about protecting and compensating workers and their families for the negative impacts of globalization. Instead, social policy needs to be tailored to fit comfortably with the new economic order, complementing economic restructuring and international competitiveness (Brown 1994; Courchene 1994; McBride 2005). Many of the areas concerned with quality of life are downplayed, and priority is given to matters of job training and skills redevelopment. The guiding principle behind social program reforms is that they must support the work ethic and economic productivity. For many income support and social service programs, this has meant tightening eligibility requirements and increasing work-related obligations for clients.

Over the past decade, the elites have changed how they talk about the Canadian welfare state. Politicians and bureaucrats now seem to view citizens as consumers with choices and responsibilities, rather than as clients or beneficiaries with entitlements and rights. The public hears less about welfare and a national social security system, and more about workfare, "making work pay," and the social union. Economic change is viewed as rapid and fundamental – as a shakedown (Reid 1997) – rather than simply as progress or growth. The metaphor of the social safety net, with its images of security and protection, is given less emphasis than the metaphor of a social trampoline or springboard, with its "active" programs enabling people to catapult back into the workforce. In addition, the discourse has shifted away from universality towards selectivity. We are told that social policy can remain compassionate but that "Canadians cannot afford to maintain their traditional level of concern over the distribution of income. Instead, they must reorient their policy mind-set towards the objective of providing meaningful work for all" (Brown 1994, 124–5). Social policy, in other words, should end its focus on insuring against major risks, as outlined by the Marsh Report and others, and instead aim to diffuse opportunities.

The Fiscalization of Policy Discourse

In the contemporary discourse of the welfare state, the dominant theme has been the fiscalization of social policy. Other factors, such as Quebec nationalism and economic globalism, have also had a voice; but the paradigm of fiscal restraint and balanced budgets has been the organizing framework for social issues, programs, and policy processes. Social policies have always been made in a context of limited budgets and competing claims; what is *new* is that financial and monetarist values have become the guiding standard in Canadian social policy discussions and reforms. Since 1975, when the Bank of Canada adopted monetarism as formal policy and the federal cabinet adopted a budget restraint policy, "virtually all discussion of social policy in Canada has been couched in the language of fiscal capacity" (Lightman and Irving 1991, 71; Lewis 2003).

Fiscalization refers to periods when financial concerns – especially considerations of expenditure restraint and deficit reduction – dominate deliberations on public policy priorities and social reforms. Fiscal discourse portrays deficit reduction as an imperative – that is, as a pressing problem that demands action by governments. The response to the 2008 economic crisis (see chapter 7), and claims that the rising deficit must be dealt with no matter what the pain, are examples of this line of analysis. From this perspective, the need to reduce program spending and generally downsize the state is not a matter of ideology, but rather a commonsense response to financial problems. This is quite different from O'Connor's critical and structural analysis of the "fiscal crisis of the state" (see chapter 4). The simple arithmetic of compounding interest on the debt makes it utterly necessary to tackle deficit reduction. Proponents of fiscalization believe that the budgetary facts speak for themselves, despite some evidence to the contrary. The concept of reducing the debt is one that anyone can grasp. It follows almost as easily that social programs based on "ideological dreams" must be cut because they comprise such a large portion of federal and provincial government budgets. In this way, social policy is placed in the context of financial responsibility, affordability, and the long-term sustainability of essential services and benefits such as health care and pensions.

Public budgeting systems in Canada and other countries had largely abandoned program-planning processes by the mid-1980s, adopting instead systems built on spending limits and restraint targets. Great emphasis is now being placed on the aggregate amounts of spending in the social policy envelopes of governments. Budgeting for social programs has become a top-down process concerned more with total sums than with service priorities. Looking at totals focuses attention on the size of social expenditures relative to other program areas. Moreover, "in a period of ideological polarization, quantities come to stand for qualities" (Wildavsky 1988, 204). For politicians and bureaucrats as well as for client groups and academics, social expenditure totals serve as crude indicators of the degree of compassion and social justice in a jurisdiction.[2]

Finance departments set the outer limits of social policy reform through their analyses of, and arguments about, fiscal imperatives (Lewis 2003). These are bolstered by pressures from business interests, the money markets, and international agencies such as the IMF and the OECD. Debates over "social investments strategy" offer a more politically acceptable language than the old rhetoric of "tax and spend." Estimates of revenues, expenditures, interest rates, and deficit reduction targets set the boundaries for social policy making. Priorities relating to human well-being must be negotiated within the constraints imposed by the assumptions and overall goals of a government's fiscal framework, which is largely controlled by central finance agencies.

A budgeting system is about making choices; it is never a neutral allocation of resources and values. The fiscalization of budgets and social policy discourse tends to promote certain ideas and objectives over others, to favour some interests in government and in the economy over others, and to encourage some program designs and institutional arrangements over others. Consider, for example, the following:

1 *Fiscal discourse erodes the legitimacy of the social security system.* Government deficits and growing debts have been attributed, in large part, to social programs and the rising costs of welfare. Social spending is seen as spending borrowed money, money we do not have, thereby placing a burden on future generations. The argument continues that we must cut social programs in order to save them and to be fair to our children, grandchildren, and great-grandchildren.

2 *Fiscal discourse diverts public and media attention from other critical issues that need to be on governments' agendas.* This relates to issues such as the consequences of monetary policy, the effectiveness of industrial grants, and who benefits from social and business tax

expenditures. Major social policy reform exercises in Canada have been based on a narrow conception of public sector social welfare, precluding other programs, options, and possible future directions. At the same time, the fiscal debate encourages welfare pluralism – the meeting of social needs through the efforts of other sectors and charitable giving by individuals. A *Globe and Mail* (2010) editorial made similar points when it observed that Canada strutted on the international stage when it talked about its deficit controls and encouraged other countries to accept a deficit reduction protocol as part of the G-20 summit but that it obstructed the process of policy development at the Copenhagen climate change summit. The rhetoric of fiscal constraint won out over that of environmental stewardship.

3 *Within federal and provincial governments, fiscalization has concentrated power in finance portfolios while weakening the influence of social policy departments and their clientele, as well as that of social advocacy groups.* Finance officials have essentially determined the development, deadlock, and decline of social policy making in Canada over the past two decades. As a consequence, groups wanting to affect the social policy process have had to aim more of their efforts at officials in economic and finance departments and treasury boards.

4 *In an age of government austerity, fiscalization changes policy discussions from ones with a socially redistributional outlook to ones with an inward-looking reallocation of resources.* Through the 1980s and 1990s, deficit reduction was the governing objective of social programs, overshadowing the goals of reducing poverty and fostering social integration. Among other effects, it intensified competition among social programs, between levels of government, and among community groups desperate for funding.

5 *The emphasis on spending cuts in aid of deficit reduction has constrained and at times divided as well as co-opted segments of the social policy community.* Many human services organizations and workers have more or less accepted the fiscal discourse and have tacitly supported governments' restraint agendas. Regarding social policy groups, Gordon Ternowetsky (1987, 386) has written that "we have been asked to participate in the process of consulting on ways and means of further rationalizing expenditures on social programs." The Chrétien government's Social Security Review of 1994–5 was a striking example of this sort of structured and hurried process. At other times, reforms have been introduced with little or no public

consultation. Either way, in the face of strong neoliberal reforms, progressive social policy advocates have found themselves in the awkward position of defending status quo programs, many of which advocates have long criticized.

6 *Fiscalization has made community development and social policy planning subservient to economic management.* Strategic planning and resource allocation are oriented to controlling costs and finding new revenue opportunities rather than assessing needs and addressing public issues. At its extreme, the fiscalization of social policy ignores the substantive aspects of programs, disregarding questions of their impacts and results, and concentrates on the degree to which a program's budget is growing or not and thereby contributing to deficit and debt reduction.

Canada's Labour Market

Economic globalization has serious implications for domestic labour markets. Canadian economist Harvey Lazar (1991, 149) has written that "global market forces have come to play a growing role in determining the supply of and demand for different kinds of labour." Globalism's growing impact has repercussions for the quantity and quality of paid work available, the distribution of income in society, and the overall performance of the economy. It also raises questions of the proper function of social policy, especially human resource development programs, in light of several disturbing trends in Canada's labour market.

Workplaces are downsizing throughout North America as a result of corporate mergers, plant closures, and the "re-engineering" of firms. The consequences have included rising unemployment and involuntary retirements, dashed career plans, and changes in the skills required for the jobs that remain. A 1990 report by the Economic Council of Canada titled *Good Jobs, Bad Jobs* drew national attention to a widening disparity in the quality and security of jobs available for many Canadians in the middle and working classes. More and more work was becoming what the council called "non-standard employment" – that is, more workers had temporary part-time jobs, were self-employed, or held multiple jobs. Ralph (1994, 75–6) described "bad jobs" as low-paid, dangerous, insecure work with few rights or services for employees. With industrial and technological sectors requiring higher-skilled workers, "the availability of relatively low-skilled jobs in Canada is being reduced," according to Brown (1994:111), but he added that "demand for less-skilled work will continue, although at lower wages."

A federal discussion paper on reforming social security (Canada 1994, 9) frankly noted that since about 1980 "our society increasingly has begun to be polarized between well-educated, highly-skilled Canadians in demand by employers – today's economic elite – and less educated people without specialized, up-to-date job skills, who have been losing ground." Other studies have examined the bifurcation of Canada into economically secure and insecure classes. Research by Rene Morissette, John Myles, and Garnett Picot (1995) on earnings polarization in Canada between 1969 and 1991 found that earnings and wage inequalities were partly a structural feature of the economy and not simply a cyclical phenomenon associated with recessions. They concluded (1995, 24) that this trend was "being driven by growing inequality in the distribution of working time. More workers are working part-time, but, more importantly, more are also working longer than the usual thirty-five to forty-hour work week." Other alarming trends have been the growth in underemployment, in long-term structural unemployment, and in economic disparities (Broad 1995; Lazar 1991). Statistics Canada reported in 2008 that according to the 2005 census, Canada's rich were getting richer while the poor were getting poorer and the middle class was stagnating. Research by Davis and Harrigan (2011) makes the point that while trade liberalization has increased aggregate efficiency, it has also led to the loss of many "good" jobs and to a steady-state increase in unemployment. The economy has become more efficient, but at the cost of people working.

For far more people than in earlier decades of the postwar welfare state, unemployment is a prolonged interruption of earning capacity. Those who first envisioned Canada's social security system saw family needs arising from the gap between a family's income, even at reasonable levels, and the large number of children they might have. Today, the need arises from an inadequate or unstable income even when there are just one or two children in the family. Today, the risks of the labour market, in Leonard Marsh's words, "are constantly making their appearance as realities" (1943, 21).

The inherent trends and risks of economic globalism have a direct bearing on social policy because several benefits, in terms of their access and value, are based on paid employment and occupational status. Examples include benefits relating to pensions, unemployment, disability and workplace injury, dental care, extended health care, and maternity and family leaves. The availability and adequacy of these occupation-related social programs vary by sectors of the economy, size of workplaces, and whether workers are full-time or part-time, unionized or non-unionized, self-employed, an employee, or an owner. For instance, a person working full-time in a unionized setting in either the public sector or a large private-sector firm is far more likely to have an employer-sponsored pension plan. When we reflect on the fact that governments and large corporations have been downsizing, and that most new jobs over the past twenty years in Canada have been in small, typically non-unionized service businesses, then potentially large social problems appear concerning retirement income security in the near future.

In response to these global forces, in recent decades Canada has entered into social security agreements with more than thirty countries.[3] This is an example of Canadian federal programs being linked explicitly to policies in other welfare states. The purpose of these agreements, from Canada's perspective, is to coordinate old age benefits and the CPP with comparable programs in other nations that provide pensions for retirement, old age, disability, and survivorship. The intent is for Canadians working abroad to enjoy the same rights under the social security laws of another country as the citizens of that country. Conversely, citizens from another country now living in Canada need not face restrictions here when they receive payments from the other country's pension system.

The Marketization of Social Programs

The marketization of social programs is routinely overlooked in analyses of welfare state politics. Customary themes of restructuring concern the contraction of the public sector (or "rolling back" of the state), the expansion of the private sector, the expectation that the voluntary sector can and should do more, and, in feminist analyses, the regulation and imposition of additional burdens on the domestic realm (Brodie 1995; Teeple 1995). Explorations of Canadian social policy still employ the concepts of residualism and institutionalism. The former, residualism, holds that most government social services should come into play only when the family breaks down, and/or the market does. The latter, institutionalism, asserts that the welfare state is just as integral an institution in modern life as the economy and the family (Guest 1997;

Prince 1996b). These mini-ideologies imply a sharper conceptual division between the market economy and the state than exists in practice.

The politics of retrenchment are usually evaluated in terms of whether welfare state benefits and services are taken away from clients, and whether social budgets are slashed or at least significantly reduced. In a detailed examination of welfare politics in Britain and the United States, Paul Pierson (1994) concluded that there have been substantial continuities in social policies in both countries while under strong conservative administrations, with few radical changes. A limitation of this approach is that regardless of the welfare state's size or the apparent stability of policies, fundamental changes can take place within existing social programs and budgets. Indeed, major reforms of a residualist nature can and do occur even when the welfare state is expanding.

At a macro-level, marketization is one of the basic processes for mediating the relationship between our capitalist economy and liberal democracy.[4] It involves a blending of market logic (private property, competition, and profit) with the logic of the state (ultimate authority, public interest, and citizenship). This is what democratic capitalism and the mixed economy are partly about. It is also what welfare pluralism is partly about. As we noted at the outset of this chapter, the Keynesian welfare state has traditionally been portrayed as politicizing economics and as modifying the market by substituting public values and activities for private-sector ones. The market, however, also modifies the welfare state. It always has. The "marketization of social programs" is the term we use to highlight this phenomenon. External to the state, marketization entails allowing social policy and economic values to influence each other; economic logic conditioning the goals and means of social benefits and services; and market-based values shaping public attitudes as to which groups and needs are deserving and worthy of support and which are undeserving and the objects of exclusion or stigma. Internal to the state, marketization involves the culture of capitalism moving into public-sector activities. It is the injection and expansion of private-sector principles into social programs, ideas, structures, and processes. It also includes the injection of "sound business principles" into social welfare systems and public administration more generally.[5]

The marketization of welfare is quite an old process; what is *new* is the intensity with which social programs are now being designed to reflect the ethic of the economic market. Economic conditions and the values of the market are more influential today in determining social policy developments than they were in earlier periods of the welfare state (Spivey 1985; Leys 2001). The demise of two universal income programs – Old Age Security and Family Allowances – in the 1990s dramatically exemplifies the decline of communal social principles and the subordination of welfare values to market norms. Eligibility for child benefits and seniors' benefits now rests entirely on income testing. In our view, several factors underlie the rising importance of economic criteria in policy making. These include globalization, of course, as well as the importance placed on international competitiveness; but they also include related concerns about declining productivity and continuing high unemployment; the fiscal discourse of crisis and government restraint; and narrowing conceptions of what social policy can and should be about.

The following vignettes illustrate versions of marketization in a range of social policy domains. The first example is the Employment Insurance (EI) Program. A long-standing debate over this program is how much of it is insurance (a market concept) and how much is social welfare (a public policy concept). Amendments to the program by the Mulroney and Chrétien governments have pushed the program closer to market ideas, in part based on social investment strategies. This movement has been reinforced by the Harper government's tightening of eligibility requirements and reduction in benefit levels. Over the long haul, financial contributions to the program directly from the public purse have been eliminated, placing the onus for full funding on employees and employers. Both the amount and the duration of benefits have been decreased numerous times. Eligibility requirements have been tightened, penalties toughened; and disqualification provisions expanded. Such changes have been motivated by complaints from the business community as well as by the government's concern that EI has a negative impact on employee and employer incentives, the unemployment level, and the mobility of workers. The general thrust of these reforms has been to strengthen the EI program's contribution to labour market policy goals, while weakening the program's traditional income protection and macroeconomic stabilization functions. The proportion of unemployed workers covered by EI and therefore potentially protected has dropped from over 90 per cent to about 40 per cent of the labour force. This is the narrowest scope of coverage since the original legislation of the early 1940s.

Cultural policy is a second example of marketization. Thelma McCormack (1984) describes the turn in Canadian cultural policy away from a nationalist model towards a market model. The nationalist model regards the arts as central to Canada's heritage; the objective of policy, so it follows, is to foster national awareness and identity, with audiences playing the role of patriots. At times this approach has been joined by what McCormack calls a welfare model, in which the arts are viewed as a public resource belonging to everyone as a social right. The focus is on public arts, not private collections, and the role of the audience is as citizens. Under the market/investment model, which has gained ground in governmental circles, the arts are commodities to be bought and sold at auctions and showings. The laws of supply and demand set the value of art and culture. The largely public and not-for-profit art systems of the nationalist and welfare models are replaced by a profit-oriented approach. The role of the audience here is that of consumer/investor. The ascendancy of a market approach to culture, which McCormack and others (Woodcock 1985) observed in the 1980s, continues.

Here are still other examples of the marketization of social policies:

- The working conditions for many in the public services are effectively being adjusted downward to match those in the private sector. Canada's politics of deficits and debt have led to a deterioration in public-sector labour relations over the past three decades. Federal and provincial governments have imposed pay freezes and wage rollbacks; restricted what may be negotiated, and even suspended collective bargaining; and introduced back-to-work legislation. This may be the beginning of the end of public-sector collective bargaining in Canada (Swimmer and Thompson 1995).
- In Canada's education policy, the new agenda for curriculum reform and the role of schools is "technological liberalism" (Manzer 1994). The job of public education in the global economy is to prepare a competitive and highly skilled labour force. There is considerable interest in measuring performance, ranking schools, and seeking corporate donations and sponsorships for school activities and facilities (Barlow and Robertson 1994).
- Among both policy makers and the public, Canada's recent immigration policy has taken on an economic orientation. There is deep interest in (and many misgivings about) the impact of immigrants on job creation, social programs such as welfare, and other public services. A prominent theme as that immigrants, whatever their skill levels, should be viewed as human capital (DeVoretz 1995). Like some other industrialized countries, Canada has a business immigration policy, the purpose of which is to secure foreign capital

and stimulate domestic economic growth. Trevor Harrison (1996, 9) argues that such programs "reflect a growing commodification of immigration policy and of the notion of citizenship."

- Since the mid-1980s, much of Canada's foreign policy has focused on trade; this extends to international assistance, even including food aid (Freeman 1985; Charlton 1992; Pratt 1994). Development aid is now often viewed a means to pursue economic policy goals and to advance domestic, commercial, and bureaucratic interests.
- Provincial welfare reforms of the 1990s and early 2000s and related "work incentive" policies were based on a "market-oriented economic perspective" (Low 1996, 189). The focus was on financial rewards at the margin and individual choices, with little attention given to social costs and structural factors. The new discourse of welfare reform speaks of breaking dependency on welfare, making work pay, and encouraging self-reliance. More stringent work obligations are directed at single, able-bodied applicants and clients. In some provinces, single mothers with young children have been redefined as employable with the expectation that they will enrol in training courses (Evans et al. 1995). For non-participation in work-for-welfare programs, benefits are commonly reduced by a significant amount. As Eric Shragge (1997, 17) states, "Workfare represents a departure from the postwar welfare state, and is leading us in the direction of a punitive system in which welfare will no longer be a right but instead will become contingent on a type of work that is paid at a rate far below the social norm."

These market-centred approaches to social issues do not signal the resurrection of "economic man" in Canadian social policy, since market principles were never dead in the welfare state. Instead, what we are seeing is the reassertion of these principles in a number of program and service areas. The market ethos is alive and flourishing in the public sector as well as in the private sector. With the marketization of social policy currently in vogue, we have market capitalism and market welfarism in concert. State intervention does not necessarily mean a corresponding decline in market systems or values. The infusion of some market principles into the state and politics compromises the notion of absolute authority or absolute good (Offe 1984, 183) and contributes to the preservation of capitalist institutions.

Marketization should prompt us to always ask, "How social is social policy?" "In principle," writes Charles Lindblom (1977, 44), "governments can redistribute income and wealth and repeat the redistribution as frequently as wished. Their disinclination to do so requires a political explanation rather than reference to market forces." This analysis is flawed, in our view, for it draws too sharp a dichotomy between state and economy. Besides being an established institution, the market is an ideological phenomenon. Part of the political explanation for limited redistribution, we believe, rests on market interests embodied in state structures and activities. Income redistribution is frustrated by prevalent market beliefs in taxation and expenditure policies. For example, the wage-based inequalities of the economy are reproduced in tax assistance for retirement savings plans and in the Canada and Quebec Pension Plans.

The traditional arguments used to justify social services and transfers relate to meeting needs, providing compensation for certain losses, and offering insurance against specific risks. In recent years, the principal reasons advanced to justify social spending and interventions have referred to economic growth, competitiveness, and investments in human resources. Traditional concerns such as assistance to the disadvantaged are still important but have been overshadowed in the past fifteen years by initiatives more acceptable to the requirements of a globalizing economy. The policy environment and social objectives are described increasingly in terms of social investment strategies related to labour market trends, human capital development, and the imperatives of international trade. This has altered the composition of many social programs; it has also changed somewhat the meaning of human well-being and social development.

The degree to which social policies have become more reliant on an economic rationale has important implications for program design and delivery. The marketization of social policy can affect eligibility criteria for program benefits, the level and duration of benefits, disqualification provisions, program financing, and other uses of programs – as the case of EI shows. Moreover, the level of public understanding and support for programs can be affected. For social agencies, cloaking budget requests in economic terms can provoke heated internal debates as to the desirability and utility of such a strategy. Some staff may see it as selling out; others, as an essential tactic for survival in these times.

Political Impacts on Social Policy Advocacy and Client Groups

For many social policy clients and interest groups, economic globalization and the companion processes of fiscalization and marketization are debilitating. For them, the changing politics of Canadian social policy is a politics of isolation, resignation, and marginalization. Globalization has contributed to the isolation of the social policy community. Part of this is due to fiscal constraints, the limited resources of advocacy groups, and the complexity and diversity of the community itself, which poses challenges when it comes to building alliances and speaking on issues with a strong, united voice. More important, though, is the increasingly global context of social policy. Globalism has reinforced the central place of the Finance Department in defining the social agenda and de-termining policy decisions. Canadian social policy groups, according to Banting (1996), have lagged in their response to global issues, and their participation in international realms has generally been limited. Social advocacy groups are politically isolated because most are, in John Wise-man's terminology, challengers to globalization. For these groups, tak-ing part in policy reviews means fighting the discourse and concrete reforms proposed by the government and business elites, who strongly favour a social policy agenda motivated by globalism. "In a world of tightened international constraints, there is a danger that public con-sultations will heighten, not reduce, the cynicism about the responsive-ness of our political institutions" (Banting 1996, 45).

Others, too, report a growing sense, not only of cynicism, but also of resignation and political impotence (Teeple 1995; Reid 1997). Many Canadians are distrustful of politicians and governments and are dis-enchanted about the outcomes of reforms and cuts to services. Amanda Sheedy (2008) points out that "voter turnout is declining in Canada, down to its lowest since 1898 during the 2004 federal election at 60.9% and increasing only slightly in 2006." She contends that Canadians are increasingly frustrated with and disconnected from their democratic structures and processes. According to Elections Canada the turnout in 2008 was the second lowest in Canadian history at 58.8 per cent. Not only voters but also clients of social services often feel that they are dis-empowered and that they are being treated as passive recipients. These sorts of experiences and sentiments translate into a politics of resigna-tion. Social movements such as those representing labour, the poor, and women, along with the traditional left, have been placed on the defen-sive as they seek to protect universal programs, national standards, and other valued aspects of the postwar Canadian welfare state. Consider-able time and energy have been devoted to guarding social programs against cutbacks, resources that might otherwise have been directed to-wards developing a new agenda of progressive change.

Business and political elites have been attempting to marginalize both new and old social movements. Anna Yeatman (1990, 131) points out that elites are minimizing the status and importance of social movements by "denying their universal significance and making them appear vehicles of particular sectoral interests." Elites portray them instead as disaffected and disadvantaged groups, lying outside the mainstream, "for whom special provision [if any] is to be made." This politics of marginalization is readily apparent in Canada. With respect to the Canadian women's movement, Janine Brodie (1995) identifies several other methods used to attack social advocates. These include cutting funding to community groups and their associations, restricting or closing their access to government decision makers, and questioning these groups' knowledge or expertise on issues such as trade policy or the deficit and the debt. Other strategies involve weakening employment equity and related affirmative action measures; excluding particular groups, such as gays or visible minorities, from social policy reports and narratives; and emphasizing selective and targeted programs. The consequence is that services are aimed at the "truly needy" and "high-risk" groups. "Instead of exposing the structural links among race, gender, sexuality, poverty, and violence, targeting serves to pathologize and individualize differences, as well as to place the designated groups under increased state surveillance and administrative control" (1995, 74).

Conclusions

Canadian social policy today is more deferential as well as more exposed to market forces than in the heyday of the welfare state. Marketization means that government need not deinstitutionalize or privatize a service in order to extend the market system. Some elements of the welfare state have been dismantled and others sharply cut, but much of what has been and still is happening to social policy has involved a realignment for the sake of the requirements of domestic and global capital. A central goal of social reform, in this context, is changing benefits and programs so as to promote a more mobile labour force and to order a more work-ready group of welfare clients for low-wage employment. In this chapter we have examined the globalization of economies, the fiscalization of public discourse and priority setting, the marketization of social programs, and the marginalization of public interest groups and social advocates. These processes all tend to constrain and challenge the welfare state. They all illustrate the complexities of change in both the context and content of social policy formation. All are engaged in shifting boundaries among the state, market, community, and family.

Under the present regime of continental trading blocs, internationalized commerce, and transnational corporations, Canada's sovereignty to regulate and restrict capital has declined. Yet sovereignty is not an all-or-nothing affair. The state continues to exercise authority in regulating workers, welfare recipients, and women, among others in the social, moral, and domestic realms. The decline of sovereignty is just that, a comparative decrease and not a complete disappearance. Sovereignty is a relational condition set in a given place and time. Externally, colonial, continental, and capital interests have always limited Canadian autonomy. Internally, Canadian sovereignty has been divided by the Constitution between the federal and provincial governments; between the courts and the legislatures; and, under the Charter of Rights, between governments and citizens as individuals and or as members of certain groups. Jurisdiction and authority is also divided and will become more so through treaty negotiations between public governments and Aboriginal governments.

So, economic globalization has shifted the social policy debate; even so, we believe that national governments still have a role to play. Harmonization of welfare states is neither inevitable nor likely under globalization (Watson 1998). We share Drucker's (1993, 11) belief regarding the nation-state that "it may remain the most powerful political organ around for a long time to come, but it will no longer be the indispensable one. Increasingly, it will share power with other organs, other institutions, other policy makers." The authority and the capacity of the nation-state, then, may be constrained, but the state is neither impotent nor powerless (Leys 2001; McBride 2005). Canada may be a semi-sovereign state, but it continues to maintain a military. Its governments still make laws and implement them; they still enforce a national criminal code and maintain federal, provincial, and local police forces; they still make tax and expenditures policy choices; and they still uphold an independent judiciary. Social cohesion and protection remain pressing issues. Social policy advocates, analysts, and academics should therefore not ignore the state at all its levels as a site for political action and policy development.

7 The Crisis of the Market Economy: International Issues and Canadian Responses

In this chapter, we examine the financial and economic crisis that threatened the functioning of market economies between 2007 and 2010. The consequences of this crisis are still reverberating. There is social unrest throughout the developed world and increasing poverty throughout the developing world. This chapter examines the nature and causes of the crisis, the response to it that has developed around the world, and the implications for Canada. We focus on the implications for Canadian families and social policy. We suggest that this latest crisis of market economies has not meant the disintegration of economic globalism; nor has it meant the demise of neoliberalism or a wholesale resurrection of the state's social role. However, the aura of superiority that used to surround neoliberalism and economic globalism has seriously diminished, and the idea that the economic sphere is logically coherent has been undermined. This presents political opportunities for renewed debates on the market economy, the state, and social policy.

Economic crises are not new. The modern market economy, which is based on economic liberalism and self-regulating markets, has seen a long series of economic booms and busts. Each boom results in increasing employment, profits, and economic development; these in turn lead to expanded production, rising prices, low interest rates, and rapid growth. A bust that sees markets crash follows the boom; businesses go into bankruptcy and unemployment soars. Karl Polanyi examined the root causes of these economic forces in *The Great Transformation* (1944). He concluded that self-regulating markets are structured in such a way as to be self-defeating and that they eventually lead to the destruction of social order. He argued that to address the destructive forces of markets, community interests must somehow be balanced. Through their political systems, citizens must demand rules that stabilize the economy, that introduce fiscal and monetary policies to limit economic growth, and that protect workers from the ravages of unfettered markets. Citizens require programs and laws for economic regulation and social protection.

The international financial crisis of 2007 had its roots in unstable credit markets and currencies in several countries, as well as in fraudulent business activities and dramatic bankruptcies; these led to the deep economic recession of 2008–9, with its disorganized markets and sharp rises in unemployment. All of this mirrored Polanyi's (1944, 227) earlier analysis of economic failures, in which "the almost forgotten issues of early capitalism reappeared" – issues that included the tensions between the economic and political spheres and the role of government intervention with respect to capital and labour markets and the provision of social assistance. These ancient issues remain at the heart of social policy debate.

As one might expect with such dramatic and worldwide events, there is a considerable Canadian and international literature on the recent global financial crisis and economic downturn. Some works by Canadians Naomi Klein (2007) and John Ralston Saul (2009) and by British author John Gray (2002) predated the crisis, warning about the delusions of global capitalism, the rise of disaster capitalism, the collapse of globalism, and, more optimistically, the reinvention of the world. In the aftermath of the financial crisis, especially in the United States, a plethora of books by economists, business writers, and social commentators have appeared, such as *Too Big to Fail* (Sorkin 2009), *All the Devils Are Here* (McLean and Nocera 2010), *The Road from Ruin* (Bishop and Green 2010), *The Crisis of Capitalist Democracy* (Posner 2010), and *Freefall: America, Free Markets, and the Shrinking of the World Economy* (Stiglitz 2010). Other works in Canadian political economy examine bankruptcies and bailouts (Guard and Antony 2009), the structural nature of the global slump rooted in the logic of capitalism (McNally 2010), and transformative alternatives to capitalism (Panitch and Gindin 2009; Albo, Gindin, and Panitch 2010). These commentators explore what the global economic crash means for neoliberalism, free market ideology, and capitalism more fundamentally as well as possibilities for post-capitalist relations. Still other political scientists have addressed how the crisis has unsettled the legitimacy of markets, thereby creating opportunities for autonomy and authority by governments, communities, and social movements (Bernstein and Coleman 2009).

Crisis of Capitalism

The goal of any responsible economic system is to allocate its resources in such a way that it is self-sustaining. It ought to function so that people in the society benefit from its actions. It is expected to produce economic stability for the vast majority while allowing for risk taking and creativity for those who seek those things. Its rules and regulations should result in a sustainable environment, economic well-being for the vast majority of citizens. and opportunities for employment. A proficient market system balances the desires of people to pursue their own rational self-interest through a system of the private ownership of resources with rules and regulations that ensures sustainability, fairness, and security. It should, as Polanyi says, be in balance.

The roots of the latest financial crisis were in the deregulation of financial markets. Beginning during the Reagan/Thatcher era of deregulation and market liberalization, banks and other financial institutions began to loosen their lending practices and reduce their reserves. The lack of regulations stimulated the economy, causing commercial and residential properties to rise dramatically in value, but it also encouraged many people to increase their debt load, to remortgage their homes, or to buy into the housing market. To encourage people to borrow money, mortgage companies offered products that had low initial lending rates, which then ballooned when market conditions changed. Lending institutions actively encouraged people to remortgage their homes or to enter the housing market. Because these companies made their profits by selling mortgages rather than by collecting mortgage payments, they often offered loans to people who were not qualified, or they falsified applications so that people could qualify for loans. Borrowing money based on rising house prices is fine (but risky) as long as those house prices keep rising. As millions of people increased their mortgages or entered the housing market, a housing bubble developed; the housing market became unstable and house values fell (Stiglitz 2010). As those values fell, they triggered an increase in interest rates. Lenders then demanded repayment of their loans, and borrowers were often unable to meet the repayment demands. This quickly led to home foreclosures.

But all of this does not fully explain the *magnitude* of the crisis. Besides overstimulating the housing market, many banks purchased these mortgages and repackaged and sold them to investors and other international banks (Greenlaw, Hatzius, Kashyap, and Shin, 2008).

Using synthetic Collateralized Debt Obligations (CDOs) and other complex derivatives, the banks spread the problems deep into the financial sector and into the international community. The banks were making record profits selling these products in the belief that deregulation had allowed them to capture new markets. Among the main culprits in the whole process were the bond rating agencies that assessed the banks' risk levels (McLean and Nocera 2010). These rating agencies, once thought of as the watchdogs of the financial industry, looked positively on the new CDO instruments and gave many of them AAA ratings, thereby sending a message to investors that these were safe investments. Many people and institutions purchased them as part of their retirement packages or as investments.

As the U.S. housing market began to crumble, the conditions necessary for the crisis to go global were now in place. Each new mortgage default had magnified economic effects. Banks started to feel their reserves tighten up; at the same time, they were having difficulty evaluating the implications of the repackaged mortgages they already held. Rating agencies were giving these high ratings, but investors were becoming suspicious. The repackaging had mixed high-risk mortgages with low-risk ones, making entire packages more "toxic" than had been assumed. Banks started refusing to lend money to other banks and – not long after – to companies and other borrowers. Liquidity within the system dried up, starting in the United States and spreading quickly throughout the world, and the financial system entered a period of crisis.

The first crack in the financial system appeared in the United States in 2007 as banks and insurance companies faltered during the collapse of the U.S. housing market and the subprime lending crisis. Bear Stearns, a large U.S. mortgage underwriter, collapsed as its mortgage-backed assets fell in value when the mortgage bubble broke. When people could no longer make their mortgage payments, banks were faced with large write-downs and write-offs on these mortgages. Unwinding these mortgages was difficult, given the complex financial instruments used by the banks to securitize their mortgage packages. The crisis rippled through the financial industry and spread to other sectors. Lehman Brothers and Merrill Lynch had to be restructured. American International Group (AIG), the largest insurer in the United States, had to be saved from bankruptcy by the government. General Motors and Chrysler needed to be protected from bankruptcy. JPMorgan Chase purchased the assets of Washington Mutual during the biggest bank failure in U.S. history. By the fall of 2008 the ravages of the crisis had spread throughout the world as credit markets stopped working normally. Banks stopped lending money, and companies began laying off workers as demand for goods declined. Investors panicked and began moving their investments to safer ground.

The Impact of the Crisis

The crisis spread around the world because financial markets are highly integrated globally. Banks depend on one another for liquidity. The impact of the crisis was felt in many ways. As the economy slowed down there was a decline in GDP, people were laid off at work, and banks made it more difficult for large and small businesses to get loans. One of the most damaging aspects of the crisis was that private losses for the big banks and other private-sector companies were "socialized" through government bailouts of financial systems. In other words, governments and ordinary taxpayers were being made to bear the weight of the private sector's poor financial decisions. Because governments had increased their debt loads to bail out the financial sector, they were limited in their ability to solve social problems, including unemployment. As Stiglitz (2011) points out, "it has become fashionable among politicians to preach the virtues of pain and suffering, no doubt because those bearing the brunt of it are those with little voice – the poor and future generations." The implications of medium- and long-term fiscal discipline had direct implications for social cohesion. As Polanyi demonstrated, functioning markets need the support of courts, legal frameworks, and regulators to maintain stability. Markets depend on the social cohesion created by redistributive taxation, safety nets, and social insurance programs. When these fail, so too does social cohesion.

First Iceland, then Greece and Ireland, then Portugal, Spain, and Italy faced increasing economic challenges and social unrest. Iceland saw the largest bank collapse in its history as all three of its commercial banks had to be nationalized. Iceland's government fell as the public lost faith in it; there were riots as police arrested demonstrators upset by the projected cost of recovery. In 2009, the Greek government slashed spending, implemented austerity measures aimed at reducing the deficit by more than €10 billion ($13.7 billion), hiked taxes, raised the age of retirement by two years, imposed public-sector pay cuts, and applied tough new tax evasion regulations. This led to violent protests, with workers staging strikes that closed airports, government offices, courts,

Table 7.1. Documented Instances of Social Unrest, 2009–10

	Public protest against austerity measures (spending cuts)	Protest against govt's response to the crisis	Protest against employers[1]	Violence or property damage
Australia			X	
Canada		X	X	X
Brazil		X	X	
Bulgaria	X		X	
Chile		X	X	
China			X	X
France	X	X	X	X
Germany	X		X	X
Greece	X	X	X	X
Iceland	X	X	X	
India	X	X	X	
Ireland	X		X	X
Italy			X	
Japan	X			
Republic of Korea			X	X
Latvia	X			X
Lithuania	X			X
Mexico			X	X

	Public protest against austerity measures (spending cuts)	Protest against govt's response to the crisis	Protest against employers[1]	Violence or property damage
Portugal	X		X	
Romania	X	X		X
Russian Federation		X	X	X
South Africa		X	X	X
Spain	X	X		
Thailand	X	X	X	X
Turkey	X		X	X
Ukraine		X	X	
United Kingdom	X	X	X	X
United States	X	X		

Notes: [1] Includes public-sector workers protesting against the government in its role as employer. An X denotes an action in that area.

Source: International Institute for Labour Studies (IILS), 09/2010, based on national sources.

and schools. Spain, Portugal, and Italy were also rocked by rising social discontent over the handling of the crisis.

In October 2010, the British government cut its spending by £81 billion, mainly through drastic reductions in welfare, higher education, social housing, policing, and local government. The French government introduced pension reforms that led to riots. French citizens viewed these cutbacks as fundamentally altering French society.

It has not been just Europe that has experienced social unrest. Table 7.1 provides a list of countries that encountered turmoil in 2009 and 2010, and the role of judicial, military, and policing apparatuses of the state (Prince 2012).

During the depths of the financial crisis and the economic downturn, many forms of collective mobilization took place worldwide. Some of these political activities were disruptive; others were defensive; both forms were legitimate. These public actions can be understood as democratic critiques of market failures and of the impacts of economic and social dislocations. As counter-movements for intervention and protection, community groups and social movements were calling for state actions to address unemployment, poverty, and other issues threatening societies.[1] In Canada, the anti-government activities focused on the G-8 meetings in Huntsville and the G-20 meetings in Toronto, both held in June 2010. Many Canadians were upset over the $1 billion of public monies that the government had spent on hosting the two events, and a large number of peaceful protests took place. There was, however, violence, as police and a small group of activists became involved in street skirmishes. The police used plastic bullets and tear gas to halt the protesters; 560 people were arrested.

The financial and social impact of the crisis on Canada was weaker than in many countries. Because of tighter banking regulations, Canadian banks were compelled to be much more prudent in their decision making. The regulations required Canadian banks to have higher assets-to-capital ratios than U.S. banks; thus, they had less exposure to the leverage effect of bad loans. Some Canadian banks were exposed to U.S. subprime mortgages, but they had written down these losses before the full force of the crisis hit the economy.

Nonetheless, Canada felt the effects of the economic slowdown in the United States. There was a rise in unemployment and a decline in purchasing power and in household spending and saving. Also, the shrinking of the U.S. market cut into Canadian exports to that country. Export earnings dropped nearly 40 per cent; there were also sharp drops in corporate income and capital spending. In 2008 and 2009, Canada saw an eight-month decline in output – a postwar record; which Philip Cross (2011) has described as "a testament to the severity of the onset of the global economic and financial crisis."

During the crisis, Canada lost 486,000 full-time jobs. Thousands of Canadians were, to use Marsh's (1943, 7) earlier words, "swallowed up in the great vortex of unemployment" – that is, they were having to confront social and economic insecurity concomitant with a loss of earning power (CCPA 2010). The national unemployment rate rose abruptly from just 6 per cent in 2007 and most of 2008, to 8.3 per cent in 2009, easing slightly to 8.0 per cent for 2010. Only half these workers were eligible for Employment Insurance, given the earlier shrinkage of the system. The OECD (2009) expected economic conditions in Canada to remain challenging for the next few years, with low growth rates and limited government flexibility. The government's failure to adequately protect low-wage individuals through EI or social assistance meant that the increased financial and social risks caused by the financial crisis were being borne by those who could least carry them – low-income Canadians. A study by Chandra Pasma (2010) on the recession found that the poverty rate increased between 2007 and 2009 by more than 900,000 people. Pasma also reported that economic insecurity and debt loads had increased among Canadian families; that the proportion of precarious jobs (temporary, part-time, contract, few benefits and rights) had grown; that historic numbers of people of all ages were turning to food banks; that welfare caseloads were growing across the country; and, reflecting a longer-term trend, that the gap between low-income and higher-income Canadians had further widened.

These developments dislocated people's lives and social status and left them economically less secure. Individuals, families, and communities experienced considerable pain from this, including increasing hunger, anxiety, ill health, and misery. Also under tremendous strain, besides financial firms, were manufacturers, housing markets, neighbourhood groups, not-for-profit agencies, and other human service organizations. Many are still feeling that strain. The social picture for many thousands of families has been grim – albeit not entirely unfamiliar. In words from the 1940s that still apply, many Canadian families are facing "the hopelessness and tragedy of seeing no means of making a livelihood in sight, and no means of maintenance other than doles from municipal or provincial governments, unskilled and dispiriting relief work, or assistance from the voluntary charitable agencies in the cities"

(Marsh 1943, 6–7). Some analysts say that the recovery phase of the last recession is complete; even so, based on certain macroeconomic indicators (Cross 2011), dark memories of hard times from this or previous crises, are not completely erased.

State Responses to the Crisis

As fears of total market failure spread, governments responded. In 2008 the U.S. Federal Reserve announced that it was prepared to inject $700 billion into the economy through the Troubled Asset Relief Program (TARP), which was designed to prop up the mortgage market by buying mortgage-backed securities. The Federal Reserve hoped in this way to restore confidence in credit markets. By 2009, the U.S. government led by President Barack Obama had launched a $787 billion economic stimulus package. This program was intended to encourage economic growth by saving as many as 2 million jobs. The program provided $288 billion in tax cuts, $224 billion in extended unemployment benefits, education, and health care, and $275 billion for job creation using federal contracts, grants, and loans. The program was to be spread over ten years, with a significant proportion spent in the first three.

The Canadian government did not have to bail out any of the Canadian banks, although it did take steps to protect the banking sector. It supported the banks by buying up blocks of insured mortgages under the National Housing Act. Initially it set aside $5 billion, later increasing this to $125 billion. Jim Flaherty, Canada's Finance Minister, claimed that "Canada's banks and other financial institutions are sound and well-capitalized, and were less highly leveraged than their international peers heading into the financial crisis. In contrast to many other countries, none of Canada's banks required bailouts. Even during the worst days of the credit crisis, our financial institutions' health allowed them to continue to raise capital" (Finance Canada 2010).

On 27 January 2009, the federal government, fearing for its survival, introduced new legislation to deal with the economic crisis. Called Canada's Economic Action Plan (2009), it set out steps the government planned to take over the next two years. In general terms, this was a $60 billion economic stimulus program aimed at encouraging private-sector businesses to build infrastructure, at stimulating house construction, and at improving access to financing; it also provided more resources for skills training and EI. The government forecast that the program would create or preserve 265,000 jobs by 2010. In September

2010, Flaherty claimed that "in Canada we have a coordinated regulatory approach and that includes the Office of the Superintendent of Financial Institutions, the Bank of Canada, the Canada Deposit Insurance Corporation, the Financial Consumer Agency of Canada and the Department of Finance, all of whom work together in coordination to monitor macroeconomic issues."

Flaherty highlighted the progress made in implementing the Economic Action Plan, noting the following:

- Economic Action Plan funds were committed to more than 23,000 projects across the country.
- More than 22,500 or 97 per cent of Economic Action Plan projects were under way or had been completed.
- In 2010–11, the Action Plan delivered a further $22 billion in federal stimulus spending, complemented by $7 billion in stimulus funding from provinces, territories, municipalities, and other partners.

By 2010, the government had lowered it sights, forecasting the creation or maintenance of 220,000 jobs by the end of 2010, with 130,000 apparently produced by January 2010.

A "double movement" of sorts is evident in the Canadian government's action plan. Its aims and methods are directed, first, at stabilizing and reviving the market economy – particularly the automotive and manufacturing sectors – and with that jobs, profits, and investments, ultimately sustaining capital accumulation and economic growth again; and, second, at regulating market activities through "a coordinated regulatory approach" in order to reassure the working and middle classes that the government is committed to protecting their interests as investors, savers, employees, business owners, homeowners, and pensioners. We see here a version of the marketization of policy issues and human needs, discussed in chapter 6 – that is, the assertion of market principles and economic rationales in government policy making so as to privilege some values and identities of people and not others in economic, political, and social life.

It took more than two years to recover the jobs lost during the recession, a rate of recovery faster than in previous recessions but still with more people unemployed than before the 2008–9 recession, including a rise in the number of long-term unemployed. During the recession, public-sector employment grew, as did the rate of self-employment, while private-sector employment dropped markedly. During the recovery phase since 2010, public-sector employment has continued to increase and self-employment has declined, while private-sector employment has grown again, though fewer such jobs are full-time and more are part-time (Statistics Canada 2011). These trends illustrate a key political point, namely, that the actual composition of employment rates over time is far more informative for appreciating social and economic security (or insecurity) than simply looking at overall participation levels. The latest crisis also confirms Polanyi's insight into how market economies and societies treat human labour: as a commodity, as a factor of production, with employment as the primary source of income and financial security for individuals and families.

The Impact on Social Policy and Community Welfare

The financial crisis had important implications for well-being in Canada. The risk of unemployment went up, as did the chances of losing one's home. There was a shift towards greater reliance on part-time or casual work, greater use of food banks, and a decline in the contributions people made to charitable organizations. While the statistics are not in yet, we can expect an increase in the demand for social welfare services, with an emphasis on the need for housing supports and services for the homeless. The government's ability to deal with these challenges faces a double burden: growing needs and reduced resources.

The 2008–9 recession was the first post–Canada Assistance Program (CAP) and post–Unemployment Insurance (UI) recession in Canada. Before the present crisis, two important policy changes introduced into the social policy regime weakened the government's ability to address dramatic economic changes. First, in 1996 the federal government dismantled its core CAP, which had been designed to provide 50 per cent reimbursement of approved social expenditures to provinces for meeting the changing economic needs of families. The original program provided benefits to needy Canadians, with no pre-existing qualifications or conditions attached to eligibility other than economic need. The program's essential design provided support to "a person who, by reason of inability to obtain employment, loss of the principal family provider, illness, disability, age or other cause of any kind acceptable to the provincial authority, is found to be unable, on the basis of a test established by the provincial authority that takes into account the budgetary requirements of that person and the income and resources available to that person to meet those requirements, to provide adequately for himself, or for himself and his dependants or any of them" (Rice 1995b). In its place, the government created the Canada Health and Social Transfer (CHST), which provided a block grant to provincial governments to meet welfare, education, or health needs as they best saw fit. Under this new legislation, a provincial government could introduce welfare-to-work legislation. Eight years later, the federal government split the block grant into two programs, the Canada Health Transfer for health-related programs and the Canada Social Transfer for post-secondary education and social assistance and services.

Besides changing the nature of social assistance support, the federal government altered the basic protection provided by the EI program. A comparison between 1971 and now demonstrates how dramatically the program had been changed. In 1971, the UI program protected 96 per cent of wage or salary earners and provided coverage up to 75 per cent of insurable income (Pal 1988). To be eligible for benefits, workers had to have eight weeks of insurable earnings in the previous fifty-two weeks, with benefits extended to those who became unemployed due to illness, maternity, and retirement. Benefits could be for a maximum of 51 weeks if a person met the eligibility criteria. Starting in 1976, the federal government began tightening conditions related to unemployment. They reduced the benefit level from 75 per cent to 66.67 per cent and increased the number of weeks from three to six that a person had to wait before getting benefits if fired from their last job, did not accept suitable employment, or failed to attend placement interviews. They also reduced the age at which a person could collect benefits from seventy to sixty-five years of age. Over the next ten years, benefits rates were reduced further, eligibility criteria were tightened, maternity benefits were modified, waiting periods were increased from six weeks to between seven and twelve weeks depending on circumstances, seasonal benefits for fishers were modified, and benefit levels were reduced again to 57 per cent. In 1996, the government renamed the program Employment Insurance (EI), reflecting its primary policy objective of promoting employment rather than supporting unemployment. It also strengthened the policy design that provided lower entrance requirements and longer benefits for unemployed workers in regions with higher unemployment rates. However, the new program restricted benefits to twenty weeks within the past five years and limited maximum insurable earnings to $750 a week.

Critics claim that these changes to EI left the government unprepared to deal with the rising unemployment created by the 2007–9 fiscal

crisis. They also claimed that the new program did not provide sufficient benefits for families to weather the financial storm, nor did it provide benefits for long enough periods. Lars Osberg (2009) believes that
the changes in the employment protection program have led to a major
shift in the burden of risk that families face as victims of the 2007–9 financial crisis. EI no longer replaces as much lost income, it does it for
shorter periods of time, and it covers far fewer people than had been
covered in the 1970s and 1980s. Osberg (2009, 11) points out that "in
January, 2009 the seasonally adjusted unemployment rate in Canada
was 7.7 per cent – as it also was in February of 1990, near the start of
the early-1990s recession – but only a bit over half as many of the unemployed were getting unemployment benefits in 2009, compared to
1990."

The way that Canadians pay for their EI has changed over the past
twenty-five years. At one time, both employers and employees were
expected to contribute. The federal government took on responsibility for all extended benefits and for financing benefits when the national unemployment rate rose above 4 per cent. This meant there was a
three-way responsibility for protecting the unemployed: the employer,
the employee, and the federal government. In 1990, the government
removed its direct support for the program, thus making employees
and employers responsible for the entire program. In this way, EI became more of a "pure" insurance program, with the costs met by those
insured. The federal government no longer helped fund EI, yet it continued to appropriate any excess of income over expenditures, adding
this to general revenues with the understanding that it would pay for
any deficits in the program. Between 1993 and 2007, billions of surplus
dollars flowed directly into government revenues.

Critics of the system felt that the government should not be appropri-
ating *any* of the surpluses; so in 2008, facing political pressure, the federal government created the Canada Employment Insurance Financing
Board (CEIFB), a Crown corporation tasked with setting the premium
rate for employees and employers. The goal is to set the rates so that
there is a balanced budget.

Another area of contention is that originally the government paid for
programs in support of employment and skills training – commonly
referred to as active employment measures – out of general revenue.
Beginning in the early 1990s, the government began to shift these costs
from the Consolidated Revenue Fund, the government's general account, to the specific EI Account. Osberg (2009, 16) points out that only

about 60 per cent of the present expenditures from the EI Account provide direct support for unemployment benefits. The other 40 per cent support labour market training and the costs of maternity and family policies paid from EI premiums. In his analysis, Osberg claims that "retraining programs may (or may not) help improve future employability, but they do not help meet current income needs – and whether or not jobs will materialize to absorb the newly created skills depends heavily on future business cycle recovery, whenever it may occur. Maternity benefits help offset the financial burden of parenthood, but they do not insure against risk."

One of the challenges inherent in connecting training with EI is that those who do not qualify for EI and are most in need of help do not qualify for training and so bear the double burden of no income support and no training for future employment. Changes in the 2009 budget did introduce additional training support through a $500 million Strategic Training and Transition Fund over two years to support the particular needs of individuals who do not qualify for EI.

As we saw during the 2008–9 recession, globalization has meant that financial instability spreads quickly around the world. Even countries – like Canada – that have been relatively cautious about economic deregulation have felt the sting of the recession. However, prudence may not be enough. For countries to benefit from globalization, they must provide economic security for their citizens. They must create social policies that protect their citizens from the risk of financial instability created by economic globalization. Failure to do this will create internal political pressures for governments to protect their economies from global economic forces. We see this happening in Ireland, Iceland, Greece, and other countries ravaged by the economic crisis. The two programs that are intended to provide economic stability in Canada – Employment Insurance and Social Assistance – have come under attack and as such have raised the risks that Canadians face in uncertain economic conditions.

The challenge facing the federal government is to ensure that the costs of the financial crisis fall on those responsible for them, not on the general public, and not on the poor, who are least able to afford the costs and who are least responsible for the crisis. The cost and pain of unemployment is borne by those who become unemployed, even though the unemployment may have resulted from high risk taking by banks or other financial organizations. The role of social policy should be to mitigate these costs and pains. The evidence indicates that Canada's policy is not doing so. Low-income families have suffered more than other families, given the government's changes in social policy. Employment benefits and the number of people protected have been reduced at the same time that social assistance supports have been shrunk. The federal government's responsibility for protecting low-income Canadians has been dramatically reduced; it is no longer committed to supporting EI (all costs are now borne by workers and employers), and it no longer directly supports provincial social assistance programs, as did the cooperative arrangement between the federal and provincial governments from the 1930s into the mid-1990s.

During the latest recession in Canada, nearly half the unemployed did not receive EI regular benefits, and of those who qualified, an estimated 500,000 exhausted their benefits before finding new employment. As a consequence, many people ended up on social assistance, which is the welfare program of last resort. Between October 2008 and December 2009, major increases in social assistance caseloads took place, including 43 per cent in Alberta, 23 per cent in Ontario, and 20 per cent in British Columbia (Pasma 2010).

In the middle of the crisis the Standing Senate Committee on Social Affairs, Science, and Technology (2009) released its report, *In from the Margins: A Call to Action on Poverty, Housing, and Homelessness* (Senate Report 2009). That report described conditions in Canada's largest urban centres. It examined poverty, housing, and homelessness; social inclusion and cohesion; urban economies; and models for collaboration and cooperation among governments. The report made seventy-two important recommendations, including these: adopting a core poverty eradication goal of lifting people out of poverty; coordinating a nationwide federal/provincial initiative on early childhood learning; with the provinces, developing a national housing and homelessness strategy; establishing a basic income floor for all Canadians with significant disabilities; and using the Urban Aboriginal Strategy as a platform for greater investment and collaboration in addressing the poverty and housing problems facing urban Aboriginal peoples. The report addressed issues facing the most vulnerable Canadians living in large cities. A *Toronto Star* article (27 September 2010) pointed out that a staggering 3.4 million Canadians have been trapped in poverty by government social programs that are "substantially broken." While many of the recommendations have been made before, it was interesting to hear that these important social policy issues were still on someone's agenda.[2]

Bill Jordan (2010) suggests that the global financial crash clarified how public policy had lost its way, indicating where new approaches to social policy were needed and providing an opportunity for fresh approaches to gain political support. Jordan notes: "The significance of all this for social policy was that it gave lie to the claims of governments, especially in the Anglophone countries, that global capitalism had made the previous roles of states an anachronism" (2010, 7). Competitive individualism and the market model, Jordan claims, have been undermined by the recent crisis in global capitalism, and this has created spaces for dialogue and possibly action on (re)introducing social and environmental considerations into policy analysis and decision making. He cautions that such reform ideas "are not so much fixes for social policy as signposts for the new directions we should be taking" (2010, 16).

The financial crisis and recession highlighted the importance of human capital formation, shoving to the political centre stage the here-and-now at the time: the pressing problems of rising unemployment and increasing bankruptcies and foreclosures, alongside weakening investments and falling consumer confidence. For public policy and the social role of the Canadian state, it meant a shift away from the longer-term future orientation of the social investment state on children and youth, towards a short-term economic action plan with a discourse of "shovel ready" projects and investments in capital infrastructure, with adult workers the central figure in this stimulus agenda. The aim was short-term payoffs in economic stability and security, by protecting pension plans, regulating financial markets, reassuring investors, and assisting communities and economic sectors hit hard by the downturn.

Conclusion

Financial and economic crises of market economies raise fundamental issues about the relationship between the market and the state, and between economic management and social policy. This latest crisis reveals what Polanyi called the "utopian nature of a market society" – the idea of a natural, spontaneous, and self-regulating economic sphere that works best when it is completely separate from the political sphere and from community interests more generally. Government responses to the financial crisis and to the ensuing economic recession indicate clearly that state intervention is not artificial interference with, but rather essential stabilization for, business and industry. In chapter 5 on retrenching the welfare state, we identified paradigmatic retrenchment as one strategy, which involves weakening support for particular guiding principles for policy action. A major example is the weakening of the Keynesian paradigm for macroeconomic policy and for high and stable levels of employment (Rice 1979, 1985).

Recent government economic action plans at the federal and provincial levels have relied upon Keynesian notions of stabilization. Such thinking holds that the task of government is to use a judicious mix of changes in taxation and in the level of total public-sector spending to stimulate the demand for goods and services when demand is deficient, and to constrain demand when it is excessive in relation to the economy's productive capacity. This so-called demand management usually relates to short-term handling of aggregate demand in order to even out business cycles of booms and busts, resulting in more stable economic conditions. Through the Canada Economic Action Plan, the Harper Conservative government explicitly acknowledged a responsibility and capacity for influencing the economy, in partnership with the provinces and municipalities. At the same time, however, the typical social protection measures of our age – specifically, EI and social assistance – do not function in the way they did in previous recessions in the 1980s and 1990s. Changes to EI and to CAP gravely weakened these safety net policies, which had been intended to offset somewhat the risks of market turbulence for unemployed and low-income Canadians. As now designed, EI lacks the capacity to provide security and stability to incomes for many individuals and families; and with the loss of CAP, we have lost an automatic stabilizer, at the national level, for addressing the inevitable increase in poverty and welfare caseloads that accompany a recession.

The recent crisis has taught us important lessons. First, the Canadian government appears to be hanging on to its neoliberal views of the economy, in that it has restricted the coverage and adequacy of EI, offloaded responsibility for poverty reduction mainly to the provinces, and begun promoting charitable responses to many basic human needs. It has continued to be a *champion of globalization,* one with much less concern for the environment and for the country's social fabric. Second, the market punishes everyone when a few take big risks to satisfy their own self-interests and most working people are unable to protect themselves from major market disasters. Those who are left at the curb in the race for wealth – low-income workers, the undereducated, those who are disabled, and those living from paycheque to paycheque – suffer the pains of economic dislocation when a boom turns into a bust. And finally, the economic and financial crisis has encouraged many people to call for a more interventionist role for the government.

8 Diversity and Equality in a Pluralist Welfare Community: Issues of Social Control, Selectivity, and Universality

In a thoughtful examination of justice and the politics of difference, Iris Marion Young (1990, 168) wrote that "integration into the full life of the society should not have to imply assimilation to dominant norms and abandonment of group affiliation and culture." This statement captures a main aim of social movements advancing the claims of women, many Aboriginal peoples, seniors, persons with physical and mental disabilities, gays and lesbians, other sexual minorities, and ethnocultural groups. Among other activities, these social movements develop and promote positive self-definitions and endeavour to make group identities a matter for public policy. They seek the affirmation and recognition of group differences, the elimination of oppression and discrimination, mutual respect for different experiences and perspectives, and the social equality of individuals and groups (Young 1990). We begin this chapter by looking at some of the critical analyses of the welfare system; we then move on to look in detail at the universality/selectivity debate. Williams (1992, 209) has observed that "diversity carries with it a very different meaning to that of selectivity or targeting. The latter are associated with a top-down objective assessment: the administrator defines the selecting or targeting of need. Diversity, on the other hand, suggests a more subjective and self-determined approach to need. Diversity reveals itself in the demands or experiences of people's own actions." Later in the chapter we also examine the Universal Child Care Benefit, introduced by Stephen Harper's Conservative government as the first new federal universal income program in more than forty years.

Our purpose here is, first, to examine how the state uses social policies to manage and regulate the ways people meet their needs; and, second, to highlight the tensions felt by many community groups. The welfare state, while it provides important benefits and creates social cohesion, has a darker side. As a form of social control, it is often used to regulate people's lives and to shape how they connect with others in society. Critics from the community point out that there is no such thing as a unified category of citizen or client or caregiver; that programs and services relate differently to different groups; that policy makers cannot assume unitary interests and needs even within groups; and that various groups have been oppressed by the market economy and the welfare state even while being excluded from the full range of civil, political, and social rights. The changing politics of social policy are bringing into question the principles of universalism, standardization, and uniformity and are moving more towards particularism, fragmentation, and diversity. They are emphasizing subjectivity and difference as opposed to universal and homogeneous kinds of experiences, needs, and forms of provision. Pluralist critiques of the welfare state deconstruct universal categories and hegemonic constructions of the world.

Towards a New Order of Particular and Universal Values?

In this politics of difference and diversity, where do welfare programs fit in general and universality in particular? We argue that the changing politics of social policy will soon force governments to create policies that protect groups of citizens from the damaging impact of social change. Community groups will redefine work so that greater support goes to women who provide care in the non-paid labour force. The personal will become political as gay and lesbian communities lobby to have the Criminal Code amended so that sexual orientation is normalized. Aboriginal peoples will gather strength to rebuild the core of their nations so that their historical ways of solving social problems begin to dominate. Community activists will seek ways to ensure that income is redistributed from those benefiting from international economic development to those who work and live in the context of local economic initiatives. The self-correcting mechanism of Polanyi's "double movement" is already being felt in many areas. Jane Ursel (1997, 177) has pointed out, for example, that the number of services for victims of wife abuse grew tenfold between 1982 and 1990, and that government expenditures rose even more dramatically during a decade of fiscal constraint, in order to demonstrate that women (those who have been battered and those who are at risk) are better off today as a result of state involvement. There are other examples. In Cape Breton, community economic development initiatives have restored some small commodity capitalism to local levels of control through worker co-ops.

It has been a challenge to convince governments to support community initiatives. There are a number of views about how the process should unfold. The core question, however, is always this: whether social policies will be developed in ways that divide people, or whether policy makers will succeed in tapping universal themes that cross groups and thereby foster social cohesion. Peter Taylor-Gooby (1994, 387) has suggested, with some concern, that "a universal and ameliorative social policy conflicts with the postmodern emphasis on diversity and pluralism in views of what is desirable." He worries that postmodernist themes of difference, decentralization, and choice may pay insufficient attention to trends of growing inequality, stricter regulation of the poor, and privatization of health and social services. He fears that postmodernism is a great leap backwards for social policy. Martin Hewitt (1994, 44) is more optimistic about the fit between diversity and universality in light of the role being played by the new social movements: "These movements challenge the failure of government to apply traditional universal ethics, such as justice, need and citizenship, appropriately in identifying the needs of specific groups. Indeed it can be argued that social movements are motivated towards a new order of particular and universal values." In this context, Fiona Williams (1992, 206) has concluded that "fragmentation of class politics and the development of identity politics implies that demands upon welfare will be about meeting the specific needs of particular groups, rather than about pressing for universal provision to cover the needs of all."

Patrick Kerans (1994, 129) has made the point that "citizenship in Canada is changing from that which accrues universally and uniformly to each individual Canadian, towards a still vaguely defined sense of the equal respect which should be accorded to groups, as groups." The Canadian government's prevailing policy discourse speaks of promoting diversity and advancing equality; except when it comes to medicare and the Canada Health Act,[1] that discourse rarely mentions universality. Key federal policies related to the theme of diversity include the Aboriginal agenda for self-determination, the Canadian Human Rights Act and Commission, immigration and refugee policy, and multiculturalism policy and heritage programs. Key federal policies related to advancing equality include the Canadian Charter of Rights and Freedoms, supports to persons with physical and mental disabilities, the

Canadian Race Relations Foundation Act, and the Employment Equity Act. The Court Challenges Program, which financed groups seeking to establish or confirm their legal and constitutional rights under the Charter, was terminated by the Harper government in 2007.

Two important universal policy values relating to the diversity of needs and capacities were added to the Canadian Constitution in the 1980s. Section 15(1) of the Charter deals with equality rights and states that every individual is equal before and under the law and has the right to the equal protection and equal benefit of the law without discrimination. Section 15(2), however, adds that "Subsection (1) does not preclude any law, program, or activity that has as its object the amelioration of conditions of disadvantaged individuals or groups including those that are disadvantaged because of race, national or ethnic origin, colour, religion, sex, age, or mental or physical disability." Thus 15(1) provides for the universal application of every law, while 15(2) immediately qualifies that by validating affirmative action and equity programs – what the social policy literature has called "positive discrimination" by or on behalf of the underprivileged.

Under section 36 of the Constitution Act of 1982, which lies outside of the Charter, the federal and provincial governments are committed to (a) promoting equal opportunities for the well-being of Canadians, (b) furthering economic development to reduce disparities in opportunities, and (c) providing essential public services of reasonable quality to all Canadians. That section also states that the federal government and Parliament are committed to the principle of making equalization payments to ensure that provincial governments have sufficient revenues to provide reasonably comparable levels of public services at reasonably comparable levels of taxation.

This constitutional guarantee of equalization codifies a practice in intergovernmental financial arrangements that dates from the late 1950s. Each year the federal government makes equalization payments to most of the provinces totalling several billions of dollars. The federal payments help ensure that provinces with tax-raising capacities below a defined national average do not need to have substantially lower levels of public services or far higher levels of taxes than residents in wealthier provinces. Constitutional expert Peter Hogg (1985, 119) has said of the equalization section: "this obligation is probably too vague, and too political, to be justiciable [i.e., subject to the jurisdiction of the judiciary and enforceable by the courts], but it suggests that equalization payments will continue into the foreseeable future." Ontario qualified for equalization payments for the first time in 2009–10, sharing in the federal expenditure of close to $14 billion dollars.

The Dark Side of Welfare: Using Social Programs to Exert Control and Exclude Citizens

In chapter 4 we described the general criticisms that community groups make about the welfare state. Here we go deeper into these criticisms so that a fuller debate about the role of universal programs can emerge. Feminist writers have described the ways in which social policies construct interventions that control the private and domestic sphere of life (Pascall 1986). They suggest that the state has used social policies to maintain a specific form of the family in which men, women, and children have specific roles. Elizabeth Wilson (1977, 9) believes that social welfare policies amount to no less than the state organization of domestic life. Aboriginal peoples claim that social policies are being used against them to control many aspects of their lives. The most powerful example is how education policy was applied as an excuse to remove children from Aboriginal families, place them in residential schools, and strip them of their language, culture, and heritage. The Indian Act was used to isolate and control Aboriginal people by removing them from their homelands, suppressing their identities, and creating ongoing feelings of colonialization. The gay and lesbian community was outlawed through social policies, with people who were not heterosexual being made to live deviant lives. Even when legislation removed the "criminal" label from private sexual preferences, many other social policies maintained that stigma.

When governments use social policies to control individuals and families, they are constraining the development of civic society. Social policies then become instruments that shape how communities are organized and how people interact within those communities. The government's primary concerns are to control the public's moral and social conduct and to define a particular type of citizenship with certain rights and benefits. All levels of government play a part in creating policies that modify the statuses and roles of people within the community. Governments use four types of civic regulations that have direct implications for community groups: human rights, justice and public order, moral sexual regulation, and welfare programs and social union. This line of analysis suggests a trend towards the greater use of rules in managing social policies.

Human Rights

Social policies that address human rights shape the terms and conditions whereby people become citizens of a country. They create what T.H. Marshall (1963) called the right to the social dimension of citizenship and through it access to social benefits such as education, social security, and health care. In this way they determine the basic eligibility criteria for all social benefits. The concept of citizenship was introduced in 1947 legislation and expanded in the 1960 Canadian Bill of Rights and the 1977 Canada Human Rights Act. Citizenship was finally entrenched in the Constitution by the Charter of Rights and Freedoms in 1982. Group rights have been expanded in the Charter to include Aboriginal people, women, gays and lesbians, and people with disabilities. The naming of these groups implies that they will be treated equally in the context of the regulatory process and ensured of their entitlements to fair consideration when benefits are allocated.

The darker side of being identified as a category in the context of citizenship is that it carries with it a subtle form of stigmatization. Those who are not named hold an underlying suspicion that preference will be given to those who are. This was manifest recently in the case of young white males, who historically have been favoured when police and fire departments are hiring. Now that consideration is being given to others, they feel left out of the process and are claiming that they are being unfairly treated.

Social Order

Civil regulations concerned with social order reflect the essential functions of government as lawmaker, umpire, and enforcer. The primary institutions concerned with justice and public order are the courts, the police, law offices, prisons, and parole boards. Historically and in contemporary times, law and public order are core functions and activities of the Canadian state. Prime Minister Stephen Harper approaches these functions in a manner both politically and philosophically different than his recent predecessors. For Paul Martin, Jean Chrétien, and Brian Mulroney, issues of law and order were obviously important but certainly were not defining ones for their governments or persistently dominant items on their public policy agendas to the extent they have become under Harper (Prince 2012). There have been ongoing tensions between community groups and these regulatory institutions of the state.

For the most part, Aboriginal peoples, people of colour, and gays and lesbians have felt harassed by the justice system. The Charter has provided some increased protection against unreasonable search or seizure, but people of colour still feel a certain threat in communities such as Montreal, Toronto, and Vancouver. The gay community has also felt under attack for a long time. Even though Canada in 1969 decriminalized gross indecency between consenting adults in private, there was an ongoing struggle between the police and the gay community. In 1981 the Toronto police raided four gay steam baths and arrested more than three hundred men. As George Smith (1990, 259) points out, the scope and violence of these raids made them a cause célèbre. The gay community was both angered and perplexed by the viciousness of the raids and struggled to make sense of the behaviour of the police.

Although the law allows homosexuals to have sex in private, it does not allow them to create a "public" space in which they can come together to meet, develop relations, and create liaisons for the purpose of having sex. This means that the police, as an expression of the state's authority, treat the gay community differently than they treat the heterosexual community. Smith, in his research, wanted to determine how the regulations contained in the Criminal Code affected police behaviour in relationship to the gay community. He traced the three-step process of investigation–raid–arrest to determine the roots of harassment. The regulations allowing the police to behave in this way are deeply entrenched in the Criminal Code, and Smith believes it will take enormous energy and a long time before substantial changes are made. At a broader level, a number of challenges to the Charter have expanded the protections afforded members of groups, although critics claim there has been only a modest shift in the balance of powers from police to citizen (McLeod and Schneiderman 1994). In *The Canadian War on Queers*, Kinsman and Gentile (2010, 458) conclude by observing that "we are never simply victims or people without agency. We have the power to act, to do and to create. We can subvert and undo national security and move towards a world in which there are no others and in which we can appreciate and celebrate the differences between people."

Morality and Sexuality

The third dimension of civil regulation concerns morality and sexuality in the social policy domain. This area too has been criticized by community groups. Janine Brodie (1996, 359) and the contributors to her book are critical of the relationship between the state and non-state actors involved in developing and reproducing codes of morality. She contends that "moral regulation is the privileging of certain forms of expression that result in the subordination of other forms of self-identification and social recognition. Sexual regulation forms a crucial part of the larger project of the production of moral subjects. The legal regulation of sexual representation through obscenity laws and pornography policy is a key example of moral regulation."

Moral regulation is one of the ways in which the government seeks to create an environment of control over the way people think about certain issues and the way community members construct their relationships with one another. There are moral regulations that deal with abortion, contraception, divorce, drug use, euthanasia, family law, marriage, pornography, prostitution, reproductive technologies, and sexual orientation. All of these areas are highly contentious. Different community groups have different positions on each of these areas, and governments find it difficult and politically dangerous to venture too far from existing legislation (Campbell and Pal 1989, 150). The pluralization of the community means there is a growing array of interests and claims, and this limits the government's willingness to create new policy.

It is difficult for governments to move incrementally on issues or to bargain with stakeholder groups because the cutting of deals is viewed by many as ethically unacceptable.

Welfare Programs and Social Union

This brings us to the final area of civic regulation. Here we are concerned with the restrictive practices operating in and through federal and provincial welfare regimes. Community groups are particularly concerned with how welfare regulations control the behaviour of individuals and families. As Margaret Biggs (1996, 1) points out, welfare programs create a "web of rights and obligations between Canadian citizens and governments that give effect and meaning to our shared sense of social purpose and citizenship." All welfare programs have rules that control entitlement, regulate the flow of benefits, create conditions for withdrawal of support, and establish power and dependency relationships. As we have seen, in recent years there has been a general tightening of the rules and regulations governing almost all welfare programs. While governments have claimed to be preventing fraud (albeit with little evidence of fraud), it appears that the underlying motive is to make work more attractive relative to social benefits.

The growth in civic regulation has been one consequence of welfare state creation. Those who view this regulation as a new form of social cohesion holding a fragmenting society together may see this growth largely in positive terms; those who see it as a way of extending the forces of patriarchy, capitalism, and racism see much of it in negative terms (Chunn and Gavigan 2004; Hermer and Mosher 2002).

Divisive Debate: Universality versus Selectivity within the Welfare State

There are unavoidable tensions between the concept of universality and the increasing pluralization of the community. The fundamental question is whether there can be a universal welfare program when the community has become so diverse. The fate of universal income programs in Canada is reflected in the various editions of *Social Welfare in Canada* by Andrew Armitage, which has been a standard text in the social welfare field for more than thirty years. The first edition, subtitled *Ideals and Realities*, was published in 1975 at the end of the expansionist period of social policy in Canada. In it, Armitage examined the advantages and disadvantages of selective versus universal transfer mechanisms. The second edition, released in 1988, near the end of the crisis period, and subtitled *Ideals, Realities, and Future Paths*, again covered the debate and similarly concluded that both universality and selectivity were needed in the income security system. The third edition, in 1996, subtitled *Facing Up to the Future*, noted that the universal Family Allowance and Old Age Security transfers no longer existed in their original form. "Thus for all practical purposes this once intense debate is over" (Armitage 1996, 42). The fourth edition (Armitage 2003), interestingly with no subtitle, conveys a similar message about the end of the debate for universal income programs. Other commentators, however, have expressed guarded optimism that universality will likely reappear on the federal income security policy agenda (Segal 2008; Shillington 2005).

The decline of universality is among the most striking changes to social policy in Canada in modern times. Now that the universal family and old age benefits have been replaced by selective, income-tested benefits, two of the pillars of the universalist welfare state in Canada have fallen. "Universal health care remains standing, but there are strong pressures to allow the growth of a two-tier system which would permit Canadians to purchase some health services if they have the desire and more to the point the means to do so; ... some provinces have created *de facto* user fees by reducing the range of insured services" (Battle 1997, 38).

Fragmentation, change and uncertainty, and contradiction distinguish recent welfare policy and provision. Regarding the changing politics of social policy, Williams (1992, 202) has observed that "whilst many of the universalistic policies and assumptions of the post-war period have been eroded, they have not been replaced by an overarching commitment to individualism, family, self-help and the market. The situation is more fluid, more complex, and more contradictory." Williams's comments pertain to Britain but also apply, we believe, to Canada. The question of universality or selectivity may appear to have been decided for now in the income security system, but the question in that field as well as in education and health care and possibly other fields is never completely closed. This uncertainty and ongoing controversy is rooted in contending views of social policy, the role of the state, and a just society. In this sense, Alan Pratt (1997b, 213) has noted that "the universality–selectivity debate can also be seen as one dimension of a perennial, profound fault line in western political thought: the relationship between state and civil society, between the market and the state." In the Canadian context, another dimension in that debate is the relationship between the federal and provincial governments, which is a perennial fault line in health care policy.

Universality in Health Care: Federal–Provincial and Public–Private Dynamics

The principle of universality remains at the core of the politics and provision of education and health care in Canada; this is evident in recent reform proposals and initiatives. As described in chapter 3, the five federal principles associated with the public health care system were set out in the Canada Health Act of 1984. These principles are *accessibility* (there will be no financial barriers to insured health care), *comprehensiveness* (all services provided by hospitals and physicians deemed to be medically necessary must be covered), *portability* (all Canadians are entitled to coverage wherever they are in the country), *public administration* (health insurance plans must be administered on a not-for-profit basis by a public authority), and *universality* (all legal residents of a Canadian province or territory must be eligible after a residency period of no more than three months). Note that it is the principle of accessibility that most closely fits with the notion of universality in income support programs, whereas the principle of universality under the Canada Health Act addresses the scope of coverage of the population. This subtle difference in meanings of universality is not commonly recognized and may add to the confusion regarding what universality means in social policy.

The National Forum on Health, a panel of experts established by the Chrétien government, recommended in 1996 that a universal home care program be developed for the frail elderly. Given the aging of the population, reductions in institutional care, and the time and skill limitations of family caregivers, the case for universal home care is to ensure equality of care, to assist informal caregivers, and to reinforce medicare. This proposal relates to issues, discussed in chapters 4 and 9, of overloading volunteers with community care responsibilities and expecting family members – which usually means women – to provide essential services. Recent federal budgets have increased tax relief for people who care for infirm dependants – most of them elderly relatives – at home. Such tax relief has been fairly selective in impact, however, for many caregivers are ineligible because the senior relatives they care for receive the federal elderly income benefits (Old Age Security and the Guaranteed Income Supplement), which places them above the threshold for relief.

The Liberals' 1997 election platform committed them to work with the provinces and territories in establishing a national pharmacare program, building on the assistance programs these governments currently offer to seniors to help defray prescription drug costs. In that it seeks to ensure that people have access to medically necessary drugs in the public health care system, such a program has universalist elements. To date, however, neither the provinces nor the general public seem very interested in a national pharmacare program. This points to the provinces' mistrust of federal intrusion into their jurisdictions, given previous unilateral cuts to joint programs; it also points to the public's wariness of new and potentially large expenditure programs.

In the field of health care policy development, Canada's First Ministers signed important agreements in 2000, 2003, and 2004. This active intergovernmental engagement reflected the public's widespread expectation that the federal government play a role in health policy, at least in terms of funding; it also reflected the provinces' and territories' awareness of that expectation. Furthermore, subsequent debates and issues have pointed to the importance of enhanced federal support on health care. The three above-mentioned agreements also represented a restoration of federal funding to health care services, which had been restrained during the 1990s with reductions to the CHST – reductions that had prompted expressions of public and professional concerns over wait times for essential medical procedures. Over the forty-year history of Canadian medicare, public health care spending has ranged between 70 to 77 per cent of total spending annually.

In 2005, the Supreme Court of Canada ruled in *Chaoulli* that the Quebec government's ban on private health insurance violated patients' rights of personal security under the Quebec Charter of Human Rights and Freedoms, in situations where the public health insurance system was unable to deliver timely care (Bliss 2010; Hartt 2007). While the decision applies legally only to Quebec, five other provinces have such prohibitions on private insurance for medically necessary services. Following the Supreme Court's decision, Jean Charest, then Liberal premier of Quebec, applied for a delay – which the court granted – to enable Quebec authorities to consult with the public before responding with policy reforms relating to health care and access. In effect, the province had one year either to formulate a plan to expedite access to essential medical procedures under the public health insurance system, or to remove the ban on private medical insurance.

The Quebec health care system, like those in all other provinces, confronts a number of challenges: an aging population; problems with equitable access to services, especially in rural and remote areas; and data gaps and the concomitant need for further research and information technology innovation. And just as in other provinces, health care expenditures are the largest share of the Quebec budget, with seemingly relentless cost pressures arising from demographics, drug costs, salaries, and equipment. Studies are published periodically that address how to restructure the system, improve the oversight of health care costs, and improve health outcomes in the population. With other provinces, Quebec has called for predictable and sustainable funding from the federal government on health care. Also like other provinces, Quebec has a mixed health care delivery system that is predominantly public. There are some private for-profit clinics, but most hospitals and community clinics are publicly owned or not-for-profit private organizations.

In recent years, Quebec, along with Alberta and perhaps British Columbia, has seriously considered expanding the role of private delivery of publicly insured health care as well as the role of private health insurance for certain treatments. And with Manitoba and New Brunswick,

Quebec has a significant number of salaried doctors working in hospitals and community clinics.

In 2006 the Quebec government responded to the Supreme Court's decision on timely access to health care. Charest characterized his government's response as a choice to maintain the principles of the public health care system, within which, however, the private sector could play a specific and (for the near future at least) modest role in the delivery of health and social services for the province's people. The plan was to introduce a series of wait time guarantees. Initially, the guaranteed access list included cardiac, cataract, hip, and knee surgeries, as well as some radiation treatments. As more funds and health professional human resources became available, other procedures would be added. The Charest wait time guarantee had three phased elements: First, the Quebec government committed to offer the specified procedures and treatments within six months from the day a specialist recommended the operation. Second, if government-funded hospitals did not perform the procedure or treatment within that time, the province would pay to have it done at a certified outpatient clinic affiliated with a hospital in the province; in other words, there would be outsourcing to clinics staffed by public-sector physicians for publicly funded medical services. And third, if the operation could not be done anywhere in Quebec within nine months, the provincial government would pay to send the patient to another province or another country.

The Quebec government estimates that it will be spending about $20 million a year sending patients to private clinics. Charest sees his plan as in compliance with the Canada Health Act. In Quebec, private clinics perform less than 2 per cent of medical services, and only about 100 of the province's 18,000 doctors have withdrawn from the publicly insured health care system (Quebec 2006). The proposal for allowing private health care includes that private health insurance plans will be able to provide coverage for only hip and knee replacements and cataract surgery. Physicians who opt to do private care are excluded from doing public health care. Moreover, they are not permitted to charge patients or private insurance plans fees higher than those set under Quebec's public health insurance system. Lastly, the provincial government reserves the right to limit the number of doctors allowed to leave the public health care system. Core health care services thus remain in the public domain of Quebec's health and social services system. Prime Minister Harper has welcomed the Quebec government's announcement on wait time guarantees as an innovative approach and starting point to tackling the issue of timely access.

The Quebec government's implementation of universal day care between 1997 and 2000 illustrates the continued relevance and attractiveness of universality (Philp 1997). Building on the province's own universal Family Allowance program and related tax credits, Quebec is providing subsidies to families with young children regardless of income. Parents pay a flat $7 daily fee for child care in day care centres and home-based settings; parents receiving social assistance, however, pay a $2 daily fee. This major policy initiative seeks to reduce poverty, encourage people to move off social assistance and seek employment, and help parents balance the responsibilities of family and paid work. Over its first decade in operation, Quebec's universal approach to child care has resulted in a growth in child care spaces from 58,000 in 1997 to about 200,000 in 2006, serving over half of all children under five years of age. This investment in infrastructure has also meant a major increase in the number of child care workers employed and in the number of parents active on boards of directors of early childhood centres in the province. Quebec's child care system receives about 80 per cent of its funding from public sources, the remaining 20 per cent from parents and families (Thériault 2009, 70).

Which Social Programs Qualify for the Term "Universal"?

Differences of opinion are apparent in the media and in the academic literature concerning which social programs in Canada are universal and which are selective. There is general agreement that four important social programs are universal: medicare, public education, Family Allowance and Old Age Security (until their recent demise), and the Universal Child Care Benefit introduced by the Harper government in 2006. Even on this list, education is often forgotten in discussions and writings about social policy, as are the Veterans and Civilians Disability Pensions.[2] Beyond this, various other programs are thought to be universal, such as the Canada and Quebec Pension Plans, Employment Insurance, and Workers' Compensation. In fact, though, these are all social insurance programs. Even further afield, municipal services such as snow removal and garbage collection, transportation services, public utilities, and the services of Canada Post have been identified as universal programs (Findlay 1983). The mass media often mistakenly refer to some selective programs – tax credits, social housing, even welfare – as universal.

Traditionally, universal income programs in Canada – also called "demogrants" in federal parlance – provided benefits to persons who met certain demographic conditions regardless of their financial situation. As an instrument for allocating public resources, the key characteristic of universality is that benefits or services are provided according to criteria other than individual or family income. Access to universal programs is not determined by a test of means, need, or work. For example, in a study on the distribution of government transfers for post-secondary education in Canada, Alex Usher has defined universal transfers as ones in which "eligibility is open to all, regardless of need or income; and the amount of the transfer is not based on need or income" (Usher 2004, 12). Applying this definition, Usher includes as "universal assistance" certain tax benefits (such as the tuition tax credit and the education amount), summer employment subsidies reserved for people who are in post-secondary, and savings assistance measures, such as the Canada Education Savings Grant. Overall, government universal expenditures for post-secondary education by family income quartile go more to higher and upper-middle-income groups than to lower-middle- and lowest-income groups. The reason, according to Usher, is that on aggregate more individuals from families with middle and higher incomes participate in the post-secondary system than do individuals from modest and lower-income families. Usher concludes that "given the known problems in access for low-income students, this skew is inconsistent with a strategy to help low-income families" (2004, iii).

Social insurance programs, by contrast, pay benefits to defined groups of workers, with benefit levels usually tied to previous employment income levels. No doubt a large part of the tendency to equate social insurance programs with universality relates to the fact that, like universal programs, they commonly provide comprehensive coverage to a client group, offer benefits as a right rather than as a charity (i.e., there is no means testing), and promote the goal of social security. Social insurance programs are not universal, however, because a person's eligibility and benefits depend on an attachment to the labour force. Social insurance benefits are not based on citizenship alone, with a flat-rate benefit paid to everyone in a broad category. Rather, eligibility is based on previous contributions in the form of premiums or payroll deductions, earnings, and the ability to work.

Within the income security system, the meaning of universality has changed over the past several decades as the design and impact of programs have been adjusted. In the 1940s and 1950s, when universal family allowances and old age pensions were introduced in Canada, universality involved paying an equal pre-tax dollar benefit to everyone in these designated demographic groups. The interaction between the benefit transfer and the income tax system was not taken into account by the federal government, nor were benefits indexed to compensate for inflation, which in any case was low during those years. The important design feature at the time was the absence of a means test. Between the 1960s and the 1980s, family allowances and old age benefits became taxable income yet were also indexed. Universality shifted to mean a variable, after-tax benefit, but with everyone keeping a substantial portion. In effect, the net benefit was now income tested. This feature permitted defenders of universality to argue that redistribution to the poor could be achieved within universal programs by taxing back some of the benefits of higher-income people.

Over the 1989–91 period, a surtax or clawback was applied to family allowance and old age benefits so that while all families with children and all seniors over age sixty-five continued to receive the benefit, some families and seniors retained few or no benefits (Rice and Prince 1993). The Mulroney government insisted that universality was still alive in these programs, for everyone in the client categories still received a monthly payment in the mail. This perspective conveniently disregarded the size and incidence of the net after-tax benefit as an important element of universalism. Most social policy commentators, and we concur, declared the death of universality in family and elderly benefits as a result of the special surtaxes. Any doubt of this was removed in subsequent policy developments. The Family Allowance program was abolished at the end of 1992 and replaced by the income-tested Child Tax Benefit. Old Age Security benefits became income tested at the front end as of July 1996; benefits are now reduced before they are sent out rather than being taxed after seniors have received their cheques. Old age pensions are now, every dollar of them, a selective program. Thus today, only Medicare and public education qualify as major universal programs.

The Political Theory of Universality

Universality has been an important policy instrument in the development of the welfare state. Based on the notion of citizenship, it has conferred benefits on everyone in the same category. But as a result of community pluralization, the relevance of universal programs has come into question. Critics have wanted to know, for example, why a banker's spouse should receive the same family allowance as a woman in a low-income family. The fiscalization of social policy dictated that for economic reasons, the banker's spouse should not get the same benefit. But the changing politics has raised the question of social cohesion in a new way, and universality appears to be a policy instrument capable of meeting the fragmented demands of a diverse population. No complete theoretical framework of universality exists in social policy analysis or practice; however, the main elements of that theory are grounded in the literature, dispersed throughout many works (Larsen 2007; Titmuss 1974).

The theoretical case for universality does not exist as a well-codified set of hypotheses; instead, it is expressed in narrative form containing key ideas, arguments, and predicted relations among certain factors. What makes the narrative a theory is the effort to explain and predict events and policy outcomes. What makes the narrative a *political* theory are the beliefs and assertions that universality promotes social integration and fosters wide public support for maintaining universal programs, and indeed for improving them over time; that it ensures political protection against cutbacks; and that it creates public sympathy among the better off for adequate and quality programs for the poor. Universality is seen therefore as a powerful policy instrument for building relations among social groups and across classes, enhancing social cohesion, and tackling inequalities on the basis of a solid public consensus. Universal programs are seen to be built upon the notion of citizenship, with eligibility based simply on membership in the community.

The theoretical core of universality consists of five propositions. Each can be found, in one form or another, in the literature. Each is based on the history and politics of social policy and welfare states, especially in Canada, Britain, and the United States. The five propositions are examined here.

1. Without a universalist policy framework, selective programs for the needy will tend to be punitive and of poor quality. This first proposition contends that stigmatization of recipients, low standards of service, lower take-up rates of benefits, and greater social divisions are associated with stand-alone, selective social programs. When social benefits are targeted to those most in need, tensions and prejudices emerge. Selective social programs, the Canadian Council of Catholic Bishops has said in public statements, inevitably create divisions between those "who pay" and those "who receive," further stigmatizing the poorer members of society. Peter Findlay (1983, 19¬20) has outlined theoretically what can happen when selective programs are aimed at

clearly identifiable groups such as women, Aboriginal peoples, recent immigrants, and the poor: "pressures will arise to define the group more precisely, to lower benefits, and to build a large bureaucracy which will regulate and police more rigorously as people adjust their behaviour to ensure they fall within the policy's parameter." Thus without a universalist policy framework, the needy will be served by second-rate selective programs that punish them.

2. Universal programs in cash or in kind services fulfil various functions: social recognition, investment, economic stabilization, prevention, social integration, and stigma avoidance. The second proposition is that universal programs serve many roles, both in the economy and in the rest of society, with the vertical redistribution of income often only a secondary objective. One such role is the fostering of societal recognition of the contributions made by groups such as families with children, seniors, and veterans, with particular reference to the costs they incur and the contributions they make to society. This role relates to horizontal equity: providing financial or service support to a broad category of people with some shared characteristics, irrespective of their income differences.

A second role of universality is to encourage investment in family stability, social development, and the health, morale, and education of children. Closely related is the idea of preventing disease and sickness through public health measures and regular medical examinations. A third role is to foster economic stabilization by maintaining the flow of consumer purchasing power through the provision of monthly payments to families and seniors. The latter two roles were notable themes in the Marsh Report and in the Keynesian paradigm of government policy discussed in chapters 3 and 5.

Finally, it has been argued that universality serves the purpose of social integration and stigma avoidance by providing a general system of benefits and services, by avoiding punitive eligibility tests, by treating all clients more or less alike, and by establishing spheres of common interest and experience. Universal income programs at the federal level of government may also foster national unity. The relative weight given to these roles will depend on the prevailing values and interests in a given country. Thus there are many different functions that universal programs fulfil that are not based simply on economic redistribution. Universal programs enjoy broad public support, which serves to maintain service levels as well as to provide the political base for further social policy reforms.

3. Because they include the middle class as clients, universal programs enjoy mass public support; they also provide a political context for other progressive social reforms. The third proposition has two parts. The first holds that universal programs are widely supported by the public and that this helps maintain and improve them; for example, the middle classes have a sense of direct personal stake in the education and health care systems as well as in income security programs. When middle-income Canadians are included in these programs, as actual or potential clients, they become a strong and supportive political constituency. Findlay (1983, 21–2) elaborates: "Benefits or services will be kept at decent levels because influential groups will insist on it ... and service providers will be more accountable and less heavy-handed because they will be dealing with influential and assertive groups in the population." Furthermore, the participation of the middle classes in the National Health Services in Great Britain, with their "articulate demands for improvements, [has] been an important factor in a general rise in standards of service" (Titmuss 1968, 196).

The second part of this proposition suggests that universal programs, with their mass public inclusion and support, provide a favourable political climate for progressive reforms on other social programs such as welfare and child care. In Canada, the National Council of Welfare (1983, 26) has argued that "rightly or wrongly, many middle-income Canadians feel that they bear more than their fair share of the tax burden relative to what they get from government in return. Universal programs such as Family Allowance and Old Age Security are among the few visible benefits that most taxpayers receive from the social security system. The middle-class majority's willingness to finance improvements in selective social programs directed to low-income persons, or even to maintain such spending at its present level, could well decline if universal measures such as family allowances were dismantled." When universal programs are maintained, broad public support is gained both for maintaining present programs and for introducing new ones.

4. Universal programs, because of their broad base of public support, are less susceptible to cutbacks than selective programs, especially those for the poor. Selective social programs are viewed as serving small, politically weak constituencies, so that service reductions and benefit cuts would not generate mainstream public criticism and dissent. Conversely, universal programs with large and growing clienteles, such as the old age pension, could generate a much louder response and greater political impact. The essence of the argument is that in an era of

fiscal retrenchment, universal programs enjoy broader public support and better protection against cutbacks than do programs affecting the poor, because of their core middle-class constituency.

5. Universalism is a prerequisite for promoting social integration, but complementary selective programs are also required in order to tackle inequalities and to implement affirmative action policies. The fifth and final proposition represents an acknowledgment of the links between universal social programs and quality selective programs. Universalism is a necessary but not a sufficient condition for "reducing and removing formal barriers of social and economic discrimination, but by itself, not enough to create greater social equality in education, medical care, or income security" (Titmuss 1968, 196–7). Once it is recognized that selective programs alone are undesirable (the first proposition) and that universal programs alone are insufficient, the issue becomes one of determining what relationship between selectivity and universality would be most effective in promoting social inclusion and reducing social inequality. According to this perspective, quality (non-stigmatizing, accessible, effective) selective social programs are only possible within a framework of universal programs that provide the general values and opportunity bases for specific groups and regions.

Perspectives on Universality

The principles and practices of universality face a paradox: as a social value and policy instrument, Canadians do not universally agree upon it. Three dominant perspectives are evident: those of the anti-universalists, the administrative universalists, and the active universalists. Table 8.1 summarizes these perspectives, which appear as distinct and separate categories for the sake of this analytical presentation but which, in reality, overlap.

The rallying cry of the anti-universalists is "slaughter the sacred cow of universality." They argue that "wealthy banker's wives shouldn't get family benefits" (McQuaig 1993), or that "private funding and user fees are necessary to preserve public education," or they ask, "Why should government continue to pay for the health care of the well-to-do? Why should the state pay for the banker's coronary bypass, the retired hockey player's hip replacement, elbow reconstructions of the ladies who lunch?" (Bliss 2010, 22). Business lobby groups, conservative think tanks, some economists, historians, and editorialists, and many individuals do not agree with paying social benefits to better-off

Table 8.1. Perspectives on Universality and Social Policy

Perspective	Ideological proponents	Images of universal social programs
Anti-universalism	Conservatives, Libertarians, Neoliberals	Wasteful, expensive, and intrusive state measures, especially for income support
Administrative universalism	Progressive Conservatives, Social Liberals, Social investment proponents	Pragmatic delivery systems and policy instruments in health, education, some income programs
Active universalism	Social democrats, New social movements	Express core social values and citizenship relationships Unrealized potential in addressing some social risks and community needs

Canadians. The universality of income support programs is regarded from this perspective as a huge waste of money, as unfair to the poor, and as irresponsible in a fiscal context of high public deficits and accumulating debt loads. Anti-universalists would make income- or needs-tested benefits the primary instrument of the income security system rather than universality or even social insurance. It is often unclear whether anti-universalists want to use the "savings" generated from deuniversalizing programs to reduce the deficit or debt, enrich selective social programs, or finance economic initiatives.

Most anti-universalists in Canada focus their opposition to universality on the federal income support programs while favouring universality in the health insurance and education. Undoubtedly, some hard-core anti-universalists are also anti-government – that is, they are generally against the state having a role in the social policy field, want sections of the health care system to be privatized, and want voucher schemes to be introduced to the school system.

The position of administrative universalists can be summed up in a quintessential Canadian way as "universality if affordable, but not necessarily universality." People and groups holding this viewpoint support universality in principle but believe that the nation can no longer afford to pay family or elderly benefits to middle- and upper-income households. Some administrative universalists support the idea of a surtax on higher-income recipients, perhaps on a family rather than an individual basis, while others have called for the replacement of the universal Family Allowance and Old Age Security. For administrative universalists, the universal distribution of benefits is more a convenient technique than a cherished principle; no intrinsic normative superiority is assumed either for universality or for selectivity. The choice is a pragmatic one based on what seems to work in a given policy setting.

Active universalists are vigorous defenders of universality in the Canadian welfare state. They call for existing universal programs to be retained and (typically) for new ones to be introduced. Proponents of this viewpoint include seniors groups, church and faith groups, most social policy organizations, organized labour, social democrats, some liberals, many child care advocates, most women's groups, and health care, education, and social work professionals. For these groups, universality is not simply about common accessibility and non-financial eligibility; it is also about social relations, community values such as equity and sharing, and political forces of citizenship and solidarity (Redden 2002; Shillington 2005). With regard to income security, active universalists believe that all parents with children and all seniors should receive a family benefit or an elderly benefit from the Canadian government in recognition of their contributions to Canadian society; they are also energetic defenders of national health insurance and public education. Active universalists contend that there are far better ways than abandoning universality for "taking from the rich to help the poor." They favour eliminating regressive tax breaks and introducing a wealth tax, an inheritance tax, and other reforms to establish a more equitable system of taxes and transfers.

The coexistence of these three orientations to universality suggests an ongoing controversy in the politics and formation of social policy. Indeed, public opinion trends over the past twenty years show that Canadian public attitudes towards universality are well formed and significantly divided. Through the 1980s and into the 1990s, for example, about 60 per cent of Canadians were of the view that only those persons who have financial need should be eligible for government benefits such as family allowances, while about 40 per cent of Canadians believed that everyone should receive such benefits (Prince 1991). Less certain, however, is whether universality is the dominant value in various social policies.

While universality is a major value undergirding health care and education policy, the contributory principle of social insurance and the selectivity principle are also significant precepts in pensions, disability benefits, unemployment benefits, social housing, and welfare benefits. Strong public support for the notion of targeting is also apparent in public and governmental preferences regarding day care policy. While most Canadians agree that day care services should be available to anyone who needs them, there is relatively little support for the principle of a universal national child care system for all families. Most Canadians and their governments favour a targeted approach to spending on child care based in part on the ability to pay of the parent or parents (Phillips 1989; Bach and Phillips 1997). Even on the left in Canada, there are differing views on how best to develop child care (Rosenblum and Findlay 1991).

The Dismantling of Universal Income Security Programs

The forces of globalization have undermined the economic reasons for universal programs. Here we examine how the two major universal programs came to an end, as well as the economic arguments put forward at the time. Events of recent years have severely tested all kinds of income security programs and other social policies in Canada. A series of cuts to the Unemployment Insurance program in the 1980s and 1990s culminated in its transformation into the Employment Insurance program in 1996, with yet further cuts in the level and duration of benefits. The formation of the Canada Health and Social Transfer in 1996 involved a substantial cut in federal transfer payments to other governments for health care, post-secondary education, social services, and welfare. The income support program of last resort, welfare, now has but one federal condition attached to it, and the provinces and territories are not under any obligation to spend transfer payments on welfare. As of 1998 the Canada Pension Plan's contributions were to rise faster than previously planned while retirement and disability benefits for future retirees were to be cut back.

Contrary to the political theory of universality, universal income programs have not been untouchable or irreversible in the face of neoconservatism and government retrenchment.[3] In particular, the Old Age Security and Family Allowance programs have not been endowed with superior protection against restraint. These universal programs' basic benefit rates have not been raised since 1973, the year that marked the end of the expansionist era of the welfare state in Canada. In 1979 a cutback in Family Allowance benefits was used to help fund a new, selective Refundable Child Tax Credit. The Family Allowance and OAS programs had their indexation provisions capped in 1983 and 1984 by the Trudeau Liberal government, thereby limiting their guard against inflation. The Family Allowance was partially deindexed as of 1986, and both programs were subjected to a clawback of benefits, phased in between 1989 and 1991 by the Mulroney Conservative government. The Conservatives then terminated the Family Allowance in 1992, replacing it and two other family-related benefits with the selective, income-tested Child Tax Benefit (Battle 1993). The Chrétien Liberal government introduced income testing of Old Age Security payments in 1996, marking the formal end of the universality of this elderly benefit.

The one exception to the dismantling of universal income programs has been veterans' financial benefits. The universal Veterans and Civilians Disability Pension and the income-tested War Veterans and Civilian War Allowances have both been improved over the past fifteen years. This may reflect the impact of a universalist framework in this benefit system, but the child and elderly systems had similar frameworks. The special treatment of Veterans Disability Pensions more likely reflects public opinion and that of politicians. Canadians have long regarded disabled military veterans as highly deserving of compensation, and the state is more than willing to show its appreciation for their sacrifices. In fact, the Pensions Act of 1919, which offered disability pensions for soldiers, was "the first significant and continuing [federal] intervention in the social welfare field" in Canada (Bryden 1974, 8). The 1943 Marsh Report noted that social security provisions for the armed forces and their dependants were more advanced in scope and in benefits than those for Canadians in ordinary civilian life. It is the status of veterans and the nature of their needs, more than universality itself, that has made their program enduring and politically resistant to restructuring.[4]

After it had been an important feature of Canadian social policy for close to fifty years, recent Conservative and Liberal federal governments eliminated universality as a central principle of income support for families and seniors. The income security system is once again a residual sector of the welfare state in Canada. Why did this happen? And how was it accomplished?

In an analysis of social policy retrenchment in Britain and the United States during the administrations of Margaret Thatcher and Ronald Reagan, Paul Pierson found that some selective programs were vulnerable to cuts while others were not and that the same was true for universal programs. The belief that universal programs are more durable than selective programs does not hold. Pierson offers two reasons why governments have gone after universal programs:

> An ideologically committed and consistent conservative government would object most strongly to governmental provisions for the middle class. It is universal programs rather than targeted programs that compete with viable private-sector alternatives. If conservatives could design their ideal welfare state, it would consist of nothing but means-tested programs. Furthermore, conservatives are very concerned with reducing spending, and it is hard to squeeze much spending out of marginal, means-tested programs. The largest potential targets are bound to be those that include the middle class; budget cutters will find their attention drawn to universal programs. (1994, 101–2)

In an examination of the administration of Brian Mulroney, Ken Battle and Sherri Torjman (1995) echo these factors in suggesting that Conservative social policy reform was motivated equally by deficit reduction and anti-welfare state ideology. Conservatives argued that it defied common sense and fiscal prudence for Family Allowance benefits to go to middle- and upper-income households (McQuaig 1993). The political vulnerability of Old Age Security pensions was linked to the aging of the Canadian population and to the slower growth of the labour force, with an anticipated budgetary crunch associated with the greying of the "baby boomers," who would have to be supported by the smaller "baby bust" generation. As the largest transfer program to individuals and families in Canada, OAS was a big target for cutbacks. The discourse of federal policy makers justifies targeting old age pensions to those who need public assistance, making the program affordable and thus sustainable for future generations.

Universal programs live in a selective policy world and in a stratified market economy and society. These structural factors limit the political potency of universality. Only a handful of the more than one hundred programs in the Canadian income security system are based on universal principles. Income support programs such as social assistance, tax expenditures, and social insurance (which has defined contributors and recipients) reflect and reproduce societal divisions. Within the framework of the child benefit and elderly benefit systems, selective programs have grown over the past three decades both in absolute terms and in relation to Family Allowance and OAS, and this has de-emphasized the universal nature of these benefit regimes. Universality may generate a clientele attached to those programs that operate on that principle, but it is uncertain whether such programs create a strong sense of solidarity across groups and classes in society. According to Canadian pollster Angus Reid (1997, 276), "government safety nets may be more important than ever during tough times, but a sizeable percentage of the population is determined to cut some of those nets adrift before too many more Canadians start depending on them." Public opinion surveys by the Angus Reid Group and other polling firms have found that most Canadians believe that the welfare system is being abused and that a majority of middle-class and wealthy Canadians accept or enthusiastically support social program cutbacks. Universal programs, then, play a partial role in our everyday worlds, not a total one; such programs are inconsistent with, or in partial tension with, other practices and beliefs, and they are subordinate to more dominant interests in our liberal democracy and capitalist economy.

Another reason for the political vulnerability of universal income programs has been the old argument – which became increasingly persuasive during the rising government deficits and debt loads of the 1980s and early 1990s – that large universal spending programs cannot pursue effectively a redistributive vertical equity role at the same time as they attempt to serve the purposes of horizontal equity. This argument runs that if income support programs are to tackle poverty more vigorously, then something has to give – namely, universality has to be eliminated and funds redirected to those in need. Contrary to the theory of universality, the very demise of universal Family Allowance and Old Age Security, rather than their continuance, was viewed as an opportunity for social policy reform. Regarding the child benefits system, Ken Battle (1993, 421) observed that "with existing resources, it is simply not possible to increase substantially the benefits for low-income families and maintain the same level of benefits for middle- and high-income families."

Battle's own thinking on universality for income programs reflected the shift away from universality towards a new orthodoxy on selectivity in the 1990s. Once a strong supporter of universality in the social security system, Battle is now what we would term a progressive selectivist with respect to income security, although he remains an active universalist for health care and education. A former director of the National Council of Welfare and currently president of the Caledon Institute of Social Policy, an independent think tank, Battle does not mourn the loss of the Family Allowance and Old Age Security programs "because they were replaced by fairer and more sustainable income-tested programs" (1996, 17). Far more damaging than the abolition of universal child and elderly benefits, Battle believes, have been the cuts in federal transfers to the provinces and territories, the partial indexation of the tax system and certain benefits, and the changes to unemployment insurance.

A New Universal Income Benefit: Harper's Child Care Benefit

As introduced in July 2006 by the Harper Conservative government, the Universal Child Care Benefit (UCCB) was the first new federal universal income program in more than forty years. Regarding political preferences for selective versus universal income programs, Pierson suggests (as we noted earlier in the chapter) that conservative governments prefer targeted and means-tested programs over universal ones. Indeed, the previous Conservative administration at the federal level, the Mulroney government, eliminated the universal Family Allowance program, replacing it with a selective program, albeit an income-tested rather than a means-tested one.

How do we account for the apparent paradox of a Conservative government introducing a universal income benefit that parents receive as a kind of right? In particular, a Conservative government that harshly criticized the Chrétien and Martin Liberals as ensnared in a political culture of entitlement? Is there a contradiction between the policy tool of universality and the political tenets of conservatism? Is it a case of the Harper government being philosophically inconsistent and less than ideologically committed, as Pierson might infer? To be sure, a political ideology like conservatism is a complex body of ideas and interests that are not necessarily in harmony. We suggest, however, that other considerations were in play that presented this decision not as ideologically inconsistent but rather as coherent with Harper's party and with his government's agenda (Prince and Teghtsoonian 2007).

The Conservatives' framing of the Chrétien/Martin record on child care amounted to a flaming partisan attack. The frame was obviously unsympathetic, rhetorically strident, and filled with considerable spin. Harper and other Conservatives ridiculed the Liberal policy agreements with the provinces on early learning and child care as impractical and as bureaucratically restrictive, declaring that the Liberal plan was for "politicians to pay other politicians." They dubbed the Liberal

plans as representing huge promises of $5 billion over five years to cre-
ate 625,000 new spaces, strongly implying that the public could not
count on those promises actually happening. The Conservatives asserted that the Liberal plans would limit the choices of parents concerning child rearing, adding that "Liberals don't trust Canadians with
their own money ... to make the choices that are best for their families."
Conservatives claimed that the Liberal Early Learning and Child Care
(ELCC) agreements suited only parents in traditional nine-to-five jobs
and excluded 67 per cent of families who wanted care for their children
that was not institutional day care. They also expressed contempt for
child care and early learning researchers, academics, and policy advocates, depicting them as self-interested and interfering. Harper stated
during the 2006 election campaign that "there are only two experts, and
their names are Mom and Dad."

Immediate reaction came from then Prime Minister Paul Martin as
well as from Ken Dryden, the Minister for Social Development. Martin used Harper's announcement on child care to reiterate the Liberal
theme that there was a stark choice between the two main parties over
Canadian values and that the Liberals believed in child care and early
learning. Martin described child care as a public right, along the lines
of medicare, for Canadian families and their children. He responded to
Harper's platform by announcing that the Liberals would extend the
ELCC agreements from five to ten years, adding a further $6 billion
for a total investment of $10 billion, which presumably would create
more than 1 million new child care spaces by 2015. Dryden said that
the Conservative cash allowance was just that: a modest financial benefit to families, but not child care. Others called it child care delivered
through the mailbox (Bezanson 2010). Indeed, Dryden pointed out that
after taxes, the benefit would be about $1,000 a year per child, or about
$20 per week, not much even for babysitting. This meant, he reasoned,
that the Conservatives did not see the need for accessible, affordable,
and quality child care. The Liberals described their plan as the only
realistic way to address the fact that more than 70 per cent of parents
with children under the age of six were both in the workforce and thus
required affordable child care spaces of high quality.

When the Harper Conservatives came to power in early 2006, federal funding commitments for child care and child benefits were the
Canada Child Tax Benefit, the National Child Benefit Supplement, the
ELCC, and the Childcare Expense Deduction. Conservative decisions
on child care and child benefits included these: serving notice that the

ELCC agreements would be cancelled; folding the CCTB supplement into the Universal Child Care Benefit (UCCB); launching the UCCB; starting a Child Care Spaces Initiative; enhancing the Child Disability Benefit; and introducing a Child Fitness Tax Credit.

UCCB payments are unconditional, which means they can be spent on anything. They are not linked to child care. As a taxable benefit, the UCCB has resulted in some revenue gains by the provinces and territories. Moreover, as a taxable benefit, it has created an inequity between families on social assistance and working-poor families; the latter keep a smaller amount (possibly $200 less a year) than those on welfare. This represents a work disincentive or welfare wall. As a benefit taxable to lower-income spouses, the UCCB tends to favour one-earner couples over single parents and two-earner couples, thus creating significant horizontal inequities: unequal treatment in distribution of net benefits between different types of families with the same income level (Thériault 2009).

Several factors help explain why universality has been the Harper government's preferred policy instrument for a child care allowance. Although it is a universal cash benefit, the program is a new form of residual thinking in social policy. That is, the UCCB represents a deliberate shift away from provincial and territorial governments and public providers towards families, friends and neighbours, and firms and employers. The first line of provision, then, is to be families, along with the local community and the private sector. The part envisaged for spaces created under the auspices of the public sector is an auxiliary one. Adoption of a universal benefit by the Conservatives is not all that radical a change from the federal child benefit policy. The Canada Child Tax Benefit (CCTB) introduced by the Chrétien Liberals in 1997, which initially targeted about 75 per cent of families with children, had, through some enhancements and reforms, extended coverage by 2005 to about 90 per cent of all Canadian families with young children; in effect, it was a mass benefit reaching into the upper-income levels. Thus, the UCCB has not been a sharp break with social policy practice. In a sense, the UCCB has incrementally extended the coverage offered by the CCTB. The UCCB is unconditional, which means that recipients are not obliged to use the benefit for certain prescribed purposes. This fits with the conservative belief in "freedom of choice" that enables parents to "choose what's best for their children." Again, to a conservative this is an attractive virtue of the program as it has been structured.

Universal income programs have long been viewed as a form of progressive social policy; that view is still held by many Canadians. It is possible that in the run-up to the 2006 federal election, the Conservatives calculated that announcing a universal child care allowance would soften widely held views that they threatened social programs. Clearly, Harper needed something to offer Canadians now that he had announced he would be terminating the Liberals' child care commitments with the provinces. Tactically, then, the UCCB allowed the Conservatives to argue, with some credibility, that they were putting forward a positive agenda and that their plan for families was rooted in Canadian values. As Luc Thériault notes, the UCCB "minimally supports the demand for childcare and is marketed as promoting flexibility in childcare choices. What the child care benefit is properly structured for is to be compatible with the maintenance of a commercial child care sector" (2009, 74).

The Harper government's child care policy is a story of retrenchment and replacement. It has entailed terminating a major intergovernmental agreement on early learning and child care and replacing it with a new universal cash program for families with pre-school children. The termination of the ELCC agreements was a pivotal social policy change and a significant political event. The death of these agreements has meant a delay in, if not the demise of, expanding public child care spaces and services across the country. A leading pollster submits that "in the long run, the Canadian values landscape will lead us to a national, public child-care infrastructure" (Adams 2006, A15). That may be so, now that detailed plans for universal child care are available (Friendly and Prentice 2009); but in the current politics of Canadian social policy, the long run looks very far away.

Conclusions

In liberal social policy regimes such as Canada's, "while there may be a commitment to universalism, it is universalism with an equal opportunity focus" rather than an equality of results or outcomes (O'Connor, Orloff, and Shaver 1999, 223). In our discussion of the social control aspects of the welfare state, we questioned whether equal treatment under and by the law are concepts of equality that many marginalized individual and groups actually experience in their everyday lives. For almost a quarter-century, the Court Challenges Program offered resources to equality-seeking organizations that enabled them to participate in legal cases dealing with equality rights and constitutional questions of the relationship between citizens and the state, and between the Charter of Rights and governments. The Harper government's termination of the Court Challenges Program shut down a vital judicial vehicle for attaining full citizenship and a fuller measure of equality (Prince 2009). Public safety and social assistance eligibility are two further locations where the law, vulnerable peoples, and the politics of exclusion all interact in significant ways (Hermer and Mosher 2002). At the same time, the ideas and practices of selectivity and universality remain powerful currents in the politics of Canadian social policy, federalism, and relations between the state and market.

The extinction of the universal Family Allowance was a pivotal social policy change and political event of the 1990s; so was the death of universal Old Age Security. The loss of these two programs marked not only the demise of a social transfer mechanism but also a serious challenge to the political theory of universality that we have outlined in this chapter. The death of universal income programs came not with a crash but with a clawback. Family allowances and old age pensions were victims of the artful practice of social policy reform by stealth, effectively carried out by the Mulroney Conservatives and later also by the Chrétien Liberals. Battle (1993, 439) has pointed out that "the main reason the Conservatives got away with their cuts to social programs ... is that most Canadians have no idea what has happened to them because the policy changes are so arcane and technical. This also makes the public more susceptible to government propaganda, which has become more bold and blatant in recent years." The partial deindexation of the Family Allowance program and the clawback imposed on both Family Allowance and Old Age Security benefits was conducted through federal budgets by the Department of Finance with no prior consultation, little media attention, and minimal public debate. Thus stealth as a policy instrument and process of covert change helped the government deuniversalize these two programs and cut federal social spending with little political harm at the time.

Key institutional features of the Canadian political system have enabled governments to retrench universal programs. Under federalism, cuts in intergovernmental financing for universal health care and education, either from the federal government to the provinces and territories or from the provinces to school boards, municipalities, and hospital boards, have allowed one level of government to offload costs and shift the burdens of restraint onto other levels, often with little political harm to the higher level. Under our parliamentary cabinet system of governance, the political executive is dominant and a majority government usually prevails in making policy changes. This tendency is only reinforced when those changes are developed under the shroud of budget secrecy and the pre-eminence of the Finance Department.

Social policy groups and women's organizations active in defending universality and in challenging the Conservatives' changes to universal child and elderly benefits had a marginal impact on the government's agenda. Social sector groups lacked sufficient political organization and mobilization to counter the moves towards selectivity (Moscovitch 1990). Meanwhile the Mulroney Conservatives appealed to their own constituency of anti-universalists and administrative universalists, using the discourse of deficit reduction and the need to reduce social expenditures to justify targeting limited resources to those in greatest need. Equality rights are a prominent item on policy agendas, and, in relation to postmodernist politics, the terms of the debate may be shifting towards reconciling universal policies and practices with the realities of diversity and group differences.

The politics and programming of universality in Canadian social policy has gone through several stages: the creation of universal benefits and services from the 1940s to the 1970s; the attacks on and defence of them in the 1970s and 1980s; the tactic of stealth in ending universal income benefits in the late 1980s and early 1990s; and, now, a new orthodoxy of selectivity regarding who should be targeted for financial assistance and on what basis and terms. In addition, the new social movements and the postmodern politics of identity and difference pose challenges and opportunities for universal values and policies.

The most recent stage in the politics of universality arrived with the universal child benefit that the Harper Conservatives established in 2006. The framing and design of the UCCB suggest that the Harper government views universality as a political tool, one that can serve a number of ideological interests and partisan purposes in addition to public policy. While the UCCB is universal in coverage, it is modest in government spending commitments (it is being financed in part by the cancellation of previous Liberal government spending plans); it is also relatively simple to administer. Also, the UCCB offers acknowledgment through public policy of parents caring for their children at home – an acknowledgment that social conservatives within the Conservative Party have insisted on for years. The actual workings of the UCCB and its interactions with other programs – particularly the Child Care Expense Deduction – have resulted in the advantaging of traditional families, that is, stay-at-home mothers supported financially by bread-winning fathers.

At the subnational level, there have been three additional developments: (1) the restoration of health care spending as a percentage of provincial economies and provincial government budgets, following a decade of decline between 1990 and 2000; (2) the introduction or reintroduction of universal full-day kindergarten for five-year-olds and, in some jurisdictions, four-year-olds, in public education systems; and (3) the establishment of anti-poverty reduction strategies in several provinces and territories, with elements of both selective and universal policy initiatives (see chapter 11). In addition, policy ideas with overtones of universality circulating within political systems across the country are embracing a public pharmacare program with catastrophic drug insurance; the goal of universal access to post-secondary education; a national basic income program for adults with severe disabilities, along the lines of the federal elderly benefit system; and a more generic guaranteed annual income for all low-income Canadians (Prince 2009; Segal 2008; Usher 2004). The universality/selectivity debate is never really over as an economic, political, or social issue in Canada, whether it relates to income security, public health care, or public education.

9 Gender and Social Policy: His and Her States of Welfare

The welfare state is highly gendered and always has been. Men and women have distinctive sets of relationships to the health care, labour market, and social security systems. Women, for example, experience a different welfare state and social world than do men. These life experiences include having the greatest responsibility for the family, child care, and elder care; being victims of male violence; and generally being poorer. There also are differences in the causes and experiences of death. Since men tend to marry younger women, who tend to live longer, more than half of Canadian women will be widows, whereas only 20 per cent of Canadian men will be widowers. With respect to family formations, women head over 80 per cent of all single-parent families in Canada. Women now constitute almost 60 per cent of the seniors population and 70 per cent of all persons aged eighty-five and older. Differences in work experiences include continued occupational segregation for women in many sectors of the labour force as well as lower rates of earnings, benefits, and pensions. In the world of politics and governing, women remain significantly underrepresented in legislatures, cabinets, and the courts and in senior levels of public bureaucracies and business corporations. In social programs, there are gender inequalities regarding benefit levels, redistributive outcomes, and access to many services and rights. Women also experience disproportionately the adverse consequences of social service cutbacks and other policy reforms (Bashevkin 2002; Brodie and Bakker 2008; Wallis and Kwok 2008).

Our purpose here is to examine the gender dimension of the Canadian welfare state, including differences in the roles, rights, and duties of men and women in relation to families and caring, jobs and workplaces, and the political and governmental systems. We discuss both feminist perspectives on social policy and the contemporary processes of restructuring and retrenching the state. We examine the gendered division of work, women's roles in the welfare state, and women's experiences with social programs.

Mainstream Literature and Feminist Thinking

Caroline Andrew (1984, 667) asserted that to understand adequately the welfare state, "it is necessary to examine the question of gender, the relations of women and the welfare state." She described the overall relations between women and the welfare state as ambiguous and contradictory yet also vital to women's well-being. Lois Bryson (1992, 159), among several other feminist writers, has demonstrated that "the conventional literature has been male-stream and the provisions of the welfare state were developed by men from within the dominant male perspective, to solve problems as men perceived them. The significant point is that this is rarely acknowledged." Despite Andrew's call a generation ago for more feminist thought concerning the welfare state, gender analysis has not fully permeated mainstream texts in Canadian public administration, public policy, or political science in a significant way (Brooks and Miljan 2003; Doern and Phidd 1992; Howlett, Ramesh, and Perl 2009; Pal 2010). In other words, such texts contain little on gender, women, and the women's movement; and none of them treat feminism as a distinct analytic approach to studying and explaining policies and programs. Feminist perspectives and critiques are more evident in social policy and social work literatures (Armitage 2003; Mullaly 1997; Pulkingham and Ternowetsky 1996; Samuelson and Antony 2007; Tester, McNiven, and Case 1996; Westhues 2006). This is especially so of some works (Baines, Evans, and Neysmith 1991; Brodie 1995), while others have little or no gender analysis (Banting and Battle 1994; Courchene 1994; Mishra 1990b; Teeple 1995). In the mainstream literature on social policy, the principal models of social policy are the residual and institutional conceptions, first articulated more than fifty years ago (Wilensky and Lebeaux 1958) and still applied and widely discussed by social policy and social work academics (Armitage 2003; Boychuk 1998; Guest 1997; McKenzie and Wharf 2010), including feminist scholars (Brodie and Bakker 2007; Sainsbury 1996; Williams 1989). Variations on and additions to these models include industrial achievement (Titmuss 1974) and social development

(Callahan, Armitage, Prince, and Wharf 1990). These models all focus on government–market relations and on the degree of state intervention and responsibility for meeting needs. Perhaps the best known typology of welfare states today is in Gosta Esping-Andersen's *The Three Worlds of Welfare Capitalism* (1990), in which the three regimes are defined along a continuum of scope of coverage and level of generosity of benefits. The continuum moves from the least extensive liberal welfare states (e.g., Canada, Britain, and the United States), to conservative welfare states (e.g., Austria, Germany, and France), and ultimately to social democratic welfare states (e.g., Sweden and the other Scandinavian countries).[1] Having been criticized for basing his three-regime framework on a male model of citizenship and for overlooking fundamental issues of gender politics (for example, see Sainsbury 1996), Esping-Andersen (2009) more recently has examined what he calls the incomplete revolution of adapting welfare states to women's new roles and advancing the goal of gender equality.

The ideologies of social welfare commonly examined in the mainstream literature reflect the focus of these typologies and models on state intervention and matters of political economy. These ideologies are those of the anti-collectivists (social Darwinists, neoconservatives, neoliberals, the new right), the reluctant collectivists (liberals, modified individualists), social democrats (the old and the new left), and the Marxists (George and Wilding 1976, 1985; Djao 1983; Mishra 1984). These ideologies of welfare range along a traditional right-to-left political spectrum, yet they all feature a male breadwinner and dependent-family model.

Feminist Perspectives on Social Policy

The feminist literature identifies a number of limitations inherent in these models, typologies, and ideologies. Diane Sainsbury (1996, 40) notes that "feminists have underlined the importance of ideology in shaping welfare policies but they have cast light on a completely different set of values than the residual and institutional models. Rather than ideologies of state intervention or distribution, feminists have made familial and gender ideologies pivotal to the analysis of the welfare state."

In this vein, feminist writers have named and proposed several alternative models of social policy to replace the male breadwinner model: the universal breadwinner model, which encompasses women as well as men; the female caregiver model; a parity model whereby caring is recognized and given remuneration; the male pauper model, which points out that amidst the feminization of poverty across societies, a portion of the male population also experiences destitution; and, finally, the individual model, in which family roles are shared and employment, wage taxes, and social policies are aimed at individuals rather than at heads of families or households (Baines, Evans, and Neysmith 1991; Sainsbury 1996). Some of these models are more fully developed conceptually and theoretically than are others, but all offer new ways of thinking about the gendered division of social programs and social rights and duties. With respect to ideology, women writers have added liberal, radical, socialist, and Marxist streams of feminist analysis to the traditional ideologies. Other ideological perspectives include black feminism, disability feminism, and lesbian feminism, as well as neomaternalism and pronatalism. Feminist works on Canadian social policy and the welfare state are devoting close scrutiny to the links among gender, race and ethnicity, and social status. In particular, this line of inquiry examines the experiences of Aboriginal women as well as those of new and recent immigrant women, highlighting the limitations of the labour market and the social safety net when it comes to providing economic opportunity and security (Dossa 2009; Stasiulis and Bakan 2005; Wallis and Kwok 2008). As a newer perspective on social policy, this literature relates to the politics of identity and cultural recognition that we discussed in the introduction to *Changing Politics*.

Deploying the concept of gender regimes, and related ideas of citizenship regimes and social policy regimes, feminist writers are widening the focus of analysis beyond the welfare state itself to include economic, cultural, social, and political structures (O'Connor, Orloff, and Shaver 1999; Pascall and Lewis 2004; Sainsbury 1996). Gender regimes draw attention to the organization of gender-differentiated roles and resources, norms and values, and relations of power and knowledge in a given political community, as working in and around governments, labour markets, families, and cultural practices of the feminine and masculine. In the Canadian context, as well as in Europe and other settings, feminist scholars are describing, explaining, and assessing the current gender regimes at different scales or levels of social organization.

Women-centred analyses of public policy in Canada are an active preoccupation among feminist social scientists; the issues and impacts addressed are wide in scope and critical in orientation (Bashevkin 2002; Briskin and Eliasson 1999; Brodie and Bakker 2007, 2008; Cohen and Pulkingham 2009; Dobrowolsky 2009; Gavigan and Chunn 2010;

Newman and White 2006). A related line of investigation concerns the project of "gendering the state," which entails women's political mobilization, engagement with public authorities, and direct representation within the structures and processes of government, as strategies for advancing gender equality (Abu-Laban 2008; Brodie 1995; Chappell 2002; Rankin and Vickers 2001; Rebick 2005; Trimble and Tremblay 2005).

Feminist writers and advocates have also surfaced, shattering ideologies that have long remained hidden or taken for granted in society, such as the public–private divide and the ideology of separate spheres (Boyd 1997). The ideology holds that there is a clear separation between the private sphere of family, home, and unpaid work of women on the one hand, and the public sphere of paid work, the market, and the state on the other.

Familism

Another ideology of great importance to social welfare and gender equality is familism, which Neysmith (1991, 285) describes as "the idealization of what we think a family should embody: a conflict-free domain where emotional and physical needs are tended to." Within this haven, family care is seen as natural, positive, and therefore intrinsically superior to most kinds of care offered by other sources in the public or private sectors. The belief that families (i.e., women) are the fitting venue for the care of young children, elderly relatives, and other dependent members is widespread in social policies across Canada. Underlying this family ethic is the assumption that women will be available and responsive to others; this includes volunteering for work outside the home and being undemanding for themselves (Aronson 1991; Williams 1989). The welfare state built from the mid-1940s to the 1970s was based on a particular notion of the family. "It presumed a stable working-/ middle-class nuclear family supported by a male bread-winner, a dependent wife and children, and the unpaid domestic labour of women" (Brodie 1995, 39). A characteristic of the changing politics of social policy is that ideas of marriage, family, and what represents "normal" family life are under intense debate and shifting in different directions. The feminist literature describes how important the family, the community, and social relations are to the maintenance of social cohesion, but it also emphasizes that these social relations need to be constructed in ways that promote an inclusive civil society that is respectful of the role of women.

Feminist writers have framed new conceptions of the welfare state that challenge traditional notions of citizenship, universality, and the boundaries of social policy. Carole Pateman's (1988) notion of the "patriarchal welfare state" draws attention to male privileges reflected in family–state–market interactions. Pateman was among the first feminist writers to challenge the idea that social citizenship, as a bundle of rights and duties based on membership in the community, was politically neutral and universally available to all groups. Thelma McCormack (1991) notes several essential differences in the ways men and women envision the welfare state. McCormack suggests that for most men, "welfare state" means government-supported health and social services and assorted social insurance programs, as well as public investment and countercyclical budgeting for stabilizing the economy. Men also see the welfare state as a limited set of administrative and economic measures, a number of which are temporary responses to economic crises.

In contrast, McCormack claims that for women, "the welfare state includes social insurance for the vulnerable groups – the unemployed, the sick, and the aged – but goes beyond these to include education, the arts, and cultural life. This viewpoint reflects women's experience as cradle-to-grave caregivers, doing unpaid or underpaid work outside the competitive, profit-driven economy" (1991, 3). This women's concept is a welfare society model with an emphasis on culture, society, and demographic trends, including "groups that fall outside the definitions of the workforce – the aged, children, the disabled, victims of sexual abuse, immigrant groups – rather than economic ones" (i.e., groups inside the paid workforce) (McCormack 1991, 39). In addition to social insurance and other income support programs, this perspective also features services, laws, and regulations. Although the two models overlap somewhat in terms of concerns and policy instruments, what we have in Canada is a retrenched but still existing welfare state, not a welfare society, within a mixed economy and a patriarchal social structure.[2]

Social Reproduction and Social Provisioning

Gendered labour, neoliberalism, and the status of women have become key points of analysis among Canadian feminists and others. Notable themes include the challenges, insecurities, hard times, and struggles of women in everyday life, in both domestic and market settings. These struggles are examined from various social locations and intersectionalities that include race, religion, and poverty; disability, paid work, and unwaged labour; and welfare (Dossa 2009; Vosko 2006). There are two conceptual approaches to much of this literature: one relates to social reproduction (Bezanson and Luxton 2006; Bezanson 2006; Luxton and Corman 2001; Braedley and Luxton 2010); the other deals with social provisioning (Neysmith and Reitsma-Street 2005; Neysmith, Reitsma-Street, Baker-Collins, and Porter 2009; Power 2004).

The term "social reproduction," as used by female political economists and others, refers to "work that is involved in the daily and generational reproduction of the population." This growing body of writing points to the vitality of Canadian feminist political economy scholarship. As a multifaceted process linked to the modern welfare state, social reproduction is concerned with "ensuring that labour power is produced, cared for, skilled and disciplined appropriate to the needs of capitalism" (Williams 1989, 183). Institutionally, the work of social reproduction takes place across several social structures and economic classes, including working-class and middle-class families and households, labour markets, voluntary organizations, co-ops, informal networks, and government agencies (Bezanson and Luxton 2006). A principal reason in applying this concept to social policy is to emphasize how much of the labour that women undertake is unpaid, undervalued, and unrecognized. As Susan Braedley and Meg Luxton (2010, 14) observe, "women have typically been responsible for most of the unpaid work of social reproduction that gets done in private households." This unpaid labour, such as child rearing and adult caregiving, is crucial to the functioning of the paid labour in market economies everywhere. Clearly, social reproduction is more than a contribution to labour power and economic capital; it contributes to the creation and transmission of cultural capital in the form of attitudes, beliefs, values, and knowledge, as well as to social capital in the form of relationships of love and trust and networks of friends and colleagues.

Social provisioning is a related concept for contextualizing the significance of women's labour and is especially useful in mapping the full extent of resources and relationships involved in economic, human, and social development. The feminist economist Marilyn Power has elaborated on the term "social provisioning" to describe a methodology with five components. These five are "incorporation of caring and unpaid labour as fundamental economic activities; the use of well-being as a measure of economic success; analysis of economic, political, and social processes and power relations to better understand human agency; the validity of ethical goals and values as an intrinsic part of the analysis; and interrogation of differences by class, race-ethnicity, and other factors" (Power 2004, 3). We like how Power explains the intention behind this concept:

> "Social provisioning" is a phrase that draws attention away from images of pecuniary pursuits and individual competition, and toward notions of sustenance, cooperation, and support. Rather than be naturalized or taken as given, capitalist institutions and dynamics become subjects to be examined and critiqued. Social provisioning need not be done through the market; it need not be done for selfish or self-interested reasons, although neither of these is inconsistent with social provisioning, either. Thus, the concept allows for a broader understanding of economic activity that includes women's unpaid and nonmarket activities and for understandings of motivation that don't fall under narrow or tautological notions of self-interest. The term also emphasizes process as well as outcomes. The manners in which we provide for ourselves, both paid and unpaid, are included in the analysis. And social provisioning emphasizes the importance of social norms. (Power 2004, 6–7)

Power views these components of social provisioning as methodological starting points and a broader world view to underscore the intrinsic interdependencies of the human condition and to support feminist approaches to policy and practice.

A stream of research by Sheila Neysmith and Marge Reitsma-Street, and their colleagues, has added greatly to our understanding of provisioning and to our conceptions of the work women do (Neysmith and Reitsma-Street 2005; Neysmith, Reitsma-Street, Baker-Collins, and Porter 2009). Neysmith and Reitsma-Street offer the concept of "provisioning communities" to describe "groups of women who come together in local initiatives, such as a community resource centre or a women's employability program, to address fundamental sources of impoverishment as well as practical livelihood needs" (Neysmith and Reitsma-Street 2005, 381).

The Dual-Welfare Thesis

Feminists point to a gendered division of income security provisions embodied in welfare states – a line of analysis called the dual-welfare thesis. This division is also referred to in the literature as the two-channel welfare state, two-tier welfare, and double-standard welfare.[3] Whatever the name, the common idea is that the welfare system is divided with reference to men and women. From this perspective, welfare states are complex systems of differentiation and stratification. The dual-welfare model has both a more critical and a less critical line of this argument, as well as a narrow and wider scope of application. The less critical version of the model is that women as welfare state clients and beneficiaries predominate in certain services and benefit programs, while men are the primary claimants in other social programs. The more critical version asserts that men's and women's bases for entitlement to benefits, and the benefits themselves, are sharply segregated: "Women and men are channelled into separate programs, resulting in a system of dual welfare. Men's maintenance by the state is through social insurance schemes based on claims as earners, while women make their claims on the basis of domestic work and rely more heavily on public assistance programs" (Sainsbury 1996, 129). This dualism is rooted in a second division: the traditional division of work between men as earners in the public sphere and women as unpaid caregivers in the private sphere.

In the narrow version of the dual-welfare model, the analysis focuses on selective income support programs provided by the state. Programs for men tend to be based on labour force attachment and include unemployment insurance, workers' compensation, and other social insurance programs. Programs for women tend to be means- and income-tested programs based on weak conceptions of need, such as public assistance, mothers' pensions, and survivors' benefits. A wider approach to welfare dualism goes beyond public income programs to encompass occupational welfare in the workplace and fiscal welfare provided through the tax system. The dualism here is between public and private provision.

As we now show, differences in the labour market status of men and women are changing, but slowly; occupational and fiscal welfare programs still favour men. The retrenchment of the welfare state in recent decades (traced in chapters 4 to 7) has different consequences for women and men. As the dual-welfare model underscores, these cutbacks have intensified the gendered dualism of social entitlements and reinforced many inequities and disadvantages facing women.

Gendered Division of Work and Positions of Power

The struggle led by feminists to influence how governments create and implement social policies has only partly succeeded. A sexual division of roles and resources is still evident in the activities of informal caring and work in the home, paid work in the labour market, and holding public offices within the Canadian state.

Caring and Working for the Family

In the private or domestic sphere, most informal care for children, relatives with disabilities, and the elderly is still provided by women, whether or not the woman is participating in the labour force. A growing number of men are primary caregivers, but it is still the exception to the general pattern of women addressing the needs of their families (Baines, Evans, and Neysmith 1991). This duty to care continues throughout the woman's lifespan. Adult daughters, for example, are expected to be the natural caregivers for aging parents. Public programs and social services have always depended on the care provided by women in families, and this reliance is growing under the guise of community care and deinstitutionalization. Traditional gender roles and imbalances also persist in the division of work in and around the house. In addition to child care, where applicable, women still shoulder the principal responsibility for meal preparation and cleanup, cleaning, laundry, and shopping, while men have responsibility for house repairs, maintenance, and yard work.

Little has changed over the past twenty years. A 1990 survey found that among dual-earning couples working full time with dependent children, only 10 per cent shared the responsibility for housework equally. For 80 per cent of these couples, women had all or most of the responsibility for household chores (Marshall 1993). A 1992 study revealed that employed women with a spouse and at least one child under age five spent 5.3 hours a day on household and child care activities; about two hours more each day than their male partners (Statistics Canada 1995b, 9). "Without a more equal division for housework, women will have to continue to juggle employment, household chores and family time" (Marshall 1993, 14). Many women consequently work a "double shift" each day, one shift at home, the other in paid work, resulting in serious "time crunch" problems, which in turn lead to stress, poor health, absenteeism, and guilt about their parenting.[4] Women are far more likely than men to lose outside work time due to family responsibilities. In 1994, female workers missed six days of work on average because of family duties compared to less than one day for men, with subsequent collective effects circling back on women's careers and on their labour force participation. The equal or fair allotment of housework and caregiving labour remains remote in most Canadian families (Kershaw 2005; Luxton and Corman 2001).

The Canadian Labour Market

It is in the area of women's labour market involvement that the women's movement arguably has had the greatest impact. This area continues to be a topic of critique by feminist academics and activists. Canada has introduced employment equity legislation at the national level (and in Quebec) as well as pay equity programs (at the federal and provincial/territorial levels of government). In 1986 the federal government introduced employment equity, a law meant to overcome discrimination in the workplace by encouraging employers to hire people from four designated groups: women, people with disabilities, Aboriginal peoples, and members of visible minorities. The law, which was updated in 1995, requires that any employer in the federal domain with 100 employees or more create and file with the federal government a statistical profile of the population, indicating the proportion of the designated groups in their community. They must then submit a plan for hiring people so that their workforce reflects the general population. Pay equity, for its part, was meant to provide a process of revaluing the compensation paid for work and removing from such evaluation the sex stereotypes that are built into job descriptions. The steps, which are complex, are meant to have employers, in consultation with employees (and unions), work out a way to revalue jobs based on skill, effort, responsibility, and working conditions.

This legislation was introduced at a time when there was a dramatic increase in the participation of women in the paid labour force, a growing unionization of women workers, and an expanding share of non-standard forms of employment. Concurrently, men's labour force participation and unionization rates have declined in recent decades. In 2009, 58 per cent of all women aged fifteen and over were in the labour force, representing 48 per cent of all paid workers – up from 42 per cent in 1976 (Ferrao 2010).[5] Since the mid-1980s a majority of single women, married women, and separated and divorced women have been employed in the Canadian labour force. Only a small proportion of widowed women are employed, and this number has been declining over the past few decades. The reasons for women's increasing participation rates include their wish for a decent job and good family care; and/or financial necessity, especially if the man is unemployed or the woman is separated, divorced, or unmarried with children. The general public's expectation today is that women can and should work – indeed, the welfare reforms enacted by many provincial governments seek to cajole and coerce single mothers on social assistance into obtaining work.

In Canada since the late 1980s, the unemployment rate for women has been somewhat lower than the rate for men. In 2009, for example, the unemployment rate for men was 9.4 per cent while for women it was 7.0 per cent. Interestingly, the unemployment rate for women born in Canada was 6.3 per cent; for immigrant women it was 9.6 per cent; and for Aboriginal women it was 12.7 per cent (Ferrao 2010). Over the past thirty-five years or so, the employment rate for women has risen while the rate for men has declined. Between 1976 and 2009, the employment of women in the labour force rose from 42 to 58 per cent; for men, it declined from 73 to 65 per cent. Despite these long-term trends, women are still less likely to be employed than men.

For many years now, most part-time jobs in Canada have been held by women. In 2009, women accounted for 68 per cent of all part-time employment: 2.2 million women. Also in 2009, 27 per cent of employed women worked part-time – that is, less than thirty hours a week – compared to only 12 per cent of employed men. Significant growth in part-time employment has occurred in accommodation and food services, in personal services such as cleaning, and in the retail trade. Many men and women "choose" to work part-time for family reasons or other considerations, but a sizeable minority, one in three, do so involuntarily because they cannot secure full-time employment. Working part-time can help people juggle family responsibilities and work demands, but the trade-off often is lower earnings, weaker job security, and fewer occupational benefits.

From the Kitchen Table to the Boardroom Table (Lochhead 1997) is a useful examination of the costs of raising and caring for children, and of the pressures on families to manage the often competing demands of home and paid work. The report's title inadvertently suggests that women have left the home and housework (the kitchen table) and entered the upper echelons of corporations and government agencies (the boardroom table). As we have seen, comparatively few women are in executive positions in either the business or the public sector. Significant occupational segregation endures in the economy, with substantial wage gaps between men's and women's work.

At the start of the 2010s, most employed women are still in occupations that historically have been female jobs. Men still dominate managerial

Table 9.1. The Gender Wage Gap: Female-to-Male Hourly Wage Ratio and Gap, Selected Years, 1988 to 2008

Year	Percentage ratio	Percentage gap
1988	75.7 ·	24.3
1993	79.4	20.6
1998	81.1	18.9
2003	82.5	17.5
2008	83.3	16.7

Source: Drolet (2011).
Note: Hourly wages expressed in 2007 dollars. Wages refer to salaries and other usual earnings before taxes, as well as to bonuses, commissions, and tips.

positions; women are overrepresented in clerical and administrative roles. In 2009, 67 per cent of all employed women, compared to just 31 per cent of employed men, were employed in secretarial, clerical, or sales positions, or in teaching, nursing, and related health occupations such as physiotherapy (Ferrao 2010, 21). Far more women than men work as dental hygienists, nutritionists, social workers, elementary and secondary school teachers, and child and youth care workers. Men predominate as dentists, engineers, physicians, community college instructors, university professors, senior executives, judges, and cabinet ministers. Several other traditionally male-concentrated sectors remain so: construction, manufacturing, mining, forestry, fisheries, and politics. Some fields are changing, such as law, medicine, and accounting; others, such as sales and personal services, are more or less balanced between men and women. This pattern of employment segregation has ramifications for earning levels, poverty, and occupational benefits.

For years, statistics have shown that the average earnings of women in the paid labour force are significantly lower than the average earnings of men. As Table 9.1 shows, the gender wage gap has been narrowing over the past twenty years, but progress is slow. The persistence of this earnings disparity is evident at all levels of educational attainment. A number of factors influence this gap; among these, sexual discrimination is certainly an important one (MacIvor 1996). In 1995, women employed on a full-time, full-year basis earned 73 per cent of what men did. This progress hides the fact that in recent years, on average, men's earnings have not been keeping up with the cost of living.

Women generally have lower incomes than men because of occupational segregation, the wage gap, and the unpaid nature of providing care to family members. In 1993 the average annual pre-tax income of women from all sources was $16,500 – that is, 58 per cent of the $28,600 for men. Women comprise more than half (56 per cent in 1993) of all persons living below Statistics Canada's low-income cut-off measures, which are commonly referred to as poverty lines by the mass media and the social policy community. These lines refer to people who are substantially worse off than people with average incomes. Women also have a higher incidence of low income than men do. In 1995 the poverty rate for women was 18.2 per cent of the female population compared to 14.3 per cent for men. The incidence is even higher among certain groups of women: 57.2 per cent of single mothers, 43.4 per cent of elderly women living on their own, and 38.7 per cent for unattached women under age sixty-five (National Council of Welfare 1997, 85). The "feminization of poverty" is not a new social problem. Unfortunately, it has been a systemic feature of the society, the economy, and the welfare state in Canada, and it has been deepening (Wallis and Kwok 2008).

Occupational Welfare

Workplace benefits such as dental, medical, and paid leave are often overlooked and unexamined parts of social policy. Yet occupational welfare – the provision by employers of a range of services and benefits to employees – is a significant feature of the Canadian social security system, coexisting with public provisions. Although they are often regarded as private transactions between a union and management, or between an employer and a group of employees, occupational benefits represent an important source of support and financial assistance. These benefits supplement public programs or are substitutes for the lack of public programs. "The value of occupational welfare is magnified by the fact that it generally avoids [or minimizes] the level of taxation that is levied on ordinary earnings" (Bryson 1992, 132).

The status of a person's employment is a pivotal determinant of whether they receive occupational benefits. There are major differences between full-time and part-time workers in receiving dental, medical, or pension plans, or paid sick leave, among other benefits. Full-time workers are far better provided for than part-time workers. Two to four times as many full-time workers as part-timers in the Canadian labour force have these benefits. In this sense, there is a dual system of occupational welfare. Even among full-time workers, 30 to 40 per cent do not have one or more of these benefits. The availability of such benefits varies by sector (i.e., public or private) and with type of industry, size of the employing organization, and unionization. Consider unionization rates, for example. In 1976, 22 per cent of women in the Canadian labour force were in unionized jobs, compared to 39 per cent of men. By 2009, the unionization rates between men and women had changed significantly: 33 per cent of women were now in unionized jobs while only 30 per cent of men were in unionized employment. Regarding self-employment – another dimension of work with implications for occupational welfare – in recent years, women have represented about 35 per cent of all self-employed workers. Men are more likely to be self-employed, and thus without access to various workplace benefits, than are women (Ferrao 2010).

For full-time workers, there is not a high degree of gender differentiation in entitlement to these four kinds of benefits. Of course, this says nothing about the level of benefits actually provided to male and female employees. In view of the wage gap and occupational segregation, earnings-related benefits result in lower benefit amounts received by women. Put another way, inequalities in wages are reproduced in workplace pension plans. As successive federal governments have cut back and restrained public pensions such as Old Age Security, greater reliance is being placed on occupational pension plans. This, in turn, has contributed to benefit disparities between men and women. Among the retired population in 1993, 92 per cent of men were claiming Canada or Quebec Pension Plan benefits compared to 73 per cent of women, and 58 per cent of retired men had income from a registered pension plan compared to just 37 per cent of women.

For part-time workers, gender differentiation is detectable. Less than 10 per cent of male part-time workers and about 21 per cent of female part-time workers receive these occupational benefits. At first glance it appears that women are, relatively, far better off than men. Recall, however, that 70 per cent of all part-time workers are women. This means that the proportion of female part-time workers covered by the benefits (33 per cent) is lower than the proportion of male part-time workers covered (38 per cent). About three-quarters of all part-time workers remain in services, clerical, sales, and blue-collar jobs. For the most part, these jobs have low wage rates, little security, and few workplace benefits.

Politics and Government

A gender dualism also exists in Canadian politics and government. Political scientist Heather MacIvor (1996, 227) has observed that "women
participate equally with men at the mass level of politics, but they are
dramatically under-represented at the elite level of politics: Women
and men are both as apt to vote, attend political meetings, or work for a
party and candidate. Men are more likely to take part in the governance
of political parties, participate in trade unions and institutionalized
pressure groups, and run for and hold public office. Within the mainstream political party structures, 'men make policy, women make cof-
fee'" (1996, 253). Women engage more than men do in alternative and
grassroots political organizations such as protest actions, neighbourhood groups and community agencies, and new social movements.

Polling data over the years indicate a divergence in beliefs between
men and women on a range of topics and policy issues. Women are
generally more supportive of social policy initiatives than men are
(McCormack 1991). In the late 1990s, public opinion surveys revealed
significant differences by gender as to what the federal government
should do with any budgetary surpluses (Prince 1998b). While a similar
proportion of men and women supported cutting taxes, more women
thought that the goods and services tax should be cut first, while more
men thought that cuts should be made to personal income taxes. Men
are far more likely than women to call for debt reduction. Conversely,
more women believe that Ottawa should spend more on government
programs, particularly for education, health care, child care, and alleviating poverty. Furthermore, more women contend that the federal government went too far in cutting benefits and services. These instances of
a gender gap in public opinion no doubt are linked to women's greater
reliance on public services, fiscal transfers, and social protection, and
thus to their greater vulnerability to cutbacks. With the return of federal budget deficits since 2008, gender differences are again apparent
regarding how governments ought to manage financial deficits. "Wom-
en's greater dependency on the state," Jill Vickers (1994, 137) has noted,
"is not an essential or inevitable relationship. Rather it reflects women's
current unequal social, political, and economic situation."

MacIvor (1996, 245) indicts Canada's political system as "sexist, exclusionary, and geared towards people without constant and pressing family responsibilities." Canadian federalism is also a hindrance
to efforts by the women's movement to achieve equity and equality:

"For women's groups the costs in human and other resources to be effective at all three levels [of government] [are] extremely demanding
given women's greater family responsibilities and smaller economic
resources" (Vickers 1994, 142). As a constitutional form of governing,
federalism recognizes and structurally empowers territorial-based interests and issues over others such as gender and social class. The in-
tricate system of intergovernmental fiscal arrangements in Canadian
federalism obscures which level is responsible for which issues and
policies, making it harder for groups to advocate constructively for reforms. Executive federalism – the arena of usually closed conferences
and meetings among cabinet ministers and senior officials across the
levels of government – substantially omits women, even though executive federalism depends on women to maintain the homes and communities of the men who sit in the conferences.

Over the past twenty-five years, women have made noteworthy
progress in increasing their representation in government institutions.
Up to and including the 1980 federal election, women comprised no
more than 5 per cent of Members of Parliament. Since then, the proportion of women MPs has grown steadily: 10 per cent in the 1984 election; 14 per cent in 1988; 18 per cent in 1993; and 20 per cent in 1997. In
the 2000, 2004, 2006, and 2008 general federal elections, the proportion
of women MPs stayed at 21 to 22 per cent. In the 2011 election, sev-
enty-six women won a seat in Parliament (24.6 per cent of seats). The
current share of women MPs is a record for the Canadian Parliament:
though less than women's representation in the national legislatures of
the Nordic countries, it is more than in Australia, Britain, France, and
the United States, among other nations. Women now comprise about 22
per cent of Canada's federal cabinet and about 27 per cent of its senate.
Between 1976 and 1994, women's share of provincial legislative seats in
the ten provinces rose from less than 4 per cent to 18 per cent, and their
representation in provincial cabinet positions rose from 4 per cent to 21
per cent (Studlar and Moncrief 1997).

Women no longer have token spots in Canadian cabinets, but rather
a tangible share of the portfolios (Trimble and Tremblay 2005). In recent
years (e.g., 2007–2012), the cabinets of the Jean Charest Liberal government in Quebec have included an equal number of men and women
as ministers. In the NDP government of Ontario from 1990 to 1995,
women were 42 per cent of the cabinet – double the previous high. In a
case study of this NDP cabinet, based on interviews and documentary
research, Lesley Hyland Byrne (1997, 601) found that this historically

high share of women in power did make a difference to institutional reforms and policy outcomes in the Ontario government. Byrne also found, however, "that those transformations were not as dramatic as the feminist progressive components might project nor as extensive as the women's movement had hoped." Byrne concluded that in terms of deconstructing "hierarchical gender-based power," the overall impact of these female cabinet ministers was "extremely limited" (1997, 611).

Women cabinet ministers in Canada are concentrated in social policy departments, in what some might consider "feminine portfolios." Typically, women head departments of health, welfare, education, family, culture, and recreation. They infrequently oversee "masculine portfolios" such as agriculture, industry, finance, natural resources, and transportation. A similar pattern is discernible in the membership of parliamentary committees (MacIvor 1996, 280–4). In municipal politics, women are also substantially underrepresented. A study of Quebec urban governments, for example, found that women had made some gains, increasing their presence on municipal councils from 11 per cent of all councillors in 1985 to 21 per cent in 1995 (Gidengil and Vengrof 1997). The same study found that many municipal councils had no women members at all. Another study reports that in 1996, women held 25 per cent of council seats in the eight major cities in Canada: Halifax, Montreal, Ottawa, Toronto, Winnipeg, Edmonton, Calgary, and Vancouver (Graham, Phillips, and Maslove 1998). There is a distance to go before federal, provincial, and local political institutions reflect fully the Canadian electorate, including women's participation in political parties, legislatures, and cabinets (Young 2009).

Women, Men, and the Canadian Welfare State

In a comparative analysis of gender relations and welfare states, Ann Shola Orloff (1993) has concluded that the social provisions offered by the state not only affect women's material circumstances but also shape gender relationships and contribute to the mobilization of identities; they may also offer political resources to women. In a feminist perspective on the caring work done by women, Carol Baines, Patricia Evans, and Sheila Neysmith (1991, 26) have observed that "women's relationship to the welfare state is an ambivalent one. It is the source of both protection and control." Women's relationship to the welfare state is a constellation of roles and interests: women are citizens, activists and advocates, workers, clients and consumers, non-clients, taxpayers, informal caregivers, formal volunteers, and grassroots service providers.

Citizens

Over the twentieth century, Canadian women fought hard for and eventually obtained a cluster of political, civil, and social rights of citizenship. For much of the century, women were excluded from full citizenship, illustrating that this has not always been a gender-neutral ideal. Today, women have the right to vote and seek office, to receive equal treatment before and under the law, and to access a range of economic and social security programs. In these times of state and economic restructuring, the Canadian women's movement finds itself defending existing rights of social citizenship and seeking to develop new rights dealing with matters such as multiculturalism, reproductive technologies, and the rights of same-sex couples (Briskin and Eliasson 1999; Newman and White 2006; Rankin and Vickers 2001; Rayside 2008). Feminist writers are rethinking the concept of citizenship to see if and how it might be squared with the diversity and equality discourses examined in chapter 8.

Activists and Advocates

In groups outside state structures and in occupational groups within those structures, women have long advocated social policy measures. Women activists and their organizations were crucial to the development of social programs and welfare agencies in the reform era from the 1880s to the 1920s: "Child Care, Mothers Pensions, the Kindergarten Associations, the Home and School Associations, reforms for juvenile delinquents and, of course, temperance campaigns – all can be seen, at least in part, as women's issues. They were women's issues because women were seen as particularly affected by the problems but also because women had been involved in the solutions. Furthermore, it was women that were pressing for change" (Andrew 1984, 673).

In modern politics, women's groups form coalitions, appear before parliamentary committees and cabinet ministers, interact with bureaucrats and the media, and intervene before tribunals and the courts in Charter of Rights and Freedoms cases. Besides participating in political parties and unions, women are deeply involved in community groups, other local agencies, and national and international coalitions, all seen as worthwhile sites for collaborative action (Dobrowolsky 2009; Rebick 2005). An important stream of contemporary feminist writing in Canada sets out proposals, agendas, and strategies for public policy reforms and progressive social changes (Braedley and Luxton 2010; Brodie and Bakker 2007, 2008; Hankivsky 2004; Vosko 2006). Reform ideas include gendering governance arrangements; fostering shifts in public values; offering new ways of understanding social risks and relationships; and tackling precarious and exploitive labour market conditions whether in the public or the private sector.

Workers in the Welfare State

For women, the welfare state has been an important source of employment, unionization, and relatively good benefits. Regarding women as state employees, Andrew (1984, 678) has pointed out that "women play a very major role as workers in the welfare state but their power is limited. They provide many of the front-line direct services but they do not determine the form of these services. They care for the clients of the welfare state but they have little influence on the direction of the welfare state." While on one level we agree with Andrew's observation, on another it narrowly conceptualizes the welfare state as its policies, failing to treat seriously its practices (McKenzie and Wharf 2010). We believe that what gets done is often determined by what women continue to do *despite* budget cuts to welfare programs; and that as welfare state employees and as volunteers and informal caregivers, women do influence the direction of the welfare state.

Clients and Consumers of the Welfare State

For many social programs and services, women are the primary clients. Prominent examples include anti-stalking laws, social assistance, old age pensions, maintenance enforcement programs, day care subsidies, and social housing. Linda Gordon (1990, 15) has written that as consumers of welfare, "women continue to do the work of consuming welfare, always vastly underestimated – waiting in lines, making phone calls, processing applications, scrimping when checks are late, begging help and favours when checks are inadequate, etc." Under the male breadwinner model of social policy, women were defined as clients in a dependent relationship to a man in their role as mother, wife, widow, victim of male violence, and so forth. As women have entered the labour market in greater numbers over the past thirty-five years, they have become eligible as clients of Employment Insurance (EI), Workers' Compensation, and other benefits on the basis of being paid workers (Bashevkin 2002; Cohen and Pulkingham 2009; O'Connor, Orloff, and Shaver 1999).

Non-Clients

Inaction and non–decision making by governments and state agencies, as well as by other economic and social structures, do a great deal to establish the scope and quality of women's relationships to the welfare state. When governments choose to not intervene, to not extend a right or enforce a law, or to not grant a benefit or provide a service, they produce non-clients. Out of the denial of benefits or the non-recognition of needs arise struggles and experiences of marginalization of women and men alike. "The absence of policy has also threatened women's interests, the dearest example being the refusal of police authorities to intervene in cases of wife battering" (MacIvor 1996, 311). Such inactions reinforce existing institutional rules, practices, and values. The status of non-client therefore reflects the presence of laws and norms in regulating the lives of women and men. Those laws and norms serve as the vehicles whereby authorities define identities as deserving or non-deserving, deny eligibility, and thus delimit the meaning of citizenship. These inactions contribute to the residualization of social care and provision; that is, public assistance becomes a last resort. State inaction amounts to an expectation that key human needs ought to be met somehow by family members, the kindness of friends, the compassion of charities, or the calculations of private markets. Inaction and non–decision making by governments and state agencies also thwart the efforts of individuals and groups to make claims, improve their lives, and promote social change (Dossa 2009; Gavigan and Chunn 2010).

Taxpayers

Because their numbers in the labour force are increasing, more and more women are paying personal income taxes and payroll taxes for EI and the Canada/Quebec Pension Plans (C/QPP). If they are running a business, as more women are, they pay corporate income taxes and federal and provincial retail sales taxes. As major clients of public services, women also pay user fees or charges. Until recently, divorced parents receiving child support payments and alimony, overwhelmingly women, were required to declare those payments as taxable income. Over 60 per cent of two-parent families today are dual-earner households. Women's income is critical for paying the bills and taxes, including property and school taxes. Despite what many Canadians may assume, women in poverty pay taxes, whether they are on welfare or are working.

Informal Volunteers

Women are the principal caregivers within families and other networks of personal relationships; this entails both caring for and caring about the emotional, physical, mental, and spiritual needs of others. Baines, Evans, and Neysmith (1991, 13) state that "the welfare state has served as a powerful reinforcer of women's caring" by emphasizing, through a familial ideology, the importance of women providing care to children, the sick, the elderly, and the terminally ill. In these settings, social policy is informed by a gendered ethic of care as well as by the interplay of neoliberalism and everyday life (Braedley and Luxton 2010; Hankivsky 2004; Kershaw 2005). The concepts of social reproduction and social provisioning, discussed earlier in this chapter, clearly emphasize the multiple kinds of work that women undertake in the informal economy and the domestic sphere as well as in civil society structures.

Formal Volunteers

Women's activities as volunteers and charity workers have a long history in Canadian health and social services. The voluntary sector is closely linked to the modern social security system. As volunteers, women extend companionship, offer supports to people who need assistance, and offer a voice for their cause. They also raise funds for local agencies and projects that help strengthen communities (Rice 1995a). As the state withdraws from providing support through social policies, it shifts additional burdens of caring for others onto women. While women are only slightly more likely than men to volunteer, as we discuss in chapter 10, a gendered division of roles and responsibilities tends to prevail in the voluntary sector.

Grassroots Service Providers

Outside the welfare state and the conventional voluntary sector, many women are engaged in providing services, raising consciousness, and offering mutual aid through collectives, women's shelters, rape crisis centres, and alternative bookstores and cafés. "Many grassroots groups do not choose to engage directly with the state; they do not believe that a patriarchal state can really help women, or reject the hierarchy and bureaucracy that characterize state organization" (MacIvor 1996, 332). For feminists, politics is far more than government and public administration.

The mainstream literature's discussion of women's relations with the welfare state – as clients, caregivers, and volunteers – has tended to portray women as relatively powerless. The role of women as policy advocates, taxpayers, citizens, and state employees has often been downplayed or ignored. Yet these roles represent women as active agents of change with some independent command over economic resources. These various roles encompass different kinds of claims and issues, and all are worth noting in order to appreciate the ambivalent association between women and the welfare state.

Women's and Men's Experiences with Social Programs

In delineating the significant and persistent extent to which women and men differ in their connections with the welfare state, we examine five social policy areas: health care, education, income support, the criminal justice and legal systems, and the tax system.

Health Care

Front-line health care in Canada is provided by women in the so-called private domain of everyday family life. With respect to the formal health care system, women are slightly more likely than men are to be in contact with the system at least once in a year. Women are more likely than men to visit a physician, and they do so more frequently; they are also more likely than men to consult with a wider range of conventional medical personnel and alternative health care providers. Also, women are more likely to be hospitalized, in large part because of pregnancies, childbirth, and care needs in later life. Women, more often than men, are diagnosed with mental disorders (and with different mental illnesses), and they are more likely to be hospitalized in psychiatric institutions. Women also seem to experience contested illnesses more than men do – that is, with illnesses that Pamela Moss and Katherine Teghtsoonian (2008, 7) describe as "dismissed as illegitimate – framed as difficult, psychosomatic, or even non-existent – by health researchers, practitioners, and policy makers operating within conventional paradigms of knowledge." Contested illnesses include anorexia nervosa, chronic fatigue syndrome, and workplace depression. The two leading causes of death for both men and women are cancer and heart disease, and these can also be experiences of contestation between patients and professionals. For men, lung cancer is more common; for women, it is breast cancer.

Education

Since the 1990s, women had made up the majority of full-time and part-time students in Canadian community colleges and universities, and across most faculties. As Table 9.2 shows, over the past four decades, women have overtaken men in university attendance. They also outnumber men two to one in education and health-related programs. The percentage of women and men with university degrees rose from 3 and 7 per cent, respectively, in 1971, to 10 and 13 per cent in 1991. As of 1993, around 205,000 women and 165,000 men worked full time as teachers, instructors, or professors in the education system.

Indeed, for twenty years now, most students at Canadian universities have been female. Likewise, the majority of community college enrollees in Canada are women. At the elementary and secondary-school levels, teaching remains a female-dominated profession (60 per cent of all full-time educators). In 2004–5, 53 per cent of elementary school principals were female while 68 per cent of secondary school principals were male. At the community college level, and especially at the university level, men prevail, particularly at the higher levels. In 2004–5, men accounted for 68 per cent of all full-time teaching positions in Canadian universities.

Income Support

The Canadian income security system is a network of federal, provincial/territorial, First Nation, and municipal programs. That system provides direct financial benefits to individuals and families. Major programs include seniors benefits, public pensions, EI, workers' compensation, veterans' benefits, social assistance, and various tax credits. To this list can be added labour market policies dealing with minimum wages, equal pay, and employment equity. Compared to men, women receive a larger part of their total income from income security programs. For

Table 9.2. University Students in Canada by Sex, 1971–2006

Year	Male percentage	Female percentage
1971	68	32
1981	54	46
1991	49	51
2001	42	58
2006	40	60

Source: Statistics Canada, Cat. no. 81–0040XIE (2008).

men aged fifteen to sixty-four, 8 per cent of their total incomes in 1993 were from government income programs, while for women it was 13 per cent. For men over sixty-five, 47 per cent of their income was from government benefits; for senior women, it was 62 per cent. The differences are even more striking by family types. For two-parent families with children, 9 per cent of their income came from government income benefits in 1993, compared to 19 per cent for single-father families and 37 per cent for single-mother families.

Women rely on certain income security programs more than men do – especially on social assistance programs, which are the provincial/territorial and municipal welfare programs of last resort. These programs are marked by social stigma, inadequate benefits, and the administrative control of clients. There are many reasons why women are overrepresented in poverty and welfare programs. Women receive low wages and lower earnings in the paid labour force. They are employed in non-standard jobs and are underemployed in part-time work. Quality child care is expensive or unavailable. The work and caring provided by women in the family and the community is unpaid. Moreover, low-paid workers, both men and women, receive little if anything from the more lucrative and stigma-free workplace benefits and tax advantages.

Senior women are less likely than are senior men to have income from private pension plans, Registered Retirement Savings Plans, or the C/QPP. When they do have such income, women receive smaller average amounts than men because of lower labour force participation, lower earnings, and lower coverage by workplace plans. The C/QPP illustrates how assumptions about women as dependants are embedded in the social security system. For the first decade or so they were in effect (1966–77), neither public pension plan allowed pension credits earned during a marriage to be split in the event of a divorce or a marriage annulment. Not until 1980 was employment of a spouse in an unincorporated family business considered pensionable employment. The QPP in 1984 and the CPP in 1987 removed a provision that survivors' benefits ceased on remarriage. In addition, in 1987 the CPP – and two years later the QPP – extended the pension-splitting provision to include common law spouses and separated partners.

Under EI, women are almost exclusively the recipients of maternity and parental benefits; they are also the main users of its adoption, compassionate care, and sickness benefits. By contrast, women obtain 40 per cent or less of training, job creation, work sharing, and self-employment assistance benefits (as well as fisher benefits) under EI. The most common benefit for men and women who receive EI is the regular benefit. As a percentage of total EI beneficiaries, women have fluctuated between 40 and 45 per cent. Over the past twenty years, from the welfare state crisis period to the present restructuring era, women have more often than not had slightly higher levels of unemployment than men. Specific groups – Aboriginal women, women with disabilities, and visible minority women – still consistently have significantly higher levels of unemployment than men or women (Ferrao 2010).

Over the past decade, many income support reforms in social policy have entailed tax measures that depend on recipients having enough income that it is taxable to access these measures. As Janine Brodie and Isabella Bakker (2007, viii–ix) demonstrate, income benefits delivered through the tax system "do not benefit low income women since they generally do not have enough taxable income or tax liability to claim deductions, exemptions or credits. Family-directed tax expenditures, such as the Canadian Child Tax Benefit also assume that the primary breadwinner shares financial gains equally within the family, an assumption that ignores many micro studies on intra-household financial inequities."

Criminal Justice

Women and men have different experiences with the criminal justice system, legal aid, and the administration of law and order in Canada. In general, these are considered "masculine" areas of the state. In 1993 men accounted for 89 per cent of violent offenders, 83 per cent of people charged with criminal offences, and 76 per cent of adults charged with property crimes. Most drug offenders and young offenders are male. Most charges (80 per cent) against women are for minor offences. Men represent 97 per cent of all federal prisoners and 92 per cent of provincial prisoners. On the law enforcement side, a similar gendered pattern is evident: men account for about 90 per cent of police officers, 80 per cent of judges and magistrates, and 65 per cent of lawyers in Canada. However, women's share of employment in all three of these fields is continuing to grow.

While men and women are about equally likely to be victims of crime, four times as many women as men (42 per cent versus 10 per cent) worry about their personal safety. Fewer women than men are victims of homicide, but women are far more likely to be the victims of a sexual assault, and more likely by a man they know than by a stranger. Men tend to be assaulted by strangers (Statistics Canada 1995a). The National Council of Welfare (1995, 10) has pointed out that "the vast majority of criminal legal aid clients are men, while most of the beneficiaries of civil legal aid are women." Women resort to legal aid for advice on family law, welfare rights and wrongs, and landlord–tenant issues. "Single-parent mothers, and some women who still live with their husbands, need legal assistance for family matters such as separation and divorce, division of matrimonial property, child custody, and access and support payments. Some also have legal questions related to their roles as mothers, such as problems with child welfare authorities or the need to have a child's paternity legally recognized" (National Council of Welfare 1995, 12). With respect to court decisions on the custody of children involved in a divorce, in about three-quarters of cases mothers get sole custody. Over the last generation, the number of joint custodies has increased and the number of sole custodies by women and men has declined. However, "although women are usually awarded custody, few are given adequate financial resources to look after their children" (MacIvor 1996, 131).

The Tax System

Kathleen Lahey reports that "women in Canada are overtaxed, relative to men" (cited in Cassin 1993, 108). Lahey found that women paid 46 per cent of their income as taxes, while men paid only 30 per cent. Furthermore, while women had 32 per cent of all pre-tax incomes, they received only 27 per cent of all after-tax income. The overall system of taxation actually diminished women's incomes and increased men's

total share of incomes. In their analysis of how to design a more equitable tax system, the Ontario Fair Tax Commission (1993, 28) concluded
that "the impact of the tax system on women is different from its impact on men. This differential impact is not the result of any explicit
discrimination against women in the Income Tax Act. Nothing in the
letter of the law singles out either men or women for special treatment.
The income tax has differential impacts on women because of the way
provisions interact with differences in the economic position of women
and men in society." The commission noted that women have lower
earnings and lower incomes than men do and are thus more likely to
be poor. On the basis of these facts, the commission noted two effects:
"Women are less able to take advantage of subsidies delivered through
the tax system. Moreover, even when they are able to take advantage
of these provisions, women derive less benefit from them. Second, because women on average earn less than men earn, elements of the income tax that affect the economic relationships between people, and
that are technically gender neutral, are not neutral in their outcomes"
(1993, 28).

Since women have less wealth than men do, Lisa Phillips writes, "income as a proxy for ability to pay therefore obscures the full nature
and extent of gender bias in the tax system" (cited in Bakker 1996, 41).
With women constituting a majority of the poor, consumption taxes
such as sales taxes, property taxes, user fees, and even lottery revenues
are regressive forms of taxation that take disproportionately more from
people with low incomes than from people with middle and higher incomes. The absence of an estate or inheritance tax in Canada results in
preferential treatment for the accumulation of wealth and its intergenerational transfer. The lack of a wealth tax also means that governments
must rely heavily on personal income taxes and on sales taxes as revenue sources. From a gender-sensitive perspective, not having a wealth
tax in the tax policy mix favours men and promotes the idea that families are a private domain separate from the public sphere.

Conclusions

Gender has become an increasingly explicit part of welfare state politics
and social policy analysis in recent decades. However, as a gender regime – or, more accurately, in the Canadian context of federal and provincial states, a series of regimes – social policy is a mixed blessing for

women. On the one hand, the welfare state offers women benefits, jobs, and some supportive laws and services; on the other, it imposes controls, perpetuates stereotypes, and reinforces dependencies. Some notable progress has been made in gaining access to the political process, yet women remain a small portion of legislators and cabinet ministers. The welfare state does offer women, and men, resources and places for meeting needs and for engaging in acts of politics and citizenship. Many, if not most, feminists still regard the public domain, despite its contradictions and gendered features, as the sector with the most potential for women to achieve equality, equity, and diversity.

There has been important legislation regarding human rights, employment equity, and pay equity; the number of women's shelters has grown; laws against sexual harassment have been passed; and the Criminal Code provisions relating to sexual offences have been strengthened. Unfinished business includes the combating of violence against women and the strengthening of women's participation in politics.

For the Canadian women's movement and allied groups, the changing politics mean continuing to struggle for gender equality, responding to a backlash against feminism, and defending imperfect social programs and rights against welfare state restructuring. As we have argued at various points in this book, restructuring goes well beyond restraint – it is altering gender relations and the political landscape. Brodie (1995, 10) has argued that rolling back the state is "eroding the very political identities and public spaces that empowered postwar Canadian feminism." In light of women's roles as caregivers, volunteers, welfare state employees, and clients, cutbacks to public-sector services and programs fall disproportionately on women (McCormack 1991; Bryson 1992). Even before the present era of restructuring, Elizabeth Wilson (1977, 171) noted the effect of cutbacks on women in the private sphere: "Hospital patients prematurely returned home to convalesce, elderly patients denied meals on wheels or home helps, children on half-time schooling, unemployed husbands for that matter, all require more attention from Mother." In the public sphere, the downsizing and contracting out of work is threatening those education, health, and social service fields that have advanced women's earnings and their access to occupational and tax benefits. Given that women are the majority of those on welfare in Canada, cuts to social assistance are cuts to women. In the community sphere, as we noted in chapter 4, when governments talk of home care as an alternative to institutional care, they really mean more work by women. Likewise, when governments speak of community care and moving heretofore institutionalized residents into the community, it effectively means that additional burdens of care are placed on women. There is no such thing as gender-neutral restructuring.

10 Civil Society, Social Economy, and the Voluntary Sector: Links between Community Capacities and Social Policy

A key aspect of social policy concerns the relations among the Canadian state and civil society, the social economy, and the voluntary sector in terms of expressing values, providing services, and developing programs. The politics of social policy continue to look towards the community as a resource for both addressing and solving social problems. Academics, policy makers, and practitioners are trying to determine how to design social policies that encourage communities to use their local abilities and resources to solve local problems. Many people contribute to the community by volunteering in not-for-profit organizations. They provide leadership to hospitals, universities, and arts councils. They operate local homes for the elderly as well as group homes or social housing for those in need of support. As donors of money to charitable organizations, as formal volunteers working through not-for-profit agencies, as informal helpers assisting others directly, and as members of informal social networks, Canadians contribute to social cohesion, community capacity, personal development, civic engagement, and social capital. Canadians do so when taking care of the sick, shopping for people who cannot get out of the house, mowing lawns, babysitting, or looking after other people's pets. Some volunteers organize political rallies, unions, or protest groups. Others clean up the environment, debate where a road, a quarry, or a dump should be located, or fight for social justice and human rights. Many are contributing financially to causes and agencies in which they believe and possibly have some connection. The more volunteers give, the more social capital they produce, and the more "civil" the community becomes. While there is not an untapped reservoir of resources in the community, and while many communities are fragile because they face difficult problems and have limited resources, there may be room for optimism – although even that assessment is debatable.

This chapter makes the case that social policies can and must encourage people in the community to come together to identify common problems, develop local solutions, and allocate resources to address problems. Also, these processes must be opened up so that they include diverse participants in community development. We begin with a discussion of the important concepts in the literature and go on to discuss the need for the state to create supports if communities are to develop the capacity to solve some of their problems.

We then examine the local conditions *within* communities that affect the development of community capacity. Here we argue that the beliefs held by members of a community about community involvement, the structure of the community, and the resources in the community shape the ability of its members to solve problems. We also touch on the darker side of community: how communities can exclude some people and provide benefits that do not meet the needs of all. We next turn our attention to the steps that community organizers can take to develop local capacity; these include locality development, social planning, and social reform. Finally, we look at community capacity in action by examining the volunteer activities of women, men, and the elderly.

Taking Stock of Key Concepts

While all the concepts in the community capacity literature stress the role of the locality in developing community capacity, these concepts are also vague. The terminology contains what can be a bewildering number of expressions: community economic development corporations; civil society organizations; non-governmental organizations; not-for-profits; the social economy sector and social enterprises; and the "third sector," that is, voluntary sector organizations. In current discourse, these concepts remain somewhat ambiguous because they are emergent and are still being contested. In concert, when exercised in practice, the terms can have conflicting aims and contentious effects. Civic engagement, for instance, is not only about meeting needs, promoting local economic development, and delivering services, but also about questioning consumerism, challenging status quo policies, and mobilizing for shifts in power arrangements.

Thus there has been an ongoing debate, which cycles up and down the public agenda, regarding the respective roles and responsibilities of governments and not-for-profits in identifying economic and social issues and addressing specific consequences. This question is often asked: What is the place of charity and philanthropy today as responses to the needs and rights of people and communities? The very concept of the voluntary sector is problematic, because it is always shaped by governing political parties, at times with similar rhetoric though with contrary motives; because there are different ideological perspectives on the nature of society, the state, and citizenship; and because of wider contextual developments in cultural pluralization and market globalization.

To illustrate all of this, consider the idea of promoting social enterprise as a public policy strategy. In the current age, what does social economy mean for the contracting out of public services and the marketization of the voluntary sector? What are the possibilities for training and employment opportunities for individuals and social groups that have long been marginalized in the labour force? How far can an entrepreneurial approach alleviate worries by countless not-for-profit organizations regarding resource sustainability? And what are the implications of such a strategy for the advocacy and related democratic work of grassroots community groups? Luc Thériault suggests that the relationship between governments and social economy organizations is mutually reliant: "The social services of provincial governments are often strongly embedded into agreements with social economy organizations. This has created a co-dependency to a large extent. While many social economy organizations are dependent upon government funding (through various departments and agencies), it is also true that the social service mission of the state can hardly be accomplished today without the contributions of social economy organizations" (Thériault 2009, 77). We agree that the relationship interconnects, but we would add that the power relations between governments and social economy organizations are far from evenly balanced.

We have identified five concepts used in the social science literature in general and the social policy literature in particular to describe and analyse the nature of community: civil society, social economy, civic engagement, social capital and cohesion, and community capacity.

Civil Society

As Table 10.1 shows, various definitions of civil society are evident in the literature: those based on normative views of the goals of civil society; those based on an institutional and organizational analysis; and those that apply a behavioural interpretation.

Prime Minister Jean Chrétien, in a speech to a world conference on volunteerism, stated that "as a country, we have always honoured and admired the work of the volunteer sector. But, to be honest, we have not known how to harness your energy and creativity. Governments have looked upon your sector as first and foremost a preserve of high ideals and noble intentions. Not as a valuable source of insight and experience" (Chrétien 1998, 1–2). In his principal study of the social economy in Canada, Jack Quarter remarked that "the term social economy is not simply descriptive but also prescriptive. It implies a vision of social transformation" (Quarter 1992, x). That vision of a civil society infused with social enterprise includes building communities of interest, giving voice to people, providing goods and services for meeting needs, and establishing democratic forms of organization and decision making.

This normative view is also evident in Sherri Torjman's (1997b, 2) writing, in which she describes the goals and objectives of civil society: it sustains and enhances the capacity of all its members to build a caring and mutually responsible society. The underlying ideas in this definition expose its normative base. By "capacity," Torjman means the ability, resources, and willingness of people to become involved with all of their neighbours. From this perspective, civil society comprises inclusive relationships based on the notion of mutual responsibility in which people find ways to express their caring for one another. This definition goes beyond the entitlements and rights contained in welfare state policies to create a sense of reciprocity between citizens.

Eric Shragge criticizes this strand of writing on civil society as being too loose and as lacking a critical approach to understanding social policy, the state, and society. Normative conceptions of civil society, he argues, overlook patterns of divergent interests, underlying power relations, and unequal responsibilities among groups; as a consequence, the struggles for social justice of "the poor, women, and many minorities" are ignored or downplayed (Shragge 2003, 113–15).

An institutional definition of civil society draws our attention to the organizations and structures that make up society. Jamie Swift (1999), like many commentators, pictures the civil society as a space that is structurally separate from the state, the market economy, and the family, although engaged with each of these other domains through people's activities. A narrow institutional view focuses on the voluntary sector. Civil society assumes the existence of voluntary and civic

Table 10.1. Three Concepts of Civil Society and Social Cohesion

Concept	Emphasis
Normative	Societal values and goals
Institutional	Voluntary sector and other institutions
Behavioural	Civic actions and relations of cooperation and reciprocity

organizations that provide assistance to members of the community. Organizations such as the Red Cross, United Way, and service clubs are essential parts of a civil society. Wider institutional definitions include informal helping, families and kinship networks, religious institutions, political parties, and unions as parts of a civil society. These definitions usually exclude the state and the private sector. An example of this approach is that of the National Survey of Nonprofit and Voluntary Organizations, which has defined the sector as comprising organizations that are non-governmental (i.e., institutionally separate from governments); not-for-profit distributing (i.e., they do not return any profits to their owners or directors); self-governing and able to regulate their own activities; voluntary (i.e., they benefit to some degree from voluntary contributions of time or money); and formally incorporated or registered under specific provincial, territorial, or federal legislation. Consequently, unincorporated citizens' groups and grassroots coalitions were not included in this survey. Nonetheless, the survey, conducted in 2003, estimated that about 161,000 not-for-profit and voluntary organizations were part of Canadian civil society (Statistics Canada 2005).

Robert Putnam suggests a more behavioural definition of civil society. For him an active, public-spirited citizenry that is involved in community activities marks a civil society. People connect in ways that create egalitarian political relations and that enhance community members' trust and cooperation. Putnam contends that horizontal relations of reciprocity and cooperation, not vertical relations of authority and dependency (1993, 88), are what bind a civil society together. A more conservative behavioural definition views civil society as a social arrangement in which morally and economically autonomous individuals, seeking their own self-interest, come together with other individuals seeking their self-interest. The interactions of these self-regarding individuals form the basis of the civil society (Seligman 1992, 119).

A politically oriented behavioural notion of civil society emphasizes mechanisms of democratic accountability. Brad McKenzie and Brian Wharf suggest that "one of the essential attributes of civil society is the ability to hold others, including institutions, accountable for their actions. This may occur through informal actions, formal complaints, the influence of public opinion, redress through the legal system, and elections to replace them in power" (2010, 36–7). In this context, voluntary agencies are a form of community governance with links to active citizenship in public affairs and public participation in the making of social policies.

Our own theoretical approach, presented in the introductory chapter, inclines us to view civil society as encompassing all three dimensions: goals, institutions, and actions. A full understanding of the activities and potential of the civic sphere requires careful consideration of the actual values, organizational arrangements, and methods of interrelating that are taking place. We regard civil society, both historically and in the current age, as serving important roles in human and social development, including the expression and protection of a public good (Swift 1999, 147), but we do not wish to romanticize and exaggerate either its caring capacities or its level of social inclusiveness. We also perceive civil society in Canada as an organizational sector that is not detached from the state, but rather is closely linked with public-sector agencies and other institutional domains, often as a junior partner with the state and the market economy.

Social Economy

In theory and in practice, multiple types of economies exist. All of them involve producing, distributing, exchanging, and consuming goods and services. All of them also involve power dynamics and beliefs. The informal economy refers to activities unreported to governments for taxation purposes and also unregulated by the state. The underground economy (or black market) refers to transactions deemed illegal by public authorities and laws. Traditional economies in the Canadian context refer to historic ways of life and customary practices by indigenous peoples. In capitalist market economies, private interests own the means of production and distribution and are motivated for the most part by profit accumulation; whereas in socialist economies, ownership, production, and distribution – particularly for major industries – are in the hands of the state. Approaches between capitalist and socialist economies are the mixed economy. And there is the social economy.

A substantial literature exists that conceptualizes and defines the social economy in Canada, especially in Quebec, where there is a long tradition of such organizations in practice and in research (Quarter 1992; Quarter, Mook, and Armstrong 2009; Shragge and Fontan 2000; Vaillancourt and Tremblay 2002; Vaillancourt 2008; Vaillancourt and Thériault 2008). Quarter (1992, ix), for instance, calls the social economy the third sector in the mixed economy, alongside the private business sector and the state sector; for him, it includes "independent organizations created to provide a service either to the public or to a defined membership."

There is considerable diversity within the social economy; that said, many organizations in this sector share the following features:

- They are structurally located in civil society between the state and the market economy, and commonly have a relatively low public profile.
- They are grassroots and community-based.
- They have a not-for-profit orientation.
- They follow democratic or inclusive practices in decision making, informed by values of mutual respect, voluntarism, and empowerment in governance.
- Their mission is to improve community conditions, often with a focus on equity and social justice.
- Often, their clientele are marginalized groups.
- They typically face issues and challenges of capacity building (funding, staffing, space), relationships with other sectors (governments, business, foundations), leadership succession, effective mobilization.

Most likely, the biggest difference between organizations in the social economy and other organizations in the voluntary sector relates to the practices of *entrepreneurship*. Community economic development corporations, social businesses, and social firms seek to create jobs and to provide opportunities for labour skill development by members; they also produce goods and services for other kinds of customers in order to generate alternative revenue sources for their social mission. One specialist in cooperatives and other forms of social enterprise has observed that "the stereotypical non-profit in public service is for people in need (due to poverty, disability, disease) who either are unable or are not expected to pay for the service" (Quarter 1992, 62).

Why would not-for-profit organizations deliver services with commercial goals and techniques (such as user payment fees) for people in need? Is it a case of member preferences, or financial pressures, or governmental requirements, or donor expectations? How often might it be an unplanned contingency rather than a strategic choice? Disability organizations that undertake more entrepreneurial activities often do so reluctantly and cautiously rather than eagerly and quickly. Some have likely felt the push to do so from funders in government, foundations, or the private sector. And some others may well have adopted such moves on their own initiative. To be sure, discussions are needed, and more research must be done on these matters.

Civic Engagement

In a speech to the World Urban Forum, Prime Minister Stephen Harper spoke of civic participation in relation to city life: "Healthy cities have voluntary, neighbourhood-based groups at the very core of their political organization. They're variously known as community leagues or community associations. Service clubs and faith- and school-based volunteer organizations perform similar functions" (in Graham 2009, 43). The concept of civic engagement expressed here is of a particular kind: a traditional notion of voluntarism and mutual aid that emphasizes local area and place-based service activities.

Civic engagement takes place at any scale or level when people become involved in self-governing associations made up of members who understand how to organize and run these organizations (Lee 1992). Members of effective associations learn how to cooperate, manage mutual tasks, come to some agreement about goals and objectives, be respectful to one another, and maintain loyalty. Self-governing association have an effect on the community because they encourage people to take positions, debate issues, support causes, and become involved in community activities. These forms of engagement foster the pursuit of the public good at the expense of purely individual and private ends (Putnam 1993, 173–6).

Civic engagement encourages an understanding of broader public needs, an appreciation of others' interests, and an acceptance of obligations for others. Hence, the concept relates closely to the ideas of active citizenship, community involvement or voluntary action, and political participation. Measures of civic engagement can include the turnout in elections, the number of people who join self-governing organizations, the number of neighbourhood associations, and the levels of volunteering in the community. These activities often operate on the principle of equality among participants, and they assume that group members can meet their common interests through social interaction. People who belong to community associations display more political sophistication, social trust, and political participation than non-members.

Social Capital, Cohesion, and Inclusion

The concepts of social capital and social cohesion are the most abstract in this cluster of ideas. Putnam, following James Coleman's (1990) lead, defines social capital as trust that flows through social networks. Thousands of small, everyday acts contribute to the social capital of a community. Someone who helps another person cross the street, gives him or her directions, or helps fix a flat tire, is creating social capital. Putnam suggests that social capital is strongly correlated to social cohesion (or social inclusion).

Many social scientists, community activists, and government administrators are infatuated with the concept of social capital. Margaret Somers posits that theories of social capital are popular because of claims that it can "insulate society against both the coercion of states and the individualism of markets, as well as to better explain social prosperity and economic prosperity" (2005, 5). She adds, however, that "laws, citizenship rights, compulsory associations and political institutions do a much better job of the former, while large-scale civic movement[s] … are the historic keys to democratic prosperity and social confidence." Echoing Shragge's critique of normative conceptions of civil society that we earlier noted, Somers points out that Putnam's version of social capital excludes both relations of public authority and the exercise of private power in local and global markets.

Citizens build social cohesion out of the interactions of sharing, caring, and giving. These small acts build themselves into networks of social engagement and norms of reciprocity, which in turn strengthen the community's fabric. As people interact, each deed adds to the trust and respect that community members have for one another, and this in turn engenders interlocking relationships and social solidarity. Jane Jenson (1998, 38) concludes from a literature review that "the distinguishing characteristic of the concept of social cohesion is the theoretical proposition that shared values must underpin processes of social ordering."

How, in Canada today, does social capital relate to cultural pluralization? Extended and reunited families of immigrants – for example, kinship networks, friends, ethnoracial community agencies, and faith-based organizations – all can and do contribute to social capital formation. Yet at the same time, immigrant homelessness is increasing in Canadian urban centres (Tanasescu and Smart 2010). In an examination of recent immigrants' housing challenges in Calgary, Alina Tanasescu and Alan Smart (2010) conclude that there is "unwarranted optimism about social capital as a mechanism to facilitate the housing of immigrants" (97–8). Kinship, friends, and ethnocultural community networks can act as a buffer against absolute homelessness; however, there are limits to social capital.

In a study on immigrant settlement and social inclusion in Canada, Ratna Omidvar and Ted Richmond (2003) treat social inclusion as both a valued norm and a process of behaviours. As a normative concept, social inclusion embraces ideas of acceptance, recognition, and belonging. Omidvar and Richmond see social inclusion as an important set of practices – as "sharing physical and social spaces to provide opportunities for interactions, if desired, and to reduce social distances between people. This includes shared public spaces such as parks and libraries; mixed income neighbourhoods and housing; and integrated schools and classrooms" (2003, ix). Laforest (2009a) and Prince (2009), among others, extend this notion of social inclusion to encompass shared economic and political spaces, such as participation in the mainstream labour force and active participation in political structures and public policy processes.

Community Capacity

Community capacity refers to the existence of individuals, local groups, and associations that are prepared to voluntarily provide assistance, time, or resources to others in the community. This entails people providing care for others, helping others find needed services, solving common problems, and sharing information. Community capacity includes being a good friend or neighbour but goes beyond this to include informal and formal volunteering. Informal volunteering takes place when a neighbour shovels the snow off another person's walk because he or she is ill or too old to go out. They may help with shopping, put their neighbour's groceries away, and help clean the local skating rink or prepare a field for a game of baseball. Formal volunteering takes place when people give freely of their time, energy, skills, or knowledge through the auspices of an organization.

Capacity commonly is described in terms of human resources, financial resources, and structural and systems competence. Not surprisingly, capacity varies on a number of dimensions. A notable gradient in capacity is between urban and rural communities in Canada: charities in rural areas tend to have fewer paid employees and smaller boards of directors and to be less well funded. Also, rural charities are less likely to be educational or health care organizations and are more likely to be religious based or faith-oriented (Friesen, Alasia, and Bollam 2010).

We can also illustrate different notions of capacity by comparing service provision organizations with new social movement organizations. When we think of the community as a cluster of organizations, capacity relates to the ability of agencies, charities, and service clubs (in the traditional segment) to provide programs and supports to different constituencies of people. Capacity concerns aspects of organizational performance, such as the effective management of funds, staff, and volunteers. From this perspective, an extended notion of capacity – and one increasingly proposed by advocates – is the ability and willingness of traditional service agencies to reach out and build partnerships with other community groups engaged in social action. In this sense, capacity includes reviewing and redesigning services and programs so that they more fully respond to and include people with debilities and their families in decision making.

In the context of new social movements, augmenting the capacity of the disability community (for example) involves enhancing such activities as social critique and consciousness raising among people in the movement and wider society; celebrating and communicating in a positive manner the experiences and varied identities of persons with disabilities; and challenging the ableist attitudes, beliefs, and actions at play in society and striving to institute progressive changes that address exclusion, cultural prejudice, and discrimination. In an important sense, building the capacity of a community as a social movement concerns cultural politics and recognition, discussed in our introduction – that is to say, unsettling prevailing systems of values and celebrating alternative norms (Young 1990).

The concept of "social reproduction," examined in the previous chapter on gender and social policy, relates to this discussion on community capacity. Specifically, social reproduction highlights the role of support networks and caregiving in households and families. The lack of recognition of and support for informal caregiving is a recurring and central issue in feminist analysis; yet because of traditional family ideologies, it is only a periodic and marginal issue on the policy agenda of most governments in Canada. Indeed, this aspect of community capacity often involves taken-for-granted activities, relations, and labour done by women. As Luxton (2006, 287) points out, "the health-care system was built on, and continues to rest on, the assumption that families, particularly women, will provide basic health care. The long tradition of relying on unpaid work in the home, usually by women, with its related practices of low status and low pay for employees who provide paid home care, has subsidized health-care systems in most welfare states for decades."

Creating a Policy Context for the Not-for-Profit and Voluntary Sector: The Chrétien and Martin Liberals and the Harper Conservatives

Creating, expanding, and relying on community capacity is a prominent idea in contemporary social policy thinking in Canada and other countries. It offers a strategy for bringing community members together to form community-based organizations to address local issues, and it assumes that there is a solid economic base on which community activities can take place. Since the 1970s, federal and provincial governments have been increasing their reliance on not-for-profit organizations for social service delivery. For the most part, these not-for-profit organizations are incorporated, self-governing entities that exist primarily to provide a social good to community members. Governments "partner" with these organizations through contractual arrangements in which the government sets the conditions of the contract and the fees to be paid and the not-for-profit organizations deliver the services. Government partnerships with not-for-profit organizations have been an effective and increasingly popular approach to shifting service delivery from the public sector to the not-for-profit sector. This reflects the neoliberal ideology of downsizing government. Contracting with not-for-profit organizations has allowed governments to specify the outcomes to be achieved by those organizations and to control the level of resources committed to any particular social problem.

Yet as Peter Elson (2011, 3) points out, "the relationship between this country's federal government and its voluntary organizations has long been weak and/or turbulent: rarely has it been mutually supportive and productive." Part of the tension between governments and the not-for-profit sector relates to the conditions that governments place on not-for-profit organizations. First, the federal government does not want to fund advocacy work and so is not prepared to enter into agreements with not-for-profit organizations that carry out advocacy activities. The government is also reluctant to support community development activities by not-for-profit organizations. Second, in the 1980s, governments shifted their support for not-for-profit organizations from a "core" funding model to contracted, program-based funding. Richmond and Shields (2004) make the point that this contractual relationship has undermined the ability of not-for-profit organizations to meet their community development and advocacy responsibilities on behalf of the citizens they serve. They contend that the contractual relationship "is serving to transform the non-profit sector, moving it away from its core mission, commercializing the sector's operations and compromising its autonomy" (2004, 53).

Torjman (1996, 8) points out that while most Canadians derive their economic security from paid employment, governments play an essential role in ensuring a stable social environment, and that they do so through their social policies, which affect community organizations. These policies allow community groups to involve themselves in activities that create community capacity to solve social problems. These activities include building and strengthening caring communities, promoting economic security, and promoting social investment. Groups and organizations that are trying to encourage civil society believe that communities must build on the existing government welfare system by encouraging partnerships and collaborative working arrangements to ensure the creation of civil society (Torjman 1997b, 3). These partnerships should include governments, business, labour, education, foundations, and social agencies.

From the 1960s to the 1980s, government support to not-for-profits and related agencies in the voluntary sector grew in financial terms, although often in a segmented fashion. Also, public policy makers paid more attention generally to these organizations, although again, often in a fragmented manner. Then, during the crisis years of the welfare state – and certainly during the years of the Mulroney Conservative governments (1984–1993), as well as during the first government of the Chrétien Liberals (1993–1997) – the voluntary sector faced cuts to core funding and program grants, in addition to growing criticisms by politicians regarding charities' inefficiency and lack of accountability. By the mid-1990s, relations between the federal government and the voluntary sector in Canada were badly strained (Phillips 2001). To begin improving relations, in 1995, a Voluntary Sector Roundtable comprising thirteen national voluntary sector organizations was founded. This coalition of national organizations established a task force in 1997 to examine issues of tax treatment of charities and their advocacy work; it also established a panel chaired by former NDP leader Ed Broadbent to examine the sector's accountability and capacity. The panel's 1999 report offered a wide range of recommendations for improving the relationship between the voluntary sector and the federal government.

Chrétien, during his second and third governments (1997–2000 and 2000–3), took a series of steps to enhance the relationship, addressing issues of policy capacity, research and information, and regulatory reform for the voluntary sector. Starting cautiously, the Chrétien Liberals committed $15 million between 1998 and 2001 to create VolNet, a dedicated network tasked with linking 10,000 voluntary arts organizations, faith groups, and health and social service organizations to one another and to the Internet. The Chrétien government also established in 1999 a series of joint tables (and other organizational bodies and committees), with equal membership of federal officials and voluntary sector representatives, to examine key issues of common interest. Still more ambitious was the Voluntary Sector Initiative (VSI), introduced in 2000, a five-year $95 million undertaking with three main objectives: to improve the relationship between the sector and the federal government; to build sector capacity in areas of finance, human resources, policy, and knowledge and information management; and to improve the regulatory and legal framework under which the sector was operating. With 2001 being the International Year of Volunteers, the Liberals established the Canada Volunteerism Initiative that same year (the Harper government would end this program in 2007). Work under the VSI produced, in 2001, *An Accord between the Government of Canada and the Voluntary Sector* and, in 2002, a *Code of Good Practice on Policy Dialogue* and a *Code of Good Practice on Funding*.

Gathering reliable information about the sector – its size and scope, its organizational composition, and the situation of its agencies – is an important element in creating a supportive policy context. With this in mind, the federal government sponsored the National Survey on Giving, Volunteering, and Participation in 1997 and 2000 (replaced by the Canada Survey on Giving, Volunteering, and Participating, conducted in 2004 and 2007); it also conducted the 2003 National Survey on Non-profits and Voluntary Organizations. These surveys shed fascinating light on many aspects of the sector (Friesen, Alasia, and Bollam 2010; Hall, Lasby, Ayer, and Gibbons 2009; Statistics Canada 2005).

During Paul Martin's Liberal government (2004–6), federal policy on the voluntary sector continued along similar lines, with a few new wrinkles. One notable development was Martin's personal interest in the social economy, which figured in his government's budgets and throne speeches. Martin's interest in social economy enterprises no doubt reflected his political base in Quebec and his familiarity with the social economy there; his predilection for distinguishing himself from Chrétien, his predecessor and long-time rival; and his own business background, which was sympathetic to community-based entities that produced goods and services for the market economy while pursuing social goals.

Martin's attention to the social economy, as part of Canadian social policy and community economic development, prompted varied reactions within the voluntary sector and related social movements. A number of groups within the disability community, for example, explored the idea closely, wondering if it offered a way out of sheltered workshops and segregated employment for people with intellectual disabilities. Other perspectives regarded the social economy as a political fad or as a traditional practice in new clothes, or even as a menace. Susan Phillips explained: "For most organizations outside of Quebec that define themselves as part of the 'voluntary sector,' the concept of the social economy is generally seen as either a separate and distinct entity or as a potential threat. Rather than viewing the essence of social economy as entrepreneurship, many voluntary organizations see it as a different organization form (as cooperatives and for-profits) that has little relevance to their own work. They often do not see that what they are doing by way of being innovative and entrepreneurial in diversifying funding could be seen as part of the social economy. The perceived threat came from the Martin government's sudden interest in the social economy, giving the impression that it felt it had finished its work and closed the chapter on the voluntary sector" (Phillips 2009, 15). As a follow-up to the VSI, the Martin government did introduce in 2005 a four-year $12 million Voluntary Sector Strategy (VSS), though with a reduced mandate and narrower scope of activities than the VSI. The VSS's objectives were to build awareness of the Accord and the Codes and of the role and value of the voluntary sector in Canada; to enhance the capacity of the sector to engage in policy dialogue with federal partners; and to support conditions for innovation, partnerships, and strategic alliances within the voluntary sector (Human Resources and Skills Development Canada 2009).

How has the voluntary sector fared under the Harper Conservatives? Harper's record is often in continuity with many Liberal policies and ongoing societal challenges facing the sector. But there have been some notable shifts in policy approach by the Harper governments towards not-for-profits and voluntary organizations. According to Rachel Laforest, "the opportunities for the voluntary sector did not crystallize as many had anticipated under the Liberals. In many respects, the Conservatives have simply picked up where the Liberals left off, drifting along the same policy currents" (2009b, 155–6). She adds that "by the time the Conservatives were elected in 2006, the voluntary sector's voice had significantly weakened in the federal policy arena" (Laforest 2009b, 157). Many other sectors and groups have experienced this weakening of voice, given the declining role of federal social policy departments in relation to the central agencies of Finance, Treasury Board, and the Prime Minister's Office in Ottawa.

Regarding the financial crisis and economic recession of 2008–9 (which we discussed more fully in chapter 7), "the Harper government's response simply reinforces the invisibility of the [voluntary] sector in Canada compared to other countries" such as the United States and Great Britain. Of the $28 billion economic stimulus plan in the 2009 federal budget, just $95 million (or 0.3 per cent) was targeted to the voluntary sector, mainly for infrastructure costs for libraries, museums, and theatres as well as for funding to hire young people as interns or summer help (Phillips 2009, 28).

The Harper government's approach to the sector reflects the traditional voluntarism of the Victorian age. Ideologically, it connects to their stance on low taxation, their opposition to a national child care strategy through public services, their promotion of a law-and-order agenda in Parliament, and their reluctance to involve themselves in many aspects of social issues today, including poverty reduction. One part of the regulatory reform agenda for charities, the Not-for-Profit Corporations Act, which had died on the parliamentary order papers in 2004 and 2006, finally passed in 2009. As well, the Harper government has eliminated the capital gains tax on donations to registered charities and has promoted the role of philanthropic foundations, while emphasizing that federal funding will not support policy advocacy or certain forms of public awareness and education.

In 2010, Harper introduced the Prime Minister's Volunteer Awards: a set of seventeen awards to be given each year, on a national and regional basis, to recognize individual volunteers, innovative charities, and forward-thinking private-sector companies that are partnering on new approaches to social challenges. The policy intent behind these awards is to encourage altruistic and charitable responses to numerous public needs and problems in contemporary Canada.

John McKnight (1992) believes that from a community development perspective, the development of civic society rests on the creation and maintenance of self-defining associations. By these, he means groups of people who come together to try to solve mutual problems, provide resources to local communities, and stimulate debate about local issues. Community organizations can creatively address social problems by developing new methods for providing goods and services. McKnight argues that to achieve this, governments must shift their welfare expenditures away from a maintenance orientation towards an investment capital orientation. Governments must find new ways to finance not-for-profit organizations while not undermining the economic security of community members. Governments can contribute to the development of community organizations by providing start-up funds, training sessions, and access to private capital through bank guarantees or tax incentives for investors.

Torjman (1997b, 4) cautions that promoting more active citizenship can inadvertently encourage governments to abrogate their responsibility for economic, social, and environmental well-being. When this happens, community groups often feel as if the government is dumping problems onto them without providing the resources to deal with them. There was a strong reaction in Ontario when the provincial government sharply cut social assistance benefits in the mid-1990s: community-based food banks struggled under the demands for support. The government had unloaded its costs onto the community without providing the supports that groups required to address the problem.

If local activists and groups are to develop community capacity, governments must not undermine feelings of trust within communities. Many people are reluctant to help if they think that their voluntary work or charitable giving will weaken or remove public responsibility for pressing social issues. Similarly, if the problems are too large and overwhelming, and if community groups do not have the resources to

solve them, then agencies and volunteers can end up feeling like failures. Governments can help prevent this from happening by promoting citizens' well-being through adequate economic and social policies.
Once community groups meet this basic condition, they can work to
solve some of their local problems.

Local Conditions for Community Capacity

Communities are people linked together through kinship, locality, shared ideals, and/or common beliefs. Wharf (1992, 16) says that
whatever the size or complexity of a community, its essential common
denominators are a pattern of relationships among people and the existence of needs shared by these individuals. Wharf analyses the conditions within communities that affect their members' ability to come
together and solve local problems. In his summary of findings, he includes a range of examples, from First Nations communities that have
developed locally controlled child welfare services through to women's
groups that have fought for women's abortion rights. Wharf states that
"most social reform organizations do not have the power to put into
place the reforms they see as desirable. Neither do they have the funds
to devote to expensive public relation campaigns or to hire equally expensive lobbyists to act on their behalf. To add to their woes, social reform organizations are not usually well connected to policy makers,
and their reforms represent causes that, if not downright unpopular,
are at best of marginal interest to policy makers" (1992, 187).

To overcome these limitations and to develop their ability to solve
problems, community organizations must develop new capacities that
will allow them to rely more on their own abilities and less on the government. Developing these capacities depends on three factors: the beliefs that community members hold about cooperation, the nature of
the connections among community members, and the existing level of
community resources.

Beliefs about Cooperating

Community members have different views about whether they should
cooperate with one another. If members believe there is a shared sense
of community, and if they feel mutual obligations, then the capacity of
the community is nurtured. If, on the other hand, members believe that

the community is made up of relationships among self-interested individuals, then it will be difficult to create and use internal capacities.

Amitai Etzioni takes the first view, offering a *communitarian* definition of community: "A community is a group of people who share affective bonds and a culture. It is defined by two characteristics: Communities require a web of affect-laden relations among a group of individuals (rather than merely one-on-one relations or chains of individual relations); relations that often crisscross and reinforce one another. And being a community entails having a measure of commitment to a set of shared values, norms and meanings" (Etzioni 1995, 14). This definition highlights the relations among community members as they share resources and create a sense of connection and feelings of mutual commitment. This sense of community reflects the pre-industrial communities that Polanyi described in chapter 1.

A dramatically different view of community is provided by the *neoliberal* perspective. From this perspective, individuals have no moral sentiments towards other members and the only grounds for sharing resources are self-serving: "I will help you if you will help me." From this perspective, there are no affect-laden relations or measure of commitments. Philip Selznick (1995, 34) argues that in the liberal imagination, people are fundamentally separate, unencumbered by obligations they did not choose; they are responsible for their own fates, authors of their own opinions, makers of their own worlds; group membership is voluntary; and a contract based on mutual consent is the preferred principle of social organization.

Selznick has criticized the liberal tradition as excessively individualistic in both theory and practice. The image of people who are autonomous and self-distancing is radically incomplete as a convincing or attractive portrayal of what participation in a moral community should entail (Selznick 1995, 34). If communities are to liberate their internal capacities, they must find ways to go beyond absolutist notions of self-interest and encourage participation and cooperation based on notions of collective survival. Communities must find a balance between the individual and the collective, between liberty and equality.

Etzioni (1993, x) contends that to maintain a balance between the abstract rights of the individual and the social entitlements created by the mutual-welfare community, members must imagine the course of a community as akin to that of a bicycle, forever teetering in one direction or another – that is, either towards the anarchy of extreme individualism and the denial of the common good or towards the collectivism that views itself as morally superior to its individual members. Like Polanyi, Etzioni believes there is a tense relationship between the centripetal forces of community and the centrifugal forces of autonomy – forces that must be kept in balance if the social system is to operate successfully. Neither the individual nor the community must dominate the other.

Canadian survey research on volunteering suggests there is a mix of individual and collective reasons why people participate in community affairs. Individual-oriented reasons include exploring personal interests; networking with people to establish contacts; developing skills such as in communications, administration, or caregiving; and gaining experiences that will help bolster one's résumé. More frequently reported reasons for volunteering by Canadians are communitarian in nature: making a contribution to the community; using skills and experiences, such as in mentoring or education, to assist others; and having been personally affected by the issue or problem that the organization addresses. Along similar lines, in making financial donations to not-for-profit organizations, the main motivations Canadians report, in addition to religious convictions, are "feeling compassion for those in need, wanting to help a cause in which the donor personally believes, and wanting to make a contribution to the community" (Statistics Canada 2009). Thus, beliefs about formal volunteering and financial giving to a large degree reflect feelings of connection and mutual commitment.

Community Connections

The nature of the connections among people in a community is a second factor affecting the ability of communities to come together and share resources. Community members can be tightly bound and interdependent or they can be loosely bound and primarily independent. The tighter the ties that bind people together and the greater the interdependence among members, the stronger the social cohesion within the group and the deeper the sense of community. One need only think of the members of a religious order or a motorcycle gang to imagine the structure of a tightly bound community. In both exists a high level of interdependence and strong social cohesion.

In communities that are loosely bound, members share relatively weak connections with other members. They often belong to more than one community, and their loyalty is spread across a number of groups. A person may belong to a tennis club, a home-and-school association, a union, a community association, and a religious group, as well as to a service club and a political party. These overlapping connections create a rich network of relationships that reflect civic engagement and represent social capital.

Differences between tightly bound and loosely bound communities are important to the development of community capacity. A motorcycle gang is a closed community with a tightly knit social network and a strict code that controls membership and access to resources. Members often share resources with one another but seldom outside the group. The new members to the club must make an unflinching commitment based on the very fundamental perception of a shared common fate, and this extraordinary commitment is based on the universal, generic, social processes of networking and bonding, which themselves are the cornerstones of any genuine community (Wolf 1994, 321). When membership becomes as closed as it does with this type of community, entries and exits are difficult and loyalty to the club and to one another is paramount. The community can develop considerable capacity, but it flows inward rather than outward.

In contrast are community associations that invite members to join freely. Service clubs provide an example: members share many of the common feelings of friendship, but the bonding is much less formal, the membership is much more open, and the focus is as much outward as it is inward. While these associations may have more difficulty in developing community capacity, when they do it flows both within the community and to members outside the community. Most communities are loosely tied together through informal connections. People can come and go as they please, there are few formal arrangements that force people to interact, and there are no binding regulations for membership. Communities have the remarkable feature of being nourished by many layers of connections – families, groups, institutions – which characteristically claim respect and protection. Selznick believes that people prize open communities, ones in which members do not seek unity of any sort at any price but rather unity that preserves the integrity of the parts (Selznick 1995, 34). The ability of people to use community resources to help others, therefore, depends on the balance between being both inward- and outward-focused.

Over the past twenty years or so, the pluralization of the community has involved many people looking to one another for help and support. The feminist movement asks women to turn to one another for recognition and support. Some women's groups want young girls to have the right to attend all-girls' public schools and to be taught by women. Ethnic groups are demanding social services in their language, with services provided by people from their culture. While such demands may be reasonable and fair, they turn communities inward. The Deaf community has gone the furthest perhaps in seeking to close its ranks and formalize its community: for many in the Deaf community, being Deaf is a source of pride, and an increasing number of people have said they would not choose to be hearing. Andrew Solomon (1994) claims that for some Deaf people, the term "Deaf" denotes culture, as distinct from "deaf," which is used to describe a pathology. People who are Deaf now often wear Deaf Pride T-shirts or buttons (one woman claimed she wanted her children to be born Deaf so that they could be part of her culture) (1994, 44). This turning inward by community groups strengthens the internal social cohesion and increases the ability of communities to deal with internal problems. At the same time, however, it can splinter the larger collective and limit the ability of communities to solve common problems.

Community Resources

Another factor affecting the community's ability to develop internal capacity is the level of resources within it. In recent years, several interrelated trends have presented a rather confusing and challenging environment for community organizations in Canada. There have been (and there continue to be in some jurisdictions) drastic and at times abrupt cuts in government funding to community agencies. At the same time, public benefits and services to agency clients have compacted. Efforts at increasing revenues through fundraising are confronting the phenomenon of donor fatigue and an ever competitive charitable sector. Meanwhile, needs and demands for community services have risen, and this is reflected in growing caseloads and overburdened staff. When to all of this we add rising expectations, among donors and governments, for accountability and performance by community organizations in a context of tremendous complexity, stress and contradiction result.

Insufficient, unpredictable, and declining resources have serious consequences for community organizations. A study of Canadian disability organizations identifies two such consequences. "First, sponsors may divert their attention to resource mobilization rather than supporting the activities that are necessary to promote citizen participation.

Second, the lack of resources may create organizational instability and make positions insecure, thereby decreasing staff effectiveness" (Boyce et al. 2001, 13).

For local not-for-profit agencies that do not want to see their public funding decline and shift away from ongoing operational funding towards time-specific project funding, several strategies are possible, some of which resemble social economy practices. Each of these strategies is a response to the challenge of ensuring adequate resources to deliver goods and services to persons with disabilities. Each has potential advantages and disadvantages for an agency's mandate, its working culture, and its clientele as well as for the broader value system of society. Take the strategy of pooling resources to achieve economies of scale. An example of this on the administrative front is a large organization in the City of Winnipeg that provides a clearinghouse of secretarial and clerical services for a number of smaller agencies and self-help groups. An example on the policy development and advocacy front is the establishing of forums – often by a provincial or national disability organization – that invite various groups and activists to come together to explore issues and common approaches.

McKnight (1992, 6) believes that the first step in community development is for members to carry out a thorough inventory of the community's current resources, skills, and capacities. Resources include financial, natural, and human assets within a community; skills include the talents and expertise of individuals and organizations that can be brought together to address problems; and capacity is the ability to join resources and skills together in ways that allow the community to address its own problems. The Aspen Institute Rural Economic Policy Program (1996) has identified eight outcome measures that examine the level of resources in a community. These measures are based on the following questions:

- Does the community foster expanding, diverse, and inclusive citizen participation?
- Does it have an expanding leadership base?
- Does the community offer ways of developing and strengthening individual skills?
- Do community members share a common vision of the community?
- Do community organizations share a common strategic community agenda?
- Does the community get things done?

- Are community organizations well organized?
- Are resources balanced between self-sufficiency and the use of outside resources?

Everyone in a community has abilities, skills, and productive motives. All of these are powerful, but they must be identified and applied if the community is to develop the capacity to solve local problems. Equally important, from McKnight's perspective, is the recognition of locally controlled associations. The basic power of associations lies in their problem-solving capacity. Unlike systems and agencies, these associations command local loyalty; they do so because they are self-governing (McKnight 1992, 8). It is essential to regenerate associational capacities and authority if productive neighbourhoods are to emerge (or re-emerge) and flourish. This regeneration of community associations is one step in the development of a civil society capable of drawing upon local communities to help address local problems.

The Darker Side of Communities

As we stated earlier, communities also have a dark side: they can be cruelly authoritarian, unfairly discriminatory, oppressively traditional, and rigidly conservative. A collection of studies on community organizing efforts in Canada concludes that "community activities are not always progressive and do not always serve the interest of all community members" (Ng, Walker, and Muller 1990, 309). Likewise, community groups can find state policies, programs, and procedures to be domineering and coercive. In some cases, government funding, regulations, employment programs, and administrative and managerial processes "further fragment the already marginalized groups (women, immigrants, and native people), creating new divisions and contradictions within these groups" (Ng, Walker, and Muller 1990, 314). Government policies on contracting for community-based services can produce unhealthy competition rather than cooperation among agencies, resulting in "agency turfism" that adversely affects clients and the community. These contracting practices also produce what Susan Phillips and Karin Levasseur have aptly dubbed "the snakes and ladders of accountability" that confront agencies in Canada's voluntary sector (Phillips and Levasseur 2004). Even within groups with shared experiences and identities, such as HIV/AIDS groups or ethnic communities, power differentials and dynamics exist that may well reproduce larger forms of patriarchy or other types of discrimination within the local group. That said, both marginalized and mainstream communities can influence and affect social programs and the administrative practices of government officials (Lee 1992; Wharf 1992; Wharf and Clague 1997).

This darker side has important implications for how community capacity is used. For community members to be willing to share resources, they must believe that the person receiving the assistance deserves to be helped. This often means that the recipient must be from the local community, be of sound moral character, and have no other visible means of support. Local communities will be unwilling to help strangers or others they believe can help themselves. The darker side of community takes social policy back to fundamental questions of legitimacy and the rights of recipients to receive help from the community.

The movement back to the community weakens the universal rights implied in national social programs. Social rights are replaced with bare minimums of social assistance, and even these are based on need rather than entitlement. Also, local initiatives are more expensive than national ones. While it is possible to reduce benefit levels so that they fit with local conditions, a community can only go so far before it impoverishes some of its members. Local programs often require duplication of administration; they are difficult to administer, given size considerations; and they are labour intensive. Thus, administration often falls into the hands of people – such as those in Charles Dickens's *Oliver Twist* – who are rewarded for keeping the costs of programs low. This makes them wardens of the poor and undermines those democratic notions of equality that are foundational to the modern state.

While the state in Canada can be properly thought of as deeply embedded in society (Cairns 1986), the state is not a homogeneous entity. Furthermore, the state is not equally connected to all communities and groups in Canadian society, nor has it similar relationships with all groups and communities. As community activists, policy analysts, and some administrators and politicians well know, relations between community organizations and government agencies can be primarily cooperative or conflictual, stable or highly fluid, restrictive or supportive. Some of the recent literature on civil society and civic community, in speaking of social partnerships and mutual responsibility, tends to ignore inequalities in power distribution and thus tends to simplify these complex and contradictory relationships between locally based groups and active or inactive governments. State support of community organizations can be a mechanism for social control and social change.

Wharf (1992, 21) describes a paradox: responsibility for social policy has largely been passed to senior levels of government, yet social problems are experienced and played out in local communities. This means there is often incongruence between the interventions designed within federal or provincial bureaucracies and the needs of local communities. This asymmetry has led many social policy analysts to believe it would be more effective if the services designed to address these issues were embedded in local communities (Davies and Shragge 1990). But governments often know little about the capacity of local communities to solve difficult social problems. A governmental plan to simply cut things and let the chips fall where they may is extremely dangerous. At every point in every policy decision there is the choice between two paths, one encouraging respect and trust and the other discouraging it. When governments or other institutions make decisions that discourage the development of respect and trust, they push the community down a destructive path.

Developing Community Capacity

When they develop community capacity, community workers use three types of activities: locality development, social planning, and social action (Rothman 1974). Locality development – which entails helping individuals and groups identify and meet local needs – is based on the notion that community members have the capacity to solve their own problems. Community workers identify people in the community who have some latent skills and encourage them to draw others together to begin to develop a capacity to identify problems. The community workers provide training and support to these natural leaders so that they can form groups that will work cooperatively to solve local problems. Social planning, by contrast, is a rational, technocratic approach in which community workers use their research skills to identify and study social problems. This process assumes that community members can develop the skills necessary to influence the larger social system. The community workers use the information from the planning process to provide evidence as to why steps should be taken to solve the local problems. Finally, community workers can encourage people from the local community to involve themselves in social action, on the assumption that society is governed by an elite few who rule in their own interests (Wharf 1992, 17). Community workers encourage community members to confront the elites about the existence of problems and to force those elites to address the problems.

Community members may encourage community capacity by developing organizational partnerships to address local problems. The Caledon Institute of Social Policy, in cooperation with a number of foundations, is testing the ability of these new partnerships to address social issues. Typically, these partnerships link a business organization to a not-for-profit group. One way for such partnerships to work together is for the business to agree to promote a social cause as part of its own marketing strategy. This creates a positive image for the business; it also highlights the social concern, as well as the community organization that is trying to solve social problems. Torjman (1997b, 12) describes the partnering of the Canadian Women's Foundation with Tambrands Canada Inc. Tambrands promotes the Canadian Women's Foundation and makes an annual commitment of $100,000 over three years. In return, the Women's Foundation has developed a granting process for shelters for assaulted women on behalf of Tambrands. Another example is Chevron Canada Resources, which allows employees to volunteer eight hours a year on company time. Most formal volunteers in Canada – 65 per cent, according to a national survey (Statistics Canada 1998) – are employed, and one in four takes time off from work, with the support of the employer, to volunteer.

The not-for-profit sector can offer businesses a multitude of resources (Pante 1996, 28), including these: knowledge about the community and consumers' interests, access to community members, credibility in the local community, an enhanced public image, an opportunity to act in a socially responsible fashion, the vitality of working with people who believe that their work can contribute positively to the community, the skills of volunteers, and insight into different management styles. In return, the private sector can offer not-for-profit organizations skills and expertise, financial resources, public relations and accounting skills, the use of equipment, access to business community members, influential voices with particular audiences, an improved image (i.e., credibility) through association, and insight into different management styles.

Community partnerships range from traditional financial arrangements where a business provides resources to the community group, through to partnerships that attempt to bring about fundamental social change. The first type is based on the donation of money; the second type may focus on alleviating poverty, creating social housing, providing access to capital, or advocating for major social intervention. As earlier chapters pointed out, governments have long played the major role in combating poverty, providing low-income housing, and developing major social service interventions. Programs designed to deal with these issues have been made available to large segments of the population and have not been focused on the community level. The development of new partnerships is changing this long-standing approach.

Community development, as a social policy tool, alleviates problems as part of the larger process of fostering community-based economic, social, and democratic development. This process integrates economic and social goals by combining job training and placement, job creation and retention, and self-employment. Besides helping people obtain more skills, community development tries to develop long-term assets in the community, such as a stock of low-income housing, child care centres, health clinics, services for elderly people, and physical assets such as parks and sports facilities.

While community interventions are perhaps best focused on local problems, there are examples of community capacity processes targeting larger problems, such as poverty.[1] Four essential strategies for community-based poverty reduction are as follows: meeting basic needs, removing barriers, building skills, and promoting economic development (Torjman 1998). Before skills development can begin, people must be able to meet their basic needs for food, housing, clothing, clean water, and sanitation. These basic issues can be met through government-supported programs such as social assistance benefits, employment benefits, child benefits, and old age security. Community programs such as food banks, clothing outlets, community gardens, community health clinics, and community-based social housing can support public social programs.

Once people's basic needs have been met, community organizations can think about removing barriers that prevent them from obtaining employment. This can include offering literacy programs, child care, support for transportation, work clothing, and other supports that make it easier for people to seek employment. It can also include removing attitudinal barriers that limit or prohibit access to people who are disabled; as well as accreditation barriers, so that people who have learned their skills outside Canada are not hindered from finding employment (Torjman 1998, 12). Once as many barriers as possible have been removed, community organizations find it much easier to focus on building skills, ranging from life skills through to particular employment skills, including job search skills. In Nova Scotia, for instance, the provincial government has collaborated with the federal government to create community resources dedicated to connecting people with workplaces. The two levels of government have created the position of "job developer," whose role is to act as a broker, linking people looking for work with companies looking for employees.

Community-based poverty reduction also involves promoting economic development. This includes creating permanent jobs (including self-employment opportunities) and providing access to capital and technical assistance. Each step is meant to strengthen the community's capacity to create conditions supportive of job generation. Partnerships between businesses and community organizations, however, are no substitute for a solid public sector. Collaborative partnerships must complement and supplement the public sector; they should never be expected to replace the government's role in redistributing income, making essential social investments, and building caring communities through the promotion of citizenship (Torjman 1997b, 14–15).

Joining an association offers intrinsic rewards for both the individual and the community. To be a member of an association is to participate in public life and to have a public identity outside of oneself. This public identity makes a statement about how a person cares about his or her community. People who join together to form a community group are creating a sense of equality – part of the implied metaphysical equality that is assumed to exist among people in modern democratic states. Membership, like citizenship, carries with it rights and responsibilities, and the manifestations of those individual rights and responsibilities are part of a person's public persona and part of the fabric of community capacity.

Community Capacity in Action

Community capacity can be defined as the ability of people to help one another meet the demands of daily living and seize opportunities to realize their hopes and goals. This capacity includes people helping one another provide care, find resources, solve problems, and share information. Community capacity includes being a good neighbour but goes beyond that to include informal and formal volunteering, joining community associations, and otherwise contributing to society. This helping capacity often lies dormant until events encourage people to come forward or demand that they do so. The Red River flood of 1997 (and, again, serious flooding in southern Manitoba and in Quebec in 2011) and the ice storm of 1998 were just such events in Canada. International relief efforts to which Canadians similarly responded have included the Indonesian tsunami of 2004 and the Haitian earthquake of 2010.

During the 1997 flood in Manitoba, thousands of people helped their neighbours by filling sandbags, cooking food, and taking care of people who had been forced from their homes. Others from across the country donated money, food, and supplies to help people in need. Jim Silver (1997, 87) points out that the flood epitomized Canada itself – an often harsh environment supporting a people who have learned the merits of responding to its demands with collective action in the interests of the community.

The same pattern repeated itself during the ice storm of 1998. The storm went on for several days, causing a power failure that eventually affected more than three million people from Kingston, Ontario, to the Annapolis Valley in Nova Scotia. Municipal water systems failed, hospitals lost their primary power, there were no streetlights or subway systems, banks closed, and the Canadian Forces were asked to provide assistance as one community after another declared a state of emergency. While workers from official organizations such as the police, fire departments, and hydro companies maintained order and repaired the hydro system, the public responded with both informal and formal help. Neighbours invited one another into their homes, volunteers staffed community centres and provided food and accommodations, and strangers pitched in and helped cut firewood for home heating in rural communities. Help lines were inundated with calls offering to take people into their homes, and people from across the country donated material, generators, and money.

At the simplest level, community capacity expresses itself when neighbours look out for one another. Jane Jacobs, in her 1961 classic *The Death and Life of Great American Cities*, described this aspect of community capacity. For her, one of the key ingredients of community life was the "eyes on the street": neighbourhood people, usually elderly ladies peeking out from behind front window curtains, keeping an eye on everything that takes place within their view. This "neighbourhood watch" was not organized by some outside agency, nor was there any external reward for looking out for the neighbourhood. However, Jacobs credited "eyes on the street" with keeping many dense urban neighbourhoods safe.

Jacobs's analysis of community involvement directs our attention towards invisible or underlying forces that become manifest as community capacity. These forces are organized through the development of community connections, informal self-help groups, community associations, and not-for-profit organizations. People come together and form organizations that perform every type of task, from providing child care to counselling recent immigrants. These organizations have become interlocking networks with political, economic, and social significance (Baum 1996).

As it is put to use, community capacity expands. It is, in other words, a renewable resource. Two neighbours decide to organize holiday fireworks for their street. They purchase firecrackers, make popcorn, and advertise the event by having their children drop notices off at neighbours' houses. The two organizers hold the event on the street in front of their homes. Neighbours of all ages come with their lawn chairs and watch the fireworks. Families contribute a little money towards the cost of the fireworks, so it is cheaper than if each parent bought their own. By the second year, other parents have taken responsibility for safety by keeping the children organized and away from the fireworks site. Still others obtain barriers to block the street from traffic and organize the popcorn and other refreshments, and one parent offers to make up a flier on her computer and have her children advertise the event. By the fifth year there are two hundred people attending the fireworks display. Sparkler parades, singsongs, and a seniors viewing area on a neighbour's front veranda are all established. The result is an event that remains informal, that draws upon the abilities of many people, and that provides a wonderful evening for the immediate community.

In a 2007 national survey on volunteering, 84 per cent of Canada's adult population (those aged fifteen and over) reported that they were involved in informal volunteering – that is, in helping others directly, who live outside their own household. These spontaneous activities included visiting the sick or elderly, shopping for or driving others, baby-sitting, writing letters, clearing snow, offering advice or personal care, helping solve problems, assisting with outside work, and a whole variety of other activities. The same survey found that 46 per cent of Canadian adults had formally volunteered during the previous year. Formal volunteers work under the auspices of a group or organization, are involved in it on a regular or planned basis, and often make long-term commitments to community organizations.

In 2007 around 12.5 million Canadians volunteered their services to the more than 175,000 not-for-profit organizations that make up the formal voluntary sector. The average number of hours volunteered formally per year was 166 (and the median hours volunteered per year was 56) for a total of nearly 2.1 billion hours. That is the equivalent of more than 1 million full-time jobs (Phillips 2001; Statistics Canada 2009). These organizations use the services of volunteers to provide a wide variety of activities such as counselling, teaching, coaching, preparing food, performing the arts, and fundraising. Most volunteer hours went to sports and recreation, social services, education, and religious organizations. The rate of volunteering between immigrants and native-born Canadians is similar across several organization types, including arts and culture, hospitals, development and housing, and the environment. Regarding religious organizations, the volunteer rate for immigrants is higher than for native-born Canadians; the opposite is true for sports and recreation organizations in the voluntary sector (Statistics Canada 2009).

Statistics Canada reports that in 2006, 84 per cent of the adult population – nearly 23 million Canadians – made a monetary donation to a not-for-profit organization. Canadians contributed $10 billion in that year, almost half of which (46 per cent) went to religious organizations, followed by health organizations (15 per cent) and social services (10 per cent). Religious organizations received the largest share of volunteer hours (18 per cent), followed by sports and recreation (17 per cent) and social services (16 per cent). Among donors, while those with higher household incomes donated larger actual dollar amounts, those with lower incomes gave more as a share of their total income (Statistics Canada 2009).

Gender and the Voluntary Sector

Evident in the Canadian voluntary sector are gendered divisions of participation, labour, and structures that are similar in some respects to the ones operating in the economic, domestic, and state domains. Men and women are different in the types of help that they provide and that they receive (Schellenberg and Turcotte 2007). Gender lines are easily identifiable among the largest voluntary organizations in the country: Big Brothers and Big Sisters, the Kinsmen and Kinettes, the Guides and Scouts, the Young Men's Christian Association (YMCA) and Young Women's Christian Association (YWCA), the Lions Club, and the

Women's Institute. The 1987 and 1997 national surveys of volunteer activity found that women were slightly more apt than men to volunteer: some 55 per cent of all volunteers were women. In the 2007 survey, the formal volunteer rate of men was 45 per cent, and for women, 47 per cent. The rate of informal helping of others was 84 per cent for both men and women, although the frequency of helping over the year was higher for women than for men. A 2010 Gallup poll in Canada reported that over the previous month, women had been somewhat more likely than men to give money to an organization; to volunteer time to a community organization, charity, or place of worship; and to help a stranger or someone they did not know who needed help (Charities Aid Foundation 2010, 28–30).

Among seniors who volunteer, 61 per cent are women. For women generally, the rate of participation was also slightly higher – 29 per cent of all adult women volunteered, compared to 25 per cent of men. This proportion of female volunteers is lower than would have been suggested by the classic stereotype: married, older, well-to-do women who are not in the workforce and who are regularly engaged in charities. Another way to look at this is to recognize that despite a substantial increase in labour market participation, women are still the main source of informal and formal volunteers. To be sure, paid employment may well influence when women can volunteer, why they do, and how many hours they can give; but this has not resulted in a dramatic decline in women's volunteering. Feminist writers speak of the double shift; in actuality, for many women it is a triple day consisting of paid work, housework and family caring, and volunteer work (Catano and Christiansen-Ruffman 1989, 4).

Women predominate as volunteers in several service areas and for certain client groups. Women outnumber men two to one or more as formal volunteers in the fields of health care, international agencies, and education and youth development, as well as in religious organizations. More women than men participate in formal mutual-aid and self-help groups. As well, women form the majority of volunteers in the arts and culture, in law and justice organizations, and in informal helping. Men predominate as volunteers in the fields of the environment and wildlife management; fire services; and leisure, recreation, and sports; as well as in economic and employment interest groups such as chambers of commerce, industrial associations, and trade unions.

Patricia Evans (1991, 178) notes that much of the work that women do in the labour market "mirrors their work in the household and incorporates a significant component of personal service." Likewise, a great deal of the voluntary work women do reflects caring and household chores. Comparing men's and women's formal and informal volunteer activities reveals a number of traditional sex role differences. As formal volunteers, women are more likely than men to prepare and serve food, provide care and companionship, collect or distribute food and other goods, and make and sell items for raising funds. As informal volunteers freely offer help to people outside their own families, women are more active in helping with shopping, cooking and cleaning, driving someone to appointments or stores, babysitting, and visiting the sick or elderly. Both women and men are active in organizing events, teaching or educating, collecting information, and writing letters for neighbours.

As formal volunteers, men are more likely than women to coach, referee, or judge events; repair, build, or maintain facilities; provide advice; and do public speaking. As informal volunteers, men are most likely to help by doing outside work or by assisting with the operation of a business. The 1987 national survey found that 33 per cent of men volunteers sat as board members, compared to only 21 per cent of women; also, 41 per cent of men volunteers said they helped run the organization, compared to 31 per cent of women. Within the health care part of the voluntary sector, women comprised 77 per cent of volunteers, yet more than two-thirds of the board members were men (Kent 1989). Kelly Thompson (1989, 2) has suggested that men prefer voluntary positions with a visible power base. Perhaps men thereby make themselves more available to be elected and to hold influential volunteer positions. The result, whatever the motives, is a specific form of patriarchy – the underrepresentation of women in the policy governance and decision-making positions of voluntary organizations.

The Volunteer Sector's Contribution to Community

Governments have identified the voluntary sector as one of the primary untapped sources in the community for additional social care. In 2004, nearly $68 billion in transfers from governments went to organizations in Canada's voluntary sector. Provincial governments accounted for 71 per cent of those transfers; the federal government for 26 per cent; and municipal governments for 4 per cent. Charitable donations from individuals to voluntary organizations totalled $8.5 billion. Also, the sector provided 2.4 million full-time and part-time jobs and an estimated 3 to

7 per cent of the Canadian GDP in 2004 (Friesen, Alasia, and Bollam 2010; Human Resources and Skills Development Canada 2009).

At a time when some governments are withdrawing from social activities, questions obviously arise about the ability of not-for-profit organizations to take on more responsibility for delivering social programs. In trying to assess how community capacity could be increased, Judith Maxwell (1995), a prominent policy adviser, has posed this question: If more of the elderly population is healthy but inactive, are there ways to tap that energy to provide social and community services needed by families and the elderly?

The analysis of older adults as a potential source of community capacity provides a useful way of determining whether there is a large pool of untapped resources in the community or whether the vast majority of those resources are already being used (Prince and Chappell 1997). The 2007 national survey on volunteer activity found that 46 per cent of Canadians volunteered with formal agencies and organizations. For Canadians aged fifty-five to sixty-four, the volunteer rate was 40 per cent; for those aged sixty-five and over the rate was 36 per cent. While lower than the national rates, these age groups gave the highest average annual volunteer hours of all Canadians. Compared to the national average of 166 hours, for those aged fifty-five to sixty-four it was 205 hours, and for those aged sixty-five and over it was 218 hours (Statistics Canada 2009). Senior volunteers spend much of their time visiting the sick and elderly. More seniors than non-seniors are involved in activities related to providing care, companionship, and friendly visiting, as well as activities related to the preparation or serving of food; younger volunteers are more involved than seniors in teaching, coaching, and refereeing. Elderly women are the most likely group to be involved in service delivery; this is consistent with the wealth of caregiving literature demonstrating that women provide more hands-on care than do men.

For the most part, seniors provide direct care for other elderly people; they are less interested in providing management services for not-for-profit organizations, and they have little interest in providing programs and services to young adults. They are involved in the arts and culture groups, health organizations, international activities, and religious organizations, so these areas provide the greatest potential for future development. In terms of helping others directly, through informal support networks, in 2007 the national rate of helping was 84 per cent. For those aged fifty-five to sixty-four it was just below that average, at

81 per cent, while for those aged sixty-five and over, the rate of helping others directly was 70 per cent – the lowest rate of all age groups
(Statistics Canada 2009). Other research suggests that the rate of helping among seniors varies significantly between younger seniors aged
sixty-five to seventy-four and older seniors aged seventy-five and over
(Schellenberg and Turcotte 2007).

Both an opportunity and a challenge exist in drawing senior volunteers deeper into providing services to community members. Those
who did give time spent approximately two hours a week on average
volunteering for an organization. When asked if they would give more
volunteer service, a majority of elderly people said they would be willing to give more time. This should not be surprising: those who volunteer report higher levels of satisfaction with their life than do their
non-volunteering peers. The 2007 survey also found that people are
more likely to donate money to charities and to volunteer time to community organizations later in life if they participated when younger
in giving, helping, and volunteering activities. Thus it appears there is
some potential for even greater voluntary action by seniors in Canada,
especially if we adopt an intergenerational approach and encourage
community engagement among younger Canadians. Such an approach
is fundamental to building sustainable community capacity.

Conclusions

The emergence of apparently new concepts such as "civil society," "social capital," and "community capacity" is part of the changing politics of social policy. Definitions, though, are never politically innocent.
We must always ask not simply what these terms mean, but also what
they exclude. Furthermore, we must ask who is doing the defining and
for what purpose, as well as who benefits and who does not from a
given discourse. Community activists, volunteers, and human service
workers are increasingly aware of and interested in policy. The reasons
for this include government moves to devolve services to municipalities and local groups; initiatives on healthy and safer communities; and
the rhetoric of community care that arose out of the crisis politics of
the welfare state in the 1980s and early 1990s. In our present age, the
mixed economy approach to state–market relations and public policy
making remains entrenched in important ways. Its key features include
a reduction in the role of governments in economic and social affairs;
a lowering of expectations for community groups, concomitant with a

discrediting of the claims they make; the encouragement to privatize certain health and social services; and – tapping into voluntary initiatives, community care, and charitable impulses – the offloading of service responsibilities onto the voluntary sector.

Community capacity is created through mediating institutions. These include self-help groups, not-for-profit organizations, religious congregations, professional associations, and other local organizations where people come together to meet their needs. Through these institutions, community members develop leadership skills, improve their problem-solving abilities, develop ideas and strategies for solving local problems, and draw together the resources they need to achieve community objectives. These practical skills are underpinned by community trust and cooperation. Mediating institutions bring together people with different skills, values, and ideas about how to solve problems.

Both the welfare system and the voluntary sector address social problems and provide protection to vulnerable Canadians. Both offer services and support to people who need assistance, and they share many of the same goals. There are many overlaps between the two systems, and in many ways they have become mutually dependent. When governments reduce benefits to families, there are longer line-ups at voluntary agencies. Rising unemployment increases the demand for counselling and the informal help of family members. Social assistance recipients turn to the voluntary sector for help when food runs low. As the government "deinstitutionalizes" people from facilities that have historically cared for them, demands on community organizations to offer more services rise dramatically.

Increasing the use of volunteers in providing health and social services poses some dilemmas for social policy as well as for the essence of citizenship in Canada. Mishra (1990a, 111) points out that using volunteers to provide essential services undermines the structure of the welfare system. Since charity is voluntary action, the nature and scope of assistance remains unspecified and uncertain. Conversely, those in need do not have any right to assistance from private sources and must be grateful for whatever they receive. Our position is that placing greater emphasis on the role of communities in solving social problems must not mean the abandonment of the traditional goals of the welfare state. Reducing poverty, offering economic security, and investing in people through education and health care remain as important now as they were when the Canadian welfare state was envisaged in the 1940s. Looking to local communities, therefore, should not result in letting go of essential public services. The capacity of communities, and marginalized groups in particular, to tackle serious public issues and risks of everyday living are closely linked with the broader context of social policies and other state policies.

It is said that the social economy offers opportunities for meaningful employment; for upgrading skills; for earning income and getting off welfare; for demonstrating personal capacity; and for expanding social networks and a sense of belonging. Certainly, these are all attractive for social groups, including Canadians with disabilities, who disproportionately face low incomes, high unemployment, and poverty, and who routinely face exclusion, stigma, and discrimination. Perhaps the social economy perspective may help advance the economic component of citizenship for marginalized people by promoting inclusion in regular employment and earning a living wage. If adopted more widely, perhaps social economy activities can shift thinking away from the "individual limitation," "welfare dependent," and "personal tragedy" images of people towards images of people as workers, producers, service providers, taxpayers, consumers, and customers; this would offset old stereotypes of people with disabilities as permanently unemployable and non-productive. At the same time, a concern is that social enterprises for those on the margins may result in reproducing marginal employment with marginal salaries, benefits, and rights. Yet perhaps the social economy can lower some social and economic barriers; perhaps it does represent an opportunity, not fully realized yet, of giving recognition to a wider spectrum of abilities and aspirations among Canadians.

In tracing the federal policies of the Chrétien, Martin, and Harper governments towards the voluntary sector, we discern some differences but also some underlying continuities. Conservative and Liberal federal governments over the past thirty years have been ambivalent regarding the legitimacy of voluntary organizations when it comes undertaking policy critiques and public protests, and to making demands for economic betterment and social justice. In contrast to the social investment state policies of Labour governments in the UK, federal governments in Canada have not had a sustained and ambitious agenda of modernizing governance arrangements with civil society groups (Dobrowolsky 2003). Canadian tax laws continue to place strict limits on the advocacy and public education work of registered charities. In addition, governments have cut funding for policy research to groups representing literacy issues and women's interests. These limits restrict the democratic potential of the voluntary sector and depoliticize social life (Graham 2009; Shragge 2003; Young 1990). Instead, governments and public service bureaucracies tend to view voluntary organizations as service providers and as noble sources of giving and helping, rather than also as important partners in policy making and governance and as essential sites of political advocacy and social citizenship (Laforest 2009a; Phillips 2001). And on top of that, federal and provincial governments have retrenched funding for the administrative infrastructure of voluntary sector groups and associations and have eliminated multi-year allocations that would enable a modicum of organizational stability and a basis for planning. At the same time, the rules and regulations for contracts and grants have expanded, with oppressive reporting requirements for rather modest funds to fairly small organizations. In many jurisdictions, small not-for-profits must undergo elaborate accreditation processes in order to remain eligible for government contracts. Conditions like these squeeze further the ability of most voluntary agencies to engage in any social policy development.

The challenge, then, is for governments and community organizations to develop and link social policy and social capital in ways that strive for a number of balances: attending to the long term *and* short term in planning and funding; committing to economic security *and* social security in national and provincial policies; addressing the needs of majority *and* minority groups; incorporating the experiences of men *and* of women, and of different groups within each gender; and paying close attention to the rights and responsibilities of citizens, to be sure, but also those of corporations, unions, voluntary agencies, the media, and governments.

11 Creating a New Policy Agenda and Rebuilding the Social Role of the State

We have viewed the contemporary politics of social policy as tensions arising from the capacity of local communities to address social problems in the face of the globalization of the Canadian economy, the decentralization of the political federation, and the pluralization of the general population. Previous chapters provided an account of the origins, nature, and implications of the changing politics facing social policy and the welfare state in Canada. We outlined the evolution of programs over the twentieth century, identifying changes in the ideas, policy instruments, interests, and institutions connected with the development of welfare.

In this concluding chapter we offer observations on the study of the welfare state and the practice of social policy. We first review the lessons we have learned about social policy, tracing a number of essential concepts and issues touched on throughout the book. We next place these lessons in the context of the welfare state in the early decades of the twenty-first century. This includes the changing role of women, the aging of the population, the changing relationship between the federal and provincial governments, and the elimination of many provincial and federal budget deficits (but not the debt). Finally, we argue for the development of a policy agenda that recognizes the new politics of social policies and the changing relationships between the market and the community and between the citizen and the state. We believe this new agenda needs to broaden the scope of social policy analysis, recognize the important role played by governments in developing social policies, and encourage the democratization of the welfare state and social agencies.

As discussed in our introduction, Canada's diverse social policies amount to a liberal welfare state. Canadian social policy as a welfare regime includes "institutional arrangements, rules and understandings that guide and shape concurrent policy decisions, expenditure developments, problem definitions, and even the respond-and-demand structure of citizens and welfare consumers" (Esping-Andersen 1990, 80). This idea of a welfare regime suggests an organized pattern of relationships among core institutions of human society, including the state, the market economy, the family, civil society, indigenous nations, and other community structures. We have suggested that the interplay among three policy orientations, associated with specific structural interests and mechanisms – economic liberalism, social protection, and cultural recognition – shape the actual complexion of Canada's social policy regime as well as its pressing issues, apparent choices, and possible directions. Our threefold typology of policy logics extends the discourse beyond the usual limiting focus on economic liberalism, the ideal type of a social investment state, or the misleading debate between redistribution and recognition politics. These three orientations represent different ways of thinking and talking about human needs, social issues, power relations, the significance of historical experiences in contemporary times, and the scope for public policy making. Devoting simultaneous attention to economic liberalism, social protection, and cultural recognition widens both the conceptual considerations and the practical possibilities for understanding social policy and changing politics. Of these three orientations the oldest is not economic liberalism, which dates from the eighteenth and nineteenth centuries, but rather relief measures of social protection, which are rooted in practices of the sixteenth and seventeenth centuries. And cultural recognition is not just a late-twentieth-century and early-twenty-first-century phenomenon of identity politics and new social movements; it traces back at least to the eighteenth and nineteenth centuries in Canada, linked with treaties between the Crown and indigenous nations as well as with the struggles and policies related to language, women, and immigrants of various races and ethnicities.

What characterizes our contemporary political condition, then, is a melange of identity struggles and claims, economic risks and opportunities, and social needs and aspirations. Consider the recent attention that some governments in Canada are paying to social economy organizations. Depending on the actors and interests involved, this can mean advancing economic liberalism by commercializing not-for-profit agencies; promoting cooperative values in community-based social service agencies; and/or creating new organizations for recognizing the needs of highly marginalized groups in society, such as people with developmental disabilities (Mook, Quarter, and Ryan 2010). This example illustrates how the three policy orientations are not simply discursive formations of ideas and values; they are also material expressions of organizations and resources.

Changing Politics and Social Policies: Where Have We Come From, and Where Are We Now?

Modern Canadian social policy, as chapters 2 and 3 point out, spans one hundred years and comprises four broad periods: the colonial pre-welfare-state phase, the period of establishing the national system of social security, the crisis period, and the current phase of changing politics. Each of these periods is associated with a particular economic context and policy direction, state form, and model of social programming. It began with the colonial period, when people turned to their neighbours and community for help during difficult times, and the local economy had a direct impact on people's ability to meet their needs – that is, people could take care of themselves if work was available. In communities where the economy was seasonal, or where there was not enough work to meet everyone's needs, communities had a difficult time helping people solve pressing problems. When the problems were too difficult for local resources to solve, community members turned to their governments for help, and the municipal, provincial, and federal governments created basic social policies to meet their most pressing needs. Early policies provided income support in a limited, means-tested fashion based on the principle of "less eligibility."

The colonial period reflected the development of local welfare programs provided by voluntary agencies and fledgling government programs that laid the foundations of the welfare state. It became clear during this period that people could not protect their own well-being without the support and help of the community. Even when the country was growing, and processes of industrialization and urbanization were creating opportunities for advancement, many people could not adapt and turned to their communities and governments for support.

This basic form of welfare lasted until the Great Depression of the 1930s – a decade that underscored the point that individuals could not on their own protect themselves from the consequences of economic failures. Every major social thinker of the time called for new programs and services to protect the population from economic ravages. New ideas began to emerge about the role governments should play in helping people meet their basic needs. The ideas of people like Leonard Marsh, Harry Cassidy, Charlotte Whitton, C.A. Curtis, and J.J. Heagerty came to define the politics of envisioning and then establishing a system of social security for Canadians. These new ideas, as we have shown in chapter 3, led to the expansionist era of social security, which in turn led to an expanded public realm. Government intervention became the norm, and between the 1940s and the 1970s, many new programs were developed. The social programs underpinning this period were based in part on Keynesian economics and stressed the comprehensive provision of a range of risks and needs. Canadians learned that in a complex society such as Canada, the federal and provincial governments must work together if they are to deal with systemic problems such as poverty, unemployment, and social dislocation, and if they are to provide universal access to education, health care, and housing.

The expansion of the welfare state came to an end by the mid-1970s, when a new period of welfare crisis and restraint began to take hold. The oil crisis and economic problems of the early 1970s resulted in a period of stagflation and economic instability, which led to a questioning of the welfare state. The old economic ideas of laissez-faire began to have greater impact on the thinking of policy makers, and a new attitude developed that called for dramatic changes to the existing system. In response, governments cut some programs, froze others, and launched only limited new initiatives over the 1970s and 1980s. The welfare state came under criticism from community members as well as from political activists on the left and the right. Critics claimed that the welfare system was overbearing, underachieving, patriarchal, too bureaucratic, and – ultimately most damaging politically – in fiscal crisis. Policy-making elites resisted introducing any further major reforms such as national child care, and various social programs were made more residual in character.

During this crisis period, provincial and federal governments began exploring ways to dismantle aspects of their welfare programs. The Canada Health and Social Transfer (CHST) replaced the Canada Assistance Plan, which brought deep cuts to federal spending; and the Unemployment Insurance program was replaced, leading to significantly reduced coverage for the unemployed. Some provincial governments made deep cuts in their social assistance programs and removed many people from their welfare rolls. By the 1990s many programs were being cut back, and this shifted responsibility from the federal government to the provincial and territorial governments, and through these governments to the community and voluntary and informal sectors.

Because of government actions and inactions, Canadians learned how exposed social programs were to economic winds of change. A number of commentators pronounced the postwar social security system – the Keynesian welfare state – dead or dying. To be sure, Brian Mulroney's Conservative federal governments of the 1980s and early 1990s, and Jean Chrétien's Liberal governments of the mid-1990s, as well as provincial administrations such as those of Ralph Klein and Mike Harris, reduced social spending, often deeply, and retreated from economic stabilization policies and the idea of a comprehensive social safety net. In this era of restructuring and retrenchment, some observers argued that the foundations of the Keynesian welfare state were disappearing in Canada (Brodie 1995; Pulkingham and Ternowetsky 1996). Other social policy writers suggest that the dismantling and privatizing of the welfare state would continue; that under economic globalism the nation-state might become obsolete; and that we needed to ponder what would come after the welfare state (Teeple 1995; Collier 1997).

Important elements of the welfare state are gone: universal income programs for families with children and for seniors; policies for, and the political commitment to, high and stable levels of employment; and a specific federal role in the financing of employment insurance and in the provision of social assistance across the country. Other elements have been reduced and residualized: economic regulation and stabilization, EI coverage, and social housing. In many respects, income support levels for those in need are less adequate today than they were a decade or more ago.

Over the past fifteen years, governments have gone beyond fiscal restraint and talk of crisis and begun retrenching social programs and restructuring the role of governments in providing social support. The neoliberal state based on monetarist economic ideas has come to dominate. Many people who support the idea of welfare are glad that certain aspects of the system have disappeared. They are pleased that sexist employment practices have been eliminated; that overtly racist immigration laws have been erased; that discriminatory regulations in social assistance, such as the "man in the house" rule for single-mother families, have been ended; and that the residential schools for Aboriginal peoples have been closed. As Alan Cairns (1986, 82–3) has said, "it is not necessary to shelter every activity of modern government in Canada under the rubric of the welfare state and thus impervious to criticism. It is far from evident that the major beneficiaries of modern state activity are the poor, the downtrodden, the disadvantaged, and the helpless."

All has not been lost, however. Much of the welfare system survives even if in an altered form. The core sectors – universal health care and education – remain. The personal income tax system continues to be broadly progressive, and several new tax credits have appeared and existing ones enriched over the past fifteen years. Another major development was the entrenchment of the Canadian Charter of Rights and Freedoms in the Constitution in 1982. Canada is the only country in the world whose constitution recognizes and protects people with disabilities. The Charter extends equal rights and freedoms to males and females; it also recognizes and affirms the existing treaty rights of the Aboriginal peoples of Canada. Human rights laws and other kinds of civic regulation (discussed in chapter 8) have been broadened in scope at the federal and provincial levels. Reforms in 1998 to the financing of the Canada Pension Plan will help sustain this important retirement income support.

In public spending terms, social policies continue to enjoy the largest share of governmental budgets. Since the 1980s, the social policy expenditures of all governments in Canada have increased in absolute terms, in per capita terms, and as a share of total program spending. In 1980–1, social expenditures by the federal, provincial, territorial, and municipal governments were $73.3 billion, representing 64.1 per cent of program spending by all governments. In 2007–8, social spending (i.e., on education, health, income security, and social services) accounted for 69.3 per cent of program spending by all governments. Between 1989 and 2007, on a per capita basis, spending on health care in Canada rose from $1,384 to $3,265, while spending on social services and income programs rose from $2,951 to $5,267.[1]

In many ways, social policies have become economic policies. Recent reforms to social programs aim to reward work effort, facilitate job searches and retraining, and discourage reliance on social assistance and EI. Investments in education and lifelong learning have become tools for improving economic adaptability and productivity. Social policies are being realigned to serve the needs of international trade and labour markets rather than the needs of people. No longer does social policy simply mean the non-market allocation of benefits and services to people; it now includes market-based provisions, or at least market-informed ones.

This latest period has opened social policy contradictions that in turn have generated struggles and debates. Fiona Williams (1992, 204) has written that "contradictions are nothing new in the state of welfare, but the 1990s marks an intensification of contradictions as well as a shifting of debates." Many social programs support economic needs; yet as we showed in chapter 6, the economic security and well-being of many citizens has been taking a hit. People on social assistance because of some debilitating condition or social disadvantage are feeling pressured or threatened into low-paid work through workfare measures; meanwhile, the real value of minimum wages has declined over time. Economic growth has been slowing, while changes in the economy have been accelerating. There has been a fragmentation of social services through contracting out, in tandem with financial restrictions on community-based services; also at the same time, provincial governments have been centralizing their authority and control. Canadian pollster Angus Reid (1997, 276) has found "far more willingness to ascribe blame to the poor these days even though it's getting much easier to sink into poverty than it used to be."

Still another consequence of this latest period is that program cuts are often intensifying inequalities even though there has been "a growing awareness and resistance to inequalities of race, gender and disability" (Williams 1992, 203). In chapter 8 we drew attention to one aspect of the changing politics: the shift away from universalism and standardization in program design and organization towards particularism and diversity. In many respects, this has been positive because it offers community recognition to groups that have been excluded by the policy process. But in other ways, it has been negative when such recognition of differences has entailed the regulation and surveillance of those who are targeted for social benefits, resulting in further stigma and marginalization.

Balancing the needs of the community with the needs of the market economy has long been a central challenge of social policy, as chapters 2, 3, and 4 have shown. Changes in the economy, be they local, provincial, or national – changes that threaten people's security and livelihood – prompt community demands for social protection. Economic globalization and civic pluralization have raised new risks and needs for the state and the community. There are competing pressures and ideas regarding the state's role in protecting its citizens. A large part of the changing politics revolves around the tensions between global economic interests, which press for the liberalization and reduction of state policies, and social movements' claims for further interventions by the state to address inequities and disadvantages.

One of the contradictions of social policy reform in Canada over the past fifteen years has been that universal income programs have been eliminated supposedly to better target benefits to those most in need, even while poverty and welfare caseloads have increased and little of the "savings" from eliminating Old Age Security payments and Family Allowance benefits have actually gone to lower-income families or seniors (Rice and Prince 1993). Behind this contradiction, however, the Canadian welfare state does perform a redistributive role, although a diminished role compared to a few decades earlier. It has been a disingenuous critique by the right and an exaggerated claim by some on the left that the welfare state has failed to eradicate inequalities or to implement a strategy of egalitarianism. In a social policy system built on universal health care and education, and on various social insurance programs – all in the context of a market economy – a modest redistribution effect is to be expected. Cash transfers and tax provisions do shift the distribution of market-based income towards greater equality. A study of market incomes and family poverty by the Canadian Council on Social Development reported that "in the absence of government income supports, many more Canadian families would be left poor by the marketplace ... [also that] government transfers and benefits rescued 557,000 families from market poverty in 1994, and brought the incomes of other poor families a little closer to the poverty line" (Schellenberg and Ross 1997, 4). We believe that income support through tax and transfer provisions is critical and needs enhancing. A new approach to improving the incomes of working-poor and welfare-poor Canadians should also place greater emphasis on job creation, child care, pay equity, and tax reforms.

Stephen Harper, Conservative Politics, the Federation, and Social Policy

With Stephen Harper and the Conservatives in power nationally for several years now, there has been a notable absence of federal leadership on many issues pertaining to social policy. The content and tone of federal politics have changed a good deal during the early years of the twenty-first century. The Jean Chrétien and Paul Martin Liberal governments addressed the place of major cities in the federation and explored tri-level relations; the Harper Conservative governments have been less concerned about urban governance, stressing instead urban issues of crime and public safety. Chrétien and Martin undertook major new social investments, building a system of early childhood learning and child care across the country; the Harper Conservatives extol the virtues of personal choices by families – thus they introduced the Universal Child Care Benefit – and at the same time question the motives of child care specialists and public services in this field. The Chrétien and Martin governments exercised the federal spending power to invest in health care and other areas; the Harper Conservatives eschew the use of this policy instrument for intergovernmental agreements on social matters. The previous Liberal governments sought a moderately new political relationship with First Nations and other Indigenous peoples; the Harper Conservatives have largely kept away from fundamental issues of self-determination and self-government, focusing rather on symbolic and service issues that are important but that on their own do not directly tackle colonial relationships.

The change in federal government from the Liberals to the Conservatives has not constituted a wholesale shift in social policy making. There have been similarities in approach between today's Harper Conservatives and the Chrétien and Martin governments from 1993 to 2006, which also had some neoliberal features. As Kate Bezanson notes: "Federal neoliberal policies in the 1990s, with the emphasis on free markets and less state intervention, and an approach that blamed the individual rather than the market for poverty and unemployment, created fertile ground for the success of the federal Conservatives" (2010, 108).

Regarding the federal role in social policy and the Canadian federation, Bezanson sees other similarities as well, contending that "the federal Liberals under Chrétien oversaw an intensification of the process of retrenchment and saw a massive realignment in federal–provincial relations, in social spending, and in philosophical commitment to the goals of the Keynesian welfare state" (2010, 108). Martha Friendly and Susan Prentice (2009, 96) contend that this decline in the federal social role has taken place "over the past three decades." This retrenchment eased a good deal in the final Chrétien government (2000–3) and in the Martin government (2004–6); during those years, there were substantial reinvestments in health care, child benefits, and housing. As well, important continuities are evident between recent Liberal and the

Conservative federal governments in some major transfer programs such as elderly benefits.

Regarding social policy, the most significant consequence under Harper's governments has been the shift in prevailing issues, in the terms of political talk, and in the underlying conception of Canadian federalism – specifically, of Ottawa's place in the political community. An old political saying on leadership suggests that "he who determines what politics is about runs the country, because the definition of alternatives is the choice of conflicts, and the choice of conflicts allocates power" (Schattschneider 1960, 68). While something of an exaggeration, this statement does capture the significance today of how issues are framed, how policy agendas are set, and how certain topics are organized into political debates while other issues are relegated to the margins, thereby shaping the opportunities and obstacles for particular changes. Harper's philosophy and action on what federal politics is about emphasizes economic matters, foreign policy to a degree, Arctic sovereignty and national defence, law and order, and public security (Harper and Flanagan 1998; Johnson 2006b; Flanagan 2007; Martin 2010). "In terms of governance," writes Rachel Laforest, "the federal role has clearly diminished within the social policy fields. So has its influence" (2009b, 160). It is now at the level of provincial governments and provincial political communities that much of the action on social policy and practice is taking place. Laforest adds: "By relinquishing and delegating responsibility to the provinces, the Conservatives have in effect changed the level at which politics around social policy will play out" (2009b, 162). Among other implications, this has meant that voluntary sector agencies, community-based interest groups, and social movements need to focus on provincial governments for their political mobilization and policy engagement.

Provincial Governments and Poverty Reduction Strategies in the Twenty-First Century

The divided sovereignty between the federal and provincial orders of government is a central and dynamic characteristic of social policy development. The federation, as always, is changing across the country. It is also diversifying. The introduction of poverty reduction strategies by several provincial governments illustrates a resurgence of provincial innovation in Canadian social policy. Between 2002 and 2010, six provinces adopted comprehensive poverty reduction strategies. Quebec established the first such strategy in 2002, passing an Act to Combat Poverty and Social Exclusion and releasing its first five-year plan in 2004. Newfoundland and Labrador followed with a poverty plan in 2006, then Ontario in 2008–9, Nova Scotia and Manitoba both in 2009, and New Brunswick in 2009–10. Poverty reduction plans are in development in Yukon, the Northwest Territories, Nunavut, and Prince Edward Island.

This rise in provincial policy action is not the result of constitutional reform to fundamental rules governing the federation. Nor is this activism the result of a transfer of legislative powers from the federal government to provincial governments. Rather, the provincialization of social policy in recent times is due to the relative increase in the activity of provinces within their own jurisdictional responsibilities. This activism is not uniform across the provinces, but a general trend is observable in terms of a new emphasis on poverty policy, with new investments in various program areas, and in the establishment of new governance structures to support these poverty reduction strategies. Associated with the wave of anti-poverty strategies across the country are altered understandings of poverty, provincial societies, and state action within Canadian federalism.

Provincial and territorial politics have always figured in social policy politics in Canada. In current times, a shift in orientation is playing out that emphasizes social citizenship at the level of the provinces. This shift derives in part from the cancellation of CAP in the mid-1990s and, since then, the reliance on loosely defined and meekly enforced conditional grants in labour market, housing, and social service areas. The profile of the provinces relates also to the relative decline or inactivity in the exercise of federal powers by the Harper Conservatives, who are disinclined to undertake major new social programs unilaterally or collaboratively with other governments. In 2010, for example, the Harper government in effect rejected all seventy-four recommendations by a Senate committee report dealing with homelessness and poverty.

In most matters of social policy, Canadian citizens are increasingly provincial citizens. Membership in a specific political community shapes their public status and human potentialities, whether that community is Nova Scotia, Quebec, Ontario, Manitoba, British Columbia, or Yukon. It is provincial governments and provincial state systems that people experience in their everyday lives. It is towards provincial political parties and leaders, and to provincial public sectors, that social movements and interest groups direct most of their social advocacy efforts. In turn, it is from provincial governments that Canadians seem increasingly to expect policy responses and provisions for education, health, housing, training, community services, and income supports. In these ways, provinces are active sovereign states, relevant political communities, and important boundaries of social belonging and inclusion.

The anti-poverty reduction strategies introduced by most provinces and territories reflect the organization and mobilization of civil society groups for economic changes and social reforms. Such campaigns, and related consultations and action plans by governments, have drawn attention to the persistence of poverty, the widening of inequalities, declining social capital and cohesion in families and communities, and the costs of long-term poverty for the market economy. If Canada is a mosaic culturally, these poverty campaigns remind us that as regards divisions in society, the country is a mosaic vertically.

Renewed provincial activity in social policy is apparent in specific legislation on poverty or on economic and social exclusion in certain jurisdictions (New Brunswick, Ontario, and Quebec, for example); in renewed budgetary investments over a number of program areas and over a number of years; in new organizational structures to support public engagement, poverty research, and policy development; and in the progress being made to establish new indicators and measures relating to housing affordability, quality of life, and deprivation. These activities represent a shift in policy orientation away from economic liberalism and towards social protection, cultural recognition, and programs to address specific disadvantaged groups, such as single mothers and persons with disabilities. Notwithstanding structural obstacles, there is a renewed belief in social reformism – that is, in the responsibility and capacity of provincial governments to tackle major societal problems effectively, in line with important policy goals such as the alleviation, reduction, and ultimately prevention of poverty.

New, comprehensive poverty reduction strategies have been launched in several provinces. Provincial governments are trying another policy path, one that differs somewhat from the poverty relief approaches of past decades. Traditional poverty relief in Canada relied heavily on means-tested welfare, and reform efforts focused on taking social assistance programs in progressive or regressive directions. Social assistance was the dominant program in provincial income policy for low-income individuals and families. Benefit levels were meagre, stigmatizing to receive, and saturated with complex rules and surveillance.

Poverty relief mainly entailed charitable and not-for-profit provision of supports; at times, it also addressed market-oriented incentives for employment. Select categories of the deserving poor were targeted – those deemed to be in greatest need. Consequently, program clients had little solidarity or social connection with the wider population, and this made both the clients and these welfare programs politically unattractive to most voters and marginal to most governmental officials. Over time, poverty relief and welfare measures developed in ad hoc and piecemeal ways, and the result was a complex patchwork of programs and purposes (Boychuk 1998; Guest 1985; Haddow 1993).

The move towards poverty reduction strategies has not meant the abandonment of core elements of the traditional poverty relief approach; however, these strategies do contain important departures and innovations in Canadian social policy. We should also note that, in keeping with the logic of federalism, across the provincial poverty reduction strategies there are differences in the scope, content, and adequacy of policy responses.

The aim of New Brunswick's poverty plan, for example, is to reduce income poverty by 25 per cent and deep income poverty by 50 per cent by 2015 and to make significant progress in achieving sustained economic and social inclusion. Ontario's poverty reduction strategy has set a goal of reducing the number of children living in poverty by 25 per cent over five years and lifting an estimated 90,000 children out of poverty by 2014. In contrast, Manitoba's poverty plan has a more general objective of continuously reducing poverty and increasing social inclusion.

As in previous poverty debates in Canada, social and economic groups and governments are looking at policy responses beyond just revamping social assistance, although this remains a focal point. Employment opportunities and work incentives are fundamental values; and the market, while taken as given, is not taken for granted as a ready source of good jobs and adequate incomes. The idea of a guaranteed annual income or basic income is a focal point for many groups, although other reform ideas are circulating in the social policy community with respect to reforming social insurance programs such as EI and CPP and to reforming tax credits. In contrast to social security reviews of the mid-1970s and the mid-1990s, two features stand out: the federal government is a far less prominent participant; and joining and pushing provincial officials are a multitude of civil society and social movement organizations.

The current wave of provincial activism on poverty policy and other social programming suggests that decentralization in the Canadian state is not necessarily a conservative phenomenon (Noël 1999). At least in recent years, the provinces more than the federal government have been developing innovative and progressive social policies, new governance structures, and promising practices. In our federation, this raises the age-old question of what role the federal government should play in addressing issues of inequality and economic and social exclusion. What might be the national dimension in poverty reduction and prevention?

Where Do We Go from Here?

In considering how to find new balances among markets, governments, and communities, we discuss three strategies Canadians can use in the study and the practice of social policy in Canada. These strategies are as follows: broadening the scope of policy debate to heighten the importance of communities in the policy process; re-establishing the capacity and social role of governments so that new ideas appear on the policy agenda; and democratizing the welfare state so that it fully includes people from a wide variety of community groups.

The welfare state as an idea is not obsolete; it remains relevant precisely because of changing economic and social conditions. Economic globalism will continue to exert a major influence on social policy. A central idea of this book, though, is the need to consider globalization in relation to social pluralization and to examine the interplay of both trends in relation to the federalized welfare state in Canada. The economic winners in the new global economy may want to restrict some decisions in some policy areas, but the modern state is not powerless. Governments must maintain their ability to direct the course of social policy. It is an exaggeration to conclude that globalism is rendering governments powerless to make policy choices and to meet social objectives.

Double Movements in Social Politics: A Multiplication of Struggles

Making and changing social policies is not a simple process of applying rational knowledge and allocating adequate resources to agreed-upon goals. The central puzzle in studying social policy, suggests Ramesh Mishra (1981, 24), "has to do with the fact that non-market forms of distribution and transaction have developed in market societies. Why? And with what consequences? Should they be developed further? And, if so, on what grounds?" Polanyi's concept of the double movement helps describe the organizational interests, power relations, and competing agendas in Canadian social policy. Polanyi emphasized how the expansion of markets and the social dislocations resulting from the fast pace of industrial change prompt a protectionist countermovement by groups in society. As Joseph Stiglitz expresses it: "Rapid transformation destroys old coping mechanisms, old safety nets, while it creates a new set of demands, *before new coping mechanisms are developed*" (Stiglitz 2001, xi). That countermovement seeks to safeguard the welfare of communities and natural environments by checking economic growth in definite directions; it mobilizes to have laws and other public measures adopted that moderate growth or even confine market forces.

Additional interpretations of the double movement in social politics arise from our analysis. A second interpretation concerns social policy in the context of crisis periods, either of the welfare state or of the market economy itself. In chapters 5 and 6, concerning the crisis of the welfare state, core social policy aims were under attack and the legitimacy of groups to claim social protection and rights diminished somewhat, with increasing prominence devoted to the marketization and fiscalization of social policy. We showed in chapter 7 how the contraction and disorganization of the economy in Canada and internationally, triggered by the financial crisis of 2007–9, was met with protests by various groups as well as by calls to contain the downturn, to more closely regulate the market system, and to take policy steps that would revive economic growth and job creation. The context here was not the problems of rapid market growth; instead, it was the problems of a sharp downturn in economic activity. Both Polanyi's original version of the double movement and this second interpretation entail support for the continuity and growth of the capitalist economic system.

The third interpretation is quite different. It concerns a countermovement primarily of intellectual thought and secondarily of political action. This countermovement involves imagining a post-capitalist society and, through a style of radical politics, transforming property rights and economic activity. In Polanyi's terms, this movement aims at changing the basic organizing principles for society in order to establish a workable form of democratic socialism. A group historically central to enacting this radical politics has been the labour movement, a sector that admittedly over recent decades has declined in relative numbers and perceived influence within many political systems, especially within liberal welfare states such as Canada, Great Britain, and the United States. In today's world, then, the old social movement of trade unionism must forge alliances with new social movements and other groups to advance effectively an agenda of democratic socialism.

All three interpretations of what we consider to be double-movement social politics imply critical roles for institutional arrangements, the exercise of power relations by interests, and a role for ideas, human agency, and distinct types of political interventions. This metaphor of movement implies that markets and welfare states are not once-and-for-all achievements; nor is neoliberalism an all-powerful reality unencumbered with resistance and alternative beliefs and interests. Polanyi's framework offers students of social policy an insightful way of examining relations among the state, the market economy, and civil society.

Broadening the Social Policy Debate

A political challenge in the coming decades is to find new ways to think about the relationship between market forces and community claims. The paradox is that, though they have contradictory logics (as Karl Polanyi among others has noted), we need both markets and communities in order to prosper and ensure a vital democracy. An essential barrier in achieving such a new relationship has been the belief, expressed most forcefully by the right, that markets are the primary institution for attaining well-being. This perspective downplays the social role of the state and often exaggerates the capacities of civil society groups. The result is that the well-being of many Canadians becomes dependent on the whims of private investors, the volatility of free markets, the fashions of foreign exchange, and the decisions of bankers and corporate presidents outside the country.

Polanyi was deeply concerned about the relationship between self-regulating markets and the community's ability to take care of its members. If he were alive today he would understand the rise of globalism and the forces for free trade. He would also understand the growing demands of community groups for recognition of their rights and interests. He would recognize the important role the state must play in balancing the forces of self-regulating markets, and he would expect the state to build social structures that protect the community's sovereignty against the impositions of market forces. We also believe that governments have the power and authority to create a new relationship between the market and the community as a way of meeting the need for social protection and the desire for cultural recognition.

Opening up a new debate about the changing role of welfare is difficult but absolutely vital because of the pluralization of society. Many more groups want a voice in how the government will address social issues but are finding it difficult to influence Canada's dominant political parties. These groups are struggling to have their issues placed on the policy agenda. They seek not only to open the debate about the policy agenda, but also to articulate how and why their issues are central to the community's well-being. To be effective, however, community groups must find ways to place their self-interest in a larger context and to relate to other interest groups. A major challenge is that there are few national forums in which community groups come together to talk about their issues or position their concerns in a more encompassing social policy vision.

New forms of Canada–indigenous nation relations, of federal–provincial–territorial relations, and of provincial–municipal cooperation must support a more inclusive policy debate. Public structures and processes must provide ways for emerging interest groups to find a legitimate voice on behalf of the communities they represent. Also, governments must find ways to help create community-based policy structures to address the changing politics of social policy. The new social policy agenda must build on a political discourse about the community and the rights and responsibilities of citizenship. It must reject the individualistic notions generated by market competition and assert the importance of social connections, social harmony, and social solidarity. It must embrace the notion of cooperation as central to a functioning society. At the deepest level, the new politics of social policy must champion the idea of interdependence and of interconnections among all communities. Moving towards a more cooperative society includes the notion that all people have value and that social differences are what make the community rich and resourceful.

The creation of a new social policy agenda must encompass the idea that we live in a finite world with limited resources existing in a fragile environment. While the search for new ways of doing things, new forms of energy, and new ways to make life better must continue, it must do so with the recognition that for a community to support economic activity, it must consider the implications of growth and development for the community and the environment. Governments must find ways to protect the nation and its citizens from the destructive forces of world trade. While there are important advantages to fostering stronger connections among producing sectors of the world economy, a country cannot allow these relationships to undermine the human rights, income security, health and safety, and working conditions of its citizens. New debates must develop that argue for trading relationships that protect people, communities, and the environment.

One way to enrich this debate is by inviting non-governmental groups into the discussions. This invitation could include those groups concerned with the environment, human rights, and the rights of particular interests. The opening of such discussions could place people with a wide variety of interests – pro-traders as well as protectionists – into debates that would make the policy trade-offs more visible and understandable to the broad public. When left to market decisions, poverty, pollution, crime, and social dislocations increase. The sum total of decisions made by self-regarding individuals or firms does not create social conditions free from the problems that governments may fail to solve. Rather, they create social arrangements that provide advantages to some and disadvantages to others. Those who are disadvantaged have a more difficult time meeting their needs and are less well off. Those who can take advantage of their position to make private decisions are able to meet their needs more effectively and also to gather more decision-making power (Finlayson 1996; Langille 1997).

The point of broadening the scope of social policy debate is to expand intellectual, political, and everyday discussions of the welfare state and public interventions. Debates should "encompass the interests of various muted groups, particularly women and oppressed racial and ethnic groups" (Bryson 1992, 4–5). Urgently required, we believe, are new dynamics among the market economy, civil society, and the welfare state. An important part of that new balance is for governments to stop offloading responsibilities onto communities and start supporting local initiatives. In the words of the Social Justice Commission (1994, 370), "government can never take the place of community: what it can and should do, however, is create political, institutional and financial frameworks which help local people rebuild their communities from the bottom up, making them safer places in which to live and generating a better quality of life which can support wider economic opportunities." We also recall that Polanyi saw cultural institutions as offering "protective covering" for individuals and groups against the acute dislocations and personal costs of economic upheavals and downturns.

The changing politics are about the waning of neoliberalism and laissez-faire market globalism, though not their demise, alongside a resurgence of the centrist liberal perspective on state intervention and social policy. Among policy leaders there is a renewed albeit cautious willingness to extend social benefits and services through the public sector. To some extent, the state's fiscal capacity is always politically negotiable. The public finance culture will most likely evolve through give and take among the viewpoints and pressures of the federal government, the provinces, public and elite opinions, and interest structures. Many leaders now refer to new social spending as "strategic investments" for enhancing economic growth and social well-being. This language is reminiscent of a vital point made long ago by Leonard Marsh (1943, 273–4): "Social security payments are not money lost, [but rather] are investments in morale and health, in greater family stability, and from both material and psychological viewpoints, in human productive efficiency. They demand personal and community responsibilities; but in the eyes of most of the people, who are beneficiaries, give a more evident meaning to the ideas of common effort and national solidarity. It has yet to be proved that any democracy which underwrites the social minimum for its citizens is any the weaker or less wealthy for doing so."

Rebuilding the Social Role and Capacity of Governments

In 1943, Marsh faced a number of questions when thinking about the social role governments should play in providing social and economic security to all citizens. What are the causes of unemployment, and what is the proper role of the government in managing the economy? What universal and employment risks do individuals and families face? How should the government share these risks? How should governments protect citizens' well-being? His answers led to a broad series of social policies that protected Canadians from the worst problems created by industrialization and urbanization. These included universal programs for families and the elderly, insurance programs for the unemployed and those injured at work, and social assistance programs for those excluded from the labour market.

We face similar questions, along with newer ones, in trying to rebuild the social role of government. What is the proper role of the government in a global economy? Under what conditions should people receive social benefits? How can the government develop new social programs in the face of an aging population in Canada and a globalizing economy? How, today, can Canada address interculturalism, secularism, ethnic differences, and race relations? To what extent, and in what ways, should governments, on behalf of the overall population, redress historic injustices towards particular groups? Recent studies by community groups, health regional authorities, city councils, medical officers of health, and foundations and policy think tanks, as well as parliamentary and legislative committees, are offering a number of answers, each focusing on a specific aspect of rebuilding social policy for the coming decades.

For us it is a matter of maintaining the essential role of government in addressing the country's social deficits. Social deficits exist when large numbers of people are on employment insurance or welfare, children and youth are going to school hungry, there are limited opportunities for skill development and retraining, and there is a lack of adequate and affordable child care and elder care. Judith Maxwell argues that rebuilding the state's social role is essential for no less a reason than restoring the political legitimacy and credibility of our governing institutions; and that one step towards rebuilding the role of government is to develop a clearly defined long-term view of cultural, economic, environmental, and social objectives that work towards a new social contract. "This means rethinking the political values that describe the obligations and rights of all the players – governments, citizens, employers, unions, and interest groups" (Maxwell 1994, 56).

Literature from academics, policy analysts, and community groups identifies many initiatives that governments could take, including the following:

- strengthening the commitment to public health care and "healthy public policy"
- lifting all Canadians out of poverty with an adequate income to meet their basic needs and to aid them in becoming financially self-sustaining
- developing country-wide, as a fundamental social investment, child care and early childhood learning networks of programs and services
- making a new commitment to affordable and secure housing of a range of types for indigenous peoples, newcomers to Canada

(immigrants and refugees), persons with disabilities, seniors, and youth
- recognizing the inherent rights of indigenous nations for self-determination and self-governance within the federation
- constructing an accessible and inclusive community for persons with mental and physical disabilities
- committing to anti-racism, inter- or multi-culturalism, and religious freedoms consistent with Canada's system of laws, rights, and duties
- acknowledging sexuality as a human rights issue and the multiple expressions of sexuality, including gay, lesbian, bisexual, and transgender persons
- making a renewed commitment to gainful employment, universal Employment Insurance protection, and active labour market benefits and measures for all who want to work, *and*
- reforming the tax system to better meet the core functions of raising adequate revenues for public services, rewarding socially valuable activities, and reducing deep poverty and inequalities.

Taking action on these or any number of other policy issues would strengthen the social roles of the government and increase its capacity to deal with social issues.

We believe the federal and provincial governments must rebuild their social roles and capacities in order to re-energize the politics of social policy. This requires that governments recommit themselves to developing a more equitable society, a society in which all Canadians have adequate income and a community in which they have a voice in the new social policy debates. Beyond this it requires governments, both federal and provincial, to work together to influence the international social policy environment so that a more global principle of citizenship develops. By taking bold steps the government will rebuild its social role and increase its capacity to govern.

While governments can choose from a long list of social problems that need addressing, we have focused on two issues: poverty at the domestic level and international social policy agreements at the global level. Poverty focuses on issues inside the country and challenges governments to develop innovative programs that help individuals and families deal with the risks of the globalizing economy. International agreements focus on broader issues and force Canadians to think about the wider policy domain and the needs of others. In both areas we have set out a policy agenda and called for renewed commitments on the part of the government in addressing social issues.

A Renewed Attack on Inequality and Injustice

Canada has an ongoing problem of inequalities and injustices with regard to housing, educational achievement, life chances, human rights, income and financial security, community inclusion, and a sense of belonging in Canadian life. Those facing the greatest challenges and social distress come from certain groups. Highly disadvantaged groups in Canadian society are indigenous peoples, recent immigrants and refugee claimants, single mothers, and persons with mental and physical disabilities. Individuals with identities associated with one or more of these groups are overrepresented among the poor (Armitage 2003; McCreath 2011; Senate Report 2009).

By a number of empirical measures, several aspects of social and economic inequality are worsening in Canada. While the actual number of low-income families has shifted over time, there has been a relatively consistent 15 to 20 per cent of the population whose incomes are near or below Statistics Canada's low-income cut-off lines. Economic inequalities result in health inequalities. The Health Council of Canada reports that "the biggest health problem in Canada is inequality. The overall improvement in our health status masks the grim reality that health inequalities among social groups are growing – as they are in most highly developed countries. In Canada, healthy life expectancy is three to four years less in low-income neighbourhoods than in high-income neighbourhoods. The infant mortality rate in low-income neighbourhoods is almost double that in high-income neighbourhoods" (Health Council of Canada 2006, 89). In a 2011 *Globe and Mail* article (5 May), Tory Senator Hugh Segal predicted that "over time, we will begin to run out of the money that we need to deal with the demographic bulge because it will be consumed in the health care requirements of the poor, which will increase. It will be consumed in the costs of the illiteracy and unemployment which relate to poverty … And it'll be unsustainable." Segal has called for increased federal attention to the problems of low-income families.

Inequalities and injustices are in the structures of market capitalism; in the rules and programs of state federalism; and in the ethnic, gender, disability, and myriad other divisions in societal pluralism. In other words, economic, political, and cultural factors shape the character and depth of disparities in society. Many inequalities in society are eco-nomic while others are clearly political and still others mainly cultural. In reality, the three dimensions overlap and interact in particular ways in multiple domains of life. Contemporary politics of Canadian social policy revolve around these institutional spheres of markets, govern-ments, and communities, and involve the contested allocation of ma-terial resources, public policy responses, and symbolic and cultural resources. While considerable evidence across numerous countries has demonstrated that equality is better for everyone's quality of life, gov-ernments tend to adopt egalitarian policies when they face crises of legitimacy and need to gain popular support (Wilkinson and Pickett 2010). One reason, as Macionis, Jansson, and Benoit (2009, 225) suggest, may be that "most members of our society are willing to accept a high level of income inequality, and may hold a harsh view of the poor."

Much of our politics of social policy is a politics of equality/inequal-ity. It is a politics about public awareness and interpretation of inequi-ties and opportunities. It is about which inequalities most people regard as acceptable and which inequalities or injustices are unacceptable or illegitimate in a liberal democracy and market society. Our politics of equality/inequality is also about the ranking, through debates and pol-icy deliberations, of such core values as merit and achievement, basic need, equal human worth, personal accountability, and shared respon-sibility. In short, as bundles of multiple values and conditions, both equality and inequality are contestable ideas and concrete activities.

Historically, economic growth reduced the number of people with low incomes by providing employment opportunities. However, the traditional relationship between economic growth and poverty seems to be weakening. As the global economy comes to have a greater influ-ence on employment, people with a good education are doing better in the labour market while people with limited skills and education are finding it more difficult to find work. The differences are widening be-tween well-paying, permanent work in the primary labour force and poor-paying, part-time jobs in the secondary labour force. The result is an increase in the number of people with jobs that do not provide a living wage. In the words of sociologists John Macionis, Mikael Jans-son, and Cecelia Benoit, "Canada is highly stratified. Not only do the rich have most of the money, but they also receive the most schooling, enjoy the best health, and consume the most goods and services. Such privilege contrasts sharply with the poverty of tens and thousands of women and men who worry about paying next month's rent or putting food on the table" (2009, 211). Others worry about finding emergency shelter or sleeping in a doorway.

While increased training and more education will solve some of these problems, some Canadians will need sustained help to ensure they do not live in poverty. The way of providing income support to the poor that best meets our goal of rebuilding the social role of governments is to develop a comprehensive social security program based on a negative income tax. This idea has been around for years. In a 1997 article, John Myles and Paul Pierson examined the negative income tax as an approach to alleviating poverty that would achieve broad political support. Under a negative income tax, people would not "apply" for social assistance; rather, when their income fell below a certain level, they would receive a top-up.

The program would be relatively simple. The government would set an income floor for eligible individuals and families: as a person's income declined, either because the individual could not work or because there was no work available, the level of the basic allowance would rise until it reached the maximum benefit level; when he or she had income from any other source, the basic allowance would be reduced so that as income rose, the amount of the allowance would fall. The government would set the rate of the reduction so that it encouraged people to seek work and thereby increased their income while not "punishing" them for finding other sources of income by removing all their benefits. At a predetermined point, depending on the tax-back rate, the benefit would disappear and the person would start to pay taxes. Since the tax-back rate would always be less than 100 per cent, some portion of benefits would still go to people with middle incomes who were firmly attached to the world of employment. This means there would be increased political support for the system from the broad middle classes.

The advantage of a negative income tax is that it can be theoretically universal while still targeting needy groups. From this perspective, everyone is a taxpayer, and therefore a negative income tax program has a universal orientation. A second advantage is that the system can give people a choice about how they earn or receive income. By providing choice the program can support work incentive programs without forcing people into workfare. People make their own decisions about how much they are able to contribute to their own well-being.

The program would not be "welfare" as we commonly know it; rather, it would act as an income stabilizer. The program would have a general appeal to the middle classes, yet it would target money where most needed: for the poor. Similarly, since it would not be based on previous earnings, it could include any number of conditions and groups. Stay-at-home parents could have the same rights and be as much a part of the system as those who worked outside the house, although their income level would reflect these choices.

Negative income tax programs could encourage any number of activities. They could support low-income parents who were taking care of other people's children, students who were going to university, or poor people who were providing volunteer assistance to social agencies. They could greatly assist low-income families who were taking care of the elderly or providing community support to those with developmental disabilities. Using the tax system to income-test social benefits would largely overcome traditional complaints that selectivity is intrusive and stigmatizing for clients and administratively complex and expensive to deliver.

The negative income tax might be the most positive way that governments could address poverty. The program would not create sharp divisions between the employed and the unemployed or between the able-bodied and the disabled. It would provide all citizens with a basic guarantee: income that does not fall below a given level.

There is yet another advantage: a negative income tax would be attached invisibly to the tax system. Governments may be losing some of their capacity to intervene in the social environment, but they will be much less willing to give up their influence when it comes to the tax system. In a social policy environment seemingly overshadowed by global interests, it is easier for governments to introduce changes in the tax system than it is to introduce new social welfare programs. The tax system is less visible than most welfare programs and does not provide the same political target for restructuring. As such, a negative income tax program could replace social insurance programs without the political protests that come when governments endeavour to introduce new welfare measures.

Negative income tax programs are well adapted to the new politics of social policy. "They rely on new political coalitions which employ new, low-profile strategies suitable for an environment of austerity" (Myles and Pierson 1997, 8). Negative income tax programs can provide a cost-effective transition from needs-based programs to income-tested programs at a time when there is resistance to any new welfare measures. The program would be structured to provide benefits to those in most need, yet those benefits would extend well into the middle-income ranges, thus generating wider support politically among the middle classes.

Developing More Inclusive International Agreements

An important step in rebuilding the government's capacity to deal with social problems is to encourage the development of a new range of international relationships and agreements concerned with the rights of citizens. John Ralston Saul points out that "the Globalization movement has produced myriad market-oriented international binding agreements at the global level and not a single binding agreement in the other areas of human intercourse – work conditions, taxation, child labour, and health and so on. The deep imbalance of the movement, however successful in its own terms, cannot help but provoke forms of disorder" (2009, 25). A more balanced relationship requires a fuller exercise of state authority through national action and international cooperation, with binding regulations on social dimensions of trade that reintroduce "the idea of the public good at the global level" (Saul 2009, 136).

Part of this strategy would be to have the Canadian government take the lead in calling for a new form of global citizenship. The underlying principle of this form of citizenship would build on the activities of the United Nations and would seek to ensure everyone's right to live a decent life. This new balance would strengthen the importance of "community" in the lives of people. This idea would encourage governments to negotiate for a more community-sensitive form of economic development. This would require negotiating limits on the unrestrained exploitation of resources, the development of global trade, and international flows of capital. The goal in this negotiation would be to highlight the social costs of unregulated economic development and to place social policy issues on the international agenda. Many observers contend that the only way to deal adequately with economic globalization is through a system of globalized democratic decision making and regulations.

This is a difficult challenge. The development of new social agreements with other countries will require a broadening of alternative policy institutions based on community interests. The European experience provides insight into how the process can develop: interest groups in Europe are working through their national governments to press for issues that are important to them; at the same time, leaders of these interest groups are developing international links with other organizations in the European Union (EU). In this way they create two paths through which they can influence the policy agenda: directly, and through local governments. The Canadian government could encourage the same type of development in Canada by supporting civil society groups in their efforts to influence the international social policy agenda through government activities and to develop international relationships with interest groups from other countries or within the UN.

There are many obstacles to developing networks that support transnational organizations. National governments must find it in their interest to have non-governmental partners concerning themselves with social issues and working to have these issues placed on the policy agenda. They must be prepared to support the agreements and social charters that will eventually emerge from a richer international debate about global citizenship. Governments must be prepared to support grassroots social movements calling for protection from labour exploitation and environmental degradation. They will need to foster connections between these grassroots community organizations and encourage them to link up with similar organizations in other countries. They will also have to increase their commitment to international organizations such as the UN, the Red Cross, and the International Court. The government must support interest groups that are prepared to question the policy directions of the IMF, the WTO, and the World Bank. Groups such as the International Labour Organization, Greenpeace, and Amnesty International need to be encouraged to open the debate about international trade and its implications for global citizens.

A global perspective on social policy could lead to international agreements that determined how market activities and social activities were to be coordinated. Social policy integration in the EU is primarily through legal instruments that unify the social policy decisions of different countries. Many of the EU's laws and regulations have been developed through intergovernmental rather than political negotiations. Over time they have resulted in a global system (in European terms) of relationships that protect civil, social, and economic rights of citizens across all EU countries. At the same time, countries have considerable autonomy on purely domestic issues.

The development of such an international approach would encourage Canada and other countries to consider the relationship between economic and social issues in different ways. New social policy agreements would force corporations to consider community needs when deciding where and when to locate new production facilities.

Corporations would have to meet international standards regarding the environment and human rights before they could invest or trade in a country. The agreements could be enforceable by punishing corporations that violated the agreements (e.g., by limiting their rights or imposing taxes).

John Wiseman (1996) has argued that a sequencing of policy initiatives is the key to developing international agreements. First, countries would need to monitor international financial flows between countries to ensure compliance with present laws. Next, governments would have to reintroduce some degree of regulation regarding exchange rates to prevent dramatic interest rate changes. Finally, Wiseman posits, governments would have to levy taxes on globalized financial transactions as a way to build the resources necessary to deal with the social implications of world trade. Pulkingham and Ternowetsky (1996) explore the idea of a financial transaction tax as a means for raising revenue and dampening currency speculation, thus stabilizing exchange rates and interest rates. A financial transaction tax as a possible policy instrument is not commonly discussed in social welfare circles, although this may be changing (McQuaig 1998).

Over time the Canadian government could evolve a set of agreements with other countries for controlling transnational corporations. Such actions could include embedding cultural, environmental, and labour clauses in trade agreements; writing stand-alone multinational social charters to regulate trade and investment relations; and building or reforming international institutions. These actions would represent varying degrees of effort at controlling capital as well as the power of transnational corporations (Broad 1995; Collier 1997). A prominent Canadian thinker on this is Marjorie Griffin Cohen, who has suggested that international institutions need to control capital, raise money, and redistribute it worldwide. Cohen (1997a, 7) adds that "there is an urgent need to recognize *economic pluralism* in international trade and investment agreements. A tolerance for pluralism requires the recognition that different goals, conditions, and cultures throughout the world require very different solutions to problems. One system, the western system based on a US kind of economy and social system, will not serve the needs of all people in all circumstances." In advocating for the continued diversity of social policy worldwide, Cohen is echoing the observations of Maxwell and Esping-Andersen on the relation between globalization and welfare states. They suggest that governments are still relatively autonomous agents, acting in a context of economic, social, and political constraints and opportunities to safeguard people and the conditions of life.

Democratizing the Welfare State, and Beyond

The fundamental characteristic of an "inclusive" welfare state is that it is democratic. For there to be a democratic welfare state, citizens must freely elect a government and have the right to change it by peaceful means if they are dissatisfied with its performance (Robson 1976, 16). Moreover, the public must be free to criticize the government if it is not meeting citizens' expectations. Democracy from this perspective requires secret ballots, competitive elections among political parties, and a popular press separate from the state. These political freedoms and many more are included in the Canadian Charter of Rights and Freedoms.

Since the 1970s crisis period of social policy, competing ideas about how the welfare state should operate have directly challenged these fundamental notions of democracy. Those on the far right have called for the rolling back of the state through reductions in laws and taxes as the route to more freedom and individual liberty. Some moderates on both the right and the left, as well as at the political centre, have viewed the increasing role of civil society institutions as a form of democratization in that this has encouraged active citizenship while limiting the need for state interventions. Others, typically on the left, have called for the constitutional entrenchment of social rights and welfare entitlements as a way to meet needs, protect individual liberties, and advance group identities; still others, increasingly through the 2000s, have called for global forms of democratic governance. While some observers have welcomed the rise of new social movements and the alternative politics of the women's movement (MacIvor 1996), others have worried that the resultant splintering of interests is threatening the general public good.

Other ideas, not just those on the desired separation or connection between the people and their political institutions, have been conditioning debates over the nature of democracy. Another critical dimension is the relation between market economics and democratic politics. Gary Teeple (1995, 123) has argued that our political system "is democratic more in form and rhetoric than in content" because it operates within a capitalist society, although "it has been possible to impose certain mitigating effects in the shape of reform on the operation of the market." Philip Resnick strikes a similar and fuller chord:

> there are significant flaws in the operation of democracy as we know it in the West, and as our elites would like to project it to the rest of the world. There is the ongoing problem of the power of capital and the control it has over our media and our political parties. One does not have to subscribe to the wooden language of Marxism-Leninism with its glib dismissal of "bourgeois" democracy as a sham; but we would be equally naive to ignore the disproportionate power which large corporations and corporate-funded media or pressure groups bring to the political arena, during not only elections but also all the time. Can there be real equality of citizen rights and far-reaching pluralism when we begin with such an uneven playing field? There is also the serious problem of voice, of citizen participation above and beyond the casting of ballots during periodic elections. This is not to disparage representative institutions, which are the privileged form which democracy needs to take in large-scale societies of the nation state variety. (1997, 70)

Resnick adds that in many long-standing liberal democracies "there has been increasing talk about a democratic deficit" (1997, 15). The origins of discontent with democracy are related, he suggests, to high unemployment, disenchantment with governing elites, and disillusionment with old-style party politics. To these we would add status anxiety and possibly moral panic associated with the politics of identity, economic and social insecurity associated with economic liberalization through free trade agreements, and the closed nature of most intergovernmental policy and administrative relations in Canada.

Some fault lies with the welfare state as a complex amalgam of organizations, professions, programs, and rules. We need to be clear about what in social policy is worth lamenting and defending and what is worth changing or letting go. We need to heed the critiques of the old welfare state – the calls for decentralization of authority, for greater racial awareness and cultural sensitivity in programming, for the de-bureaucratizing of agencies, and for the demedicalization of health care policy and provision. In a remarkable essay, Leo Panitch writes that "welfare state reforms had little to do with changing the state itself – that is, with altering the mode of administration in which social policy became embedded." From Panitch's perspective, government administration is "fundamentally undemocratic, constructed according to strict doctrines of secrecy and hierarchy that owe much to the nineteenth-century British Colonial Office, or even the Indian army on which it was modeled" (1994, 41). Consequently, the welfare state has very limited potential for mobilizing people with shared interests to come together to share common experiences and assert their beliefs and claims. One factor contributing to the success of retrenchment strategies in the 1980s and 1990s, Panitch suggests, was that "few employees or clients of the welfare state felt that the public agencies really belonged to them – were theirs to influence and control"; and we agree with Panitch's argument that "social policy can be revived only by its explicit association with social participation, empowerment, and mobilization or, in a word, with the democratization of the state" (1994, 39). The democratization of the welfare state requires a shift in ideology, changes to social policy–making structures, and the involvement of a much wider range of interest groups when social needs are being identified.

Canadian social work and social policy texts (McKenzie and Wharf 2010; Prince 2009) have called for a democratizing of social service agencies to reduce controls over clients and enhance services and supports. The struggle for workplace democratization "may take various forms, such as union activity to build and increase service user participation in the decision-making process, more peer supervision, development of a consultative relationship with supervisors rather than that of boss–subordinate, and a struggle to implement more democratic means of sharing decisions, responsibilities, and information" (Mullaly 1997, 183).

A more democratized social policy agenda would allow community groups to find ways of encouraging politicians to stop offering corporations an open-door policy in which environmental standards are overlooked, unions are undermined, wages are cut, tax breaks are given, and a blind eye is turned to working conditions. A more open policy debate would encourage community groups to find ways of supporting governments that require corporations to meet fundamental community expectations. Community groups would be able to work with governments to develop regulations that shape the ways corporations enter a community, to ensure that issues such as pollution, health and safety, and working conditions are included in corporate plans. Again, history teaches us an important lesson – that community activities can set the stage for government action. Many of the early labour codes and health and safety issues started as local initiatives adopted by provincial governments, and later expanded through dialogue and support at the national level. In the beginning the assumption was that it was impossible to regulate economic development in an industrializing country; later came the recognition that such regulations are essential to the stability, legitimacy, and growth of a market economy.

Gradually, the democratization of social policy is positioning gender, disability, sexual orientation, and race – among other social divisions – alongside traditional concerns (e.g., poverty and redistribution) when economic policies and welfare programs and practices are being considered. Feminist writers have drawn attention to limitations in the conventional models of social policy and theories of the welfare state and have generated new concepts and perspectives by emphasizing gender relations and the experiences of women. Feminist research is leading the way in the search for more democratic forms of social policy development by going beyond traditional analyses of entitlement (need, labour market status, and citizenship) to consider other issues central to women, such as motherhood and caregiving. Social reproduction and the interrelationships among the family, the market, and the welfare state are highlighted. These important themes of inquiry counterbalance the usual focus on industrial activities and the usual neglect of unpaid, caring work.

The welfare state's own history suggests that "it will be the old, the poor, the workers, women, Aboriginal peoples, the ill, and the disabled who will have to struggle for, and invent, new self-help and mutual aid methods, and the organizational arrangements to go along with them" (Collier 1997, 140).

As part of the pluralization process, many groups and social movements are looking to the public sector for recognition of their identities and needs; perhaps for compensation for past wrongs; for provision of services and resources to support their autonomy; and for the realization of citizenship rights. In contemporary identity politics, struggles for citizenship may not mean gaining equal rights and participating in a common culture, but rather attaining a bundle of equivalent individual rights and group rights. Citizenship, then, is about creating connections and defining differences. An interesting opportunity is opening up because of developments within the global community: it is now possible for community groups to communicate more effectively via the Internet, thus creating stronger local social movements, more democratic local institutions, and more cooperative local relationships.

Be we administrators or caregivers, professionals or volunteers, service users or policy makers, students or teachers of policy, there is work to do in finding a new balance of democratic social provisions within our increasingly global economy and our continuously pluralistic society.

Notes

1. Changing Politics: Social Policy in a Globalizing and Pluralizing Context

1 Official bilingualism in Canada has grown modestly over the past few generations, from 13 per cent of the population in 1971 reporting an ability to conduct a conversation in both English and French, to 17.5 per cent in 2011.

2 The regulations to the Employment Equity Act specify the following groups as visible minorities: Chinese, South Asians, Blacks, Arabs and West Asians, Filipinos, Southeast Asians, Latin Americans, Japanese, Koreans, and Pacific Islanders.

2. Early Developments in Canadian Social Welfare

1 Earlier, Parliament enacted the Annuities Act of 1908, a modest system of government-operated annuities for building pension income for old age, which few Canadians could make real use of over the next twenty years.

2 Bryden (1974, 79) adds that "veterans had an additional advantage: a higher pension was paid to a married man regardless of his wife's age and to a widower with one or more dependent children." An amendment to the War Veterans Allowance Act in 1936 provided for special consideration to veterans over fifty-five years of age who, because of "pre-aging" combined with disabilities, were incapable of maintaining themselves. A further amendment in 1938 made it possible for veterans with disabilities even younger than fifty-five to be considered for benefits. We briefly discuss this difference in policy generosity between veterans and other citizens in chapter 6.

3 Our calculations are from the Appendix, Table 1, in Guest (1985, 242–3).

4 The federal government had earlier entered the housing field in 1919 with a $25 million scheme to combat high unemployment at the end of the First World War.

5 Bennett's package of social and economic policy reforms was dubbed a New Deal after the highly popular New Deal of activist government measures unveiled in 1933 by Franklin D. Roosevelt, President of the United States.

3. Envisaging and Establishing a System of Social Security for Canadians

1 The children's allowance that Marsh recommended differed from the mothers' allowance programs then existing in Canada in several important ways. The mothers' allowances were usually targeted to widows with dependent children; seven of the then nine provinces had such programs, which were provincially financed and administered. The programs therefore had varying rules and practices across provinces; also, the mothers' allowance programs were based on the traditional public relief philosophy. Marsh's children's allowance was based on modern ideas of social insurance and was to be a national program for all families, wholly administered by the federal government and financed through general tax revenue.

2 We discuss housing policy and veterans' benefits in the war years, but because of space limitations we do not discuss these for the later periods; nor can we examine education, fiscal federalism, Indian affairs, training, or rural rehabilitation and regional development, among others.

3 The Liberals increased the maximum blind allowance effective July 1957, from $40 to $46 monthly. The Conservatives then increased the maximum allowance effective November 1957 from $46 to $55 monthly. As of February 1962, the maximum monthly allowance was raised to $65 by the Conservatives and then to $75 by the Liberals as of December 1963. That was the last time the benefit was boosted by the federal government.

4 The 1951 Blind Persons Act was finally repealed in 1983, having ceased to be necessary.

5 When the eligible age for Old Age Security reached sixty-five in 1970, the Old Age Assistance Act of 1951 was no longer operative, as persons who had been receiving old age assistance could now collect benefits under the OAS legislation.

6 The two Deputy Ministers of National Welfare in this period were George Davidson (1944–59) and Joseph Willard (1960–72). For more details on these officials, see Splane (1987).

4. The Crisis of the Welfare State: Canadian Perspectives and Critiques

1 Major works on the welfare crisis are Castles (2004), Clarke (2007), Collier (1997), Esping-Andersen (1996a), Teeple (1995), Pierson (1994), and Mishra (1984 and 1990b). This chapter is by necessity a selected review of the perspectives. Moreover, other perspectives could be added, such as those on ethnicity, race, and sexuality.

2 Armitage (1996) sees the Piven and Cloward (1971) theory of social assistance reflected somewhat in the modern history of Canadian social welfare. Moscovitch and Drover (1987, 15), by contrast, say that the theory "appears to explain little in Canada ... [but] does highlight the necessity to look at state expenditures in national historical context."

3 A political economy approach to studying the welfare state and social policy generally looks at the nature of capitalist relations of power and production; the patterns of inequality in society and the economy; and historical program developments as well as contemporary policies. The approach in Canada has drawn on neo-Marxist thinkers from Britain, Europe, and the United States. Canadian writers tend to adopt a fairly broad view of social welfare that includes the media, culture, the arts, and taxation, along with the more traditional areas of income support, health, education, and housing. Social welfare is regarded as a form of control and care and as a form of intervention that can both modify and – more important – reinforce structures of disparity and inequality.

4 The term "Fordism" is derived from Henry Ford, the American automaker who applied the assembly-line approach to mass production in the car industry. Ford thereby achieved significant productivity gains, corporate profits, and capital expansion, as well as the promotion of mass consumption of the Model T Ford, other vehicles, and commodities more generally. In part, the concept of Fordism is a synonym for twentieth-century industrial capitalism – mass production and mass consumerism, the scientific management of the workplace, urbanization, and international markets coupled with Keynesian policy, collective bargaining in certain sectors of the economy, and social welfare programs. Janine Brodie (1995, 15) adds that "Fordism also rested on a very particular model of the workplace, the home, and the gender order. It presumed a stable working and middle class, a nuclear family supported by a male breadwinner, a family wage, a dependent wife, and children, and women's unpaid domestic labour."

5 This quote is from the Fraser Institute's website, www.fraserinstitute. ca. Since its formation in 1974, the Fraser Institute has published countless critiques on such social welfare fields as affirmative action, education,

government deficits and debt, health care, housing policy, labour markets, poverty, public sector unions, rent controls, tax loads, and unemployment insurance. Other conservative policy institutes founded in this period were the Canada West Foundation and the National Foundation for Public Policy Development.

6 The reader will notice, from chapters 2 and 3, that our own view of the development of social policy in Canada differs from that of Courchene in a number of respects. We believe that traditional sources of support were not replaced or suppressed by the emergence of social programs; in fact, most public programs assumed the continued vitality and responsibility of informal supports. Second, comprehensiveness and generosity of benefits are in the eye of the beholder. Third, while some universal programs were established, most notably Family Allowance in 1945, Old Security in 1952, and national health insurance (Medicare) over the 1957–72 period, most social programs continued to be selective and targeted. Fourth, the argument that economic growth rendered social policy expansion politically costless in the 1950s and 1960s is simplistic. There were other political costs besides financial ones, namely, jurisdictional fights, constitutional amendments, and the concerns of business and producer interest groups. Finally, Courchene overlooks the forces of pluralization taking place in Canadian society at the time. Aside from economic growth or indeed economic decline as a trigger for demands, numerous claims are rooted in cultural, ethnic, regional, and gender factors. Such claims frequently are not demands for rights to the status quo but rather for a more equitable and inclusive social order.

7 Several thoughtful papers on the culture of poverty are contained in W. Edward Mann (1970). More recent works with a critical cultural perspective include Galabuzi (2006) and McCreath (2011).

8 Like other belief systems, feminism has several branches, such as anti-racist, liberal, radical, and socialist perspectives. Each takes a particular approach to social policy and women's experiences of the welfare state. The discussion here is what may be called a mainstream approach, which other branches share to some extent. On living the effects of public policies, see also Neysmith, Bezanson, and O-Connell (2005) and Dossa (2009).

9 We turn to those agencies and organizations closest to clients, such as the Canadian Council on Social Development, the National Council of Welfare, and Canada without Poverty, to hear about the concerns of those inside the system. Information can also been gathered from federal, provincial, and non-governmental studies, which have asked clients their opinions. Some academic work also provides detailed examinations of the experiences of clients and non-clients.

5. Response to the Crisis: Retrenching the Welfare State and Changing Responsibilities for Social Protection

1 There are several other measures for remixing the social economy of care and provision. These include non-intervention, deregulation, privatization, and the creation of internal markets within the welfare state; land claims settlements and self-government agreements for Aboriginal peoples; and the creation of tax policies for supporting the care of dependents and for encouraging charitable donations.

2 Margaret Biggs (1996, 1) has defined the social union as "the web of rights and obligations between Canadian citizens and governments that give effect and meaning to our shared sense of social purpose and common citizenship." She adds that "the social union has been most closely identified with the policies and programs of the post-welfare state from equalization to health care and social programs. Federal–provincial fiscal arrangements have helped nurture it." The official website for the social union is http://socialunion.gc.ca.

3 For details on these and other countries, see Esping-Andersen (1990 and 1996b), Mishra (1990b), and Pierson (1994).

4 For detailed examinations of the retrenchment records of the Mulroney and Chrétien governments, see Rice and Prince (1993); Rice (1995b); Prince (1997); and Battle (1997). On provincial governments, see, for example, Taft (1997) on Alberta and, on Ontario, Ralph, St-Amand, and Regimbald (1997), Hermer and Mosher (2002), and Lightman, Mitchell, and Herd (2010).

5 It can be argued that the goods and services tax (GST) is a form of systemic retrenchment in that, by raising the visibility of and thus hostility towards the GST, the Mulroney government raised the political cost of any future attempts to raise the tax. The apparent flip-flop of the first Chrétien government regarding replacement of the GST added to the controversial nature of this tax. The Harper government lowered the GST rate from 7 to 5 per cent, thus delivering on a campaign promise in 2006 and also reducing the flow of revenues to the public purse with which to fund services and programs.

6. Global Capitalism and the Canadian Welfare State: Impacts of Economic Integration, Fiscal Policy, and Market Liberalism on Social Policy

1 Some challengers, whom Marjorie Griffin Cohen (1997b) calls "purists," confine their critiques to opposing all new trade agreements and calling for the abolition of existing agreements. Cohen labels as "revisionists" other challengers who seek to establish strong clauses protecting the

environment, labour, and social programs in international trade arrangements. Cohen finds both approaches unsatisfactory, and presents a third
approach for establishing international control of corporate rules and behaviour. We discuss this further in chapters 7 and 11.

2 Many social policy writers focus on aggregate social spending levels as a
measure for defining and comparing welfare states. For a discussion on the
uses and limitations of this approach, see Esping-Andersen (1990), Mishra
(1990b), and Prince (1996a).

3 A complete listing of the social security agreements in effect and those
under negotiation between Canada and other countries is available from
Human Resources and Skills Development Canada's website.

4 Other processes where governments extend the state's realm into the market and community include nationalization or state ownership, economic
and civic regulation, taxation, and expenditures and public services. These
all represent the penetration of the political system into the economy. By
contrast, the processes of taking governments out of the market include
the privatization of public assets and services; the full or partial deregulation of economic sectors; tax cuts, especially for corporations; and spending cutbacks and the contracting out of public service provision to for-profit
agencies. In the latter case, the result would be a marketization of society,
by subjecting more areas of life to the influence of private-sector values and
market mechanisms.

5 The marketization of social programs can be distinguished from the concept of the "social market," which refers either to the welfare state sector or to the state and the nongovernmental provision of health and social
services in the voluntary sector. Our concept is also different from "occupational welfare" and "corporate welfare" – the development and administration of social benefits and services in the workplace, such as day care and
employee assistance plans. A related concept is "commercialization," which
is the adoption of business methods to operating public assets such as air-
ports and harbours. Like marketization, it can involve collecting user fees
from clients.

7. The Crisis of the Market Economy: International Issues and Canadian Responses

1 In the fall of 2011, the Occupy Wall Street movement began in Manhattan,
New York, prompting similar occupy groups, people assemblies, and civil
society-based occupations in scores of other cities in the United States,

Canada, and worldwide. Among the varied issues and messages that arose from these occupations, most focused on critiques of unaccountable corporate capitalism, dashed economic opportunities, and excessive wealth and power held by 1 per cent of people resulting in systemic social inequalities.

2   In reference to our framework outlined in the Introduction, this advocacy represents support for a social protection policy orientation and, at times, cultural recognition, alongside most governments acting under mainly the influence of interests and values associated with economic liberalism.

8. Diversity and Equality in a Pluralist Welfare Community: Issues of Social Control, Selectivity, and Universality

1   Under the Canada Health Act, 1984, universality is one of the conditions that each provincial and territorial health insurance plan must meet in order to receive full federal cash contributions under the Canada Health Transfer. Universality means that 100 per cent of the insured persons of a jurisdiction are entitled, on uniform terms and conditions, to the insured health services provided for by the plan. A related condition is accessibility, which requires that provincial and territorial plans provide reasonable access to insured health services unimpeded by financial charges or other means.

2   The Veterans and Civilians Disability Pensions (VCDP) program provides pensions to those with disabilities related to military service with the Canadian Armed Forces. The amount of the pension is based on the degree of disability as determined by medical examination. The universalistic feature of the VCDP relates to eligibility in that the applicant's financial circumstances have no bearing on entitlement to a pension or to the amount of the pension.

3   Moreover, the universal education and health care sectors have also experienced cutbacks and challenges. On education, see Barlow and Robertson (1994); and on health care, see Armstrong and colleagues (1997), Redden (2002), Hartt (2007), and Bliss (2010).

4   Other factors contributing to the distinctive treatment accorded veterans in federal social policy: veterans have had a specific department and minister representing them, in one form or another, since 1918; and through the Royal Canadian Legion and other associations, veterans have a highly institutionalized and effective network of interest-group representation.

9. Gender and Social Policy: His and Her States of Welfare

1 Another classification is by Ramesh Mishra (1984), who distinguishes between "differentiated welfare states" and "integrated welfare states." The first type refers to a relatively delimited group of social policies and institutions appended but largely unrelated to the economic, industrial, and public sectors. In "integrated welfare states," social policies are linked to the larger society and regarded in close relation to the economy and to the polity. Mishra also refers to this type as the "corporatist welfare state," in that the key interests represented and addressed by the state are those of business and organized labour.

2 A patriarchal social structure is one "based on male authority, male power and male privilege" (McCormack 1991, 3). Whether in a business firm, local community, family, or government, patriarchy refers to rule, exclusively or primarily, by men.

3 Besides gender divisions, other dualisms are apparent in the welfare state, economy, and larger society. These include patterns of stratification between Aboriginal and non-Aboriginal people, people of colour and Caucasians, the poor and the well off, straight people and gays and lesbians, younger and older generations, the federal and provincial/territorial governments, and so forth.

4 Dual-earner couples who share housework fairly equally tend to be younger with few children, and the woman has a university education (Marshall 1993). Employed women with children over age five, and women with no children, work fewer hours a day on household chores than women with young children, but still do more than their partners. The difference in the number of hours men and women spend on domestic work appears to be narrowing over the past fifteen years or so, though a gap remains. Women continue to do most of the household work (Bezanson and Luxton 2006; Braedley and Luxton 2010).

5 Unless otherwise noted, the following discussion on labour force trends is drawn from *Women in Canada* (Statistics Canada 1995b); and Ferrao (2010). While we are discussing overall averages for women as a group, there are differences by different categories of women. For instance, 52 per cent of all women were in the labour force in 1994. This breaks down to 56 per cent of women in a visible minority, 50 per cent of immigrant women, 47 per cent of Aboriginal women, and 41 per cent of women with disabilities.

10. Civil Society, Social Economy, and the Voluntary Sector: Links between Community Capacities and Social Policy

1 We are persuaded by the argument made by Brian Wharf (1992, 21–2) "that senior levels of government have the clear responsibility for resolving what is, after all, the most fundamental social problem – poverty. However, their continuing reluctance to attack the problem in a serious and committed fashion places a particular responsibility on social reform organizations." With local communities across Canada, large and small, the meeting ground between social problems associated with poverty and the delivery of social programs, municipal governments and voluntary agencies are increasingly engaged in social planning, research, and advocacy. The challenge, though, as Wharf identifies it, is that the grand issues of social policy, such as poverty, wealth, and redistribution, cannot be addressed adequately on a community-by-community basis; national organizations, coalitions, and sustained campaigns of policy advocacy are needed.

11. Creating a New Policy Agenda and Rebuilding the Social Role of the State

1 Our calculations are based on information in Statistics Canada, *Public Sector Statistics*, 2009, Ottawa: Statistics Canada, Cat. no. 68-213-XIE. Social policy refers to education, health, housing, income security and social services, employment and immigration, the protection of persons and property, and recreation and culture.

Bibliography

Abele, Frances, and Michael J. Prince. 2008. "The Future of Fiscal Federalism: Funding Regimes for Aboriginal Self-Government." In *Aboriginal Self-Government in Canada: Current Trends and Issues*, 3rd ed., ed. Y. Belanger. Saskatoon: Purich. 158–69.

Abramovitz, Mimi. 1988. *Regulating the Lives of Women*. Boston: South End.

Abu-Laban, Yasmeen. 1994. "The Politics of Race and Ethnicity: Multiculturalism as a Contested Arena." In *Canadian Politics*, 2nd ed., ed. James P. Bickerton and Alain-G. Gagnon. Peterborough: Broadview.

– , ed. 2008. *Gendering the Nation-State: Canadian and Comparative Perspectives*, Vancouver: UBC Press.

Abu-Laban, Yasmeen, and Christina Gabriel. 2002. *Selling Diversity: Immigration, Multiculturalism, Employment Equity, and Globalization*. Peterborough: Broadview.

Adams, Michael. 1997. *Sex in the Snow: Canadian Social Values at the End of the Millennium*. Toronto: Viking.

– . 2006. "Mr. Harper's Child-Proof Political Strategy." *Globe and Mail*, 2 May, A15.

– . 2007. *Unlikely Utopia: The Surprising Triumph of Canadian Pluralism*. Toronto: Viking.

– . 2010. *Stayin' Alive*. Toronto: Viking Canada.

Albo, Greg, Sam Gindin, and Leo Panitch. 2010. *In and Out of Crisis: The Global Financial Meltdown and Left Alternatives*. Oakland: PM.

Alfred, Taiaiake. 2005. *Wasáse: Indigenous Pathways of Action and Freedom*. Peterborough: Broadview.

Alieweiwi, Jehad, and Rachel Laforest. 2009. "Citizenship, Immigration, and the Conservative Agenda." In *The New Federal Policy Agenda and the Voluntary*

Sector: On the Cutting Edge, ed. Rachel Laforest. Montreal and Kingston: Mc-Gill–Queen's University Press. 137–53.

Anderson, Sarah, and John Cavanagh. 1996. "Corporate Empires." *Multinational Monitor* 17, no. 12: 26–7.

Andrew, Caroline. 1984. "Women and the Welfare State." *Canadian Journal of Political Science* 17, no. 4: 667–83. http://dx.doi.org/10.1017/S0008423900052537.

Armitage, Andrew. 1975. *Social Welfare in Canada: Ideals and Realities.* Toronto: McClelland and Stewart.

– . 1988. *Social Welfare in Canada: Ideals, Realities, and Future Paths,* 2nd ed. Toronto: McClelland and Stewart.

– . 1996. *Social Welfare in Canada: Facing Up to the Future,* 3rd ed. Toronto: Oxford University Press.

– . 2003. *Social Welfare in Canada,* 4th ed. Toronto: Oxford University Press.

Armstrong, Hugh. 1977. "The Labour Force and State Workers." In *The Canadian State: Political Economy and Political Power,* ed. Leo Panitch. 289–307. Toronto: University of Toronto Press.

Armstrong, Pat, Hugh Armstrong, Jacqueline Choiniere, Eric Mykhalovskiy, and Jerry P. White. 1997. *Medical Alert: New Work Organizations in Health Care.* Toronto: Garamond.

Aronson, Jane. 1991. "Dutiful Daughters and Undemanding Mothers: Constraining Images of Giving and Receiving Care in Middle and Later Life." In *Women's Caring: Feminist Perspectives on Social Welfare,* ed. Carol Baines, Patricia M. Evans, and Sheila M. Neysmith. 11–35. Toronto: McClelland and Stewart.

Arrighi, Giovanni, and Beverly Silver. 2003. "Polanyi's Double Movement: The Belle Époques of British and U.S. Hegemony Compared." *Politics and Society* 31, no. 2: 325–55. http://dx.doi.org/10.1177/0032329203252274.

Aspen Institute Rural Economic Policy Program. 1996. *Measuring Community Capacity.* Version 3. Aspen: Aspen Institute / Rural Economic Policy Program.

Azmier, Jason, and Robert Roach. 1997. *Welfare Reform in Alberta: A Survey of Former Recipients.* Calgary: Canada West Foundation.

Bach, Michael, and Marcia Rioux. 1996. "Social Policy, Devolution, and Disability: Back to Notions of the Worthy Poor." In *Remaking Canadian Social Policy: Social Security in the Late 1990s,* ed. Jane Pulkingham and Gordon Ternowetsky. 317–26. Halifax: Fernwood Publishing.

Bach, Sandra, and Susan D. Phillips. 1997. "Constructing a New Social Union: Child Care beyond Infancy?" In *How Ottawa Spends 1997–98: Seeing Red: A Liberal Report Card,* ed. Gene Swimmer. 235–58. Ottawa: Carleton University Press.

Badgett, M.V. Lee. 2009. *When Gay People Get Married: What Happens When Societies Legalize Same-Sex Marriages*. New York: NYU Press.

Badgley, Robin F., and Samuel Wolfe. 1967. *Doctors' Strike: Medical Care and Conflict in Saskatchewan*. Toronto: Macmillan.

Baines, Carol, Patricia M. Evans, and Sheila M. Neysmith, eds. 1991. *Women's Caring: Feminist Perspectives on Social Welfare*. Toronto: McClelland and Stewart.

Baines, Donna. 2010. "Neoliberal Restructuring, Activism/Participation, and Social Unionism in the Non-Profit Sector." *Nonprofit and Voluntary Sector Quarterly* 39, no. 1: 10–28. http://dx.doi.org/10.1177/0899764008326681.

Bakker, Isabella, ed. 1996. *Rethinking Restructuring: Gender and Change in Canada*. Toronto: University of Toronto Press.

Banting, Keith. 1987. "Visions of the Welfare State." In *The Future of Social Welfare Systems in Canada and the United Kingdom*, ed. Shirley B. Seward. Halifax: Institute for Research on Public Policy.

– . 1996. "Social Policy." In *Border Crossing: The Internationalization of Canadian Public Policy*, ed. G. Bruce Doern, Leslie A. Pal, and Brian W. Tomlin. Toronto: Oxford University Press.

– . 2006. "Dis-Embedding Liberalism? The New Social Policy Paradigm in Canada." In *Dimensions of Inequality in Canada*, ed. David A. Green and Jonathan R. Kesselman, 417–452. Vancouver: UBC Press.

Banting, Keith, and Kenneth Battle eds. 1994. *A New Social Vision for Canada: Perspectives on the Federal Discussion Paper on Social Policy Reform*. Kingston: Caledon Institute of Social Policy.

Banting, Keith G., Thomas J. Courchene, and F. Leslie Seidle. 2007. *Belonging? Diversity, Recognition, and Shared Citizenship in Canada*. Montreal: Institute for Research on Public Policy.

Barlow, Maude, and Heather-Jane Robertson. 1994. *Class Warfare: The Assault on Canada's Schools*. Toronto: Key Porter.

Bashevkin, Sylvia. 2002. *Welfare Hot Buttons: Women, Work, and Social Policy Reform*. Toronto: University of Toronto Press.

Battle, Kenneth. 1990. [written under Gratten Gray, pseud.]. "Social Policy by Stealth." *Policy Options* 11, no. 2: 17–29.

– . 1993. "The Politics of Stealth: Child Benefits under the Tories." In *How Ottawa Spends 1993–1994: A More Democratic Canada*, ed. Susan D. Phillips. Ottawa: Carleton University Press.

– . 1996. "Back to the Future: Reforming Social Policy in Canada." Paper presented at a Conference in Honour of Allan J. MacEachen, St Francis Xavier University, Antigonish, Nova Scotia, 6 June.

– . 1997. *Transformation: Canadian Social Policy, 1985–2001*. Ottawa: Caledon Institute of Social Policy.

Battle, Kenneth, and Michael Mendelson. 1997. *Child Benefit Reform in Canada: An Evaluative Framework and Future Directions*. Ottawa: Caledon Institute of Social Policy.

Battle, Kenneth, and Sherri Torjman. 1995. *How Finance Reformed Social Policy*. Ottawa: Caledon Institute of Social Policy.

Battle, Kenneth, Sherri Torjman, and Michael Mendelson. 1998. "Reinvest the Fiscal Dividend." *Policy Options* 19, no. 1: 19–22.

Baum, Gregory. 1996. "The Practice of Citizenship in Today's Society." Annual General Meeting of the Social Planning Council of Metro Toronto.

Begin, Monique. 1997. "The Canadian Government and the Commissions Report, Women and the Canadian State." In *Women and the Canadian State*, ed. Caroline Andrew and Sandra Rodgers. 12–26. Montreal and Kingston: McGill–Queen's University Press.

Belanger, Yale D. 2008. *Aboriginal Self-Government in Canada: Current Trends and Issues*, 3rd ed. Saskatoon: Purich.

Berman, Marshall. 1988. *All That Is Solid Melts into Air: The Experience of Modernity*. New York: Penguin.

Bernard, Mitchell. 1994. "Post-Fordism, Transnational Production, and the Changing Global Political Economy." In *Political Economy and the Changing Global Order*, ed. Richard Stubbs and Geoffrey R.D. Underhill, 216–229. Toronto: McClelland and Stewart.

Bernstein, Steven, and William D. Coleman, eds. 2009. *Unsettled Legitimacy: Political Community, Power, and Authority in a Global Era*. Vancouver: UBC Press.

Beveridge, William. 1942. *Social Insurance and Allied Services*. Cmd. 6404. London: HMSO.

Bezanson, Kate. 2006. *Gender, the State, and Social Reproduction: Household Insecurity in Neoliberal Times*. Toronto: University of Toronto Press.

– . 2010. "Child Care Delivered through the Mailbox." In *Neoliberalism and Everyday Life*, ed. Susan Braedley and Meg Luxton, 90–112. Montreal and Kingston: McGill–Queen's University Press.

Bezanson, Kate, and Meg Luxton, eds. 2006. *Social Reproduction: Feminist Political Economy Challenges Neoliberalism*. Montreal and Kingston: McGill–Queen's University Press.

Bhagwati, Jardish. 2004. *In Defence of Globalization*. New York: Oxford University Press.

Bibby, Reginald W. 2006. *The Boomer Factor: What Canada's Most Famous Generation Is Leaving Behind*. Toronto: Bastian.

Bickerton, James. 2010. "Deconstructing the New Federalism." *Canadian Political Science Review* 4, nos. 2–3: 56–72.

Biggs, Margaret. 1996. *Building Blocks for Canada's New Social Union*. Working Paper No. R 02. Ottawa: Canadian Policy Research Networks.

Bishop, Matthew, and Michael Green. 2010. *The Road from Ruin*. New York: Crown.

Black, Edwin R. 1975. *Divided Loyalties: Canadian Concepts of Federalism*. Montreal and Kingston: McGill–Queen's University Press.

Blake, Raymond B. 2008. *From Rights to Needs: A History of Family Allowances in Canada, 1929–92*. Vancouver: UBC Press.

Bliss, Michael. 1975. "Preface." In *Report on Social Security for Canada*, ed. Leonard Marsh, ix–xxxi. Toronto: University of Toronto Press.

– . 2010. *Critical Condition: A Historian's Prognosis on Canada's Aging Health Care System*. Toronto: C.D. Howe Institute.

Block, Fred. 2007. "Understanding the Diverging Trajectories of the United States and Western Europe: A Neo-Polanyian Analysis." *Politics and Society* 35, no. 1: 3–33. http://dx.doi.org/10.1177/0032329206297162.

Bloemraad, Irene. 2006. *Becoming a Citizen: Incorporating Immigrants and Refugees in the United States and Canada*. Berkeley: University of California Press.

Bouchard, Gerard, and Charles Taylor. 2008. *Report: Building the Future: A Time for Reconciliation*. Quebec: Government of Quebec.

Boyce, William, Mary Tremblay, Mary Anne McColl, Jerome Bickenbach, Anne Crichton, Steven Andrews, Nancy Gerein, and April D'Aubin. 2001. *A Seat at the Table: Persons with Disabilities and Policy Making*. Montreal and Kingston: McGill–Queen's University Press.

Boychuk, Gerard William. 1998. *Patchworks of Purpose: The Development of Provincial Social Assistance Regimes in Canada*. Montreal and Kingston: McGill–Queen's University Press.

Boyd, Susan B., ed. 1997. *Challenging the Public/Private Divide: Feminism, Law, and Public Policy*. Toronto: University of Toronto Press.

Braedley, Susan, and Meg Luxton, eds. 2010. *Neoliberalism and Everyday Life*. Montreal and Kingston: McGill–Queen's University Press.

Brawley, Mark R. 2008. *The Politics of Globalization: Gaining Perspective, Assessing Consequences*. Toronto: University of Toronto Press.

Briskin, Linda, and Mona Eliasson, eds. 1999. *Women's Organizing and Public Policy in Canada and Sweden*. Montreal and Kingston: McGill–Queen's University Press.

Broad, David. 1995. "Globalization versus Labour." *Canadian Review of Social Policy* 36: 75–85.

Broadbent, Edward. 1999. "Building on Strength: Improving Governance and Accountability in Canada's Volunteer Sector." Ottawa: Panel on Accountability and Governance in the Voluntary Sector.www.pagvs.com.

– . 2010. *The Rise and Fall of Economic and Social Rights: What Next?* Ottawa: Canadian Centre for Policy Alternatives.

Brodie, Janine. 1995. *Politics on the Margins: Restructuring and the Canadian Women's Movement.* Halifax: Fernwood.

– , ed. 1996. "Canadian Women, Changing State Forms, and Public Policy." In *Women and Canadian Public Policy.* Toronto: Harcourt Brace, 1–28.

Brodie, Janine, and Isabella Bakker. 2007. *Canada's Social Policy Regime and Women: An Assessment of the Last Decade.* Ottawa: Status of Women Canada. Cat. no. SW21–156/2007E-PDF.

– . 2008. *Where Are the Women? Gender Equity, Budgets, and Canadian Public Policy.* Ottawa: Canadian Centre for Policy Alternatives.

Brooks, Stephen, and Lydia Miljan. 2003. *Public Policy in Canada: An Introduction,* 4th ed. Toronto: Oxford University Press.

Brown, David M. 1994. "Economic Change and New Social Policies." In *The Case for Change: Reinventing the Welfare State,* ed. William G. Watson, John Richards, and David M. Brown. Toronto: C.D. Howe Institute.

Browne, Paul Leduc. 1996. *Love in a Cold World? The Voluntary Sector in an Age of Cuts.* Ottawa: Canadian Centre for Policy Alternatives.

Bryden, Kenneth. 1974. *Old Age Pensions and Policy Making in Canada.* Montreal and Kingston: McGill–Queen's University Press.

Bryson, Lois. 1992. *Welfare and the State: Who Benefits?* London: Macmillan.

Burt, Sandra. 1994. "The Women's Movement: Working to Transform Public Life." In *Canadian Politics,* 2nd ed., ed. James P. Bickerton and Alain-G. Gagnon. Peterborough: Broadview.

Byrne, Lesley Hyland. 1997. "Feminists in Power: Women Cabinet Ministers in the New Democratic Party (NDP) Government of Ontario, 1990–1995." *Policy Studies Journal: The Journal of the Policy Studies Organization* 25, no. 4: 601–12. http://dx.doi.org/10.1111/j.1541-0072.1997.tb00044.x.

Cairns, Alan. 1986. "The Embedded State: State–Society Relations in Canada." In *State and Society: Canada in Comparative Perspective,* ed. Keith Banting. 53-86. Toronto: University of Toronto Press.

– . 1991. *Disruptions: Constitutional Struggles from the Charter to Meech Lake.* Toronto: McClelland and Stewart.

Cairns, Alan, and Cynthia Williams. 1985. "Constitutionalism, Citizenship, and Society in Canada: An Overview." In *Constitutionalism, Citizenship, and Society in Canada,* ed. Cairns and Williams. 1–50. Toronto: University of Toronto Press.

Callahan, Marilyn, Andrew Armitage, Michael J. Prince, and Brian Wharf. 1990. "Workfare in British Columbia: Social Development Alternatives." *Canadian Review of Social Policy* 26: 15–26.

Calvert, John. 1984. *Government Limited: The Corporate Takeover of the Public Sector in Canada*. Ottawa: Canadian Centre for Policy Alternatives.

Cameron, Duncan, and Andrew Sharpe, eds. 1988. *Policies for Full Employment*. Ottawa and Montreal: Canadian Council on Social Development.

Campbell, Robert M. 1987. *Grand Illusions: The Politics of the Keynesian Experience in Canada, 1945–1975*. Peterborough: Broadview.

Campbell, Robert M., and Leslie A. Pal. 1989. *The Real Worlds of Canadian Politics: Cases in Process and Policy*. Peterborough: Broadview.

Canada. 1985. *Report*. Royal Commission on the Economic Union and Development Prospects for Canada. Ottawa: Minister of Supply and Services.

– . 1994. "Improving Social Security in Canada: A Discussion Paper." Ottawa: Human Resources Development Canada. Canadian Council on Social Development.

– . 1997a. "Inclusive Social Policy Development: Ideas for Practitioners." Ottawa: Canadian Council on Social Development.

– . 1997b. Message to the 36th Parliament. 10 September. Ottawa: Canadian Council on Social Development.

Canadian Centre for Policy Alternatives. 2010. *Getting the Job Done Right: Alternative Financial Budget 2010*. Winnipeg: CCPA.

Canadian Woman Studies / les cahiers de la femme. 1992. "Women in Poverty." *Canadian Woman Studies / les cahiers de la femme* (special issue) 12, no. 4.

Carniol, Ben. 2005. *Case Critical: Social Services and Social Justice in Canada*, 5th ed. Toronto: Between the Lines.

Cassidy, Harry M. 1947. "The Canadian Social Services." *Annals of the American Academy of Political and Social Science* 253, no. 1: 190–199. http://dx.doi.org/10.1177/000271624725300127.

Cassin, A. Marguerite. 1993. "Equitable and Fair: Widening the Circle." In *Fairness in Taxation: Exploring the Principles*, ed. Allan M. Maslove. Toronto: University of Toronto Press.

Castles, Francis G. 2004. *The Future of the Welfare State: Crisis Myths and Crisis Realities*. Oxford: Oxford University Press.

Catano, Janis Wood, and Linda Christiansen-Ruffman. 1989. *Women as Volunteers in Canada*, ed. Voluntary Action Directorate, Multiculturalism and Citizenship. Ottawa: Supply and Services Canada.

Chann, Steve, and James R. Scarritt, eds. 2002. *Coping with Globalization: Cross-National Patterns in Domestic Governance and Policy Performance*. London: Frank Cass.

Chappell, Louise A. 2002. *Gendering Government: Feminist Engagement with the State in Australia and Canada*. Vancouver: UBC Press.

Charities Aid Foundation. 2010. *The World Giving Index 2010*. Kent: West Malling.

Charlton, Mark W. 1992. *The Making of Canadian Food Policy*. Montreal and Kingston: McGill–Queen's University Press.

Choudry, Aziz, Jill Hanley, Steve Jordan, Eric Shragge, and Martha Stiegman. 2009. *Fight Back: Workplace Justice for Immigrants*. Halifax: Fernwood.

Chrétien, Jean. 1998. "A Global Quest for Volunteer Effort." Speech to the Biennial World Volunteer Conference of the International Association for Volunteer Effort, Edmonton.

Chunn, Dorothy E., and Shelley A.M. Gavigan. 2004. "Welfare Law, Welfare Fraud, and the Moral Regulation of the Never Deserving Poor." *Social and Legal Studies* 13, no. 2: 219–43. http://dx.doi.org/10.1177/0964663904042552.

Clarke, John. 2007. "Subordinating the Social? Neoliberalism and the Remaking of Welfare Capitalism." *Cultural Studies* 21, no. 6: 974–87. http://dx.doi.org/10.1080/09502380701470643.

Clement, Wallace. 1975. *The Canadian Corporate Elite: An Analysis of Economic Power*. Toronto: McClelland and Stewart.

Clutterbuck, Peter. 1997. "A National Municipal Social Infrastructure Strategy." *Canadian Review of Social Policy* 40: 69–75.

Cohen, Marjorie Griffin. 1992. "The Canadian Women's Movement and Its Effort to Influence the Canadian Economy." In *Changing Times: The Women's Movement in Canada and the United States*, ed. Constance Backhouse and David H. Flaherty. Montreal and Kingston: McGill–Queen's University Press.

– . 1997a. Presentation to the House of Commons Sub-Committee on International Trade, Trade Disputes, and Investment: Hearings on the Multilateral Agreement on Investment Panel on Corporate, Consumer, and Social Implications. http://www.policyalternatives.ca/maipresentation.html.

– . 1997b. "What to Do about Globalization." Toronto and Vancouver: Canadian Centre for Policy Alternatives. http://www.policyalternatives.ca/apec.html.

Cohen, Marjorie Griffin, and Jane Pulkingham, eds. 2009. *Public Policy for Women: The State, Income Security, and Labour Market Issues*. Toronto: University of Toronto Press.

Cohn, Theodore. 2005. *Global Political Economy Theory and Practice*. New York: Pearson Longman.

Coleman, James S. 1990. *Foundations of Social Theory*. Cambridge, MA: Harvard University Press.

Coleman, William D. 1991. "Financial Services and Government Intervention." In *Canada at Risk? Canadian Public Policy in the 1990s,* ed. G. Bruce Doern and Bryne B. Purchase. Toronto: C.D. Howe Institute.

Coleman, William D., and Tony Porter. 1996. "Banking and Securities Policy." In *Border Crossings: The Internationalization of Canadian Public Policy,* ed. G. Bruce Doern, Leslie A. Pal, and Brian W. Tomlin. Toronto: Oxford University Press.

Collier, Kenneth. 1995. "Social Policy versus Regional Trading Blocs in the Global System: NAFTA, the EEC and Asia." *Canadian Review of Social Policy* 35: 50–9.

– . 1997. *After the Welfare State.* Vancouver: New Star.

Commission on Social Justice. 1994. *Social Justice: Strategies for National Renewal: The Report of the Commission on Social Justice.* London: Vintage.

Cooper, Andrew E., and Leslie A. Pal. 1996. "Human Rights and Security Policy." In *Border Crossings: The Internationalization of Canadian Public Policy,* ed. G. Bruce Doern, Leslie A. Pal, and Brian W. Tomlin. Toronto: Oxford University Press.

Courchene, Thomas J. 1980. "Towards a Protected Society: The Politicization of Economic Life." *Canadian Journal of Economics / Revue Canadienne d'Economique* 13, no. 4: 556–77. http://dx.doi.org/10.2307/134641.

– . 1987. *Social Policy in the 1990s: Agenda for Reform.* Policy Study no. 3. Toronto: C.D. Howe Institute.

– . 1994. *Social Canada in the Millennium: Reform Imperatives and Restructuring Principles.* The Social Policy Challenge, no. 4. Montreal: C.D. Howe Institute.

Cross, Philip. 2011. "How Did the 2008–2010 Recession and Recovery Compare with Previous Cycles?" *Canadian Economic Observer* 24, no. 1. Ottawa: Cat. no. 11–010-X, Internet edition. www.statcan.gc.ca.

CUPE Economic Brief. 2006. *Thirty Years of Dwindling Minimum Wages in Canada.* Ottawa: Canadian Union of Public Employees Research.

Dale, Gareth. 2010. "Social Democracy, Embeddedness, and Decommodification: On the Conceptual Innovations and Intellectual Affiliations of Karl Polanyi." *New Political Economy* 15, no. 3: 369–93. http://dx.doi.org/10.1080/13563460903290920.

Davies, Linda, and Eric Shragge, eds. 1990. *Bureaucracy and Community.* Montreal: Black Rose.

Davis, Donald R., and James Harrigan. 2011. "Good Jobs, Bad Jobs, and Trade Liberalization." *Journal of International Economics* 84, no. 1: 26–36. http://dx.doi.org/10.1016/j.jinteco.2011.03.005.

Dear, Michael L., and Jennifer R. Wolch. 1987. *Landscapes of Despair: From Deinstitutionalization to Homelessness.* Princeton: Princeton University Press.

Deaton, Rick. 1973. "The Fiscal Crisis of the State in Canada." In *The Political Economy of the State*, ed. Dimitrios I. Roussopoulos. 18–56. Montreal: Black Rose.

Department of Finance Canada. 2010a. "Report to Canadians Shows Canada's Economic Action Plan Is Supporting the Recovery." Montreal, 27 September.

– . 2010b. "World Economic Forum Ranks Canadian Banks Soundest in the World for the Third Consecutive Year." Kitchener, 9 September.

DeVoretz, Donald J. 1995. *Diminishing Returns: The Economics of Canada's Recent Immigration Policy*. Ottawa: CD. Howe Institute and the Laurier Institute.

Dhamoon, Rita. 2009. *Identity/Difference: How Difference Is Produced and Why It Matters*. Vancouver: UBC Press.

Djao, Angela Wei. 1979. "The Welfare State and Its Ideology." In *Economy, Class, and Social Reality*, ed. John Allan Fry. Toronto: Butterworths.

– . 1983. *Inequality and Social Policy: The Sociology of Welfare*. Toronto: John Wiley.

Dobrowolsky, Alexandra. 2003. *Social Investment/Civil Society Interactionism: New Forms of Governance in Britain*. Fostering Social Cohesion: A Comparison of New Policy Strategies, Working Paper #9, Université de Montréal.

– , ed. 2009. *Women and Public Policy in Canada: Neoliberalism and After?* Toronto: Oxford University Press.

Doern, G. Bruce, Allan M. Maslove, and Michael J. Prince. 1988. *Public Budgeting in Canada: Politics, Economics, and Management*. Ottawa: Carleton University Press.

Doern, G. Bruce, Leslie A. Pal, and Brian W. Tomlin, eds. 1996. *Border Crossings: The Internationalization of Canadian Public Policy*. Toronto: Oxford University Press.

Doern, G. Bruce, and Richard W. Phidd. 1983. *Canadian Public Policy: Ideas, Structure, Process*. Toronto: Methuen.

– . 1992. *Canadian Public Policy: Ideas, Structure, Process*, 2nd ed. Toronto: Nelson.

Doern, G. Bruce, and Bryne B. Purchase, eds. 1991. *Canada at Risk: Canadian Public Policy in the 1990s*. Toronto: C.D. Howe Institute.

Dossa, Parin. 2009. *Racialized Bodies, Disabling Worlds: Storied Lives of Immigrant Muslim Women*. Toronto: University of Toronto Press.

Drache, Daniel, and Duncan Cameron. 1985. "Introduction." In *The Other Macdonald Report*, ed. Daniel Drache and Duncan Cameron. Toronto: James Lorimer.

Drache, Daniel, and Andrew Ranachan. 1995. *Warm Heart, Cold Country: Fiscal and Social Policy Reform in Canada*. Ottawa / Toronto: Caledon Institute on Social Policy / Robarts Centre for Canadian Studies.

Drolet, Marie. 2011 (Spring). "Why Has the Gender Wage Gap Narrowed?" In *Perspectives on Labour and Income*. Ottawa: Statistics Canada. 3–13.

Drucker, Peter F. 1993. *The Post-Capitalist Society*. New York: Harper Business.

Echenberg, Havi. 2004. "Back to the Future – the Rear View Mirror Provides Glimpses of What Lies Ahead for Income Security in the 21st Century." *Policy Options* 25, no. 7: 13–9.

Economic Council of Canada. 1990. *Good Jobs, Bad Jobs*. Ottawa.

Elson, Peter R. 2011. *High Ideals and Noble Intentions: Voluntary Sector-Government Relations in Canada*. Toronto: University of Toronto Press.

Esping-Andersen, Gosta. 1990. *The Three Worlds of Welfare Capitalism*. Princeton: Princeton University Press.

– . 1996a. "After the Golden Age? State Dilemmas in a Global Economy." In *Welfare States in Transition: National Adaptations in Global Economies*, ed. Esping-Andersen. 1–31. London: Sage. http://dx.doi.org/10.4135/9781446216941.n1

– , ed. 1996b. *Welfare States in Transition: National Adaptation in Global Economics*. London: Sage.

– . 2009. *Incomplete Revolution: Adapting Welfare States to Women's New Roles*. Cambridge: Polity.

Etzioni, Amitai. 1993. *The Spirit of Community: Rights, Responsibilities, and the Communitarian Agenda*. London: Fontana.

– . 1995. "The Attack on Community: The Grooved Debate." *Society* (July/August): 12–17.

Evans, Patricia M. 1991. "The Sexual Division of Poverty: The Consequences of Gendered Caring." In *Women's Caring: Feminist Perspectives on Social Welfare*, ed. Carol Baines, Patricia M. Evans, and Sheila M. Neysmith. Toronto: McClelland and Stewart.

Evans, Patricia M., and Gerda R. Wekerle, eds. 1997. *Women and the Canadian Welfare State: Challenges and Change*. Toronto: University of Toronto Press.

Evans, Patricia M., Lesley A. Jacobs, Alain Noel, and Elisabeth R. Reynolds. 1995. *Workfare: Does It Work? Is It Fair?* Montreal: Institute for Research on Public Policy.

Fagan, Tony, and Phil Lee. 1997. "New Social Movements and Social Policy: A Case Study of the Disability Movement." In *Social Policy: A Conceptual and Theoretical Introduction*, ed. Michael Lavalette and Alan Pratt. London: Sage.

Ferrao, Vincent. 2010. *Women in Canada: A Gender-Based Statistical Report: Paid Work*. Ottawa: Statistics Canada, Publication no. 89–503–X.

Finance Canada. 2010. *Canada's Economic Action Plan: A Sixth Report to Canadians, September*. Ottawa. http://www.fin.gc.ca.

Finkel, Alvin. 2006. *Social Policy and Practice in Canada: A History*. Waterloo: Wilfrid Laurier University Press.

Finlayson, Ann. 1996. *Naming Rumpelstiltskin: Who Will Profit (and Who Will Lose) in the Workplace of the 21st Century*. Toronto: Key Porter.

Findlay, Peter C. 1983. "The Case for Universality." *Canadian Social Work Review* 1: 17–24.

Firestone, Shulamith. 1979. *The Dialectic of Sex*. London: Women's Press.

Fisher, Robert, and Joe Kling. 1994. "Community Organization and New Social Movement Theory." *Journal of Progressive Human Services* 5, no. 2: 5–21.

Flanagan, Tom. 2007. *Harpers Team*. Montreal and Kingston: McGill–Queen's University Press.

Food Banks Canada. 2010. *HungerCount 2010 Survey*. http://www.foodbanks-canada.ca/documents/HungerCount2010_web.pdf.

Fox, Bonnie, ed. 2009. *Family Patterns and Gender Bonds*, 3rd ed. Toronto: Oxford University Press.

Freeman, Linda. 1985. "The Effect of the World Crisis on Canada's Involvement in Africa." *Studies in Political Economy* 17: 107–39.

Friendly, Martha, and Susan Prentice. 2009. *About Canada: Childcare*. Halifax: Fernwood.

Friesen, Arthur, Alessandro Alasia, and Ray Bollam. 2010. *The Social Economy across the Rural to Urban Gradient: Evidence from Registered Charities, 2004*. Ottawa: Statistics Canada. Cat. no. 21–601–M–92.

Galabuzi, Grace-Edward. 2006. *Canada's Economic Apartheid: The Social Exclusion of Racialized Groups in the New Century*. Toronto: Canadian Scholars' Press.

Gavigan, Shelley A.M., and Dorothy E. Chunn, eds. 2010. *The Legal Tender of Gender: Law, Welfare, and the Regulation of Women's Poverty*. Portland: Hart.

George, Victor, and Paul Wilding. 1976. *Ideology and Social Welfare*. London: Routledge and Kegan Paul.

– . 1985. *Ideology and Social Welfare*, 2nd ed. London: Routledge and Kegan Paul.

Gidengil, Elisabeth, and Richard Vengrof. 1997. "Representational Gain of Canadian Women or Token Growth? The Case of Quebec's Municipal Politics." *Canadian Journal of Political Science* 30, no. 3: 513–37. http://dx.doi.org/10.1017/S0008423900015997.

Gillespie, W. Irwin. 1978. *In Search of Robin Hood: The Effects of Federal Budgetary Policies during the 1970s on the Distribution of Income in Canada*. Montreal: C.D. Howe Institute.

– . 1991. *Tax, Borrow, and Spend: Financing Federal Spending in Canada, 1867–1990*. Ottawa: Carleton University Press.

Goffman, Irving J. 1968. "Canadian Social Welfare Policy." In *Contemporary Canada*, ed. R.H. Leach. 191–224. Toronto: University of Toronto Press.

Goldberg, Susan, and Chloe Brushwood Rose, eds. 2009. *And Baby Makes More: Known Donors, Queer Parents, and Our Unexpected Families*. London, ON: Insomniac.

Gonick, Cy. 1987. *The Great Economic Debate: Failed Economics and a Future for Canada*. Toronto: James Lorimer.

Gordon, Linda. 1990. "The New Feminist Scholarship on the Welfare State." In *Women, the State, and Welfare*, ed. Linda Gordon. Madison: University of Wisconsin Press.

Gough, Ian. 1979. *The Political Economy of the Welfare State*. London: Macmillan.

Graham, Andrew. 2009. "Examining Means to Build Financial Sustainable Capacity in Canada's Voluntary Sector." In *The New Federal Policy Agenda and the Voluntary Sector: On the Cutting Edge*, ed. R. Laforest. Montreal, Kingston: McGill–Queen's University Press. 35–60.

Graham, John, Karen J. Swift, and Roger Delaney. 2008. *Canadian Social Policy: An Introduction*, 3rd ed. Toronto: Pearson Education.

Graham, Katherine A., Susan D. Phillips, and Allan Maslove. 1998. *Urban Governance in Canada: Representation, Resources, and Restructuring*. Toronto: Harcourt Brace.

Gray, John. 2002. *False Dawn: The Delusions of Global Capitalism*. London: Granta.

Greenlaw, David, Jan Hatzius, Anil K Kashyap, and Hyun Song Shin. 2008. *Leveraged Losses: Lessons from the Mortgage Market Meltdown*. Report prepared for the U.S. Monetary Policy Forum.

Guard, Julie, and Wayne Antony, eds. 2009. *Bankruptcies and Bailouts*. Halifax: Fernwood.

Guest, Dennis. 1985. *The Emergence of Social Security in Canada*, 2nd ed. Vancouver: UBC Press.

–. 1997. *The Emergence of Social Security in Canada*, 3rd ed. Vancouver: UBC Press.

Gwyn, Richard. 1996. *Nationalism without Walls: The Unbearable Lightness of Being Canadian*, 2nd ed. Toronto: McClelland and Stewart.

Haddow, Rodney. 1993. *Poverty Reform in Canada, 1958–1978: State and Class Influences on Policy Making*. Montreal: McGill–Queen's University Press.

Hall, Michael, David Lasby, Steven Ayer, and William David Gibbons. 2009. *Caring Canadians, Involved Canadians: Highlights from the 2007 Canada Survey of Giving, Volunteering, and Participating*, Ottawa: Statistics Canada, Cat. no. 71–542–XWE.

Hamdon, Evelyn Leslie. 2010. *Islamophobia and the Question of Muslim Identity: The Politics of Difference and Identity*. Halifax: Fernwood.

Hankivsky, Olena. 2004. *Social Policy and the Ethic of Care*. Vancouver: UBC Press.

Harmes, Adam. 2007. "The Political Economy of Open Federalism." *Canadian Journal of Political Science* 40, no. 2: 417–37. http://dx.doi.org/10.1017/S0008423907070114.

Harper, Stephen, and Tom Flanagan. 1998. "Conservative Politics in Canada: Past, Present, and Future." In *After Liberalism: Essays in Search of Freedom, Virtue, and Order*, ed. William Gardiner. Toronto: Stoddart. 168–93.

Harrison, Trevor. 1996. "Class, Citizenship, and Global Migration: The Case of the Canadian Immigration Business Program, 1978–1992." *Canadian Public Policy* 21, no. 1: 7–23. http://dx.doi.org/10.2307/3551746.

Hartt, Stanley H. 2007. "*Chaoulli* and Universality – A Timely Charter Test Case." *Policy Options* 28, no. 2: 99–102.

Haskell, Rebecca, and Brian Burtch. 2010. *Get That Freak: Homophobia and Transphobia in High Schools*. Halifax: Fernwood.

Health Council of Canada. 2006. *Health Care Renewal in Canada: Clearing the Road to Quality – Annual Report to Canadians 2006*. Ottawa.

Hermer, Joe, and Janet Mosher, eds. 2002. *Disorderly People: Law and Politics of Exclusion in Ontario*. Halifax: Fernwood.

Hewitt, Martin. 1994. "Social Policy and the Question of Postmodernism." In *Social Policy Review* 6, ed. Robert Page and John Baldock. Canterbury: University of Kent.

Hirsch, Werner Z. 1991. *Privatizing Government Services: An Economic Analysis of Contracting Out by Local Governments*. Los Angeles: Institute of Industrial Relations, University of California.

Hodgetts, J.E. 1973. *The Canadian Public Service: The Physiology of Government 1867–1970*. Toronto: University of Toronto Press.

Hogg, Peter W. 1985. *Constitutional Law of Canada*, 2nd ed. Toronto: Carswell.

Howlett, Michael, M. Ramesh, and Anthony Perl. 2009. *Studying Public Policy: Policy Cycles and Policy Subsystems*, 3rd ed. Toronto: Oxford University Press.

Human Resources Development Canada. 1994. *Improving Social Security in Canada*. Ottawa.

Human Resources and Skills Development Canada. 2009. "Voluntary Sector Initiative Impact Evaluation: Lessons Learned from the Voluntary Sector Initiative (2000–2005)." Ottawa: Evaluation Directorate, Strategic Policy and Research Branch. Cat. no. HS4–102/2010E–PDF.

James, Carl, David Este, Wanda Thomas Bernard, Akua Benjamin, Bethan Lloyd, and Tana Turner. 2010. *Race and Well-Being: The Lives, Hopes, and Activism of African Canadians*. Halifax and Winnipeg: Fernwood.

James, Matt. 2006. *Misrecognized Materialists: Social Movements in Canadian Constitutional Politics*. Vancouver: UBC Press.

Jacobs, Jane. 1961. *The Death and Life of Great American Cities*. New York: Vintage.

Jenson, Jane. 1998. "Mapping Social Cohesion: The State of Canadian Research." Ottawa: Canadian Policy Research Networks. CPRN Study no. F/03.

Jenson, Jane, and Denis Saint-Martin. 2003. "New Routes to Social Cohesion? Citizenship and the Social Investment State." *Canadian Journal of Sociology* 28:77–99.

– . 2004. "Canada's New Social Risks: Directions for a New Social Architecture." Ottawa: CPRN Research Report no. F/43.

Johnson, Albert W. 1987. "Social Policy in Canada: The Past As It Conditions the Present." In *The Future of Social Welfare Systems in Canada and the United Kingdom*, ed. Shirley B. Seward. 29–70. Halifax: Institute for Research on Public Policy.

Johnson, William. 2006. *Stephen Harper and the Future of Canada*. Toronto: McClelland and Stewart.

Jordan, Bill. 2010. *What's Wrong with Social Policy and How to Fix It*. Cambridge: Polity.

Kent, Judy. 1989. *Volunteers in Health Organizations*. Voluntary Action Directorate, Multiculturalism and Citizenship. Ottawa: Supply and Services Canada.

Kent, Tom. 1999. *Social Policy 2000: An Agenda*. Ottawa: Caledon Institute of Social Policy.

Kerans, Patrick. 1994. "Universality, Full Employment, and Well-Being: The Future of the Canadian Welfare State." *Canadian Review of Social Policy* 34: 119–35.

Kershaw, Paul. 2005. *Carefair: Rethinking the Responsibilities and Rights of Citizenship*. Vancouver: UBC Press.

Keynes, John M. 1936. *The General Theory of Employment, Interest, and Money*. London: Macmillan.

Kinsman, Gary, and Patrizia Gentile. 2010. *The Canadian War on Queers: National Security and Sexual Regulations*. Vancouver: UBC Press.

Kitchen, Brigitte. 1995. "Scaled Social Benefits: Are They a Step Up from Universality?" In *Warm Heart, Cold Country: Fiscal and Social Policy Reform in Canada*, ed. Daniel Drache and Andrew Ranachan. 57–79. Ottawa / Toronto: Caledon Institute of Social Policy / Robarts Centre for Canadian Studies.

– . 1996. "Round Up – Ontario." *Canadian Review of Social Policy* 38: 165–6.

– . 1997. "The New Child Benefit: Much Ado About Nothing." *Canadian Review of Social Policy* 39 (Spring): 65–74.

Klein, Naomi. 2007. *The Shock Doctrine: The Rise of Disaster Capitalism*. Toronto: Knopf Canada.

Kuusisto, Nils, and Rick Williams. 1981. "Social Expenses and Regional Underdevelopment." In *Inequality: Essays on the Political Economy of Social Welfare*, ed. Allan Moscovitch and Glenn Drover, 249–74. Toronto: University of Toronto Press.

Laforest, Rachel. 2009a. "Introduction." In *The New Federal Policy Agenda and the Voluntary Sector: On the Cutting Edge*, ed. R. Laforest, 1–6. Montreal and Kingston: McGill–Queen's University Press.

– . 2009b. "Policy Currents and the Conservative Undertow." In *The New Federal Policy Agenda and the Voluntary Sector: On the Cutting Edge*, ed. Laforest, 155–67. Montreal and Kingston: McGill–Queen's University Press.

Langille, David, ed. 1997. *Exposing the Facts of Corporate Rule*. Toronto: Jesuit Centre for Social Faith.

Larsen, Christian Albrekt. 2007. "The Institutional Logic of Welfare Attitudes: How Welfare Regimes Influence Public Support." *Comparative Political Studies* 41, no. 2: 145–68. http://dx.doi.org/10.1177/0010414006295234.

Lash, Scott, and John Urry. 1987. *The End of Organized Capitalism*. Cambridge: Polity.

Laxer, James. 1984. *Rethinking the Economy: The Laxer Report on Canadian Economic Problems and Policies*. Toronto: New Canada.

Lazar, Harvey. 1991. "Investing in People: A Policy Agenda for the 1990s." In *Canada at Risk: Canadian Public Policy in the 1990s*, ed. G. Bruce Doern and Bryne B. Purchase. Policy Study no. 13. Toronto: C.D. Howe Institute.

– . 2008. "The Spending Power and the Harper Government." *Queen's Law Journal* 34, no. 1: 125–40.

Lee, Bill. 1992. *Pragmatics of Community Organization*, 2nd ed. Mississauga: Commonact.

Lee, Phil, and Colin Raban. 1988. *Welfare Theory and Social Policy: Reform or Evolution?* London: Sage.

Leroux, Darryle. 2010. "Québec Nationalism and the Production of Difference: The Bouchard–Taylor Commission, the Herouxville Code of Conduct, and Québec's Integration Policy." *Québec Studies* 49: 107–26.

Lewis, David. 1972. *Louder Voices: The Corporate Welfare Bums*. Toronto: James Lewis and Samuel.

Lewis, Timothy. 2003. *In the Long Run Were All Dead: The Canadian Turn to Fiscal Restraint*. Toronto: University of Toronto Press.

Leys, Colin. 2001. *Market-Driven Politics: Neoliberal Democracy and the Public Interest*. London: Verso.

Lightman, Ernie S. 1995. "Equity in Lean Times." In *Warm Hearts, Cold Country: Fiscal and Social Policy Reform in Canada*, ed. Daniel Drache and Andrew Ranachan. 355–62. Ottawa / Toronto: Caledon Institute on Social Policy / Robarts Centre on Canadian Studies.

– . 2003. *Social Policy in Canada*. Toronto: Oxford University Press.

Lightman, Ernie S., and Allan Irving. 1991. "Restructuring Canada's Welfare State." *Journal of Social Policy* 20, no. 1: 65–86. http://dx.doi.org/10.1017/S0047279400018481.

Lightman, Ernie, Andrew Mitchell, and Dean Herd. 2010. "Cycling Off and On Welfare in Canada." *Journal of Social Policy* 39, no. 4: 523–42. http://dx.doi.org/10.1017/S0047279410000279.

Lindblom, Charles. 1977. *Politics and Markets: The World's Political-Economic Systems*. New York: Basic.

Lipsky, Michael. 1980. *Street-Level Bureaucracy: Dilemmas of the Individual in Public Services*. New York: Russell Sage.

Lochhead, Clarence. 1997. *From the Kitchen Table to the Boardroom Table: The Canadian Family and the Work Place*. Ottawa: Vanier Institute of the Family.

Low, William. 1996. "Wide of the Mark: Using Targeting and Work Incentives to Direct Social Assistance to Single Parents." In *Remaking Canadian Social Policy: Social Security in the Late 1990s*, ed. Jane Pulkingham and Gordon Ternowetsky, 188–201. Halifax: Fernwood.

Luxton, Meg. 2006. "Friends, Neighbours, and Community: A Case Study of the Role of Informal Caregiving in Social Reproduction." In *Social Reproduction: Feminist Political Economy Challenges Neoliberalism*, ed. Kate Bezanson and Luxton, 263–92. Montreal and Kingston: McGill–Queen's University Press.

Luxton, Meg, and June Corman. 2001. *Getting By in Hard Times: Gendered Labour at Home and on the Job*. Toronto: University of Toronto Press.

Macionis, John, Mikael Jansson, and Cecelia Benoit. 2009. *Society: The Basics*, 4th Can. ed. Toronto: Pearson Education.

MacIvor, Heather. 1996. *Women and Politics in Canada*. Peterborough: Broadview.

Mann, W.E., ed. 1970. *Poverty and Social Policy in Canada*. Vancouver: Copp Clark.

Maioni, Antonia. 2004. "New Century, New Risks: The Marsh Report and the Post-War Welfare State in Canada." *Policy Options* 25, no. 7: 20–3.

Manzer, Ronald. 1985. *Public Policies and Political Development in Canada*. Toronto: University of Toronto Press.

–. 1994. *Public Schools and Political Ideas: Canadian Educational Policy in Historical Perspective*. Toronto: University of Toronto Press.

Marsh, David. 1991. "British Industrial Relations Policy Transformed: The Thatcher Legacy." *Journal of Public Policy* 11, no. 3: 291–313. http://dx.doi.org/10.1017/S0143814X00005341.

Marsh, Leonard. 1975[1943]. *Report on Social Security for Canada*. Reprint. Toronto: University of Toronto Press.

Marshall, Katherine. 1993. "Dual Earners: Who's Responsible for Housework?" *Canadian Social Trends* 31: 11–14.

Marshall, Thomas H. 1963. "Citizenship and Social Class." In *Sociology at the Crossroads*. London: Heinemann.

Marsland, David. 1996. *Welfare or Welfare State? Contradictions and Dilemmas in Social Policy*. London: Macmillan.

Martin, Lawrence. 2010. *Harperland: The Politics of Control*. Toronto: Viking Canada.

Martin, Paul. 1994. The Budget Speech. Ottawa: Department of Finance (February 22).

Maslove, Allan M., Michael J. Prince, and G. Bruce Doern. 1986. *Federal and Provincial Budgeting: Goalsetting, Coordination, Restraint, and Reform.* Toronto: University of Toronto Press.

Maxwell, Judith. 1993. "Globalization and Family Security." In *Family Security in Insecure Times: National Forum on Family Security,* ed. Canadian Council on Social Development. Ottawa.

– . 1994. "Rethinking the Social Role of Government." *Policy Options* 16, no. 3: 54–8.

– . 1995. ."The Role of the State in a Knowledge-Based Economy." In *Redefining Social Security,* ed. P. Grady, R. Howse, and J. Maxwell, 1–48. Kingston: School of Policy Studies, Queen's University.

– . 2003. *The Great Social Transformation: Implications for the Social Role of Government in Ontario.* Paper prepared for the Panel on the Role of Government. http://www.cprn.org.

McBride, Stephen. 1992. *Not Working: State, Unemployment, and Neoconservatism in Canada.* Toronto: University of Toronto Press.

– . 2005. *Paradigm Shift: Globalization and the Canadian State,* 2nd ed. Halifax: Fernwood.

McColl, Mary Ann, and Lyn Jongbloed, eds. 2006. *Disability and Social Policy in Canada,* 2nd ed. Concord: ON: Captus University Press.

McCormack, Thelma. 1984. "Culture and the State." *Canadian Public Policy* 10, no. 3: 267–77. http://dx.doi.org/10.2307/3550320.

– . 1991. *Politics and the Hidden Injuries of Gender: Feminism and the Making of the Welfare State.* Ottawa: Canadian Research Institute for the Advancement of Women.

McCreath, Graeme. 2011. *The Politics of Blindness: From Charity to Parity.* Vancouver: Granville Island.

McGilly, Frank. 1990. *An Introduction to Canada's Public Social Services: Understanding Income and Health Programs.* Toronto: McClelland and Stewart.

– . 1998. *Canada's Public Social Services,* 2nd ed. Toronto: Oxford University Press.

McKeen, Wendy. 2006. "Diminishing the Concept of Social Policy: The Shifting Conceptual Ground of Social Policy Debate in Canada." *Critical Social Policy* 26, no. 4: 865–87. http://dx.doi.org/10.1177/0261018306068479.

McKenzie, Brad, and Brian Wharf. 2010. *Connecting Policy to Practice in the Human Services,* 3rd ed. Toronto: Oxford University Press.

McKnight, John. 1992. *The Future of Low-Income Neighborhoods and the People Who Reside There: A Capacity-Oriented Strategy for Neighborhood Development.* Chicago: Center for Urban Affairs and Policy Research, Northwestern University.

McLean, Bethany, and Joe Nocera. 2010. *All the Devils Are Here: The Hidden History of the Financial Crisis*. New York: Penguin.

McLeod, R.C., and D. Schneiderman. 1994. *Police Powers in Canada: The Evolution and Practice of Authority*. Toronto: University of Toronto Press.

McNally, David. 2010. *Global Slump: The Economics and Politics of Crisis and Resistance*. Oakland: PM.

McQuaig, Linda. 1993. *The Wealthy Banker's Wife: The Assault on Equality in Canada*. Toronto: Penguin.

– . 1995. *Shooting the Hippo: Death by Deficit and Other Canadian Myths*. Toronto: Penguin.

– . 1998. *The Cult of Impotence: Selling the Myth of Powerlessness in the Global Economy*. Toronto: Viking.

Miki, Roy. 2005. *Redress: Inside the Japanese Canadian Call for Justice*. Vancouver: Raincoast.

Miller, Dorothy C. 1990. *Women and Social Welfare: A Feminist Analysis*. New York: Praeger.

Mishra, Ramesh. 1981. *Society and Social Policy: Theoretical Perspectives on Welfare*, 2nd ed. Toronto: Macmillan.

– . 1984. *The Welfare State in Crisis: Social Thought and Social Change*. Brighton: Wheatsheaf.

– . 1990a. "The Collapse of the Welfare Consensus? The Welfare State in the 1980s." In *Housing the Homeless and the Poor: New Partnerships among the Private, Public, and Third Sectors*, ed. George Fallis and Alex Murray. 82–114. Toronto: University of Toronto Press.

– . 1990b. *The Welfare State in Capitalist Society: Policies of Retrenchment and Maintenance in Europe, North America, and Australia*. New York: Harvester Wheatsheaf.

Mook, Laurie, Jack Quarter, and Sheridan Ryan. 2010. *Researching the Social Economy*. Toronto: University of Toronto Press.

Morissette, Rene, John Myles, and Garnett Picot. 1995. "Earnings Polarization in Canada, 1969–1991." In *Labour Market Polarization and Social Policy Reform*, ed. Keith G. Banting and Charles M. Beach. 23–50. Kingston: School of Policy Studies, Queen's University.

Moscovitch, Allan. 1990. "Slowing the Steamroller: The Federal Conservatives, the Social Sector, and Child Benefits Reform." In *How Ottawa Spends 1990–91: Tracking the Second Agenda*, ed. Katherine A. Graham. 171–217. Ottawa: Carleton University Press.

Moscovitch, Allan, and Jim Albert, eds. 1987. *The Benevolent State: The Growth of Welfare in Canada*. Toronto: Garamond.

Moscovitch, Allan, and Glenn Drover, eds. 1981. *Inequality: Essays on the Political Economy of Social Welfare*. Toronto: University of Toronto Press.

– . 1987. "Social Expenditures and the Welfare State: The Canadian Experience in Historical Perspective." In *The Benevolent State: The Growth of Welfare in Canada*, ed. Moscovitch and Drover. 13–43. Toronto: Garamond.

Moss, Pamela, and Katherine Teghtsoonian, eds. 2008. *Contesting Illness: Processes and Practices*. Toronto: University of Toronto Press.

Mullaly, Robert. 1997. *Structural Social Work: Ideology, Theory, and Practice*, 2nd ed. Toronto: Oxford University Press.

Murphy, H.B.W., B. Pennee, and D. Luchins. 1972. "Foster Homes: The New Back Ward." *Canada's Mental Health* 20 (Supplement 71): 1–17.

Murray, Charles. 1984. *Losing Ground: American Social Policy 1950–1980*. New York: Basic.

– . 1990. *The Emerging British Underclass*. London: Institute of Economic Affairs.

– . 1994. *Underclass: The Crisis Deepens*. London: Institute of Economic Affairs.

Myles, John, and Paul Pierson. 1997. "Friedman's Revenge: The Reform of Liberal Welfare States." *Politics & Society* 25: 443–72.

National Council of Welfare. 1976. *The Hidden Welfare System*. Ottawa: Supply and Services Canada.

– . 1978. *Bearing the Burden, Sharing the Benefits*. Ottawa: Supply and Services Canada.

– . 1983. *Family Allowances for All?* Ottawa: Supply and Services Canada.

– . 1987. *Welfare in Canada: The Tangled Safety Net*. Ottawa: Supply and Services Canada.

– . 1995. *Legal Aid and the Poor*. Ottawa: Supply and Services Canada.

– . 1996–97. *Welfare Incomes 1995*. Ottawa: Supply and Services Canada.

– . 1997. *Poverty Profile 1995*. Ottawa: Supply and Services Canada.

National Forum on Family Security. 1993. Keynote paper. In *Family Security in Insecure Times*, ed. Canadian Council on Social Development. Ottawa.

Neary, Peter, and J.L. Granatstein, eds. 1998. *The Veterans Charter and Post World War II Canada*. Montreal and Kingston: McGill–Queen's University Press.

Neysmith, Sheila M. 1991. "From Community Care to a Social Model of Care." In *Women's Caring: Feminist Perspectives on Social Welfare*, ed. Carol Baines, Patricia M. Evans, and Sheila M. Neysmith. 272–99. Toronto: McClelland and Steward.

Neysmith, Sheila M., and Marge Reitsma-Street. 2005. "Provisioning: Conceptualizing the Work of Women for 21st-Century Social Policy." *Women's Studies International Forum* 28: 381–91.

Newman, Jacquetta, and Linda A. White, eds. 2006. *Women, Politics, and Public Policy: The Political Struggles of Canadian Women*. Toronto: Oxford University Press.

Neysmith, Sheila M., Kate Bezanson, and Anne O'Connell. 2005. *Telling Tales: Living the Effects of Public Policy*. Halifax: Fernwood.

Neysmith, Sheila M., Marge Reitsma-Street, Stephanie Baker-Collins, and Elaine Porter. 2009. "A Study of Women's Provisioning: Implications for Social Provisions." In *Public Policy for Women: The State, Income Security, and Labour Market Issues*, ed. Marjorie Griffin Cohen and Jane Pulkingham, 94–113. Toronto: University of Toronto Press.

Ng, Roxana, Gillian Walker, and Jacob Muller, eds. 1990. *Community Organization and the Canadian State*. Toronto: Garamond.

Noël, Alain. 1999. "Is Decentralization Conservative? Federalism and the Contemporary Debate on the Canadian Welfare State." In *Stretching the Federation: The Art of the State in Canada*, ed. Robert Young. Kingston: Queen's University, Institute of Intergovernmental Relations. 195–219.

Oakes, Leigh, and Jane Warren. 2007. *Language, Citizenship, and Identity in Quebec*. New York: Palgrave Macmillan. http://dx.doi.org/10.1057/9780230625495.

O'Connor, James. 1973. *The Fiscal Crisis of the State*. New York: St Martin's Press.

O'Connor, Julia S., Ann Shola Orloff, and Sheila Shaver. 1999. *States, Market, Families: Gender, Liberalism, and Social Policy in Australia, Canada, Great Britain, and the United States*. Cambridge: Cambridge University Press. http://dx.doi.org/10.1017/CBO9780511597114.

OECD. 2009. *Economic Outlook March 2009*. http://www.oecd.org/dataoecd/18/1/42443150.pdf.

Offe, Claus. 1984. *Contradictions of the Welfare State*, ed. John Keane. London: Hutchinson.

– . 1985. *Disorganized Capitalism*. Cambridge, MA: MIT Press.

O'Higgins, Michael. 1985. "Inequality, Redistribution, and Recession: The British Experience, 1976–1982." *Journal of Social Policy* 14, no. 3: 279–307. http://dx.doi.org/10.1017/S0047279400014744.

Olsen, Gregg. 2002. *The Politics of the Welfare States: Canada, Sweden, and the United States*. Toronto: Oxford University Press.

Omidvar, Ratna, and Ted Richmond, eds. 2003. *Perspectives on Social Inclusion: Immigrant Settlement and Social Inclusion in Canada*. Toronto: Laidlaw Foundation.

Ontario Fair Tax Commission. 1993. *Fair Taxation in a Changing World: Highlights*. Toronto: Queen's Printer for Ontario.

Organization for Canadian Economic Development. 1997. *Beyond 2000: The New Social Policy Agenda*. Paper prepared for a Conference on the Challenges of Change in Social Policy: North American Perspectives.

Orloff, Ann Shola. 1993. "Gender and the Social Rights of Citizenship: The Comparative Analysis of Gender Relations and Welfare States." *American Sociological Review* 58, no. 3: 303–25. http://dx.doi.org/10.2307/2095903.

Orloff, Ann Shola, and Bruno Palier. 2009. "The Power of Gender Perspectives: Feminist Influence on Policy Paradigms, Social Science, and Social Politics." *Social Politics* 16, no. 4: 405–12. http://dx.doi.org/10.1093/sp/jxp021.

Osberg, Lars. 1981. *Economic Inequality in Canada*. Toronto: Butterworths.

– . 2009. *Canada's Declining Social Safety Net: The Case for EI Reform*. Winnipeg: Canadian Centre for Policy Alternatives.

Owram, Doug. 1986. *The Government Generation: Canadian Intellectuals and the State, 1900–1945*. Toronto: University of Toronto Press.

Pal, Leslie A. 1988. *State, Class, and Bureaucracy: Canadian Unemployment Insurance and Public Policy*. Montreal and Kingston: McGill–Queen's University Press.

– . 2010. *Beyond Policy Analysis: Public Issue Management in Turbulent Times*, 4th ed. Toronto: Nelson.

Palier, Bruno. 2004. *Social Protection Reforms in Europe: Strategies for a New Social Model*, Ottawa: Canadian Policy Research Networks, Research Report no. F/37.

Panitch, Leo, ed. 1977. *The Canadian State: Political Economy and Political Power*. Toronto: University of Toronto Press.

– . 1994. "Changing Gears: Democratizing the Welfare State." In *Continuities and Discontinuities: The Political Economy of Social Welfare and Labour Market Policy in Canada*, ed. Andrew F. Johnson, Stephen McBride, and Patrick J. Smith. 36–43. Toronto: University of Toronto Press.

Panitch, Leo, and Sam Gindin. 2009. "The Current Crisis: A Socialist Perspective," *Studies in Political Economy* 83 (Spring): 7–31.

Pante, Michelle. 1996. "Social Partnerships, Sustainable Social Policy, and Community Capital." In *Sustainable Social Policy and Community Capital*, ed. Caledon Institute of Social Policy. Ottawa: CISP and CMHC.

Pascall, Gillian. 1986. *Social Policy: A Feminist Analysis*. New York: Tavistock.

Pascall, Gillian, and Jane Lewis. 2004. "Emerging Gender Regimes and Policies for Gender Equity in a Wider Europe." *Journal of Social Policy* 33, no. 3: 373–94. http://dx.doi.org/10.1017/S004727940400772X.

Pasma, Chandra. 2010. *Bearing the Brunt: How the 2008–2009 Recession Increased Poverty for Canadian Families*. Ottawa: Citizens for Public Justice. www.cpj.ca.

Pateman, Carole. 1988. "The Patriarchal Welfare State." In *Democracy and the Welfare State*, ed. Amy Gutmann. 231–60. Princeton: Princeton University Press.

Peach, Ian, and William Warriner. 2007. *Canadian Social Policy Renewal, 1994–2000*. Halifax: Fernwood.

Peck, Jamie. 2010. *Constructions of Neoliberal Reason*. Oxford: Oxford University Press. http://dx.doi.org/10.1093/acprof:oso/9780199580576.001.0001.

Penna, Sue, and Martin O'Brien. 1996. "Postmodernism and Social Policy: A Small Step Forward?" *Journal of Social Policy* 25, no. 1: 39–61. http://dx.doi. org/10.1017/S0047279400000052.

Petter, Andrew. 2010. *The Politics of the Charter: The Illusive Promise of Constitutional Rights*. Toronto: University of Toronto Press.

Phillips, Susan D. 1989. "Rock-a-Bye, Brian: The National Strategy on Child Care." In *How Ottawa Spends 1989–90: The Buck Stops Where?* ed. Katherine A. Graham. 165–208. Ottawa: Carleton University Press.

– . 2001. "More Than Stakeholders: Reforming State–Voluntary Sector Relations." *Journal of Canadian Studies / Revue d'Etudes Canadiennes* 35, no. 4: 182–202.

– . 2009. "The Harper Government and the Voluntary Sector: Wither a Policy Agenda?" In *The New Federal Policy Agenda and the Voluntary Sector: On the Cutting Edge*, ed. R. Laforest, 7–34. Montreal and Kingston: McGill–Queen's University Press.

Phillips, Susan D., and Karin Levasseur. 2004. "The Snakes and Ladders of Accountability: Contradictions between Contracting and Collaboration for Canada's Voluntary Sector." *Canadian Public Administration* 47, no. 4: 451–74. http://dx.doi.org/10.1111/j.1754-7121.2004.tb01188.x.

Philp, Margaret. 1997. "Child-Care Plan Makes Quebec Distinct." *Globe and Mail*, 17 June, A1, A6.

Piat, Myra. 1992. "Deinstitutionalization of the Mentally Ill." *Canadian Social Work Review* 9, no. 2: 201–13.

Pierson, Paul. 1994. *Dismantling the Welfare State? Reagan, Thatcher, and the Politics of Retrenchment*. New York: Press Syndicate of the University of Cambridge.

Piore, Michael J. 2009. "Second Thoughts: On Economics, Sociology, Neoliberalism, Polanyi's Double Movement, and Intellectual Vacuums." *Socio-Economic Review* 7, no. 1: 161–75. http://dx.doi.org/10.1093/ser/mwn023.

Piven, Frances Fox, and Richard A. Cloward. 1971. *Regulating the Poor: The Functions of Public Welfare*. New York: Vintage.

Polanyi, Karl. 1944[1957/2001]. *The Great Transformation: The Political and Economic Origins of Our Times*. Boston: Beacon.

Porter, John. 1965. *The Vertical Mosaic: An Analysis of Social Class and Power in Canada*. Toronto: University of Toronto Press.

Posner, Richard A. 2010. *The Crisis of Capitalist Democracy*. Cambridge, MA: Harvard University Press.

Power, Marilyn. 2004. "Social Provisioning as a Starting Point for Feminist Economics." *Feminist Economics* 10, no. 3: 3–19. http://dx.doi.org/10.1080/1354 570042000267608.

Pratt, Alan. 1997. "Neoliberalism and Social Policy." In *Social Policy: A Conceptual and Theoretical Introduction*, ed. Michael Lavalette and Pratt. 31–49. London: Sage.

– . 1997b. "Universalism or Selectivism? The Provision of Services in the Modern Welfare State." In *Social Policy: A Conceptual and Theoretical Introduction*, ed. Michael Lavalette and Pratt. 196–213. London: Sage.

Pratt, Cranford, ed. 1994. *Canadian International Development Assistance Policies: An Appraisal*. Montreal and Kingston: McGill–Queen's University Press.

Prince, Michael J. 1989. *Social Policy Commissions: A Review of Findings and Implications for Housing*. Ottawa: CMHC.

– . 1992. "Touching Us All: International Context, National Policies, and the Integration of Canadians with Disabilities." In *How Ottawa Spends 1992–93, The Politics of Competitiveness*, ed. Frances Abele. 191–239. Ottawa: Carleton University Press.

– . 1995. "The Canadian Housing Policy Context." *Housing Policy Debate* 6, no. 3: 721–58. http://dx.doi.org/10.1080/10511482.1995.9521201.

– . 1996a. "At the Edge of Canada's Welfare State: Social Policy Making in British Columbia." In *Politics, Policy, and Government in British Columbia*, ed. R.K. Carty. 236–271. Vancouver: UBC Press.

– . 1996b. "From Expanding Coverage to Heading for Cover: Shifts in the Politics and Policies of Canadian Pension Reform." In *Aging Workforce, Income Security, and Retirement: Policy and Practical Implications*, ed. Anju Joshi and Ellie Berger. Proceedings of the 12th Annual McMaster Summer Institute on Gerontology. Hamilton: Office of Gerontological Studies.

– . 1997. "Lowering the Boom on the Boomers: Replacing Old Age Security with the New Seniors Benefit and Reforming the Canada Pension Plan." In *How Ottawa Spends 1997–98: Seeing Red: A Liberal Report Card*, ed. Gene Swimmer. 211–34. Ottawa: Carleton University Press.

– . 1998. "New Mandate, New Money, New Politics: Federal Budgeting in the Post-Deficit Era." In *How Ottawa Spends 1998–99: Balancing Act: The Post Deficit Mandate*, ed. Leslie A. Pal. 31–55. Toronto: Oxford University Press.

– . 1999. "Civic Regulation: Regulating Citizenship, Morality, Social Order, and the Welfare State." In *Changing the Rules: Canadian Regulatory Regimes and Institutions*, ed. G. Bruce Doern, Margaret Hill, Prince, and Richard Schultz. Toronto: University of Toronto Press.

– . 2002. "Ready or Not? Hide and Seek Politics of Canadian Federalism, the Social Union Framework Agreement, and the Role of National Aboriginal Political Organizations." In *The Social Union Framework Agreement: Perspectives and Directions*, ed. Tom McIntosh. Regina: Canadian Plains Research Centre. 99–111.

– . 2003. "SUFA: Sea Change or Mere Ripple for Canadian Social Policy?" In *Forging the Canadian Social Union: SUFA and Beyond*, ed. Sarah Fortin, Alain Noël, and France St-Hilaire. Montreal: Institute for Research on Public Policy. 125–56.

– . 2005. "From Welfare State to Social Union: Shifting Choices of Governing Instruments, Intervention Rationales, and Governance Rules in Canadian Social Policy." In *Designing Government: From Instruments to Governance*, ed. Pearl Eliadis, Margaret M. Hill, and Michael Howlett. Kingston and Montreal: McGill–Queen's University Press. 281–302.

– . 2009. *Absent Citizens: Disability Politics and Policy in Canada*. Toronto: University of Toronto Press.

– . 2011. "Federal Accountability Regimes and First Nations Governance." In *Approaching Public Administration: Core Debates and Emerging Issues*, ed. Roberto P. Leone and Frank L.K. Ohemeng. Toronto: Emond Montgomery Publications. 325–31.

– . 2012. "A Hobbesian Prime Minister and the Night Watchman State: Social Policy under the Harper Conservatives." In *How Ottawa Spends, 2011–2012*, ed. G. Bruce Doern and Christopher Stoney, 53–70. Montreal, Kingston: McGill–Queen's University Press.

Prince, Michael J., and Neena L. Chappell. 1997. "Voluntarism by Canadian Seniors: Silver Threads or Golden Opportunities for Social Care." Unpublished paper, National Welfare Grants Program.

Prince, Michael J., and James J. Rice. 1981. "Department of National Health and Welfare: The Attack on Social Policy." In *How Ottawa Spends Your Tax Dollars*, ed. G. Bruce Doern. 90–119. Toronto: James Lorimer.

– . 1989. "The Canadian Job Strategy: Supply Side Social Policy." In *How Ottawa Spends Your Tax Dollars*, ed. K. Graham. 247–87. Toronto: James Lorimer.

– . 2007. "Governing through Shifting Social Policy Regimes: Brian Mulroney and Canada's Welfare State." In *Transforming the Nation: Canada and Brian Mulroney*, ed. Raymond Blake. 167–77. Montreal and Kingston: McGill–Queen's University Press.

Prince, Michael J., and Katherine Teghtsoonian. 2007. "The Harper Governments Universal Child Care Plan: Paradoxical or Purposeful Social Policy?" In *How Ottawa Spends 2007–2008, The Harper Conservatives – Climate of Change*, ed. G.B. Doern. Montreal and Kingston: McGill–Queen's University Press. 180–99.

Pulkingham, Jane, and Gordon Ternowetsky, eds. 1996. *Remaking Canadian Social Policy: Social Security in the Late 1990s*. Halifax: Fernwood.

Putnam, Robert D. 1993. "The Prosperous Community: Social Capital and Public Life." *American Prospect* 13: 35–42.

– . 1996. "The Strange Disappearance of Civic America." *American Prospect* 24 (Winter) http://epn.org/prospect/24/24putn.html.

Quarter, Jack. 1992. *Canada's Social Economy: Cooperatives, Non-Profits, and Other Community Enterprises*. Toronto: James Lorimer.

Quarter, Jack, Laurie Mook, and Ann Armstrong. 2009. *Understanding the Social Economy: A Canadian Perspective*. Toronto: University of Toronto Press.

Quebec. 2006. *Guaranteeing Access: Meeting the Challenges of Equity, Efficiency, and Quality*. Consultation Document. February. Quebec: Ministry of Health and Social Services, Communications Directorate.

Ralph, Diana. 1994. "Fighting for Canada's Social Programs." *Canadian Review of Social Policy* 34: 75–85.

Ralph, Diana, Neree St-Amand, and Andre Regimbald, eds. 1997. *Open for Business / Closed to People: Mike Harris's Ontario*. Halifax: Fernwood.

Rankin, L. Pauline, and Jill Vickers. 2001. *Women's Movements and State Feminism: Integrating Diversity into Public Policy*. Ottawa: Status of Women Canada.

Raphael, Dennis. 2007. *Poverty and Policy in Canada: Implications for Health and Quality of Life*. Toronto: Canadian Scholars' Press.

Rayside, David. 2008. *Queer Inclusions, Continental Divisions: Public Recognition of Sexual Diversity in Canada and the United States*. Toronto: University of Toronto Press.

Rebick, Judy. 2005. *Ten Thousand Roses: The Making of a Feminist Revolution*. Toronto: Penguin.

Redden, Candace Johnson. 2002. *Health Care, Entitlement, and Citizenship*. Toronto: University of Toronto Press.

Reid, Angus. 1997. *Shakedown: How the New Economy Is Changing Our Lives*. Toronto: Seal.

Resnick, Philip. 1997. *Twenty-First Century Democracy*. Montreal and Kingston: McGill–Queen's University Press.

Rice, James J. 1979. "Social Policy, Economic Management, and Redistribution." In *Public Policy in Canada*, ed. G. Bruce Doern and Peter Aucoin. Toronto: Macmillan.

– . 1985. "Politics of Income Security: Historical Developments and Limitations to Future Change." In *Royal Commission on Economic Union and Development Prospects for Canada*, ed. G. Bruce Doern. 221–49. Toronto: University of Toronto Press.

– . 1986. "The Macdonald Commission: Social Policy Recommendations." *Canadian Review of Social Policy* 14/15: 96–106.

– . 1987. "Restitching the Safety Net: Altering the National Social Security System." In *How Ottawa Spends 1987–88: Restraining the State*, ed. Michael J. Prince. Toronto: Methuen.

– . 1990. "Volunteering to Build a Stronger Community." *Perception* 14, no. 4: 9–14.

– . 1995a. "A National Treasure at Risk: Changing the Social Security System Threatens the Voluntary Sector." In *Critical Commentaries on the Social Security*

Review, ed. Keith G. Banting and Ken Battle. Ottawa: Caledon Institute of Social Policy.

– . 1995b. "Redesigning Welfare: The Abandonment of a National Commitment." In *How Ottawa Spends: Mid-Life Crises*, ed. Susan D. Phillips. Ottawa: Carleton University Press.

Rice, James J., and Michael J. Prince. 1993. "Lowering the Safety Net and Weakening the Bonds of Nationhood: Social Policy of the Mulroney Years." In *How Ottawa Spends: A More Democratic Canada*, ed. Susan D. Phillips. 381–416. Ottawa: Carleton University Press.

– . 2004. "Martin's Moment: The Social Policy Agenda of a New Prime Minister." In *How Ottawa Spends 2004–2005: Mandate Change in the Paul Martin Era*, ed. G. Bruce Doern. 111–30. Kingston and Montreal: McGill–Queen's University Press.

Riches, Graham. 1997. "The Renewal of Social Citizenship: Right to Food Central to an Alternative Agenda." http://www.policyalternatives.ca.

Richmond, Ted, and John Shields. 2004. "NGO Restructuring: Constraints and Consequences." *Canadian Review of Social Policy* 53: 53–67.

Rifkin, Jeremy. 1995. *The End of Work*. New York: Tarcher Putnam.

Robson, William A. 1976. *Welfare State and Welfare Society: Illusion and Reality*. London: Allen and Unwin.

Rosenblum, Sidney, and Peter Findlay, eds. 1991. *Debating Canada's Future: Views from the Left*. Toronto: James Lorimer.

Ross, David P. 1986. "Local Economic Initiative: An Overview." In *Employment and Social Development in a Changing Economy*, ed. Canadian Council on Social Development. Ottawa.

Ross, David P., and Peter Usher. 1986. *From the Roots Up: Economic Development As If Community Mattered*. Toronto: James Lorimer.

Rothman, Jack. 1974. *Planning and Organizing for Social Change: Action Principles from Social Science Research*. New York: Columbia University Press.

Ryan, Phil. 2010. *Multicultiphobia*. Toronto: University of Toronto Press.

Ryan, William. 1971. *Blaming the Victim*. New York: Vintage.

Sainsbury, Diane. 1996. *Gender, Equality, and Welfare States*. Cambridge: Cambridge University Press. http://dx.doi.org/10.1017/CBO9780511520921.

Samuelson, Les, and Wayne Antony, eds. 2007. *Power and Resistance: Critical Thinking about Canadian Social Issues*, 4th ed. Halifax: Fernwood.

Saul, John Ralston. 1995. *The Unconscious Civilization*. Concord: Anansi.

– . 2009. *The Collapse of Globalism: And the Reinvention of the World*. Toronto: Penguin.

Schattschneider, Elmer. 1960. *The Semi-Sovereign People: A Realist's View of Democracy in America*. New York: Holt Rinehart.

Schellenberg, Grant. 1996. "Diversity in Retirement and the Financial Security of Older Workers." In *Remaking Canadian Social Policy: Social Security in the Late 1990s*, ed. Jane Pulkingham and Gordon Ternowetsky. Halifax: Fernwood. 151–67.

Schellenberg, Grant, and David P. Ross. 1997. *Left Poor by the Market: A Look at Family Poverty and Earnings.* Social Research Series Paper no. 2. Ottawa: Centre for International Statistics at the Canadian Council on Social Development.

Schellenberg, Grant, and Martin Turcotte. 2007. *A Portrait of Seniors in Canada.* Ottawa: Statistics Canada, Cat. no. 89–519–XWE.

Scott, Alan. 1990. *Ideology and the New Social Movements.* London: Unwin Hyman.

Segal, Hugh. 2008. "Guaranteed Annual Income: Why Milton Friedman and Bob Stanfield Were Right." *Policy Options* 29, no. 4: 46–51.

Segalman, R., and D. Marsland. 1989. *Cradle to Grave: Comparative Perspectives on the State of Welfare.* London: Macmillan.

Seligman, Adam B. 1992. *The Idea of Civil Society.* New York: Free Press.

Selznick, Philip. 1995. "Thinking about Community: Ten Theses." *Society* 32, no. 5: 33–7. http://dx.doi.org/10.1007/BF02693335.

Senate Report. 2009. *In from the Margins: A Call to Action on Poverty, Housing, and Homelessness.* Ottawa: Standing Senate Committee on Social Affairs, Science, and Technology.

Sheedy, Amanda, in collaboration with Mary Pat MacKinnon, Sonia Pitre, and Judy Watling. 2008. *Handbook on Citizen Engagement: Beyond Consultation.* Canadian Policy Research Networks.

Shillington, Richard. 2005. "Universality of Social Programs versus Targeting: Either Neither, or Both." *Perception* 27, nos. 3 and 4: 12–13.

Shragge, Eric, ed. 1997. *Workfare: Ideology for a New Under-Class.* Toronto: Garamond.

– . 2003. *Activism and Social Change: Lessons for Community Organizing.* Peterborough: Broadview.

Shragge, Eric, and Jean-Marc Fontan. 2000. *Social Economy: International Debates and Perspectives.* Montreal: Black Rose.

Silver, Jim. 1997. "Round-up, Manitoba." *Canadian Review of Social Policy* 39: 86–7.

Simeon, Richard. 1991. "Globalization and the Nation-State." In *Canada at Risk: Canadian Public Policy in the 1990s.* Policy Study no. 13, ed. G. Bruce Doern and Bryne B. Purchase. Toronto: C.D. Howe Institute.

Smith, George. 1990. "Policing the Gay Community." In *Community Organization and the Canadian State*, ed. Roxana Ng, Gillian Walker, and Jacob Muller. 259–85. Toronto: Garamond.

Smith, Miriam. 2008. *Political Institutions and Lesbian and Gay Rights in the United States and Canada.* London: Routledge.

Social Justice Commission. 1994. "Report of the Commission on Social Justice." In *Social Justice: Strategies for National Renewal*. Toronto: Vintage.

Solomon, Andrew. 1994. "Defiantly Deaf." *New York Times Magazine*, 28 August, 39–68.

Somers, Margaret. 2005. "Let Them Eat Social Capital: Socializing the Market versus Marketizing the Social." *Thesis Eleven* 81, no. 1: 5–19. http://dx.doi.org/10.1177/0725513605051611.

Spivey, W. Allen. 1985. "Problems and Paradoxes in Economic and Social Policies of the Modern Welfare States." *Annals of the American Academy of Political and Social Science* 479, no. 1: 14–30. http://dx.doi.org/10.1177/00027162854 79001002.

Splane, Richard B. 1965. *Social Welfare in Ontario, 1791–1893: A Study of Public Welfare Administration*. Toronto: University of Toronto Press.

– . 1987. "Social Policy Making in the Government of Canada, Further Reflections: 1975–1986." In *Canadian Social Policy*, rev. ed., ed. Shankar Yelaja. Waterloo: Wilfrid Laurier University Press.

Sorkin, Andrew Ross. 2009. *Too Big to Fail*. New York: Penguin.

Stasiulis, Davia K., and Abigail B. Bakan. 2005. *Negotiating Citizenship: Migrant Women in Canada and the Global Systems*. Toronto: University of Toronto Press.

Statistics Canada. 1994. *Public Sector Finance*. Cat. no. 68–212. Ottawa: Supply and Services Canada.

– . 1995a. *Education in Canada*. Cat. no. 81–229. Ottawa.

– . 1995b. *Women in Canada: A Statistical Report*, 3rd ed. Ottawa.

– . 1997. *1996 Census: Marital Status, Common Law Unions, and Families; Mother Tongue, Home Language, and Knowledge of Languages; Immigration and Citizenship*. Ottawa: Supply and Services Canada.

– . 1998. *1996 Census: Aboriginal Data; Ethnic Origin, Visible Minorities*. Ottawa: Supply and Services Canada.

– . 2005. *Cornerstones of Community: Highlights from the National Survey of Nonprofit and Voluntary Organizations*. Ottawa: Minister of Industry, Cat. no. 61–533–XIE.

– . 2006. *Families by Family Structure, Canada and Regions, 2001 and 2006*. General Social Survey. Ottawa: Minister of Industry.

– . 2009. *2008 General Social Survey: Selected Tables on Social Engagement*. Ottawa: Cat. no. 89–640–X.

– . 2010. *2006 Census of Population*. Ottawa: Cat. no. 97–559–XCB2006018.

– . 2011. "Inside the Labour Market Downturn," *Perspectives on Labour and Income* 23, no. 1. Ottawa. Cat. no. 75–001–X.

Stiglitz, Joseph E. 2001. "Foreword." In Karl Polanyi, *The Great Transformation*. Boston: Beacon. vii–xvii

– . 2010. *Freefall: America, Free Markets, and the Shrinking of the World Economy.* London: Allen Lane.

– . 2011. *New Year's Hope against Hope.* Project Syndicate.

Studlar, Donley, and Gary Moncrief. 1997. "The Recruitment of Women Cabinet Ministers in the Canadian Provinces." *Governance: An International Journal of Policy, Administration, and Institutions* 10, no. 1: 67–81. http://dx.doi.org/10.1111/0952-1895.291996029.

Swift, Jamie. 1999. *Civil Society in Question.* Toronto: Between the Lines.

Swimmer, Gene, and Mark Thompson, eds. 1995. *Public Sector Collective Bargaining in Canada: Beginning of the End or the End of the Beginning?* Kingston: Industrial Relations Centre Press, Queen's University.

Taft, Kevin. 1997. *Shredding the Public Interest: Ralph Klein and 25 Years of One-Party Government.* Edmonton: University of Alberta Press.

Tanasescu, Alina, and Alan Smart. 2010. "The Limits of Social Capital: An Examination of Immigrants' Housing Challenges in Calgary." *Journal of Sociology and Social Welfare* 37, no. 4: 97–122.

Taylor-Gooby, Peter. 1994. "Postmodernisrn and Social Policy: A Great Leap Backwards?" *Journal of Social Policy* 23, no. 3: 385–404. http://dx.doi.org/10.1017/S0047279400021917.

Teeple, Gary. 1995. *Globalization and the Decline of Social Reform.* Toronto: Garamond.

Ternowetsky, Gordon W. 1987. "Controlling the Deficit and a Private Sector-Led Recovery: Contemporary Themes of the Welfare State." In *The Canadian Welfare State: Evolution and Transition*, ed. Jacqueline S. Ismael. 372–90. Edmonton: University of Alberta Press.

Tester, Frank James, Chris McNiven, and Robert Case, eds. 1996. *Critical Choices, Turbulent Times.* Vancouver: School of Social Work, University of British Columbia.

Thériault, Luc. 2009. "Moving Back into the Shadows: Social Economy, Social Policy, and the Harper Government." In *The New Federal Policy Agenda and the Voluntary Sector: On the Cutting Edge*, ed. Rachel Laforest. Montreal and Kingston: McGill–Queen's University Press. 61–80.

Thompson, Kelly. 1989. *Volunteerism in the International Sector: Voluntary Action Directorate, Multiculturalism, and Citizenship.* Ottawa: Supply and Services Canada.

Titmuss, Richard M. 1968. *Commitment to Welfare.* London: Allen and Unwin.

– . 1974. *Social Policy: An Introduction*, ed. Brian Abel-Smith and Kay Titmuss. London: Allen and Unwin.

Torjman, Sherri. 1996. "Sustainable Social Policy." In *Sustainable Social Policy and Community Capital*, ed. Caledon Institute of Social Policy. Ottawa: CISP and CMHC.

– . 1997a. *Cash Poor, Community Rich*. Ottawa: Caledon Institute of Social Policy.

– . 1997b. *Civil Society: Reclaiming Our Humanity*. Ottawa: Caledon Institute of Social Policy.

– . 1998. *Community-Based Poverty Reduction*. Ottawa: Caledon Institute of Social Policy.

Trainor, John, Bonnie Pape, and Edward Pomeroy. 1997. "Critical Challenges for Canadian Mental Health Policy." *Canadian Review of Social Policy* 39: 55–64.

Trebilcock, Michael J., Leonard Waverman, and J. Robert Prichard. 1978. "Markets for Regulation: Implications for Performance Standards and Institutional Design." In *Government Regulations*. 11–66. Toronto: Ontario Economic Council.

Trimble, Linda, and Manon Tremblay. 2005. "Representation of Canadian Women at the Cabinet Table, 1917–2002." *Atlantis: A Women's Studies Journal*, 30, no. 1: 31–45.

Tudiver, Neil. 1987. "Forestalling the Welfare State: The Establishment of Programmes of Corporate Welfare." In *The Benevolent State: The Growth of Welfare in Canada*, ed. Allan Moscovitch and Jim Albert. 186–202. Toronto: Garamond.

Tyhurst, James S. 1963. *More for the Mind: A Study of Psychiatric Services in Canada*. Toronto: Canadian Mental Health Association.

Ursel, Jane. 1997. "Considering the Impact of the Battered Women's Movement on the State: The Example of Manitoba." In *Women and the Canadian State*, ed. Caroline Andrew and Sandra Rodgers. 155–79. Montreal and Kingston: McGill–Queen's University Press.

Usher, Alex. 2004. *Who Gets What? The Distribution of Government Subsidies for Post-Secondary Education in Canada*. Winnipeg: Educational Policy Institute.

Vaillancourt, Yves. 2008. *Social Economy in the Co-Construction of Public Policy*. Victoria: Canadian Social Economy Hub.

Vaillancourt, Yves, and Louise Tremblay, eds. 2002. *Social Economy: Health and Welfare in Four Canadian Provinces*. Halifax: Fernwood.

Vaillancourt, Yves, and Luc Thériault. 2008. *Social Economy, Social Policy, and Federalism in Canada*. Victoria: Canadian Social Economy Hub.

Vanier Institute of the Family. 1979. *Exploring Work and Income Opportunities in the 1980s: Our Future in the Informal Economy*. Ottawa.

– . 2010. *Families Count: Profiling Canada's Families IV*, Ottawa: The Institute. http://www.vifamily.ca.

Vickers, Jill. 1994. "Why Should Women Care about Federalism?" In *Canada: The State of the Federation 1994*, ed. Douglas M. Brown and Janet Hiebert. 135–51. Kingston: Institute of Intergovernmental Relations, Queen's University.

Voluntary Action Directorate. 1989. *National Survey of Volunteer Activity. Social Trends Analysis Directorate*. Ottawa: Supply and Services Canada.

Vosko, Leah F., ed. 2006. *Precarious Employment: Understanding Labour Market Insecurity in Canada*. Montreal and Kingston: McGill–Queen's University Press.

Walker, Michael. 1985. "The Welfare State." In *Free Enterprise and the State: What's Right? What's Left? What's Next?*, ed. Jan Federowicz. Toronto: CBC Enterprises.

Wallace, Elisabeth. 1950. "The Origin of the Welfare State in Canada, 1867–1900." *Canadian Journal of Economics and Political Science* 16, no. 3: 383–93. http://dx.doi.org/10.2307/137811.

Wallis, Maria, and Sui-Ming Kwok. 2008. *Daily Struggles: The Deepening Racialization and Feminization of Poverty in Canada*. Toronto: Canadian Scholars' Press.

Walzer, Michael. 1983. *Spheres of Justice*. New York: Basic.

Warrier, William E., and Ian Peach. 2007. *Canadian Social Policy Renewal 1994–2000*. Halifax and Winnipeg: Fernwood.

Watson, William. 1998. *Globalization and the Meaning of Canadian Life*. Toronto: University of Toronto Press.

Westhues, Anne, ed. 2006. *Canadian Social Policy: Issues and Perspectives*, 4th ed. Waterloo: Wilfrid Laurier University Press.

Wharf, Brian, ed. 1979. *Community Work in Canada*. Toronto: McClelland and Stewart.

– , ed. 1990. *Social Work and Social Change in Canada*. Toronto: McClelland and Stewart.

– , ed. 1992. *Communities and Social Policy in Canada*. Toronto: McClelland and Stewart.

Wharf, Brian, and Michael Clague, eds. 1997. *Community Organizing: Canadian Experiences*. Toronto: Oxford University Press.

White, Joe, and Aaron Wildavsky. 1989. *The Deficit and the Public Interest: The Search for Responsible Budgeting in the 1980s*. Berkeley and Los Angeles: University of California Press and Russell Sage Foundation.

Whitmore, Elizabeth, Maureen G. Wilson, and Avery Calhoun, eds. 2011. *Activism That Works*. Halifax: Fernwood.

Wildavsky, Aaron. 1988. *The New Politics of the Budgetary Process*, 4th ed. Boston: Little, Brown.

Wilensky, Harold, and Charles Lebeaux. 1958. *Industrial Society and Social Welfare*. New York: Russell Sage.

Wilkinson, Richard, and Kate Pickett. 2010. *The Spirit Level: Why Equality Is Better for Everyone*. London: Penguin.

Williams, Fiona. 1989. *Social Policy: A Critical Introduction*. Cambridge: Polity.

– . 1992. "Somewhere Over the Rainbow: Universality and Diversity in Social Policy." In *Social Policy Review* 4, ed. Nick Manning and Robert Page. Canterbury: Social Policy Association, University of Kent. 200–19.

Wilson, Elizabeth. 1977. *Women and the Welfare State*. London: Tavistock.

Wiseman, John. 1996. "National Social Policy in an Age of Global Power: Lessons from Canada and Australia." In *Remaking Canadian Social Policy: Social Security in the Late 1990s*, ed. Jane Pulkingham and Gordon Ternowetsky. 114–29. Halifax: Fernwood.

Wolf, Daniel. 1994. "Brotherhood in Biker Bars." In *Doing Everyday Life: Ethnography as Human Lived Experience*, ed. Mary Lorenz Dietz, Robert Prus, and William Shaffir. Mississauga: Copp Clark Longman.

Wolfe, David. 1985. "The Politics of the Deficit." In *The Politics of Economic Policy*, ed. G. Bruce Doern. 111–62. Toronto: University of Toronto Press.

Wolf, Martin. 2004. *Why Globalization Works*. New Haven: Yale University Press.

Woodcock, George. 1985. *Strange Bedfellows: The State and the Arts in Canada*. Vancouver: Douglas and McIntyre.

Woodsworth, J.S. 1972[1911]. *My Neighbor*. Toronto: University of Toronto Press.

Yeates, Nicola. 2005. *"Globalization" and Social Policy in a Development Context*. Social Policy and Development Program Paper no. 18. United Nations Research Institute for Social Development.

Yeatman, Anna. 1990. *Bureaucrats, Technocrats, Femocrats: Essays on the Contemporary Australian State*. Sydney: Allen and Unwin.

Young, Iris Marion. 1990. *Justice and the Politics of Difference*. Princeton: Princeton University Press.

Young, Lisa. 2009. "Women (Not) in Politics: Women's Electoral Participation." In *Canadian Politics*, 5th ed., ed. James Bickerton and Alain-G. Gagnon. Toronto: University of Toronto Press. 283–300.

Author Index

Subject Index

Aboriginal peoples, 33–4, 127, 182, 186–7, 190, 192, 203, 229, 293, 319; communities, 38, 125; governments, 135, 166; residential schools, 190, 292; self-government, 5, 296, 325; treaty rights, 293. *See also* First Nations; Indians
accessibility, 207; health care, 195, 327
Acquired Immune Deficiency Syndrome (AIDS), 15, 272
active citizenship, 254, 256, 265, 316
active programs, 152
active universalists, 205, 207
activists and advocates, x, 3, 10, 11, 59, 89, 92, 107, 110, 118, 134, 143, 150, 156, 165–6, 174, 187, 207, 213, 223, 229, 236–7, 241, 257, 265, 271, 284, 291
administrative universalists, 205–7, 217
advocacy groups, 36–7, 133, 150, 155, 164
affirmative action, 12, 165, 189, 205, 323
African Canadians, 33, 344
agenda, 3, 14, 15, 18, 20–1, 23, 25–6, 61, 77, 83–5, 124, 136; Aboriginal,

188; creating a new social policy, 288–320; crisis/retrenchment, 88, 94, 114, 155; feminist/women's, 100, 103, 238, 250, 260; Harper government's, 212, 215–17, 264; Liberal, 182–3, 191, 194
Alberta, 48–9, 82, 118, 182, 197, 325
alternative models of social policy, 221; dual welfare, 226–7; female caregiver, 221; individual, 222; male pauper, 222; parity, 222; universal breadwinner, 222; welfare society, 223
American: administrations, 116; central bank, 145; cities, 278; welfare state, 110. *See also* United States
Amnesty International, 314
anti-universalists, 205–6, 217
arts and culture: policy, 160; volunteers in, 280–3
Asia-Pacific Economic Cooperation (APEC), 13, 145
Asian origin, 33, 321
Aspen Institute Rural Economic Policy Program, 271, 332
assistance, social, 4. *See also* social assistance
Australia, 116, 172, 235